S0-BSP-748

Recast is the magical adventure story of a boy,

JD, who wants to be the Master of Magicians

in a world full of magical particles, BOXES.

JD is chased by assassins and monsters

because of his latent abilities, which had been secret.

God sends enemies against JD and just watches.

JD become the Master of Magicians?

JAN 1 7 2008

2803805

# *Recast* Vol. 4

## Created by Seung-Hui Kye

Translation - Woo Sok Park
Copy Editor - Stephanie Duchin & Sarah Mercutio
Retouch and Lettering - Star Print Brokers
Production Artist - Mike Estacio
Cover Design - James Lee & Tina Corrales

Editor - Hope Donovan
Digital Imaging Manager - Chris Buford
Pre-Production Supervisor - Erika Terriquez
Production Manager - Elisabeth Brizzi
Managing Editor - Vy Nguyen
Creative Director - Anne Marie Horne
Editor-in-Chief - Rob Tokar
Publisher - Mike Kiley
President and C.O.O. - John Parker
C.E.O. and Chief Creative Officer - Stuart Levy

A 🌀 TOKYOPOP® Manga

TOKYOPOP and 🌀 are trademarks or registered trademarks of TOKYOPOP Inc.

TOKYOPOP Inc.
5900 Wilshire Blvd. Suite 2000
Los Angeles, CA 90036

E-mail: info@TOKYOPOP.com
Come visit us online at www.TOKYOPOP.com

© 2004 SEUNG-HUI KYE, DAIWON C.I. Inc. All rights reserved. No portion of this book may be
All Rights Reserved. First published in Korea in 2004 by reproduced or transmitted in any form or by any means
DAIWON C.I. Inc. English translation rights in North America, without written permission from the copyright holders.
UK, NZ, and Australia arranged by DAIWON C.I. Inc. through This manga is a work of fiction. Any resemblance to
Topaz Agency. actual events or locales or persons, living or dead, is
English text copyright © 2007 TOKYOPOP Inc. entirely coincidental.

ISBN: 978-1-59816-667-5

First TOKYOPOP printing: November 2007
10 9 8 7 6 5 4 3 2 1
Printed in the USA

# RECAST™

## VOLUME 4

### by
### Seung-Hui Kye

JAN 17 2008

HAMBURG // LONDON // LOS ANGELES // TOKYO

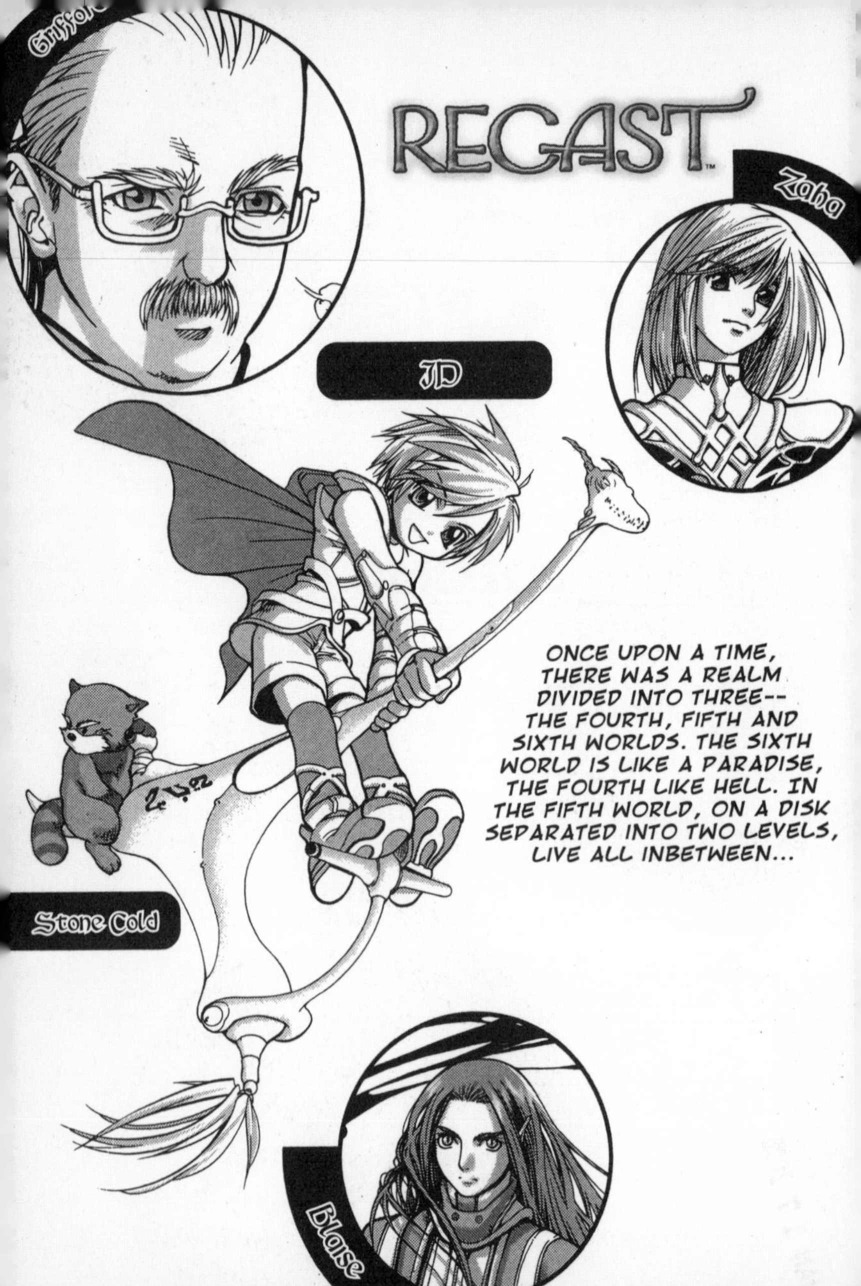

RECAST™
Griffor
Zaha
JD
ONCE UPON A TIME, THERE WAS A REALM DIVIDED INTO THREE-- THE FOURTH, FIFTH AND SIXTH WORLDS. THE SIXTH WORLD IS LIKE A PARADISE, THE FOURTH LIKE HELL. IN THE FIFTH WORLD, ON A DISK SEPARATED INTO TWO LEVELS, LIVE ALL INBETWEEN...
Stone Cold
Blaise

TWELVE-YEAR OLD JD IS A YOUNG BOY WHO WAS RAISED BY HIS GRANDFATHER, GRIFFORD, IN THE FIFTH WORLD.

Eomaia

JD HAS TWO SPELLS CAST ON HIM--AN ELECTRIFYING CHASTITY SPELL AND A MYSTERIOUS RECAST SPELL.

Lain

AFTER GRIFFORD WAS KILLED BY A PUPPET BOUNTY HUNTER, JD FLED TO THE JADE REGION TO SEEK AID FROM GRIFFORD'S FRIEND, THE VAMPIRE LORD BLAISE. BUT BLAISE COLDLY REFUSED TO HELP JD GET TO THE FOURTH WORLD, AS BLAISE'S SISTER IS POSSESSED BY ITS EVIL POWERS...

Kntor

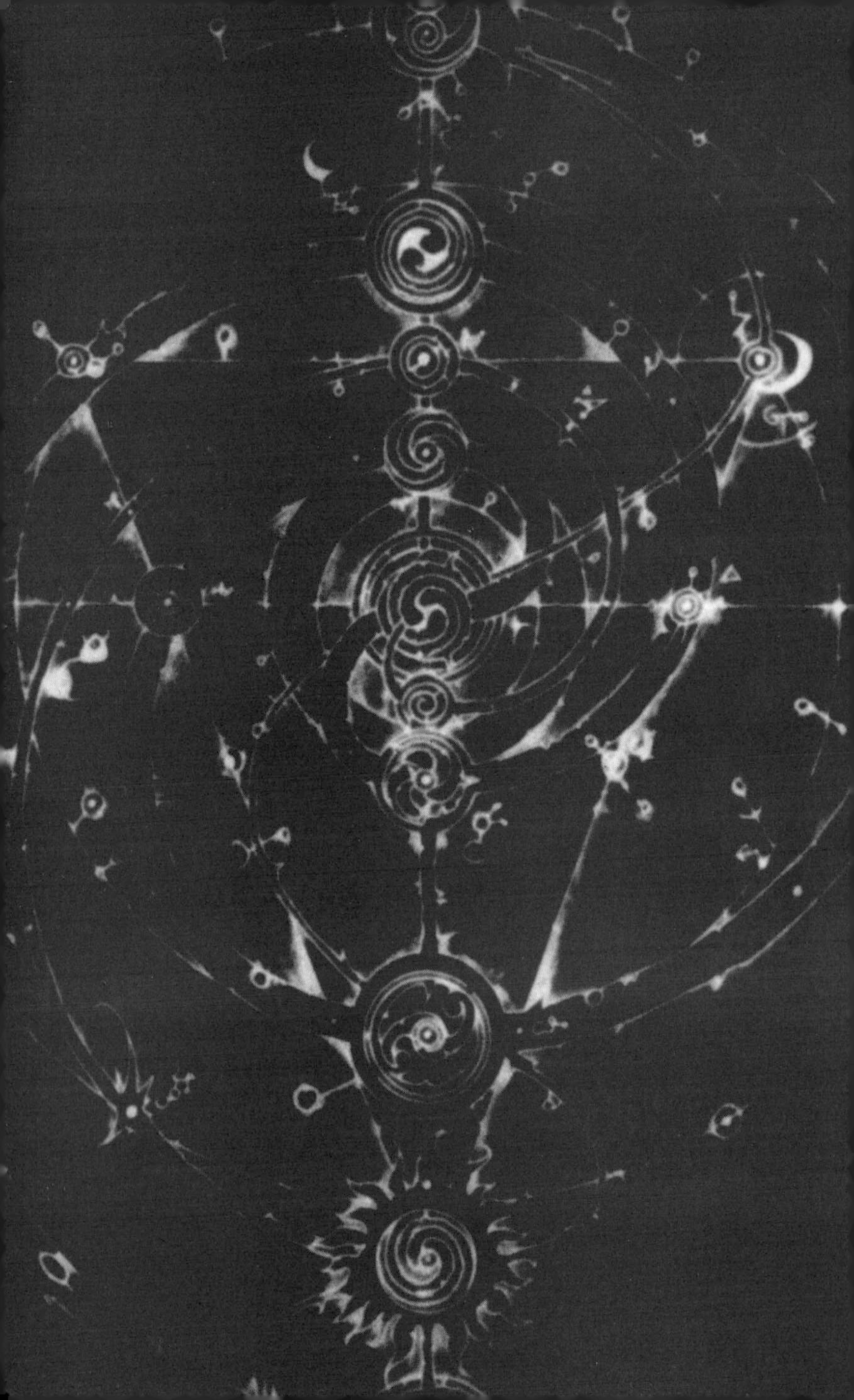

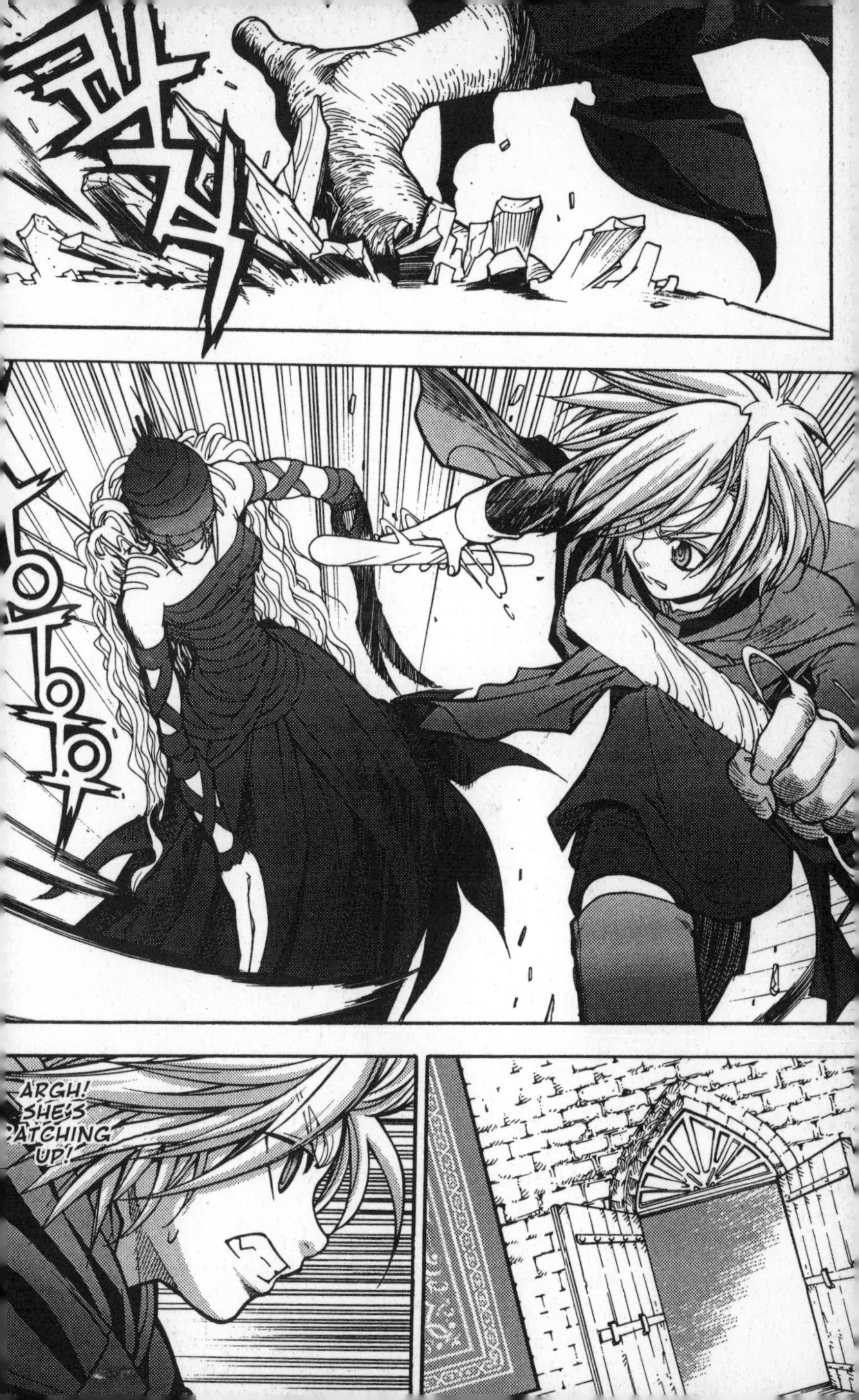
ARGH! SHE'S CATCHING UP!

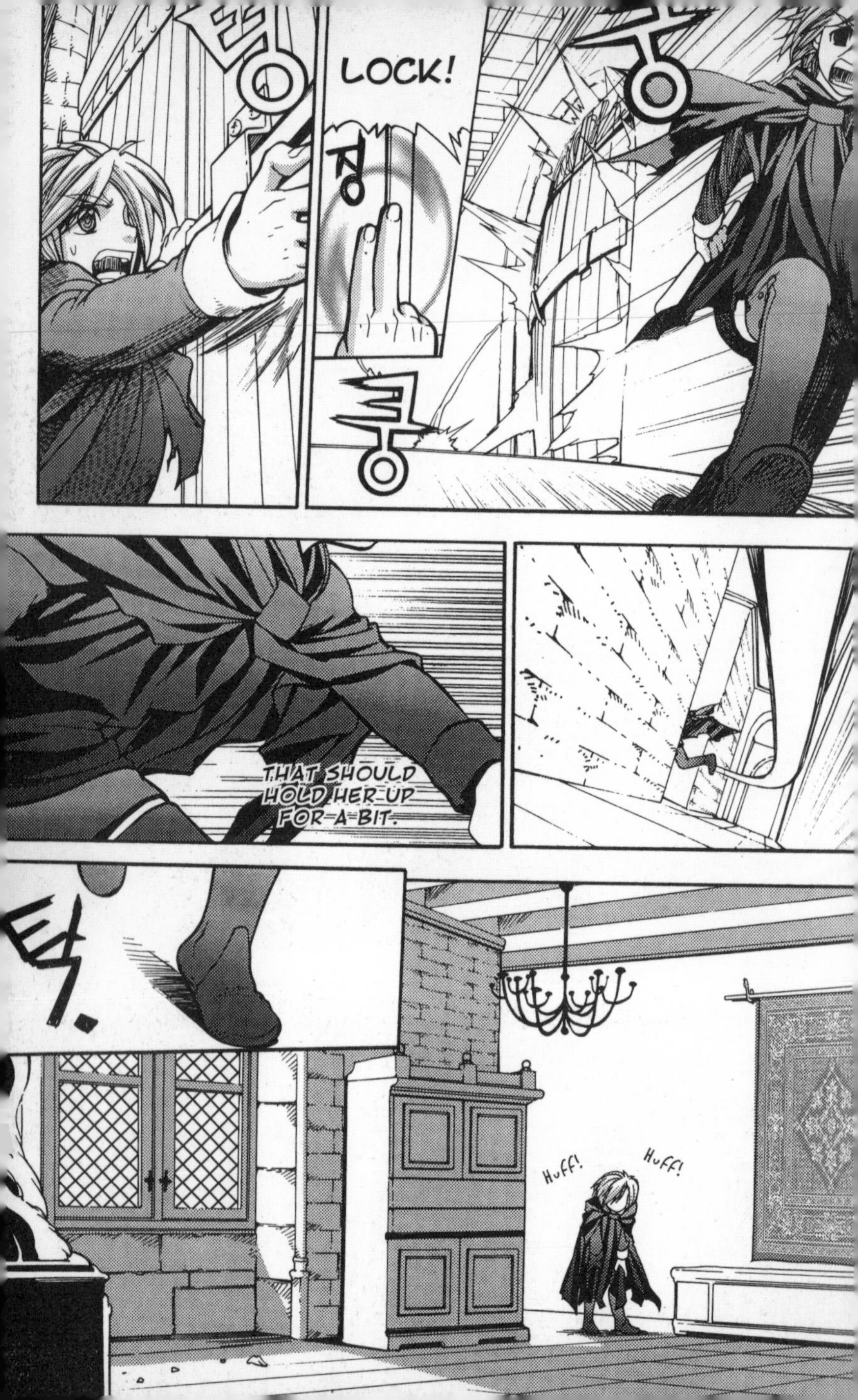
LOCK!
THAT SHOULD HOLD HER UP FOR A BIT.
Huff!
Huff!

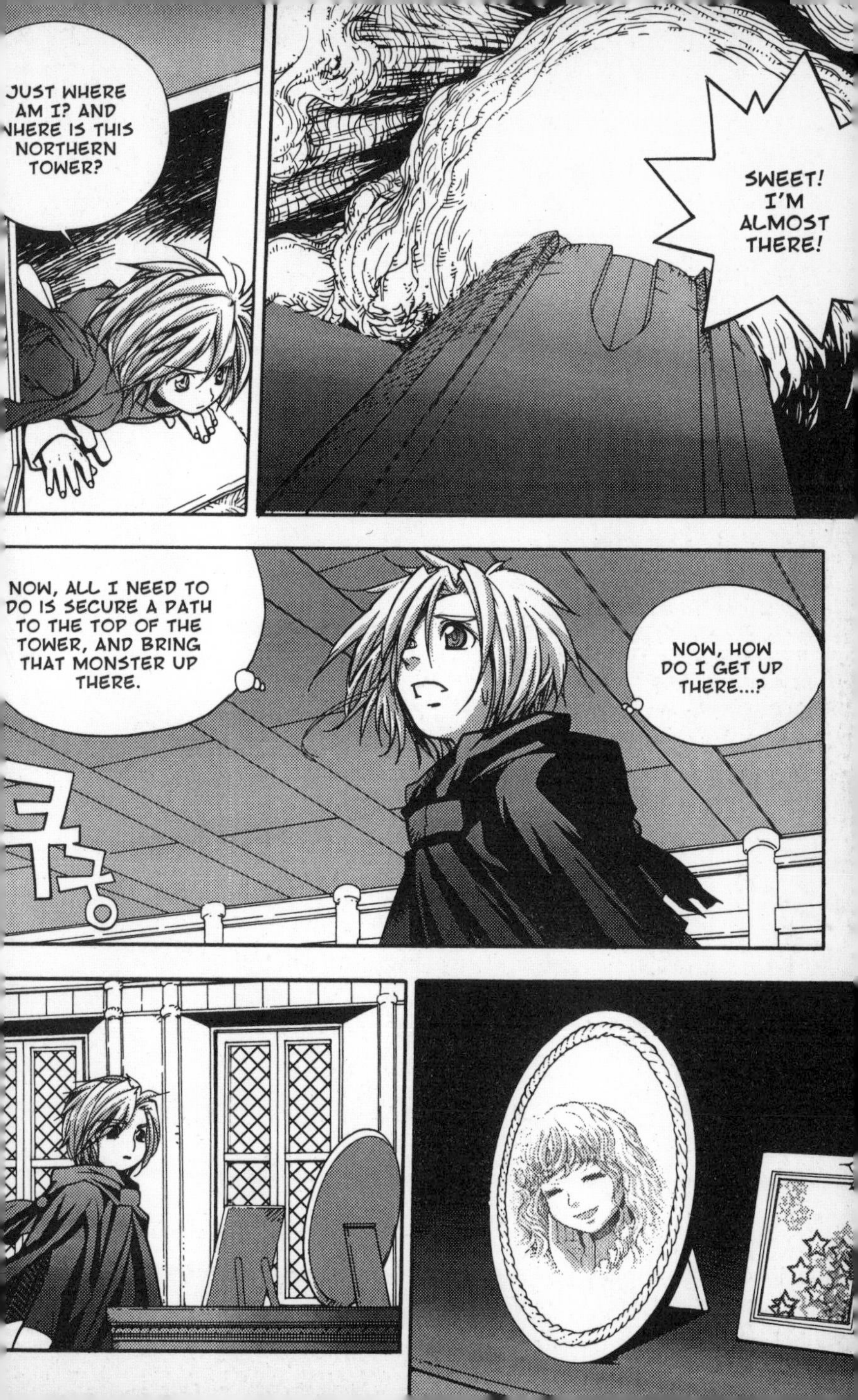
JUST WHERE AM I? AND WHERE IS THIS NORTHERN TOWER?
SWEET! I'M ALMOST THERE!
NOW, ALL I NEED TO DO IS SECURE A PATH TO THE TOP OF THE TOWER, AND BRING THAT MONSTER UP THERE.
NOW, HOW DO I GET UP THERE...?

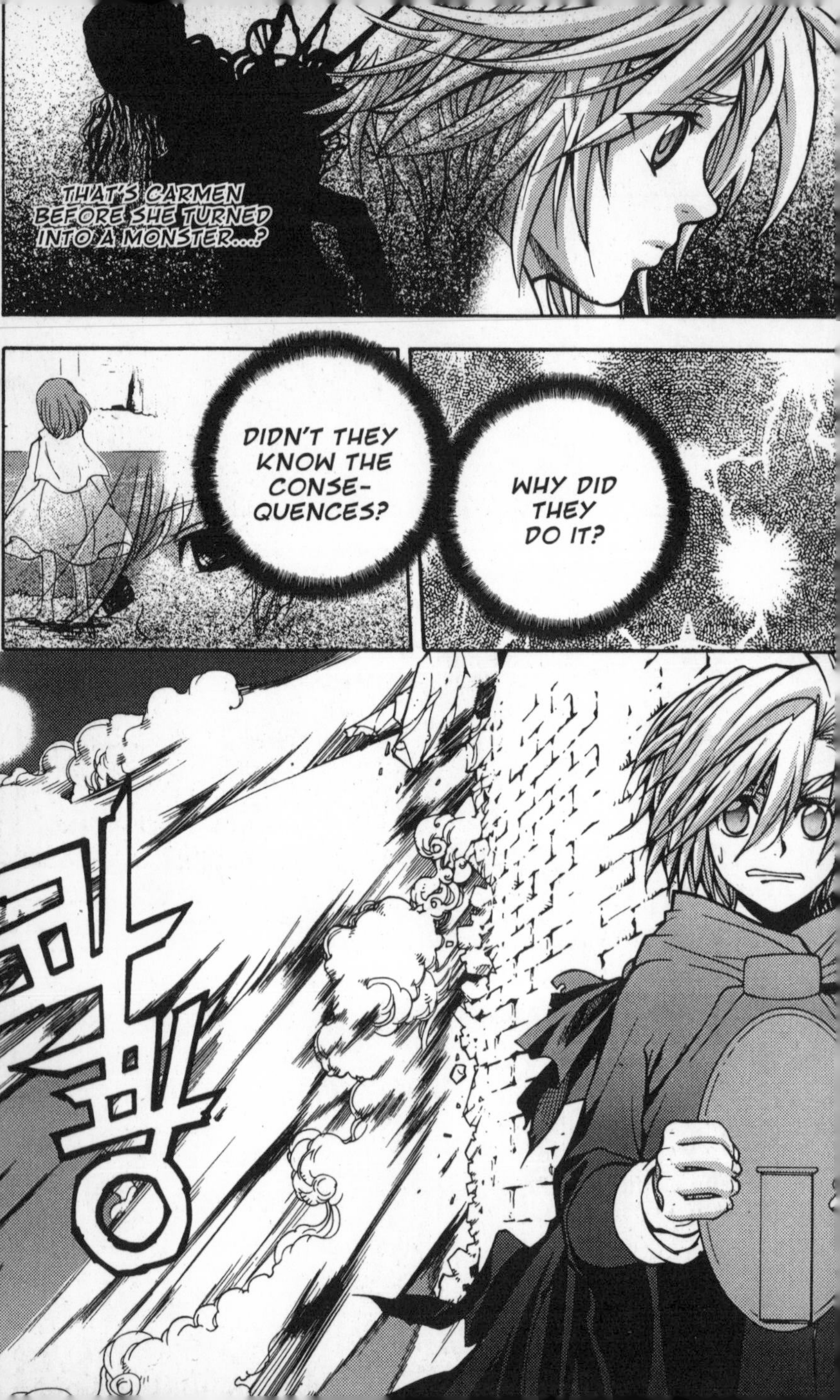
THAT'S CARMEN BEFORE SHE TURNED INTO A MONSTER...?
DIDN'T THEY KNOW THE CONSE-QUENCES?
WHY DID THEY DO IT?

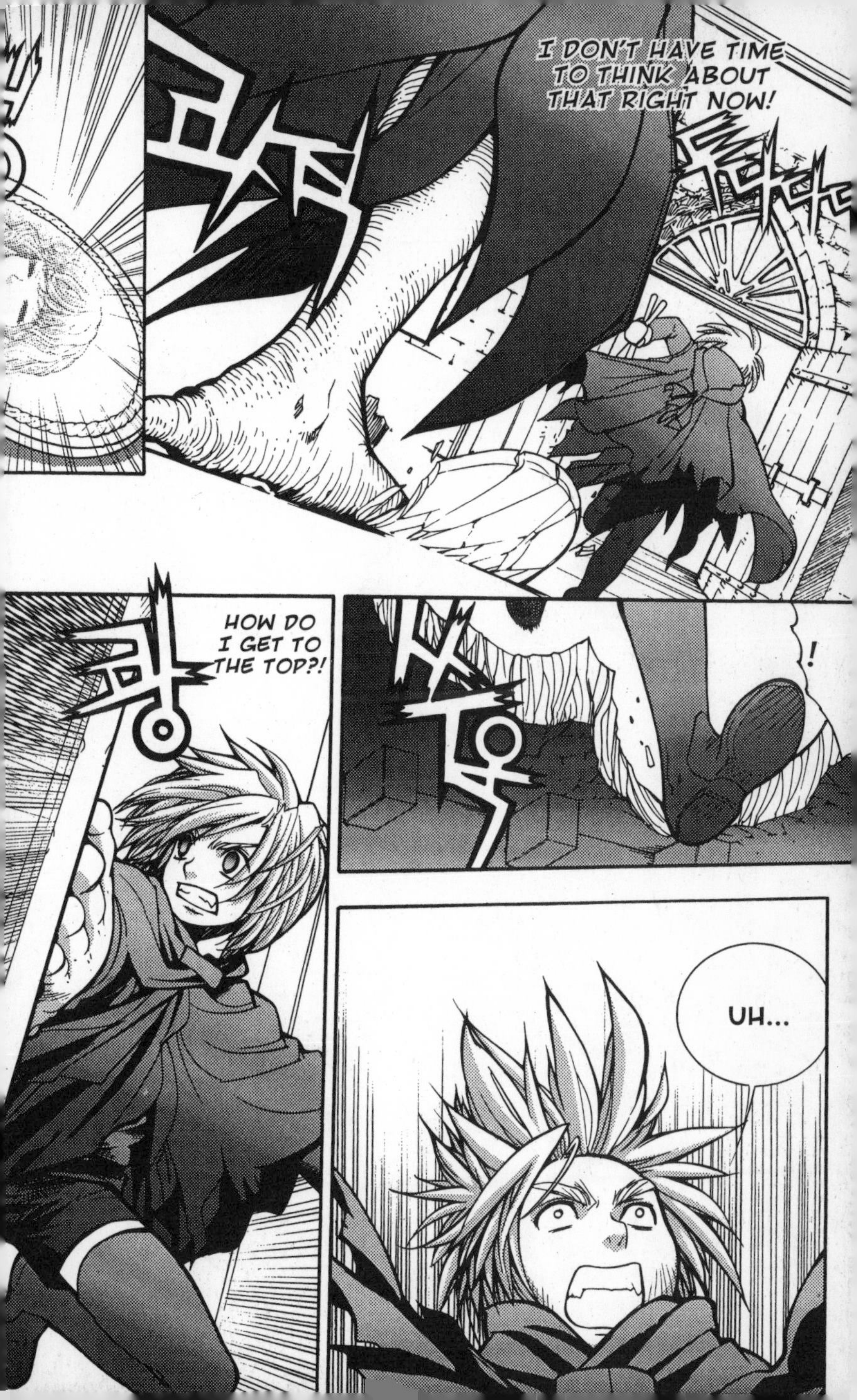
I DON'T HAVE TIME TO THINK ABOUT THAT RIGHT NOW!
HOW DO I GET TO THE TOP?!
!
UH...

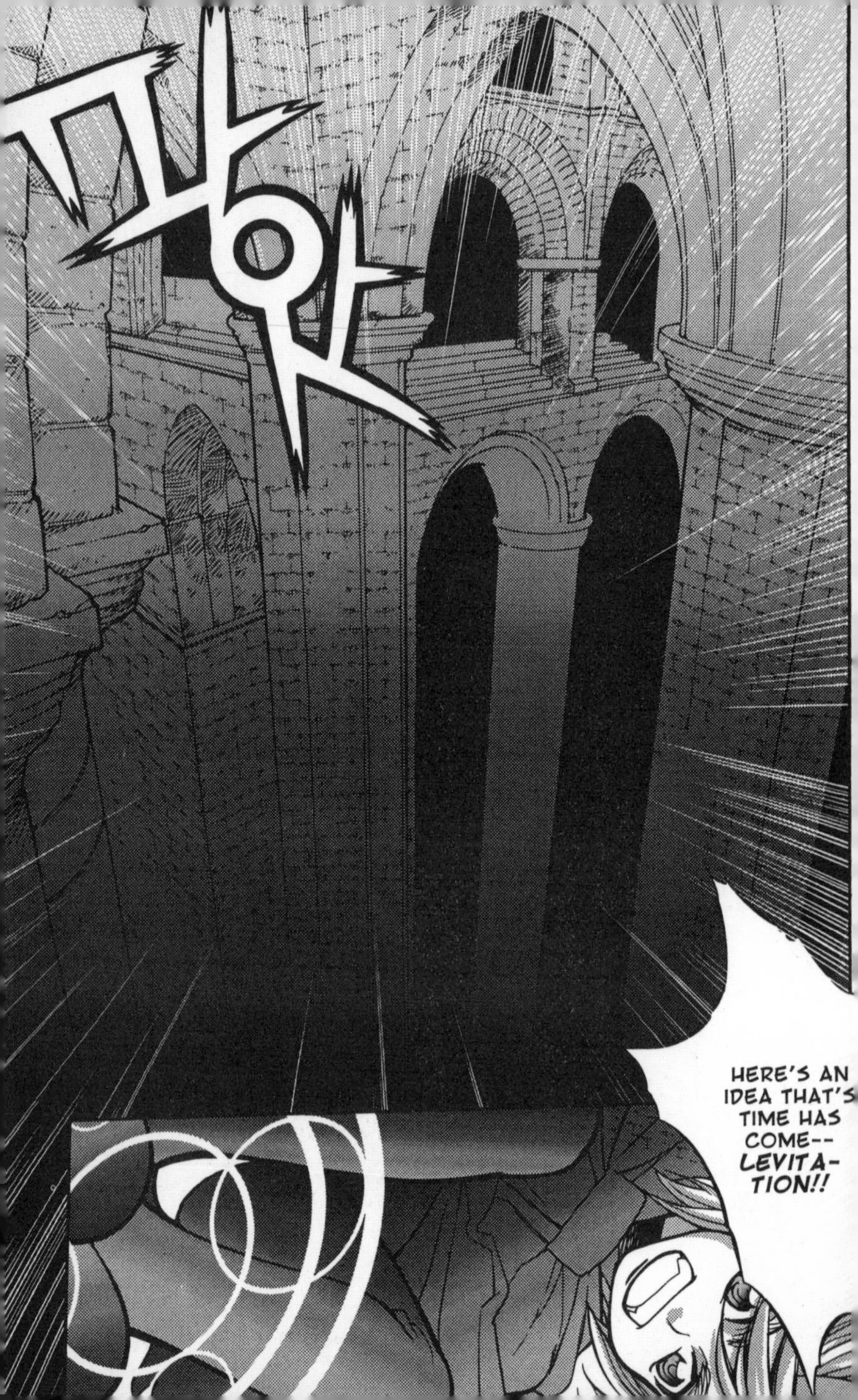
HERE'S AN IDEA THAT'S TIME HAS COME-- LEVITATION!!

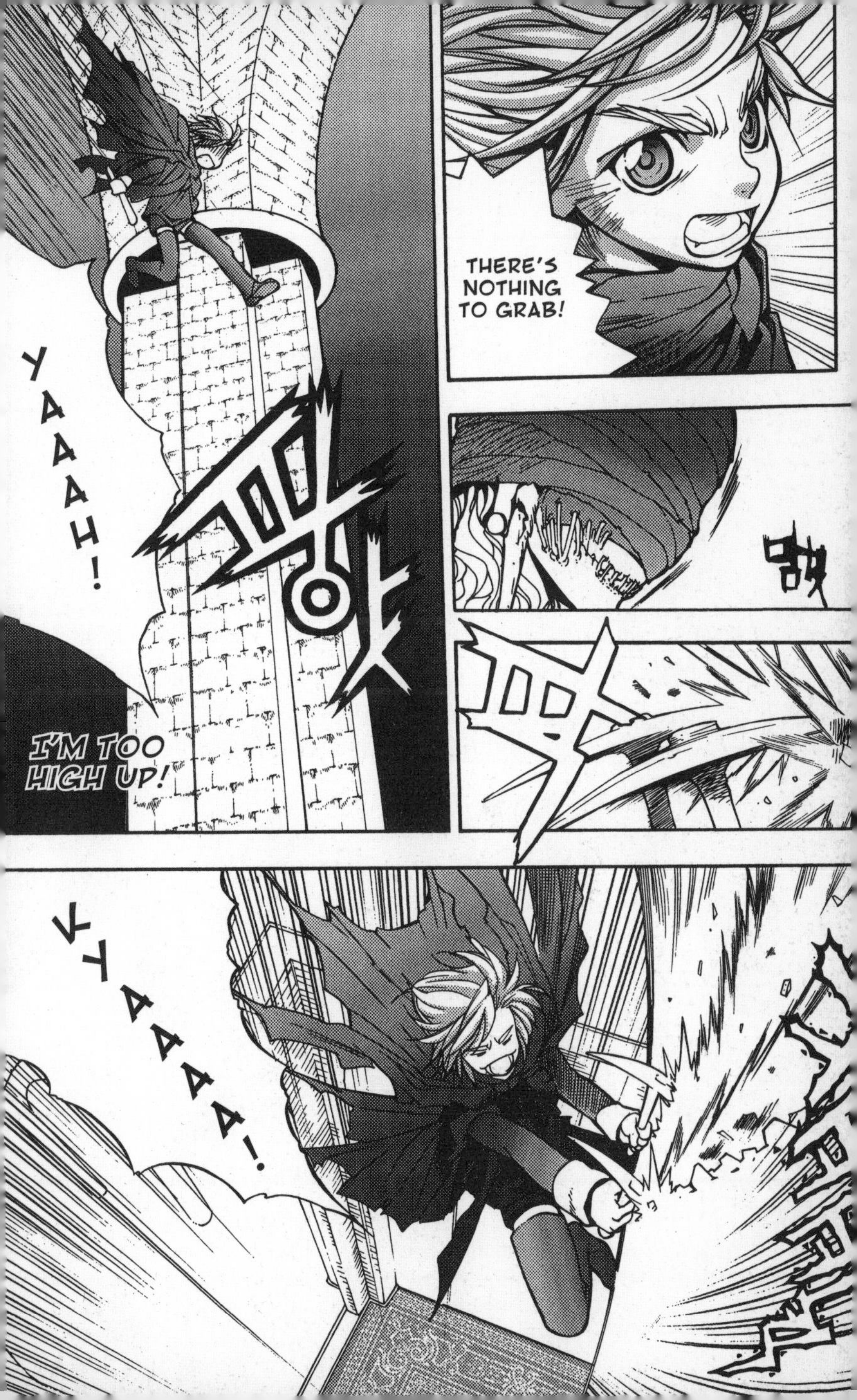
YAAAH!
I'M TOO HIGH UP!
THERE'S NOTHING TO GRAB!
KYAAAA!

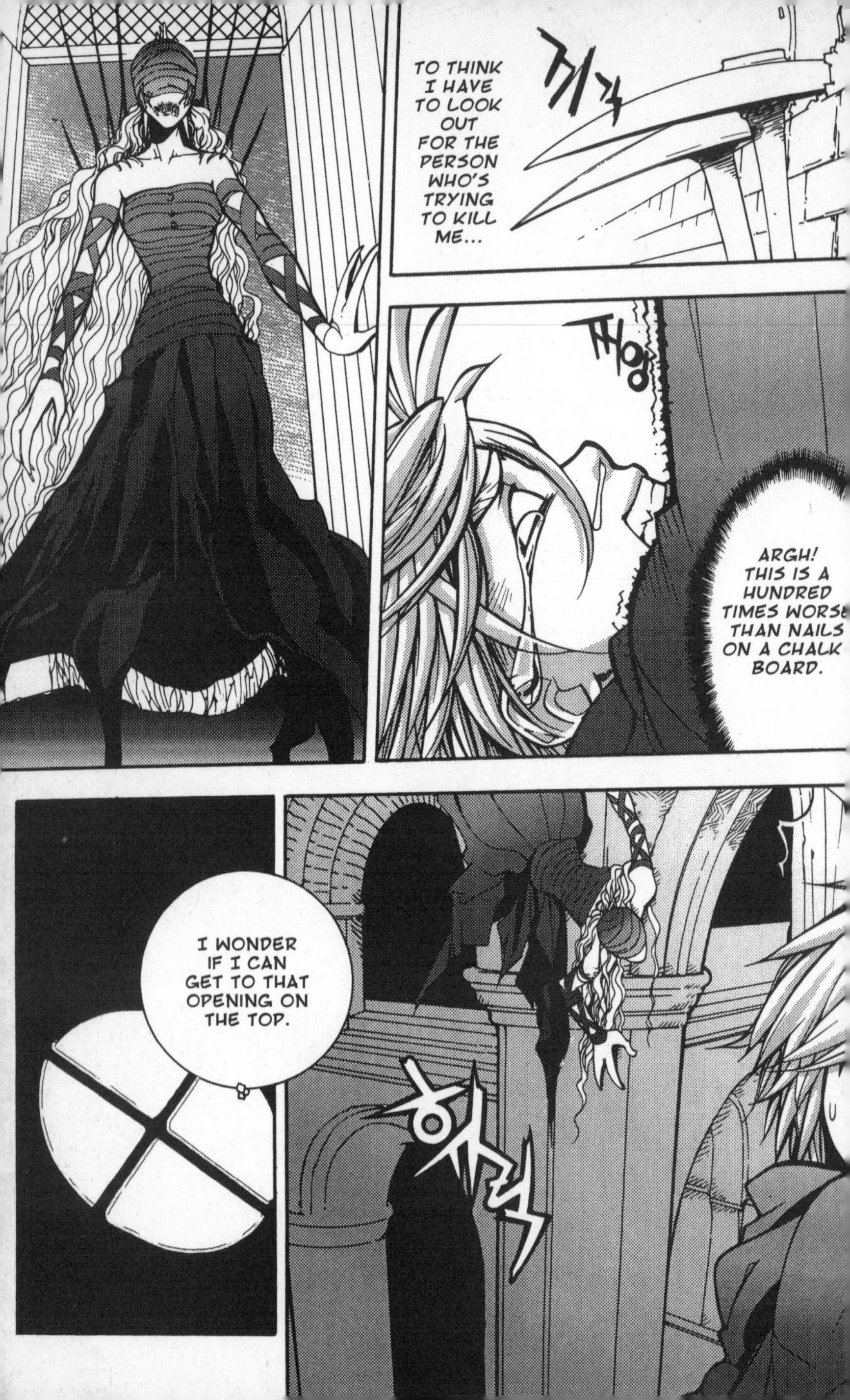
TO THINK I HAVE TO LOOK OUT FOR THE PERSON WHO'S TRYING TO KILL ME...
ARGH! THIS IS A HUNDRED TIMES WORSE THAN NAILS ON A CHALK BOARD.
I WONDER IF I CAN GET TO THAT OPENING ON THE TOP.

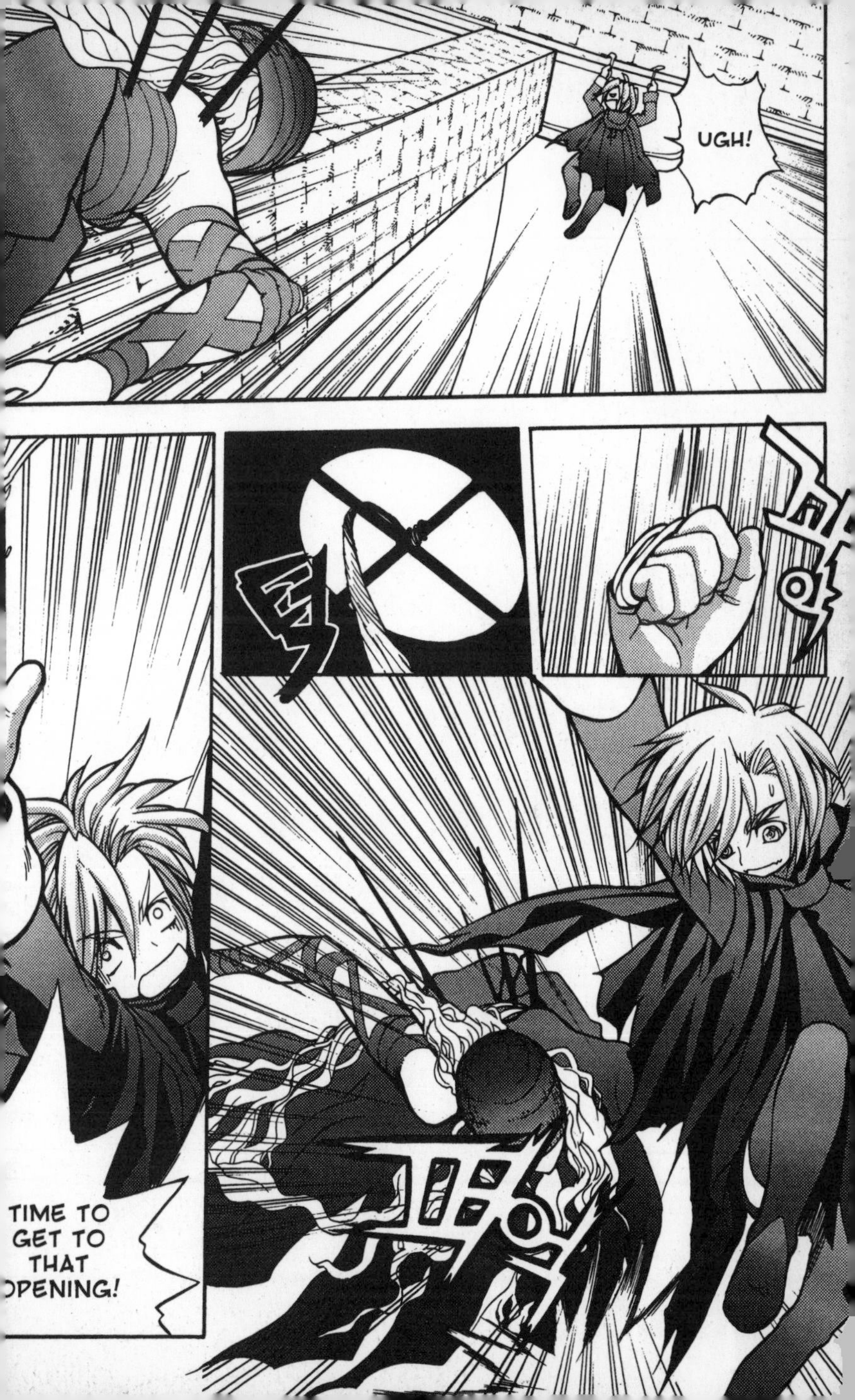
UGH!
TIME TO GET TO THAT OPENING!

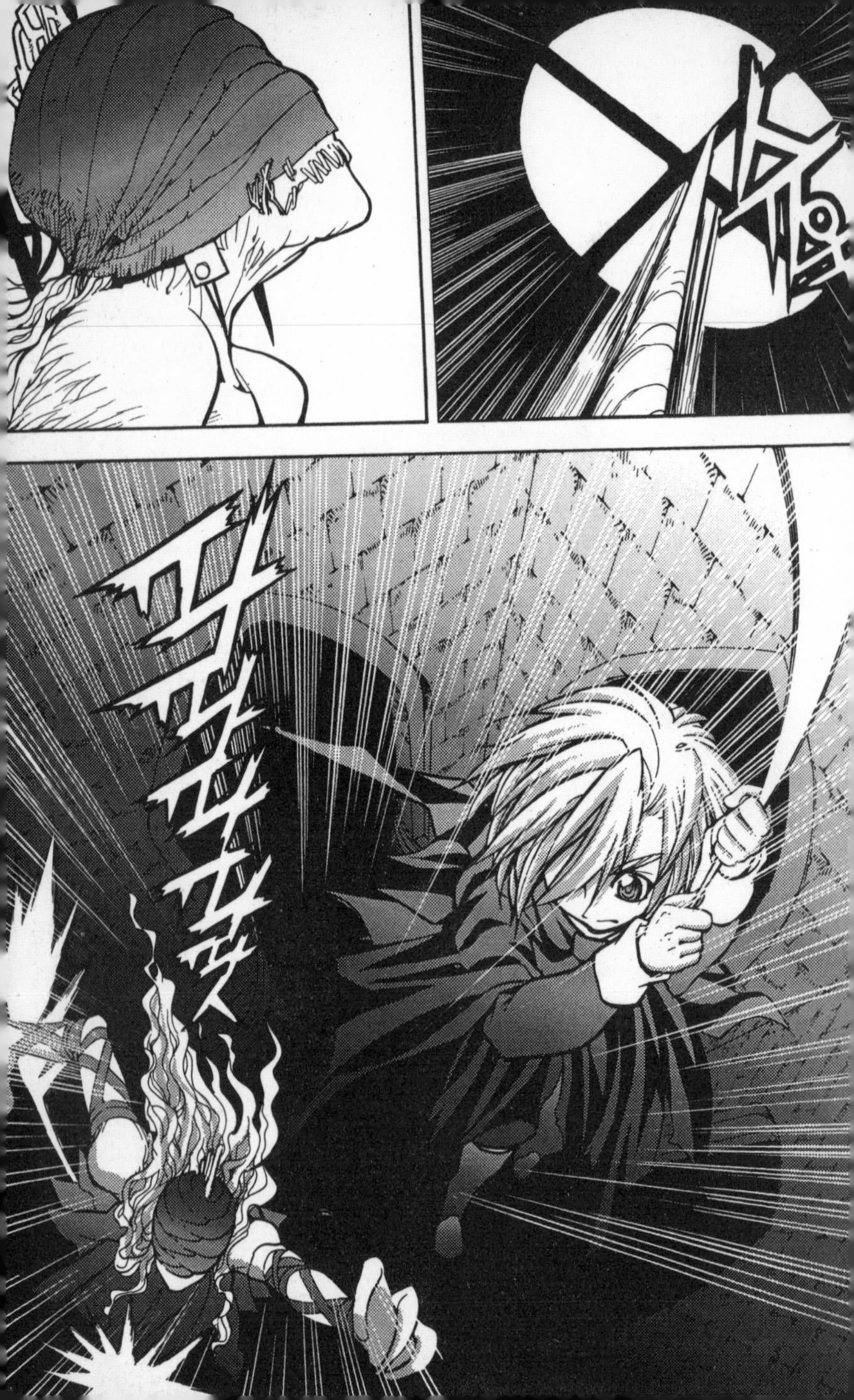

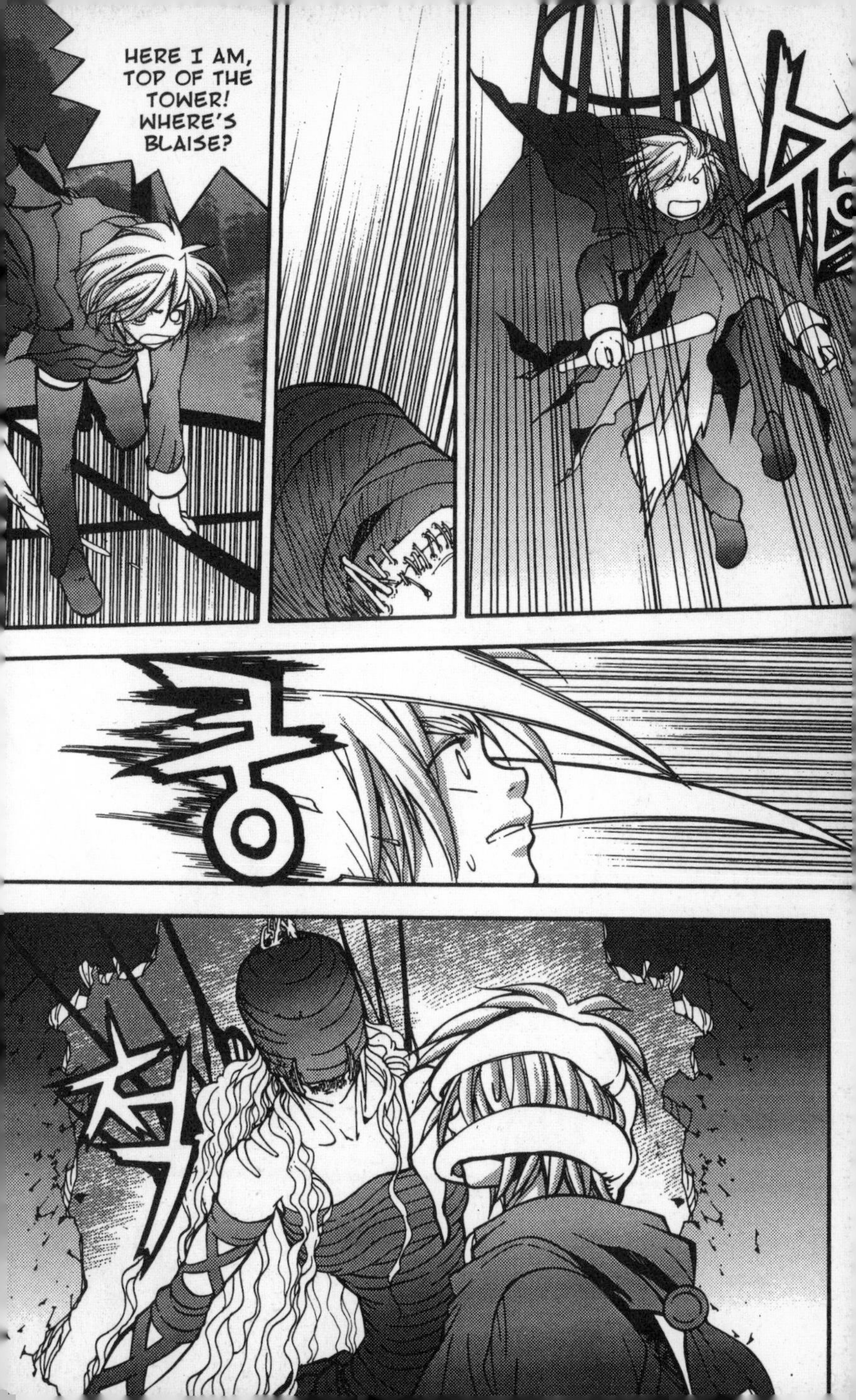
HERE I AM, TOP OF THE TOWER! WHERE'S BLAISE?

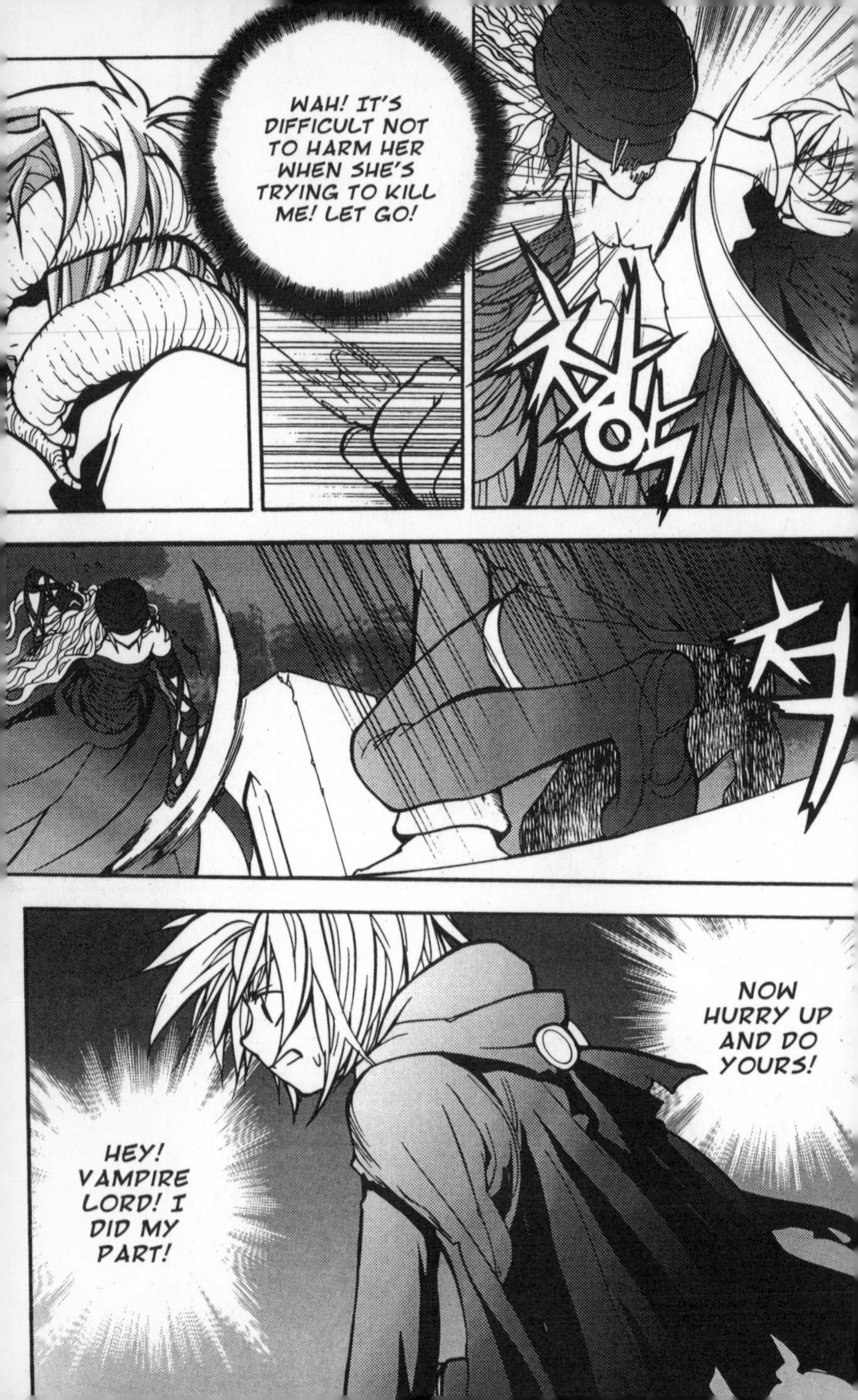
WAH! IT'S DIFFICULT NOT TO HARM HER WHEN SHE'S TRYING TO KILL ME! LET GO!
HEY! VAMPIRE LORD! I DID MY PART!
NOW HURRY UP AND DO YOURS!

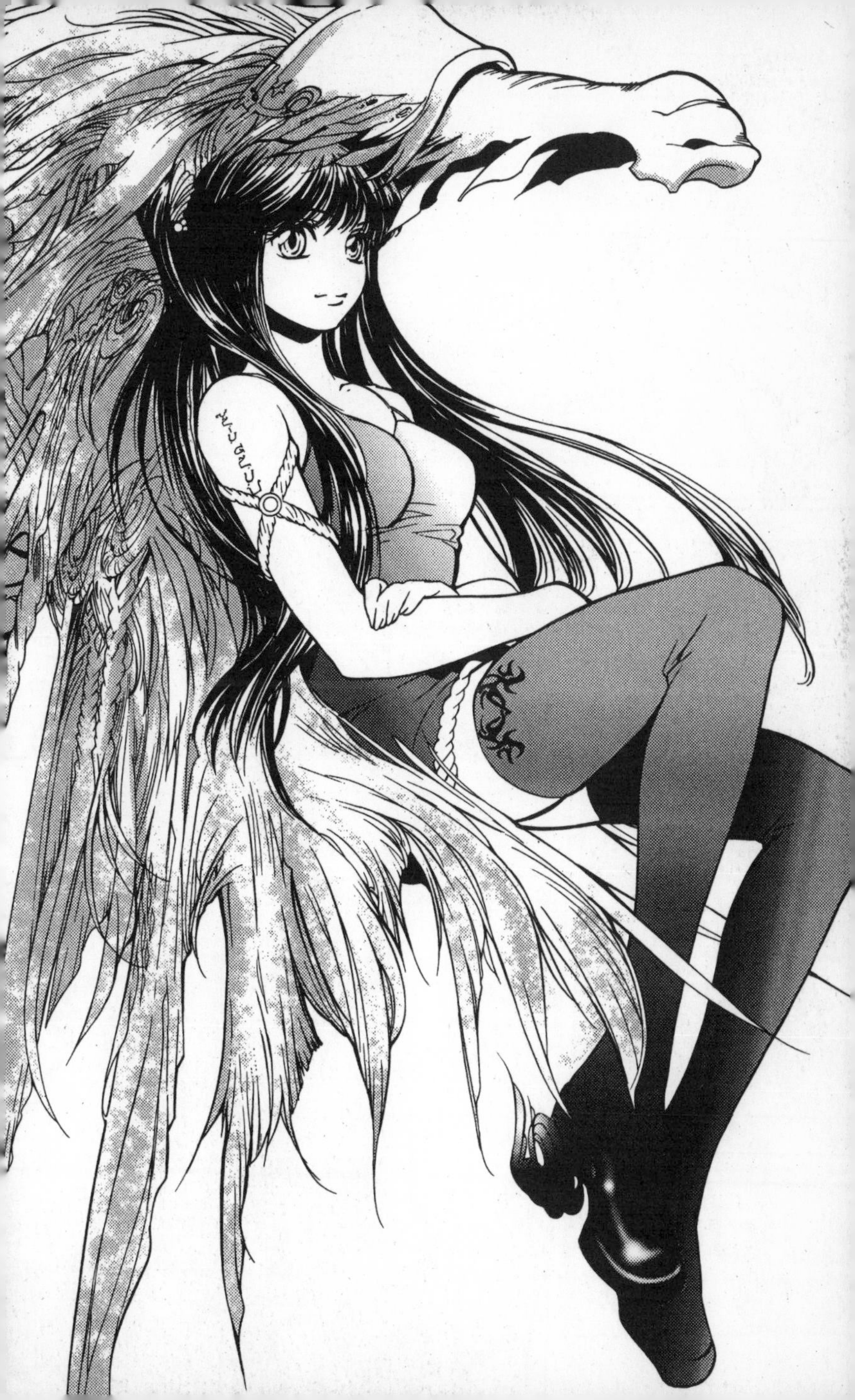

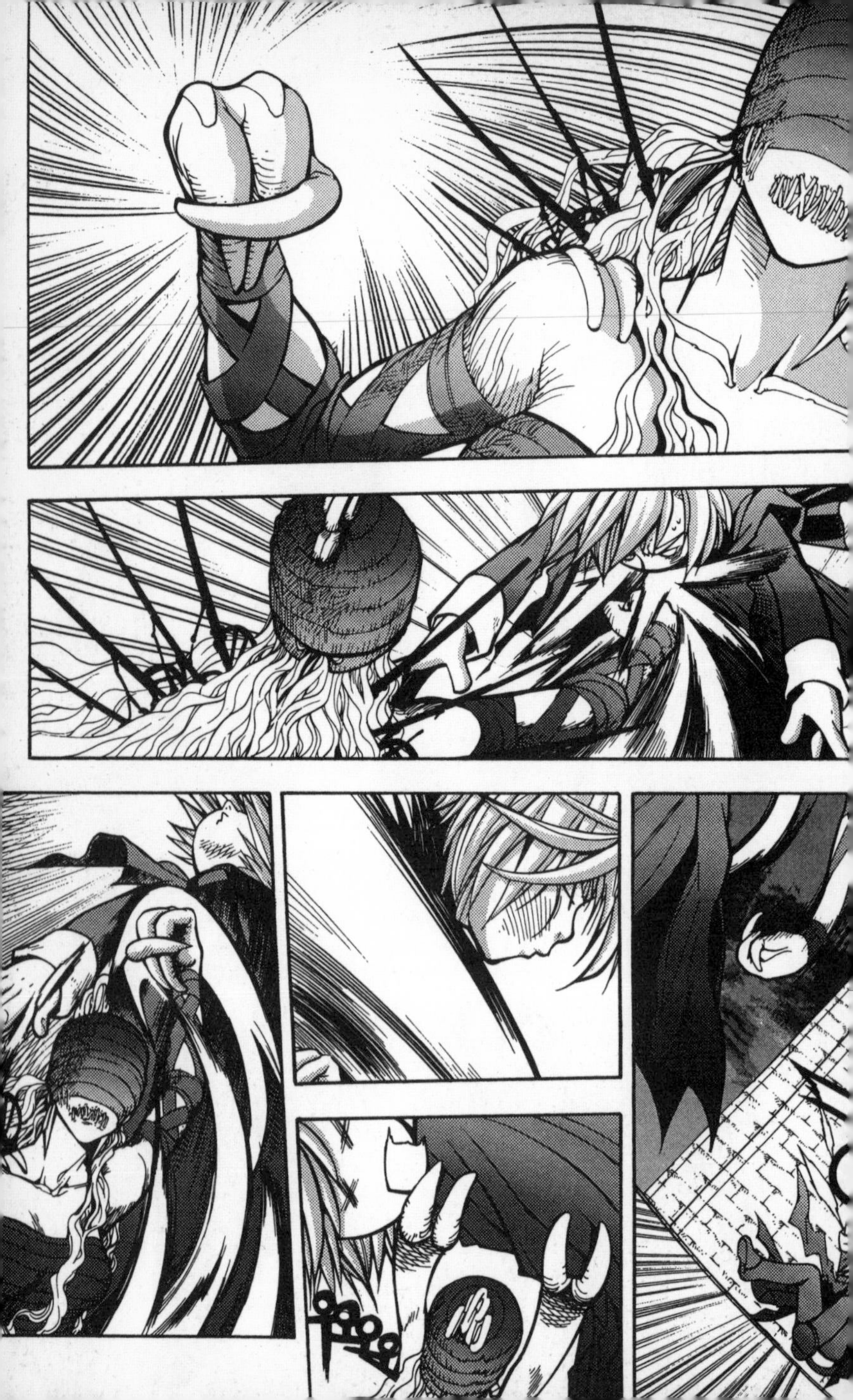

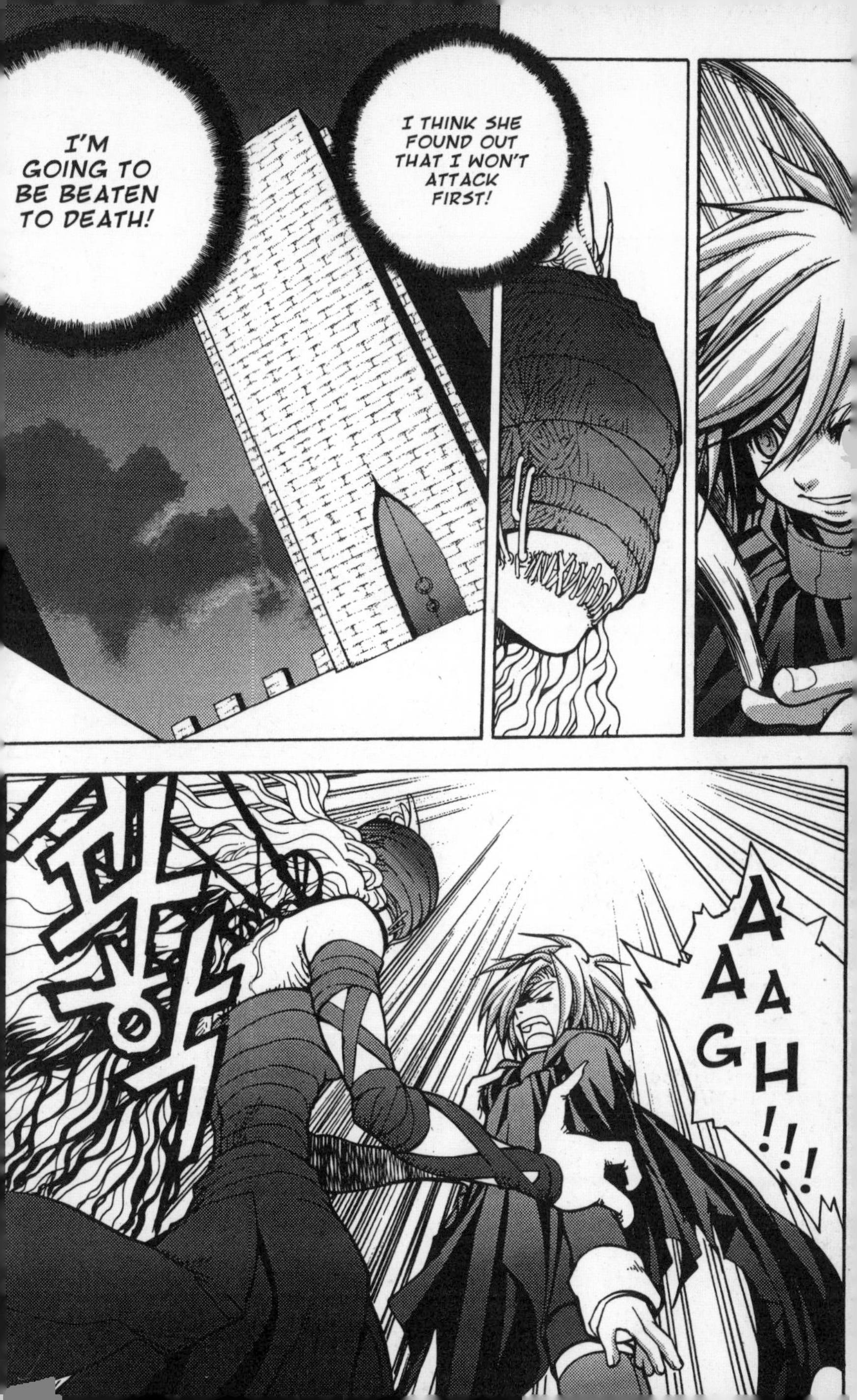
I'M GOING TO BE BEATEN TO DEATH!
I THINK SHE FOUND OUT THAT I WON'T ATTACK FIRST!
AAAGH!!!!

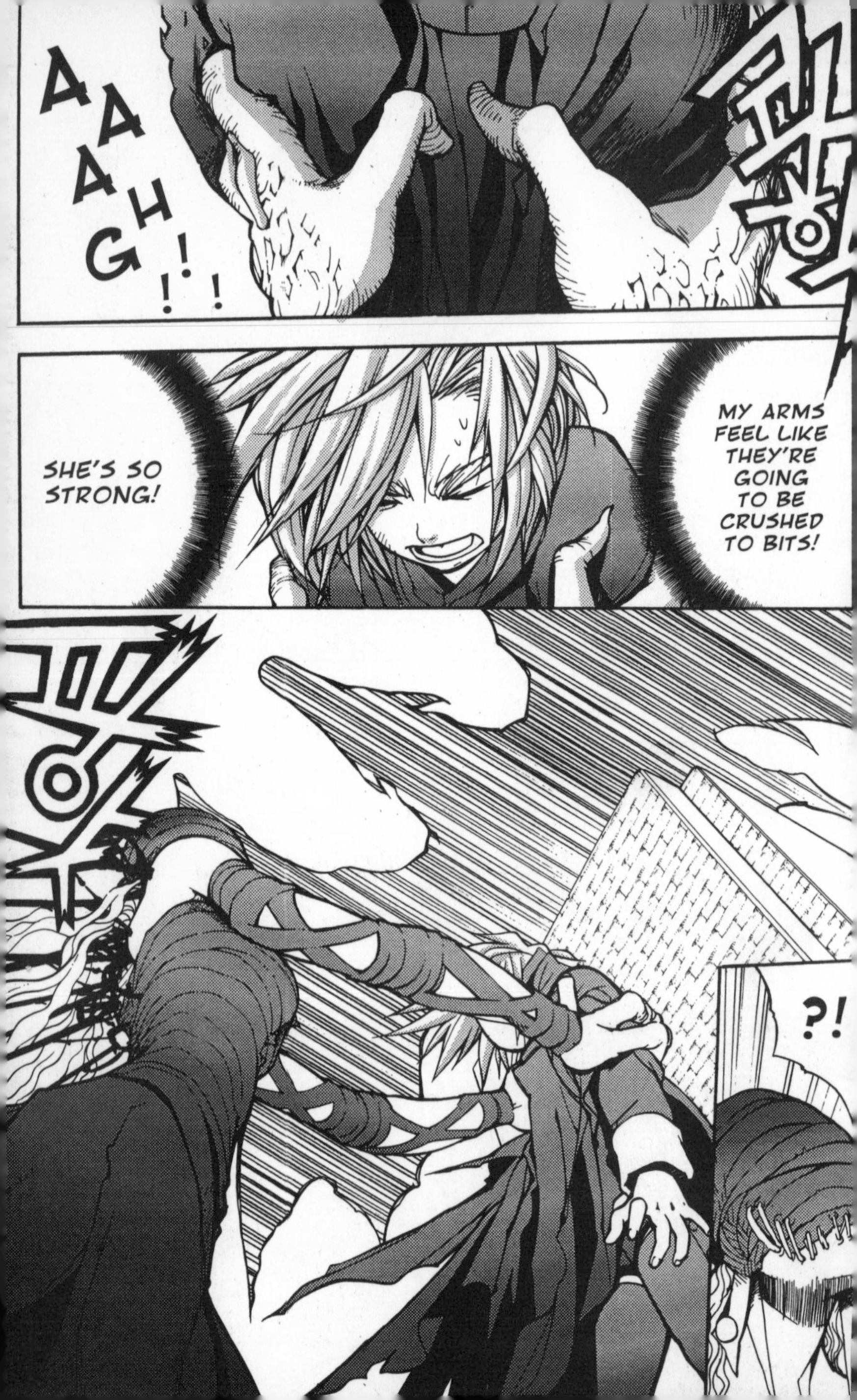
AAAGH!!!
SHE'S SO STRONG!
MY ARMS FEEL LIKE THEY'RE GOING TO BE CRUSHED TO BITS!
?!

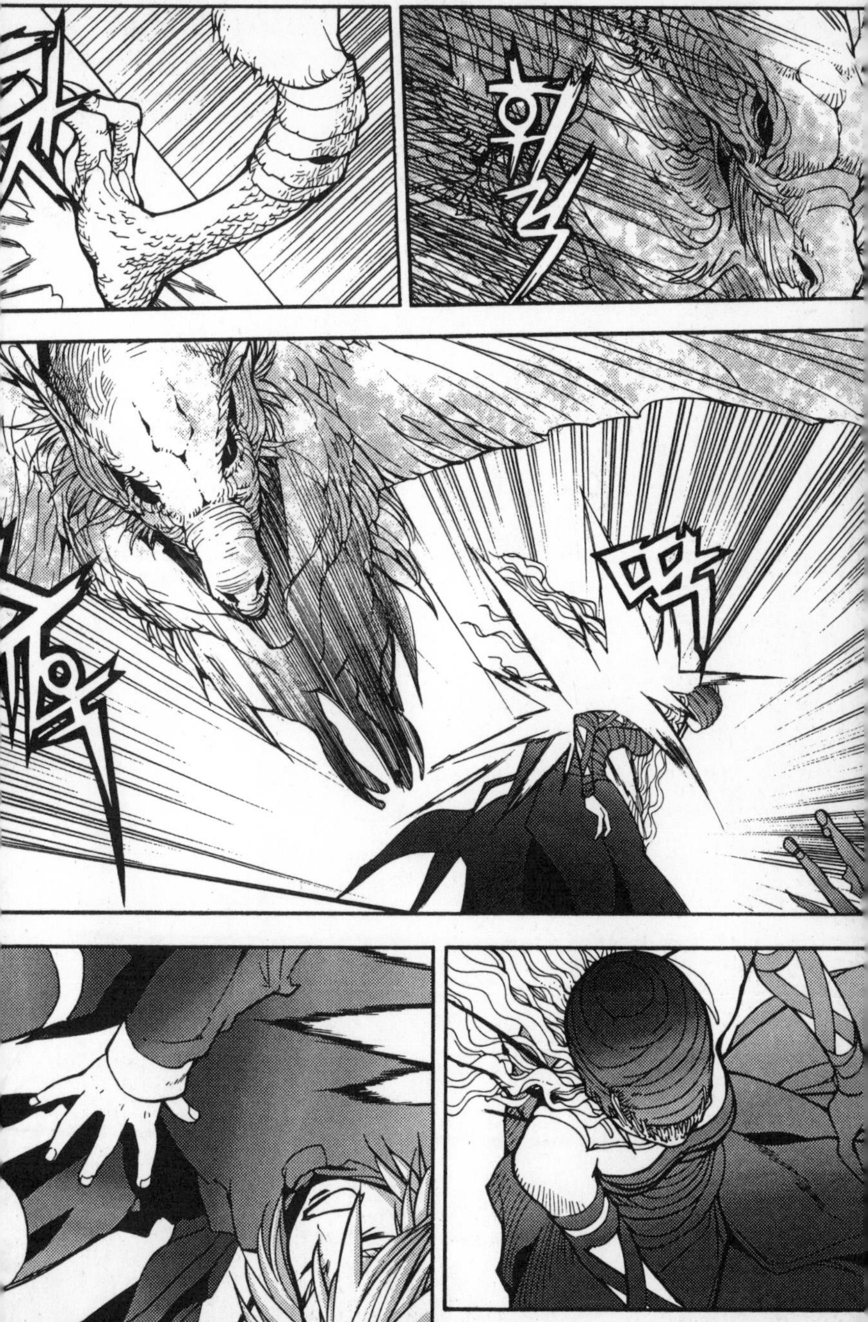

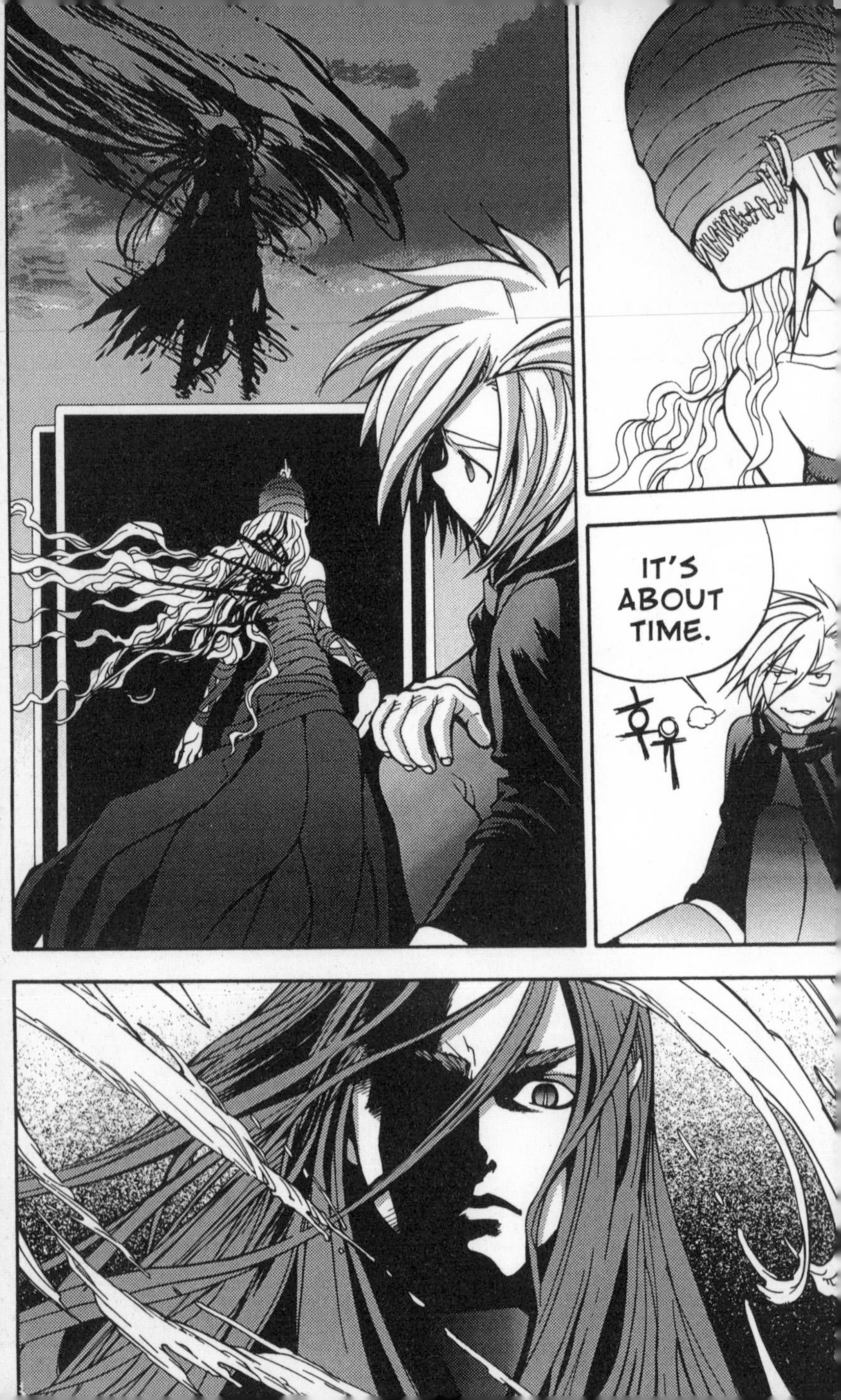
IT'S ABOUT TIME.

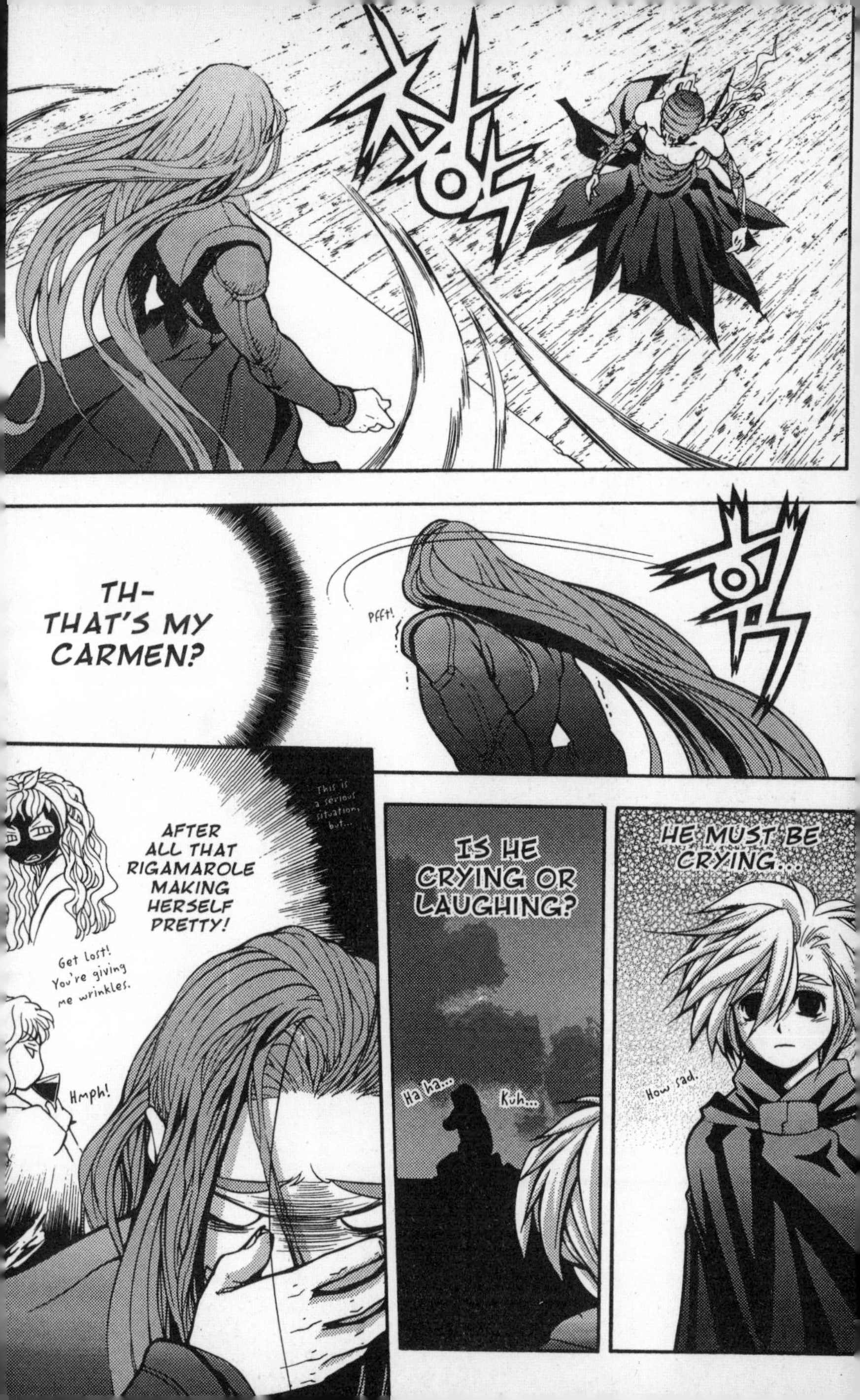
TH-
THAT'S MY
CARMEN?
Pffft!
AFTER ALL THAT RIGAMAROLE MAKING HERSELF PRETTY!
This is a serious situation, but...
Get lost! You're giving me wrinkles.
Hmph!
IS HE CRYING OR LAUGHING?
Ha ha...
Kuh...
HE MUST BE CRYING...
How sad.

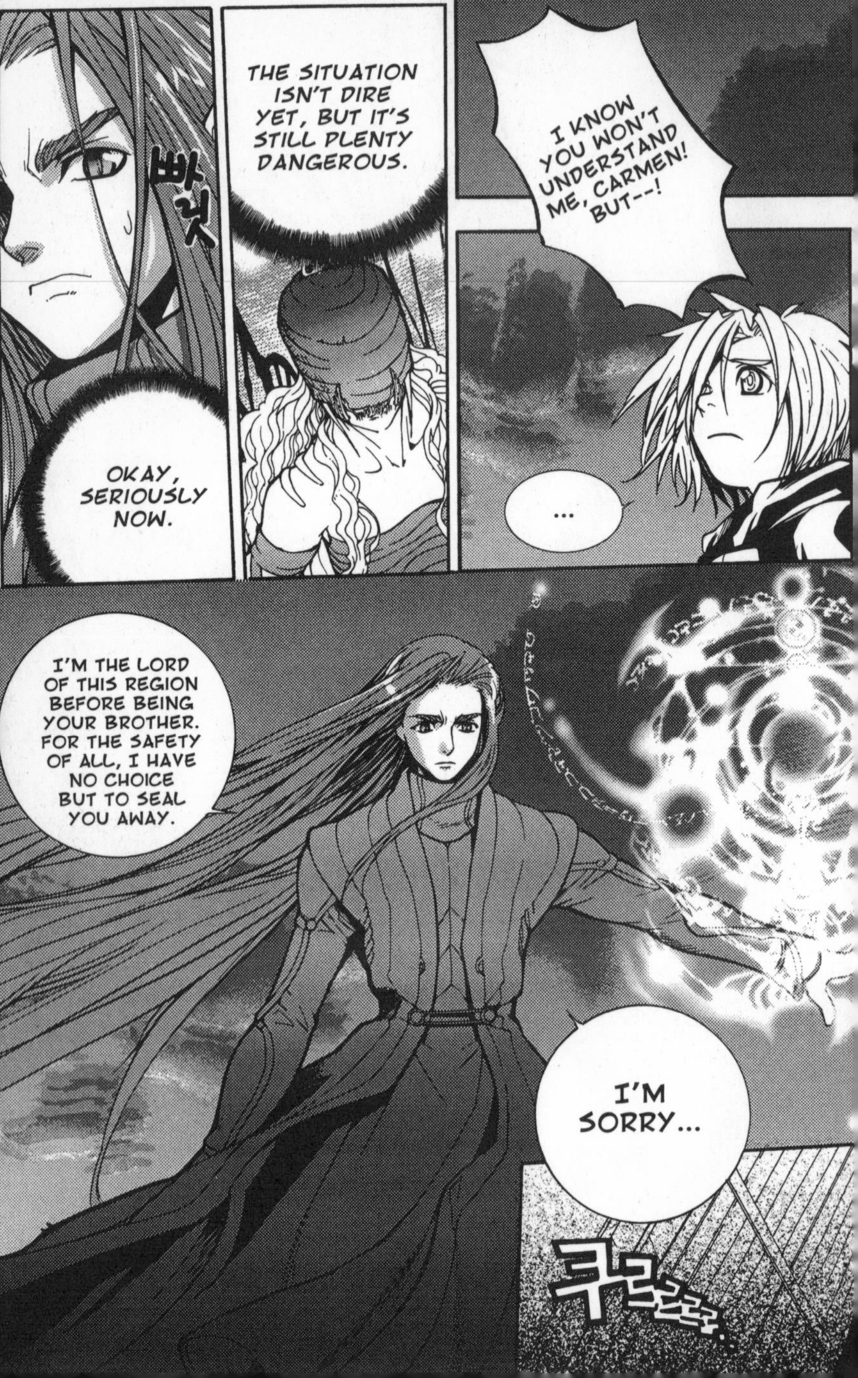
OKAY, SERIOUSLY NOW.
THE SITUATION ISN'T DIRE YET, BUT IT'S STILL PLENTY DANGEROUS.
I KNOW YOU WON'T UNDERSTAND ME, CARMEN! BUT--!
...
I'M THE LORD OF THIS REGION BEFORE BEING YOUR BROTHER. FOR THE SAFETY OF ALL, I HAVE NO CHOICE BUT TO SEAL YOU AWAY.
I'M SORRY...

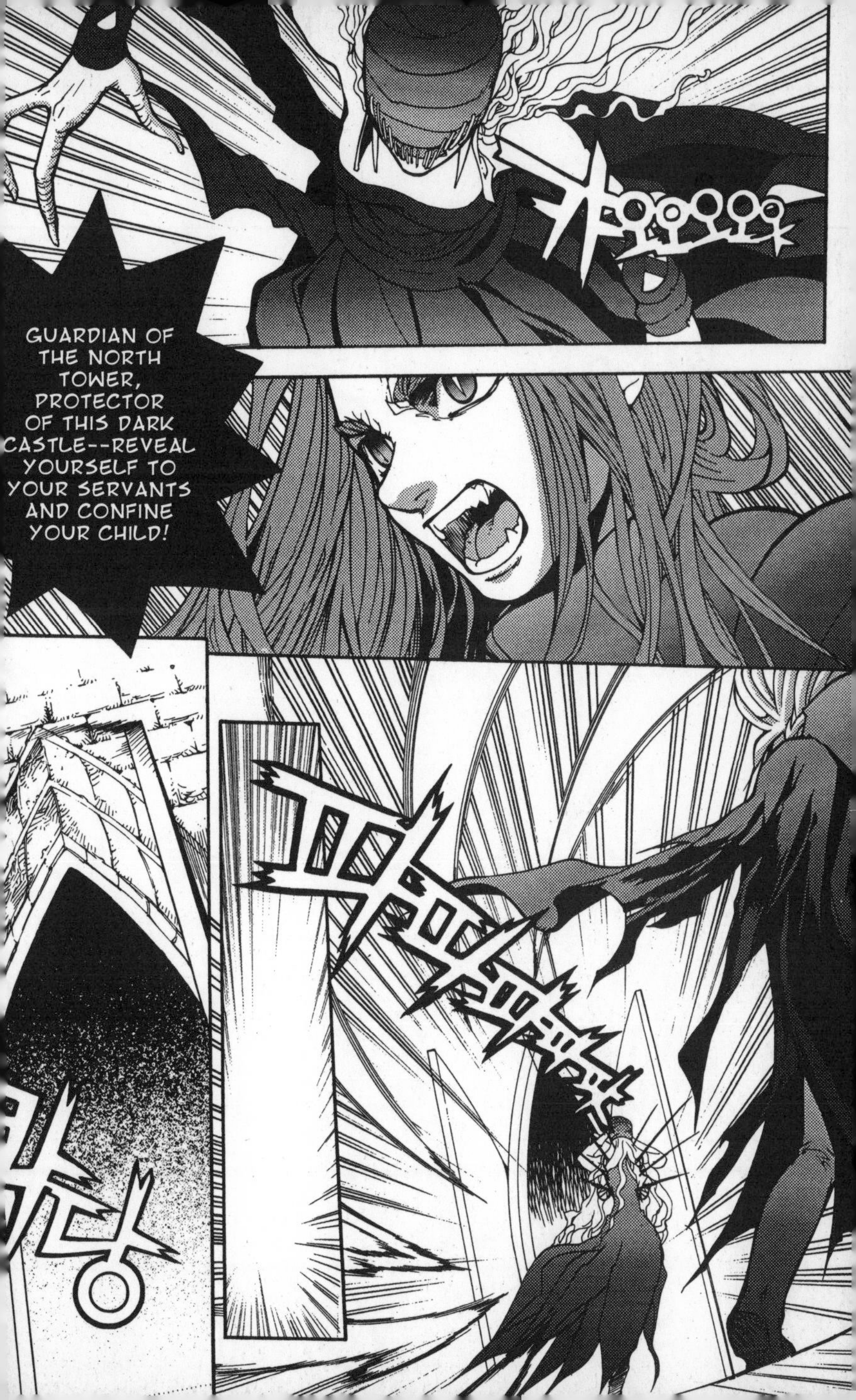
GUARDIAN OF THE NORTH TOWER, PROTECTOR OF THIS DARK CASTLE--REVEAL YOURSELF TO YOUR SERVANTS AND CONFINE YOUR CHILD!

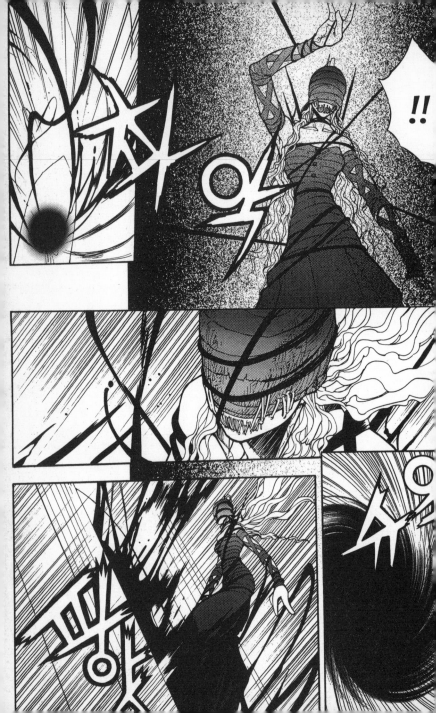

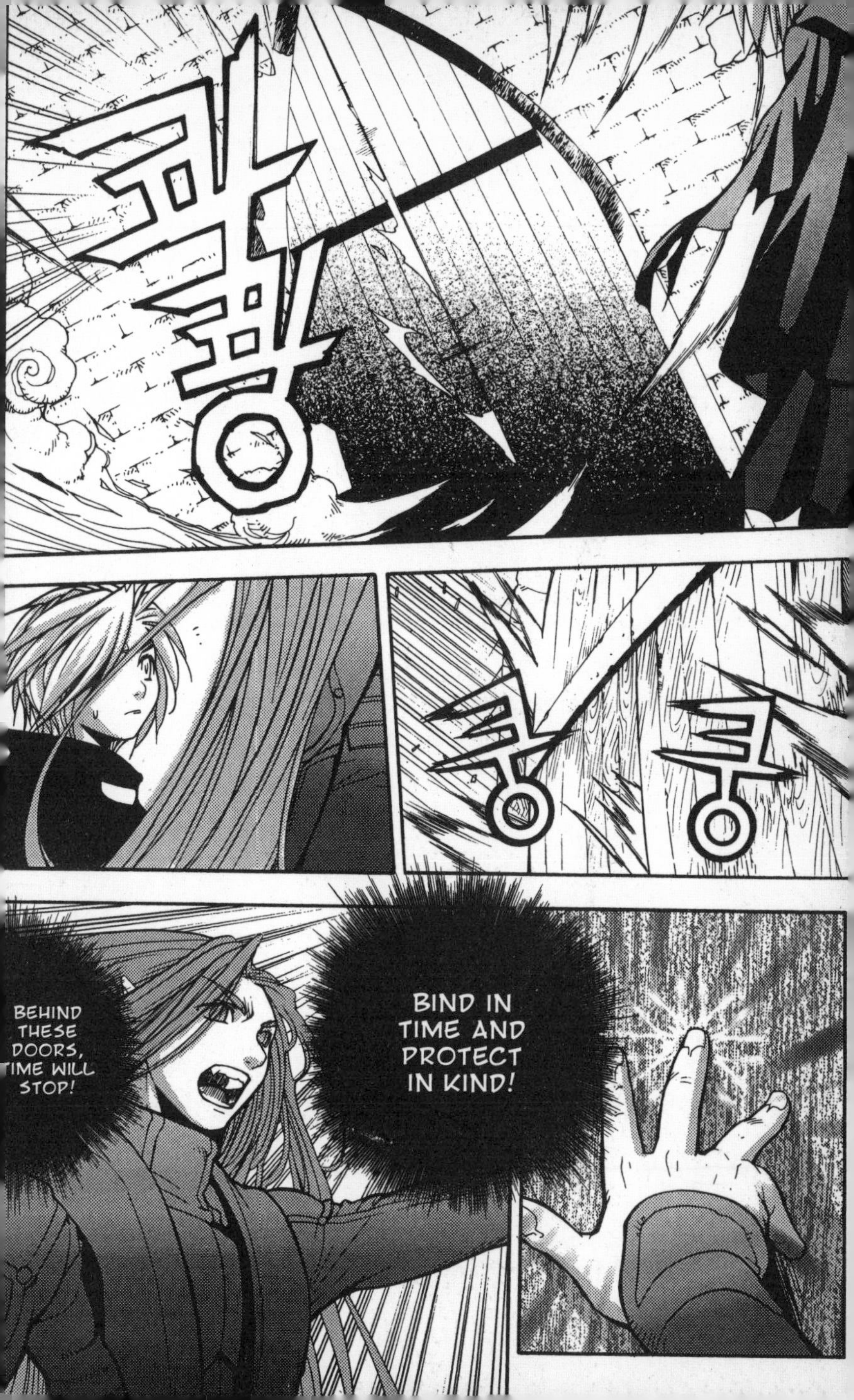
BEHIND THESE DOORS, TIME WILL STOP!
BIND IN TIME AND PROTECT IN KIND!

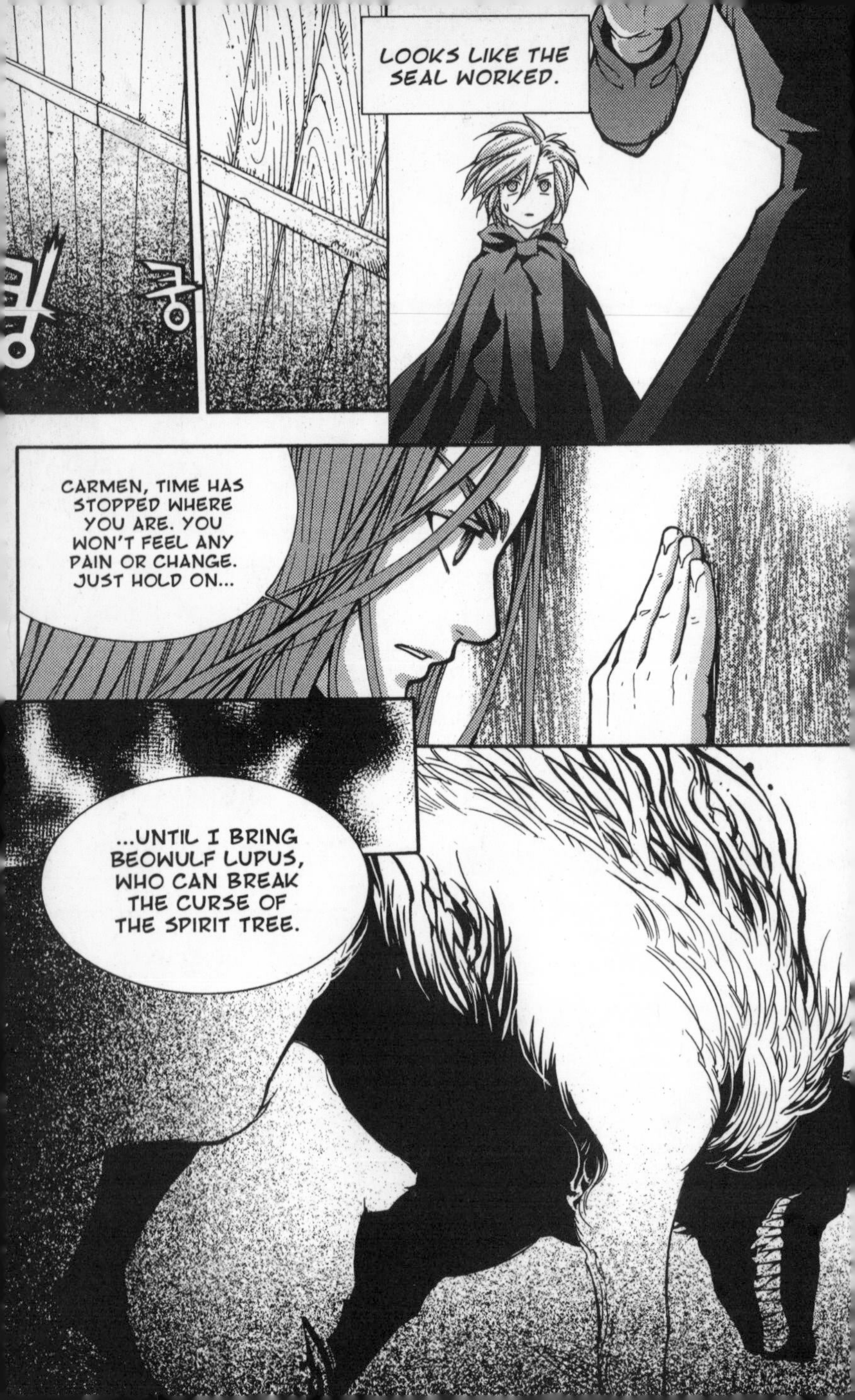
쿵
쿵
LOOKS LIKE THE SEAL WORKED.
CARMEN, TIME HAS STOPPED WHERE YOU ARE. YOU WON'T FEEL ANY PAIN OR CHANGE. JUST HOLD ON...
...UNTIL I BRING BEOWULF LUPUS, WHO CAN BREAK THE CURSE OF THE SPIRIT TREE.

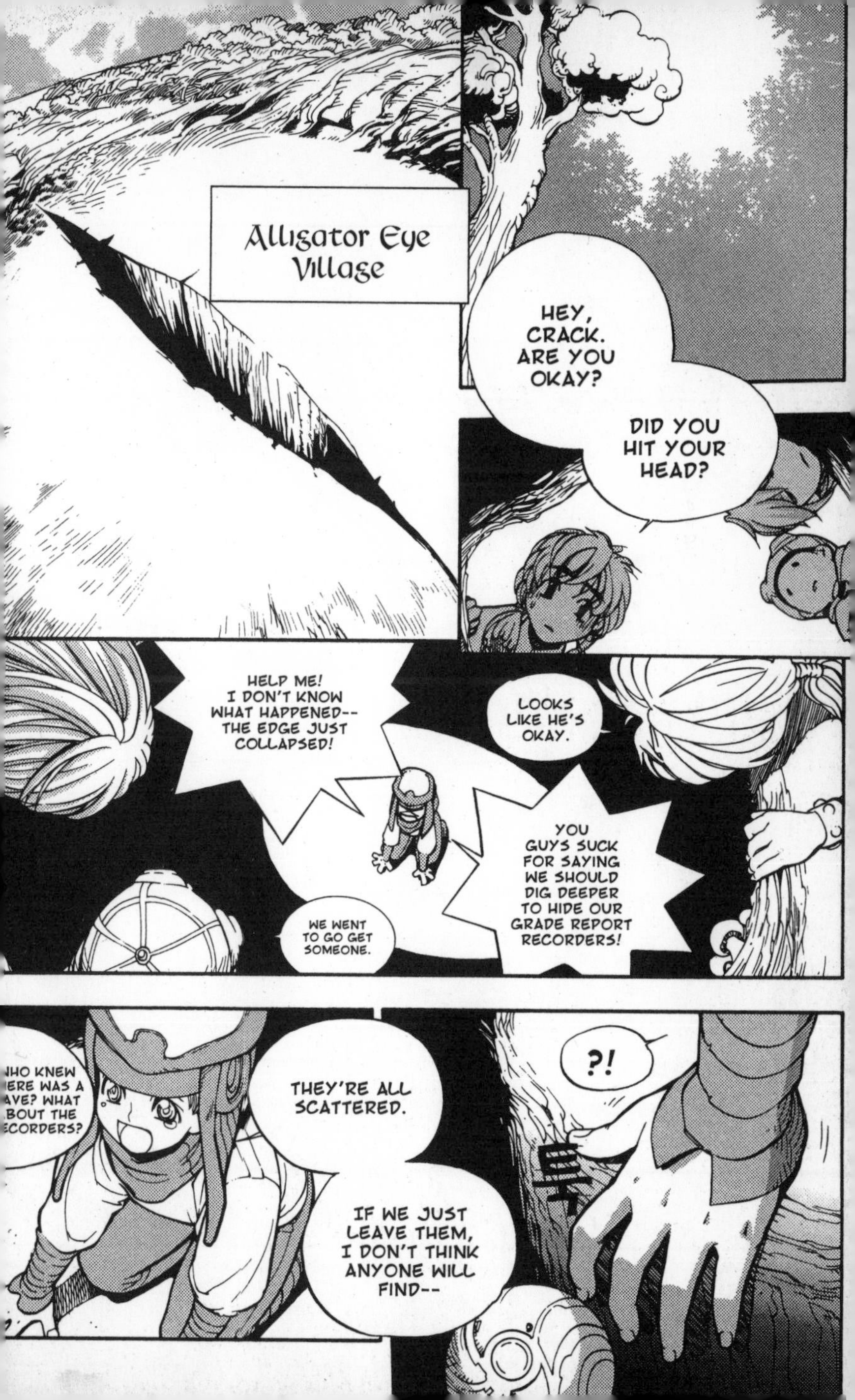
Alligator Eye Village
HEY, CRACK. ARE YOU OKAY?
DID YOU HIT YOUR HEAD?
HELP ME! I DON'T KNOW WHAT HAPPENED-- THE EDGE JUST COLLAPSED!
LOOKS LIKE HE'S OKAY.
YOU GUYS SUCK FOR SAYING WE SHOULD DIG DEEPER TO HIDE OUR GRADE REPORT RECORDERS!
WE WENT TO GO GET SOMEONE.
HO KNEW ERE WAS A AVE? WHAT BOUT THE ECORDERS?
THEY'RE ALL SCATTERED.
IF WE JUST LEAVE THEM, I DON'T THINK ANYONE WILL FIND--
?!

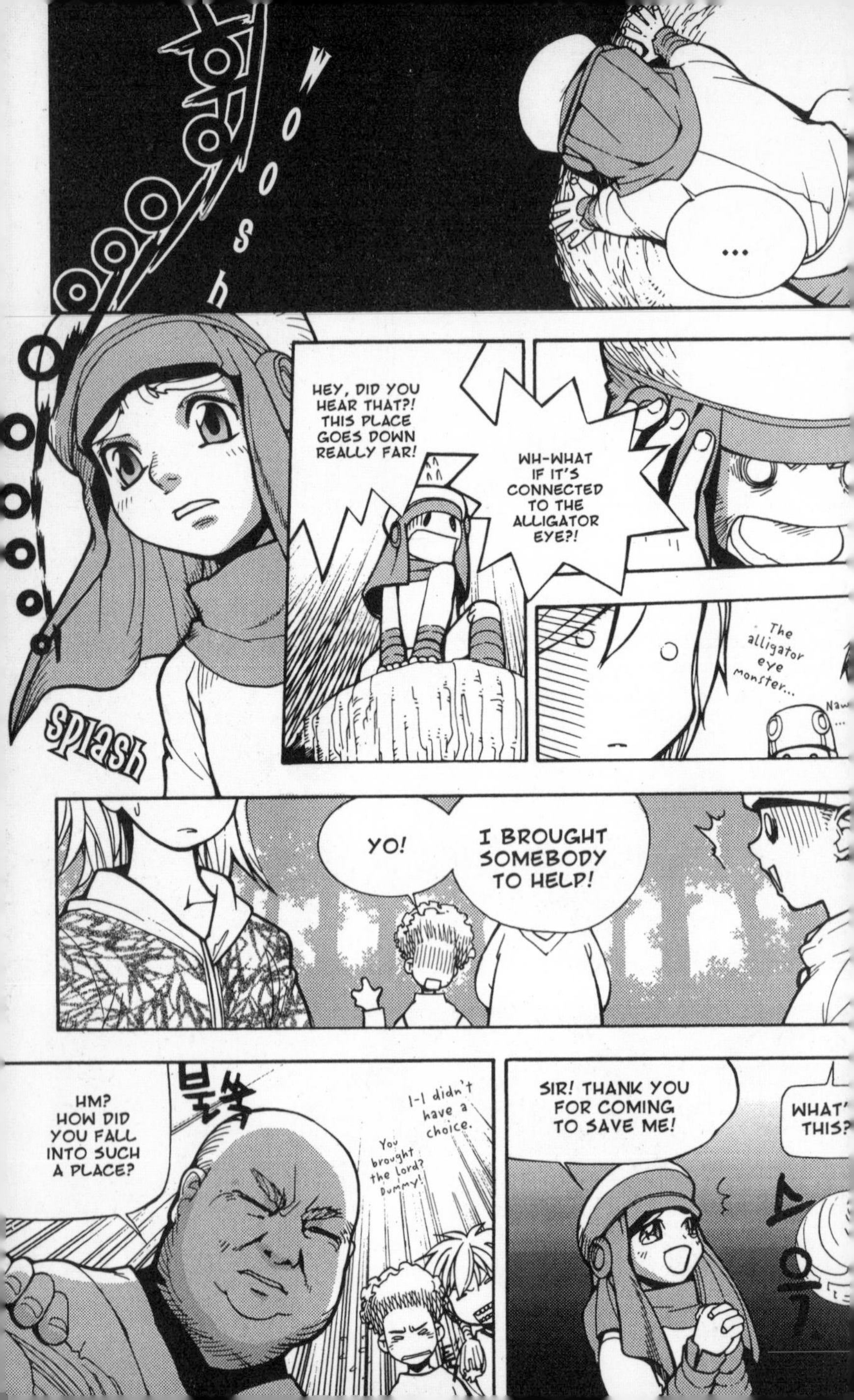

Woosh
...
splash
HEY, DID YOU HEAR THAT?! THIS PLACE GOES DOWN REALLY FAR!
WH-WHAT IF IT'S CONNECTED TO THE ALLIGATOR EYE?!
The alligator eye monster...
YO!
I BROUGHT SOMEBODY TO HELP!
HM? HOW DID YOU FALL INTO SUCH A PLACE?
I-I didn't have a choice.
You brought the lord? Dummy!
SIR! THANK YOU FOR COMING TO SAVE ME!
WHAT' THIS?

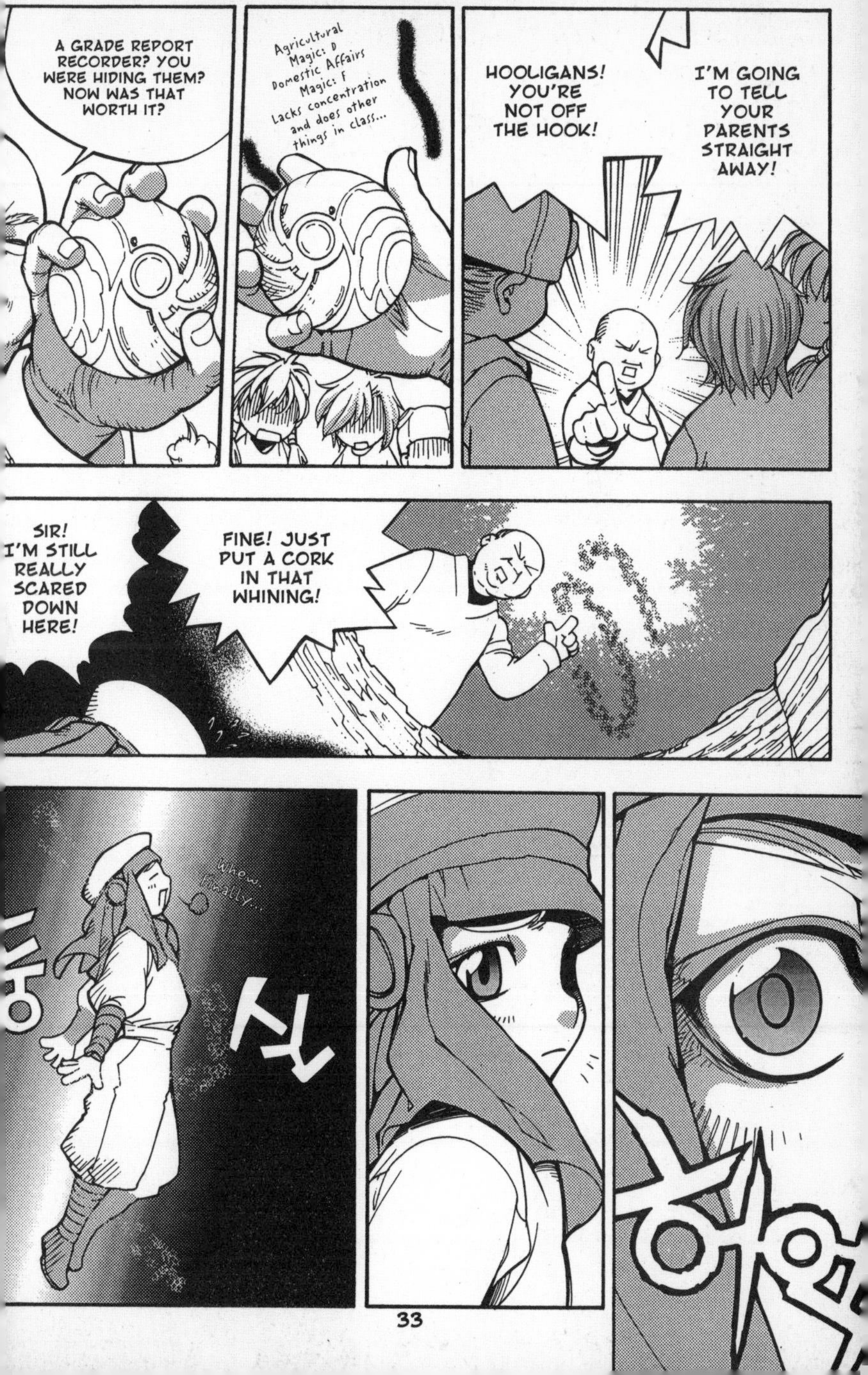
A GRADE REPORT RECORDER? YOU WERE HIDING THEM? NOW WAS THAT WORTH IT?
Agricultural Magic: D
Domestic Affairs Magic: F
Lacks concentration and does other things in class...
HOOLIGANS! YOU'RE NOT OFF THE HOOK!
I'M GOING TO TELL YOUR PARENTS STRAIGHT AWAY!
SIR! I'M STILL REALLY SCARED DOWN HERE!
FINE! JUST PUT A CORK IN THAT WHINING!
Whew. Finally...

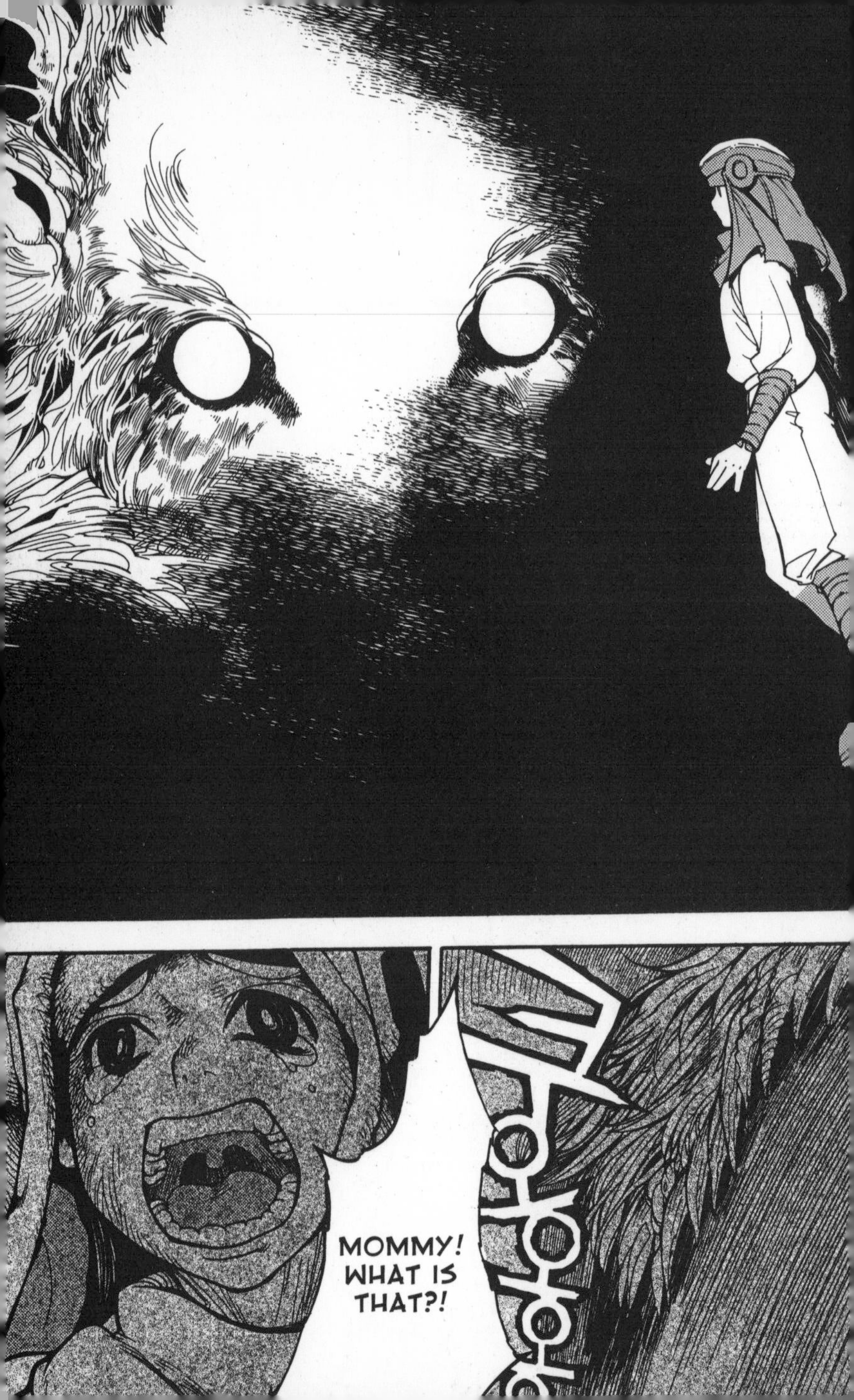
MOMMY! WHAT IS THAT?!

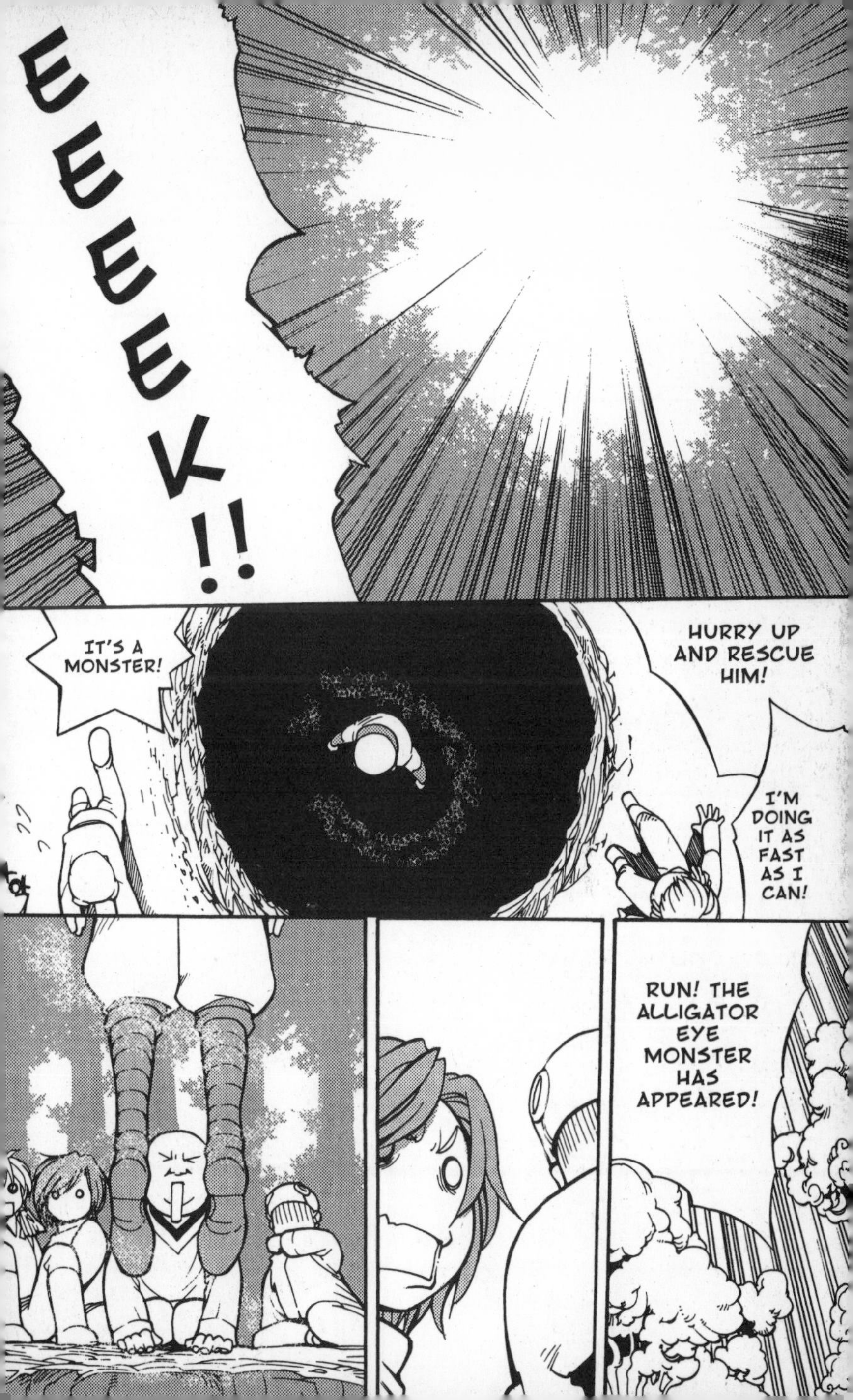
EEEEEK!!
IT'S A MONSTER!
HURRY UP AND RESCUE HIM!
I'M DOING IT AS FAST AS I CAN!
RUN! THE ALLIGATOR EYE MONSTER HAS APPEARED!

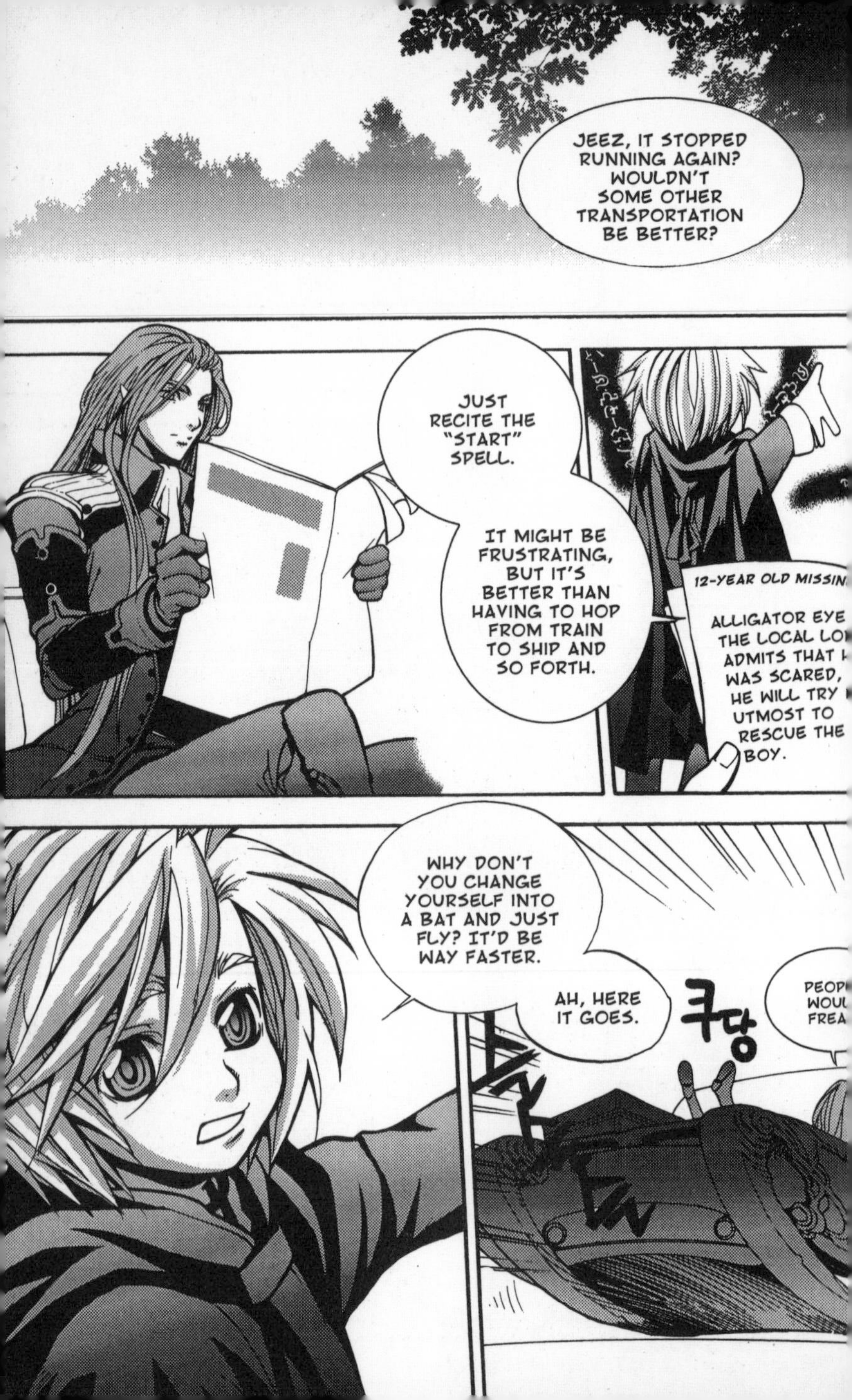
JEEZ, IT STOPPED RUNNING AGAIN? WOULDN'T SOME OTHER TRANSPORTATION BE BETTER?
JUST RECITE THE "START" SPELL.
IT MIGHT BE FRUSTRATING, BUT IT'S BETTER THAN HAVING TO HOP FROM TRAIN TO SHIP AND SO FORTH.
12-YEAR OLD MISSIN
ALLIGATOR EYE THE LOCAL LO ADMITS THAT WAS SCARED, HE WILL TRY UTMOST TO RESCUE THE BOY.
WHY DON'T YOU CHANGE YOURSELF INTO A BAT AND JUST FLY? IT'D BE WAY FASTER.
AH, HERE IT GOES.
쿠당

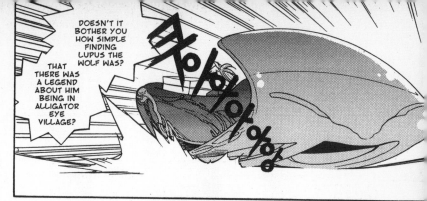

DOESN'T IT BOTHER YOU HOW SIMPLE FINDING LUPUS THE WOLF WAS?

THAT THERE WAS A LEGEND ABOUT HIM BEING IN ALLIGATOR EYE VILLAGE?

OBSERVE! FROM THE "NATIONAL INQUISITOR" OF THE CROCODILE REGION!

IT'S AN ARTICLE ABOUT THIS VERY SUBJECT!

## MONSTER WOLF RETURNS?!

A CHILD WENT MISSING IN THE RAVINE OF ALLIGATOR EYE, LIKELY A VICTIM OF THE INFAMOUS "MONSTER WOLF" OF THE TOWN!

THE BOY WAS PLAYING IN A NEARBY FOREST WITH HIS FRIENDS WHEN THE GROUND GAVE WAY BENEATH HIM AND HE FELL INTO A PIT. INSIDE THE PIT, HE CAME FACE-TO-FACE WITH A CREATURE HIGHLY SUSPECTED TO BE THE MONSTER WOLF OF LEGENDS!

C'MON, EVERYBODY KNOWS THAT PAPER'S MADE UP. MY FRIENDS CALL IT THE BALONEY PAPER.

AREN'T YOU TOO OLD FOR THAT?

!!!

DON'T YOU SPOIL MY PLEASURES OF THE OUTSIDE WORLD... MY REGION DOESN'T HAVE ANY OF THIS STUFF.

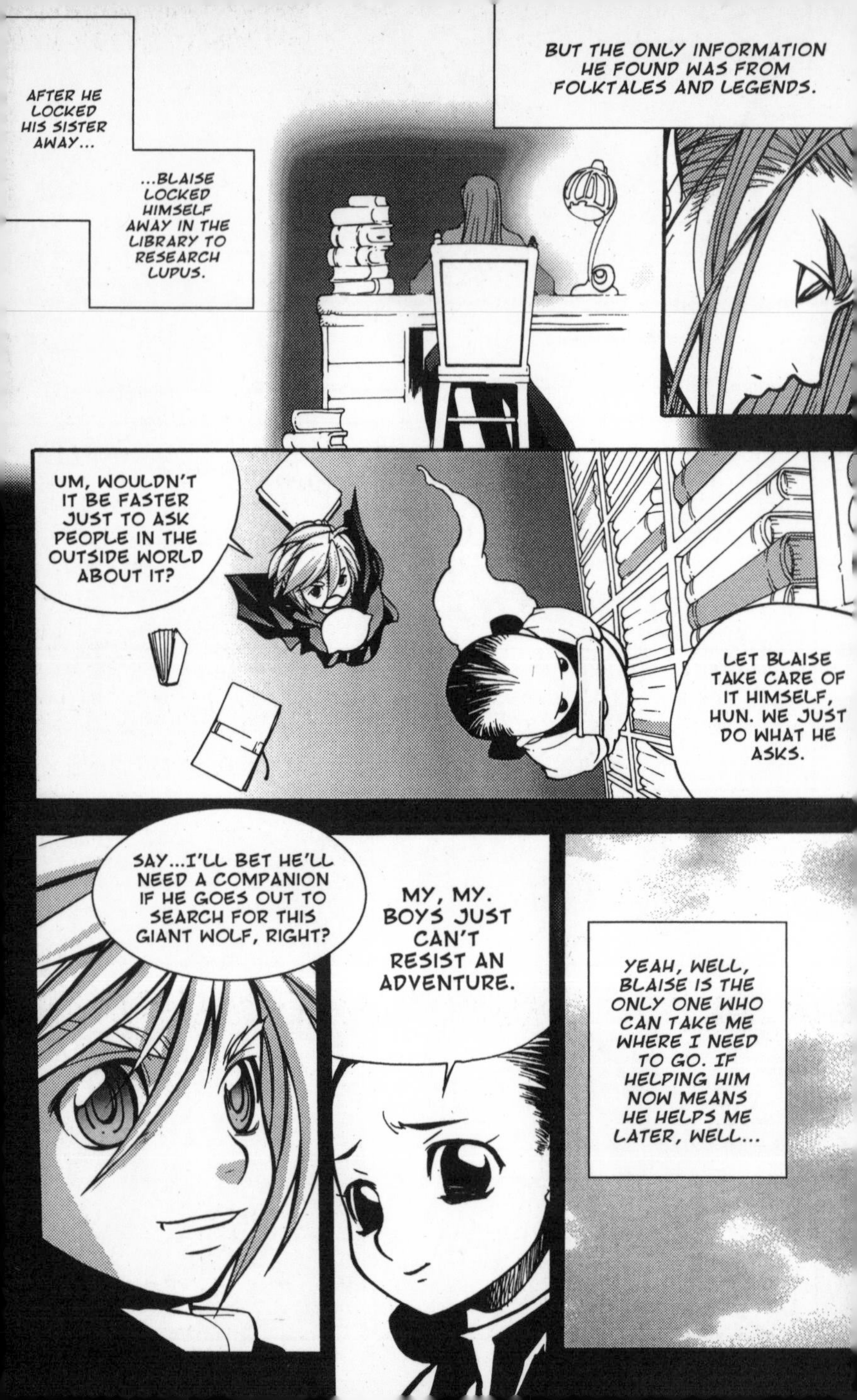
AFTER HE LOCKED HIS SISTER AWAY...
...BLAISE LOCKED HIMSELF AWAY IN THE LIBRARY TO RESEARCH LUPUS.
BUT THE ONLY INFORMATION HE FOUND WAS FROM FOLKTALES AND LEGENDS.
UM, WOULDN'T IT BE FASTER JUST TO ASK PEOPLE IN THE OUTSIDE WORLD ABOUT IT?
LET BLAISE TAKE CARE OF IT HIMSELF, HUN. WE JUST DO WHAT HE ASKS.
SAY...I'LL BET HE'LL NEED A COMPANION IF HE GOES OUT TO SEARCH FOR THIS GIANT WOLF, RIGHT?
MY, MY. BOYS JUST CAN'T RESIST AN ADVENTURE.
YEAH, WELL, BLAISE IS THE ONLY ONE WHO CAN TAKE ME WHERE I NEED TO GO. IF HELPING HIM NOW MEANS HE HELPS ME LATER, WELL...

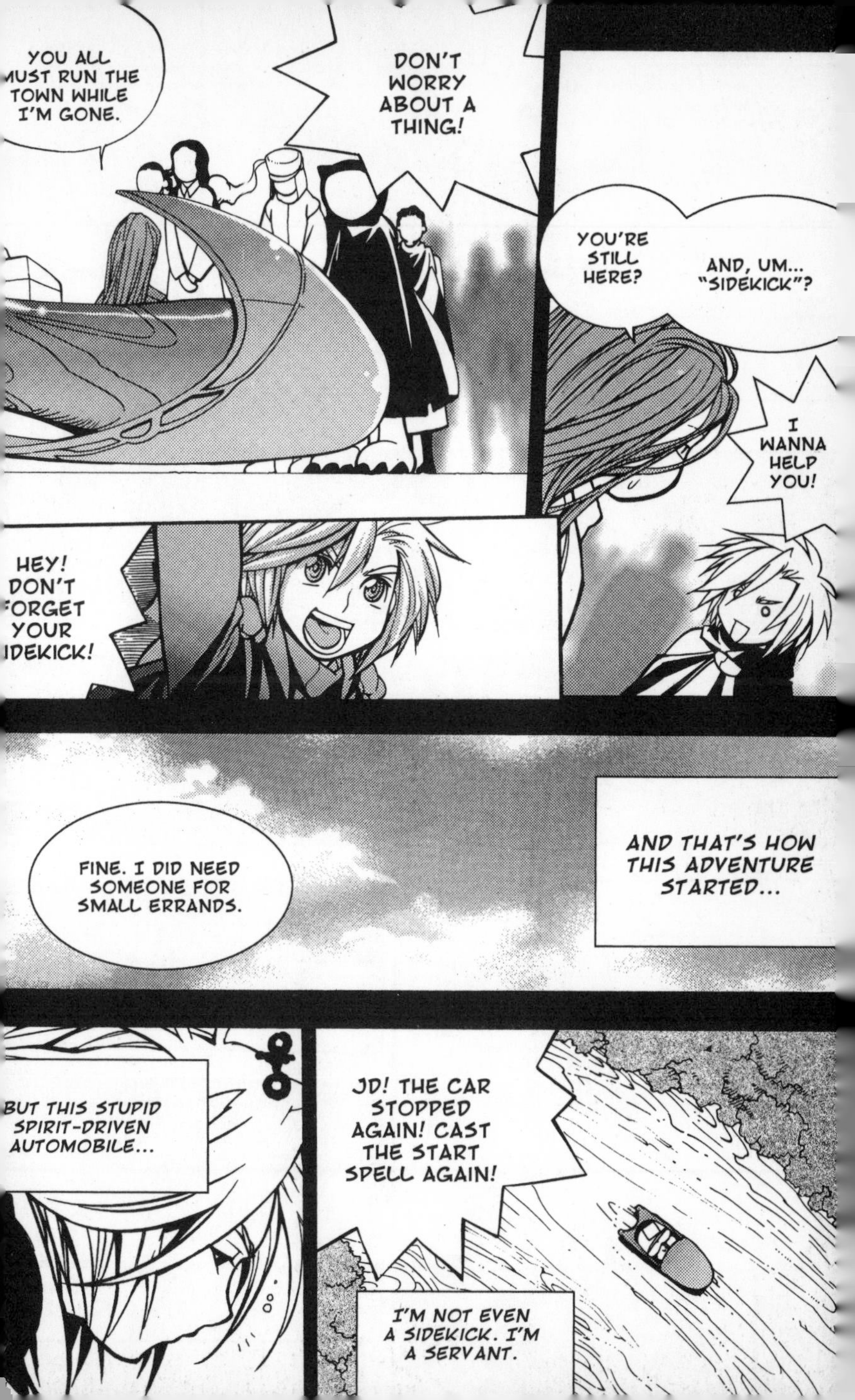

YOU ALL MUST RUN THE TOWN WHILE I'M GONE.
DON'T WORRY ABOUT A THING!
HEY! DON'T FORGET YOUR IDEKICK!
YOU'RE STILL HERE?
AND, UM... "SIDEKICK"?
I WANNA HELP YOU!
FINE. I DID NEED SOMEONE FOR SMALL ERRANDS.
AND THAT'S HOW THIS ADVENTURE STARTED...
BUT THIS STUPID SPIRIT-DRIVEN AUTOMOBILE...
JD! THE CAR STOPPED AGAIN! CAST THE START SPELL AGAIN!
I'M NOT EVEN A SIDEKICK. I'M A SERVANT.

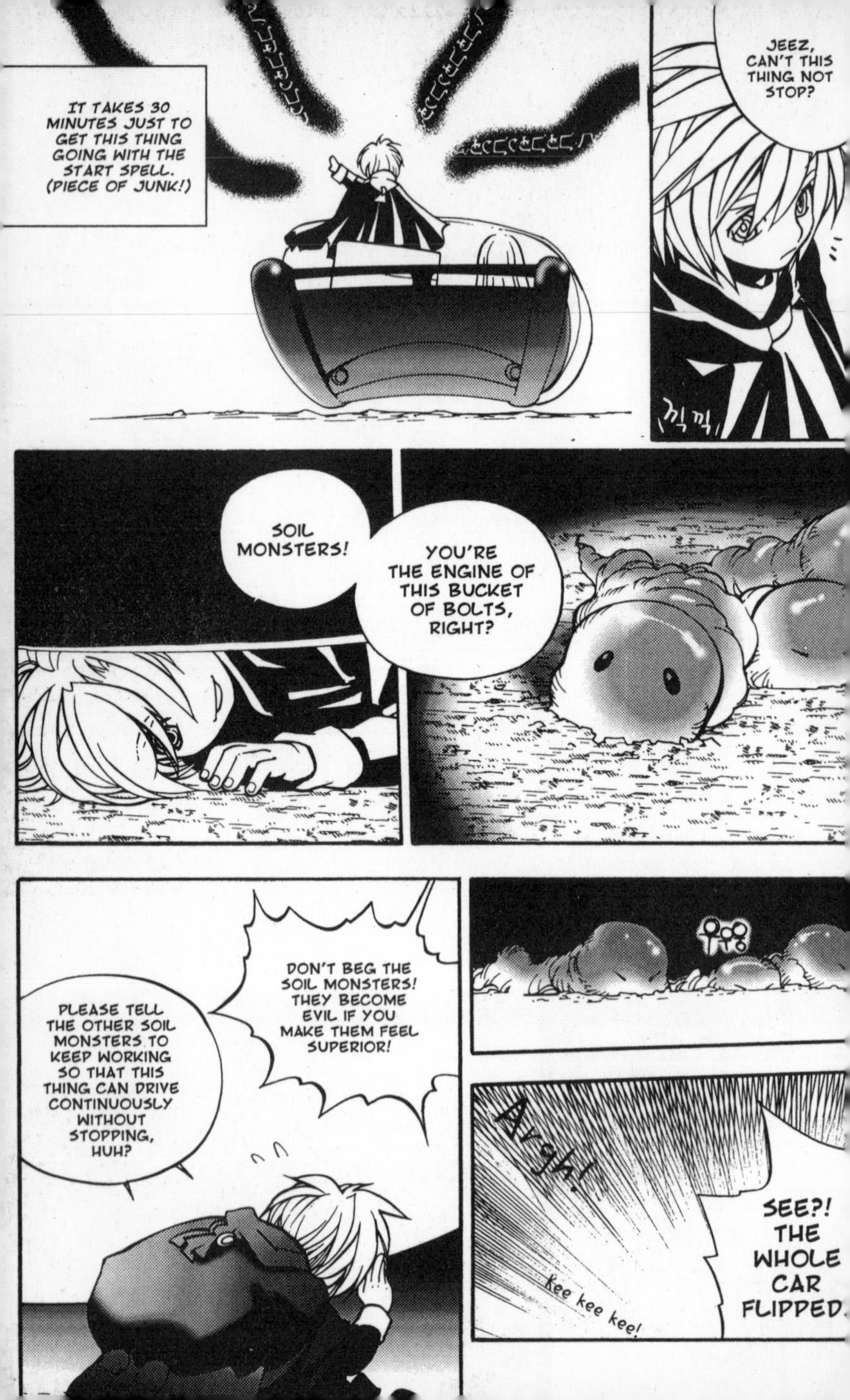
IT TAKES 30 MINUTES JUST TO GET THIS THING GOING WITH THE START SPELL. (PIECE OF JUNK!)
JEEZ, CAN'T THIS THING NOT STOP?
SOIL MONSTERS!
YOU'RE THE ENGINE OF THIS BUCKET OF BOLTS, RIGHT?
PLEASE TELL THE OTHER SOIL MONSTERS TO KEEP WORKING SO THAT THIS THING CAN DRIVE CONTINUOUSLY WITHOUT STOPPING, HUH?
DON'T BEG THE SOIL MONSTERS! THEY BECOME EVIL IF YOU MAKE THEM FEEL SUPERIOR!
Argh!
SEE?! THE WHOLE CAR FLIPPED.
Kee kee kee!

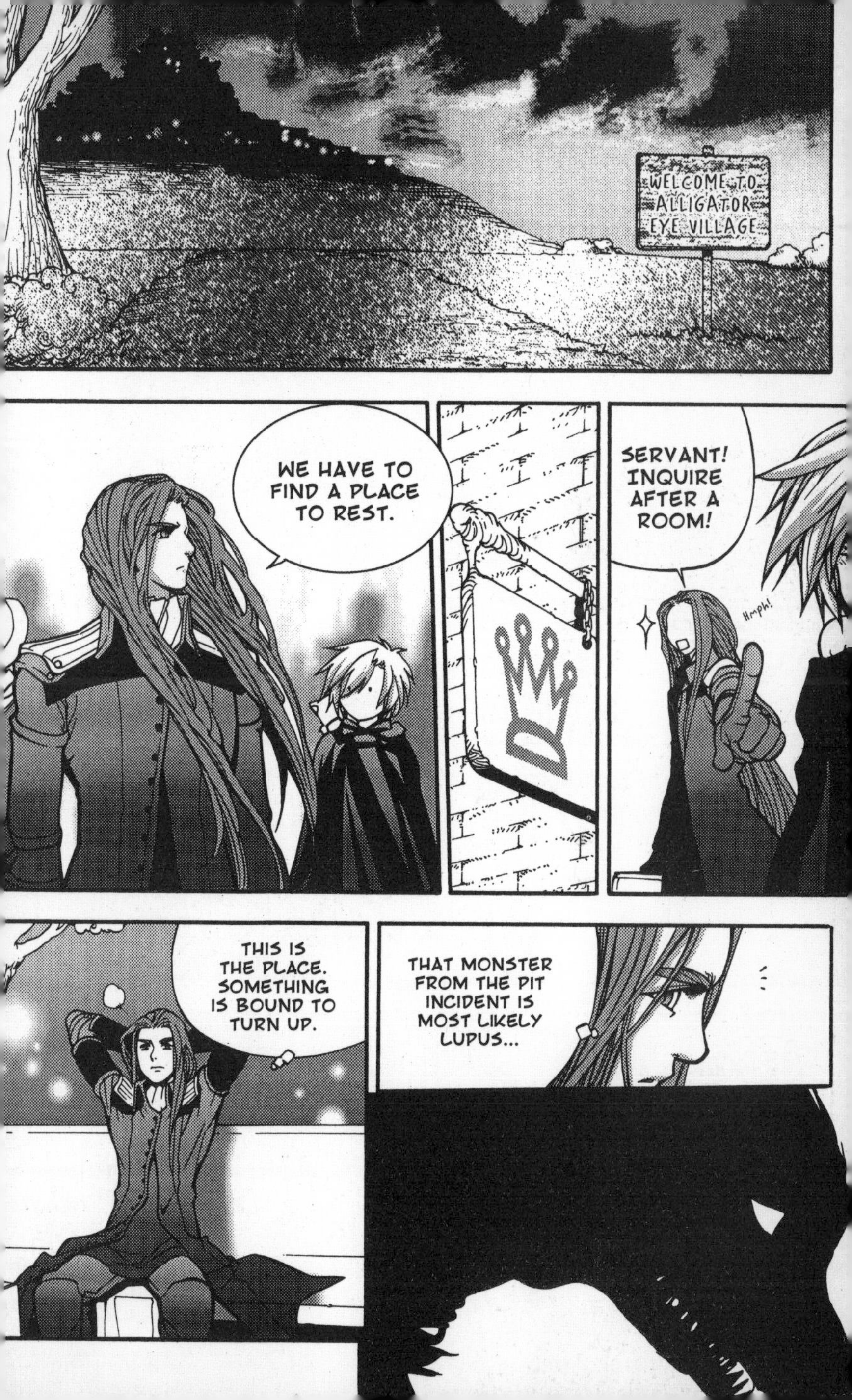
WELCOME TO ALLIGATOR EYE VILLAGE
WE HAVE TO FIND A PLACE TO REST.
SERVANT! INQUIRE AFTER A ROOM!
Hmph!
THIS IS THE PLACE. SOMETHING IS BOUND TO TURN UP.
THAT MONSTER FROM THE PIT INCIDENT IS MOST LIKELY LUPUS...

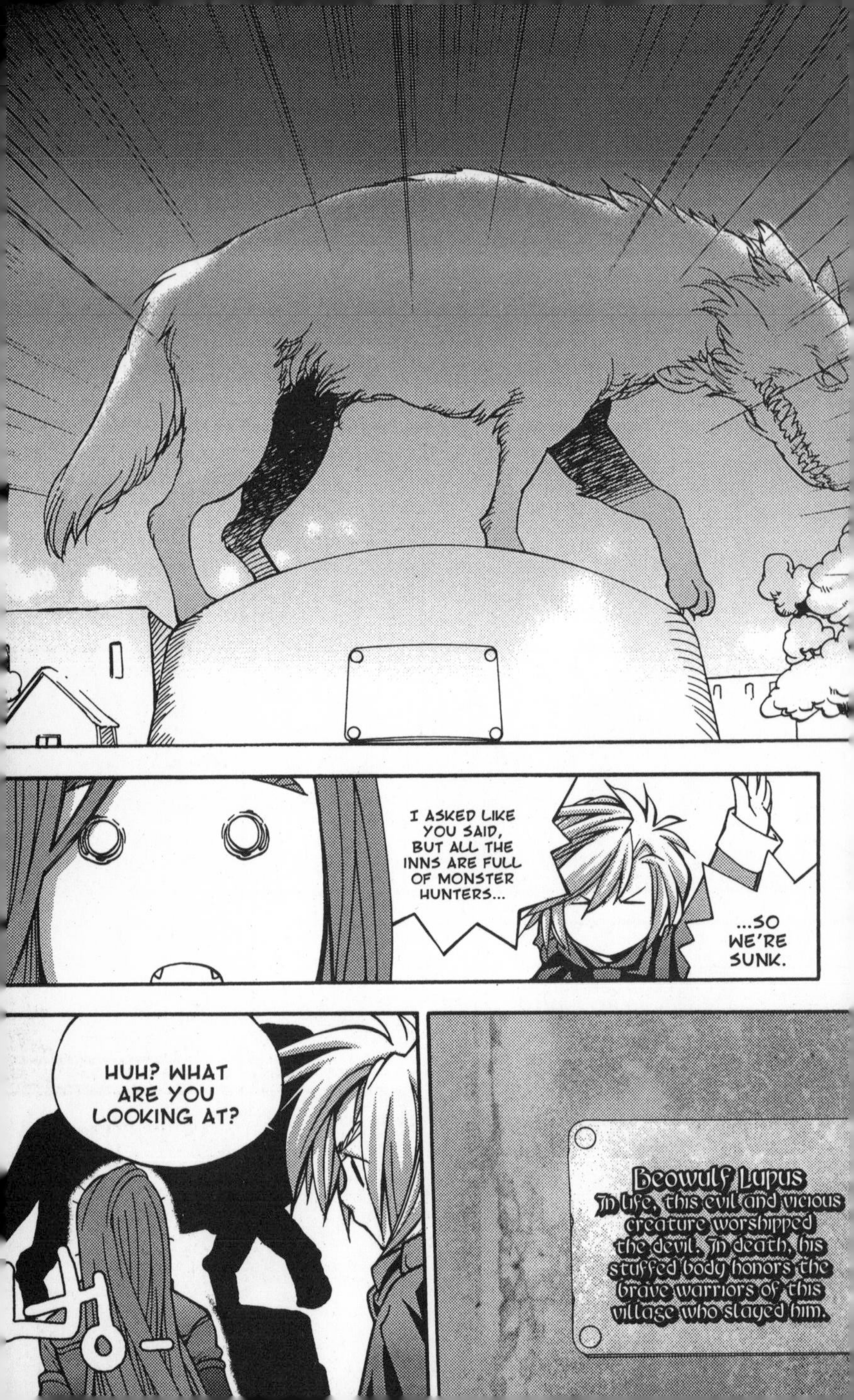
I ASKED LIKE YOU SAID, BUT ALL THE INNS ARE FULL OF MONSTER HUNTERS...
...SO WE'RE SUNK.
HUH? WHAT ARE YOU LOOKING AT?
Beowulf Lupus
In life, this evil and vicious creature worshipped the devil. In death, his stuffed body honors the brave warriors of this village who slayed him.

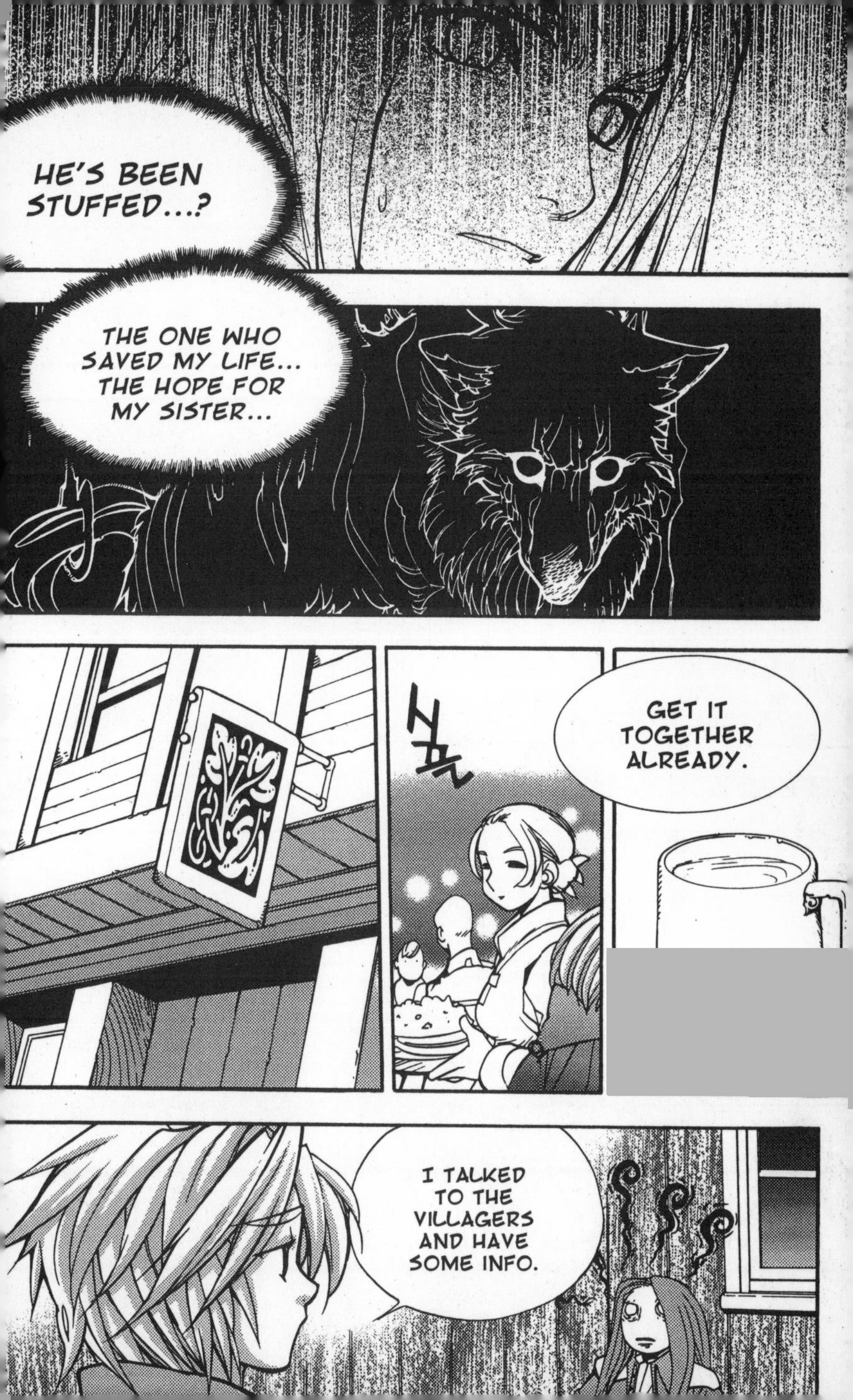
HE'S BEEN STUFFED...?
THE ONE WHO SAVED MY LIFE... THE HOPE FOR MY SISTER...
GET IT TOGETHER ALREADY.
I TALKED TO THE VILLAGERS AND HAVE SOME INFO.

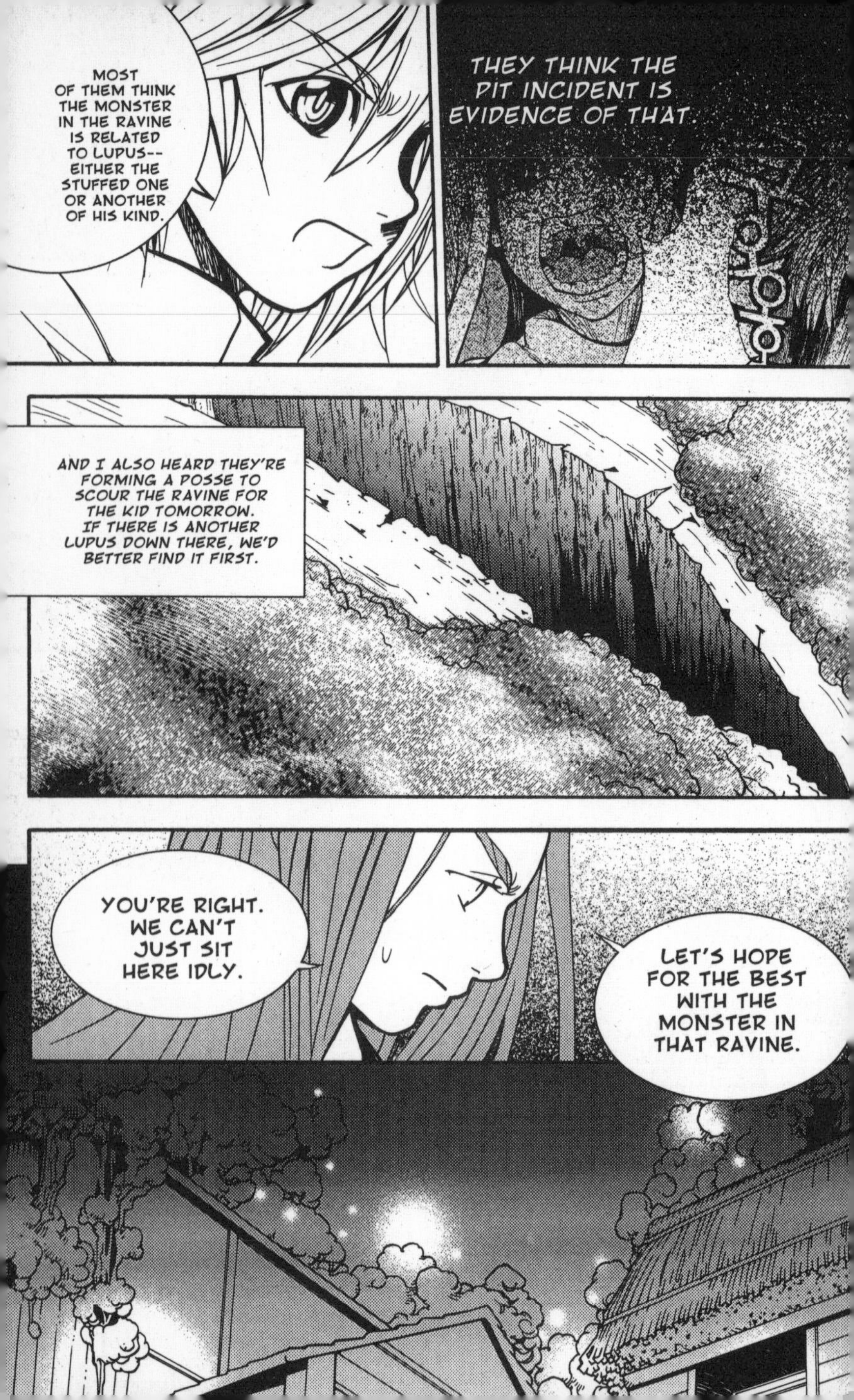
MOST OF THEM THINK THE MONSTER IN THE RAVINE IS RELATED TO LUPUS-- EITHER THE STUFFED ONE OR ANOTHER OF HIS KIND.
THEY THINK THE PIT INCIDENT IS EVIDENCE OF THAT.
AND I ALSO HEARD THEY'RE FORMING A POSSE TO SCOUR THE RAVINE FOR THE KID TOMORROW. IF THERE IS ANOTHER LUPUS DOWN THERE, WE'D BETTER FIND IT FIRST.
YOU'RE RIGHT. WE CAN'T JUST SIT HERE IDLY.
LET'S HOPE FOR THE BEST WITH THE MONSTER IN THAT RAVINE.

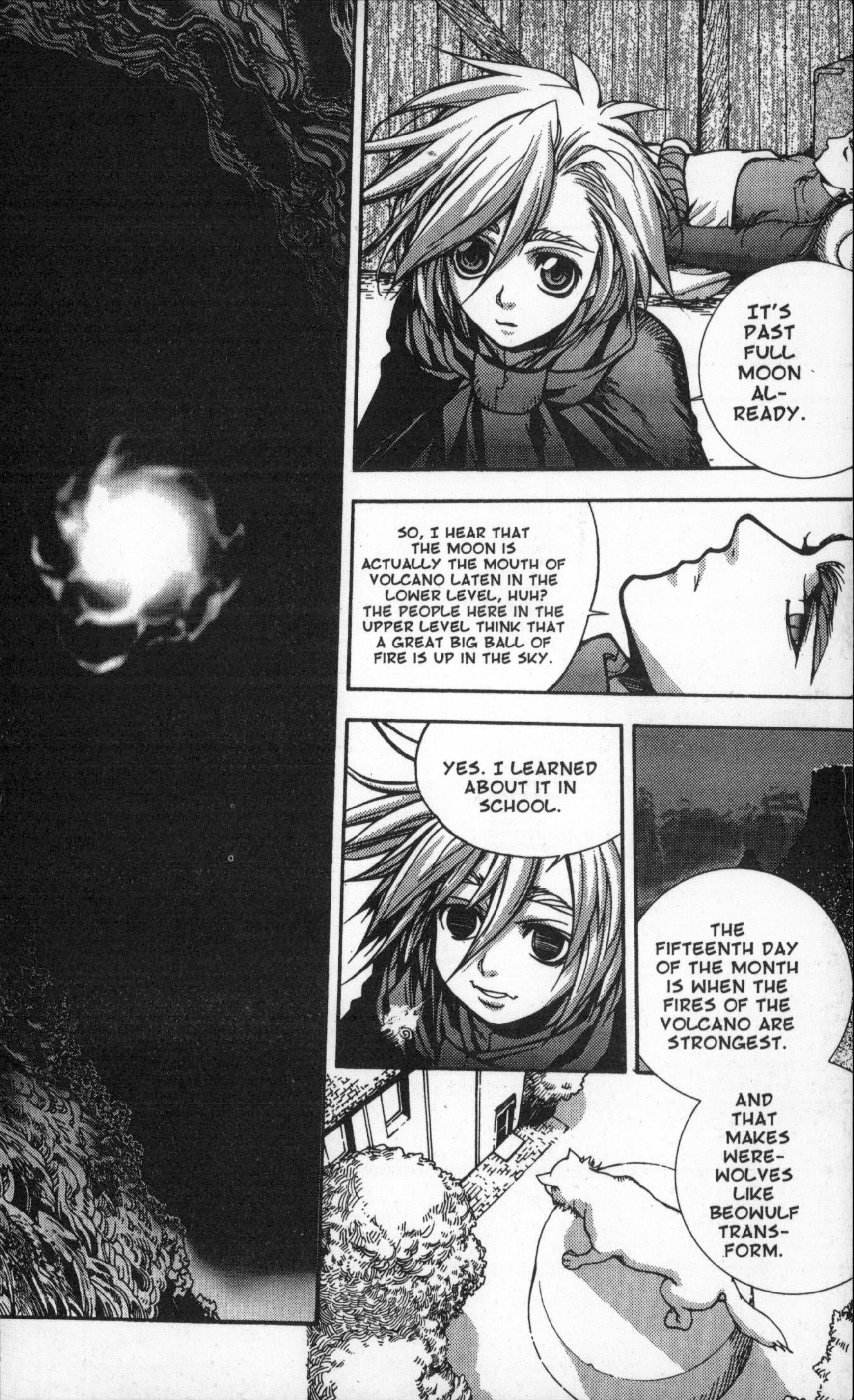
IT'S PAST FULL MOON AL- READY.
SO, I HEAR THAT THE MOON IS ACTUALLY THE MOUTH OF VOLCANO LATEN IN THE LOWER LEVEL, HUH? THE PEOPLE HERE IN THE UPPER LEVEL THINK THAT A GREAT BIG BALL OF FIRE IS UP IN THE SKY.
YES. I LEARNED ABOUT IT IN SCHOOL.
THE FIFTEENTH DAY OF THE MONTH IS WHEN THE FIRES OF THE VOLCANO ARE STRONGEST.
AND THAT MAKES WERE- WOLVES LIKE BEOWULF TRANS- FORM.

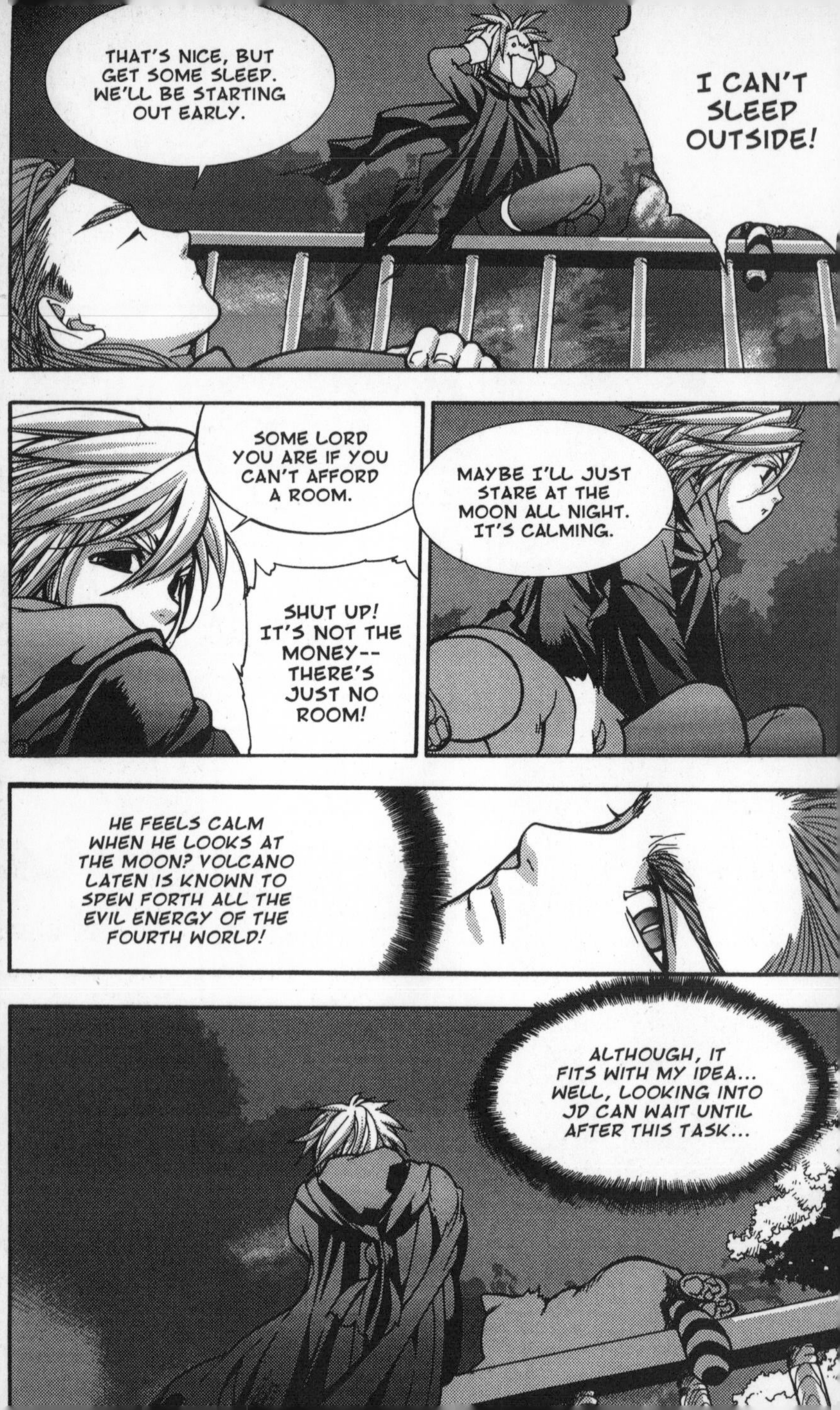
THAT'S NICE, BUT GET SOME SLEEP. WE'LL BE STARTING OUT EARLY.
I CAN'T SLEEP OUTSIDE!
SOME LORD YOU ARE IF YOU CAN'T AFFORD A ROOM.
SHUT UP! IT'S NOT THE MONEY-- THERE'S JUST NO ROOM!
MAYBE I'LL JUST STARE AT THE MOON ALL NIGHT. IT'S CALMING.
HE FEELS CALM WHEN HE LOOKS AT THE MOON? VOLCANO LATEN IS KNOWN TO SPEW FORTH ALL THE EVIL ENERGY OF THE FOURTH WORLD!
ALTHOUGH, IT FITS WITH MY IDEA... WELL, LOOKING INTO JD CAN WAIT UNTIL AFTER THIS TASK...

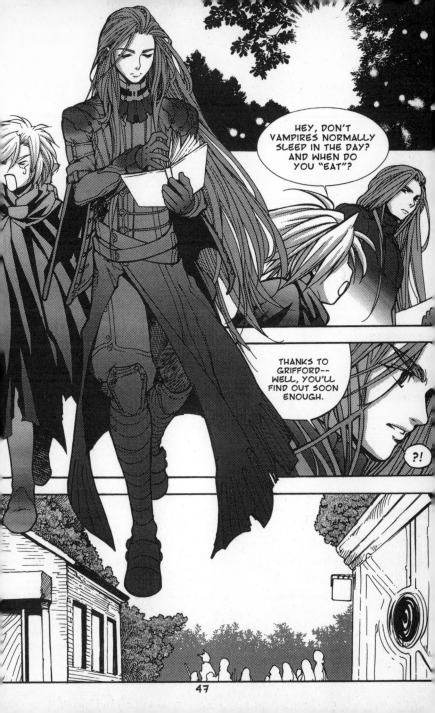

HEY, DON'T VAMPIRES NORMALLY SLEEP IN THE DAY? AND WHEN DO YOU "EAT"?

THANKS TO GRIFFORD-- WELL, YOU'LL FIND OUT SOON ENOUGH.

?!

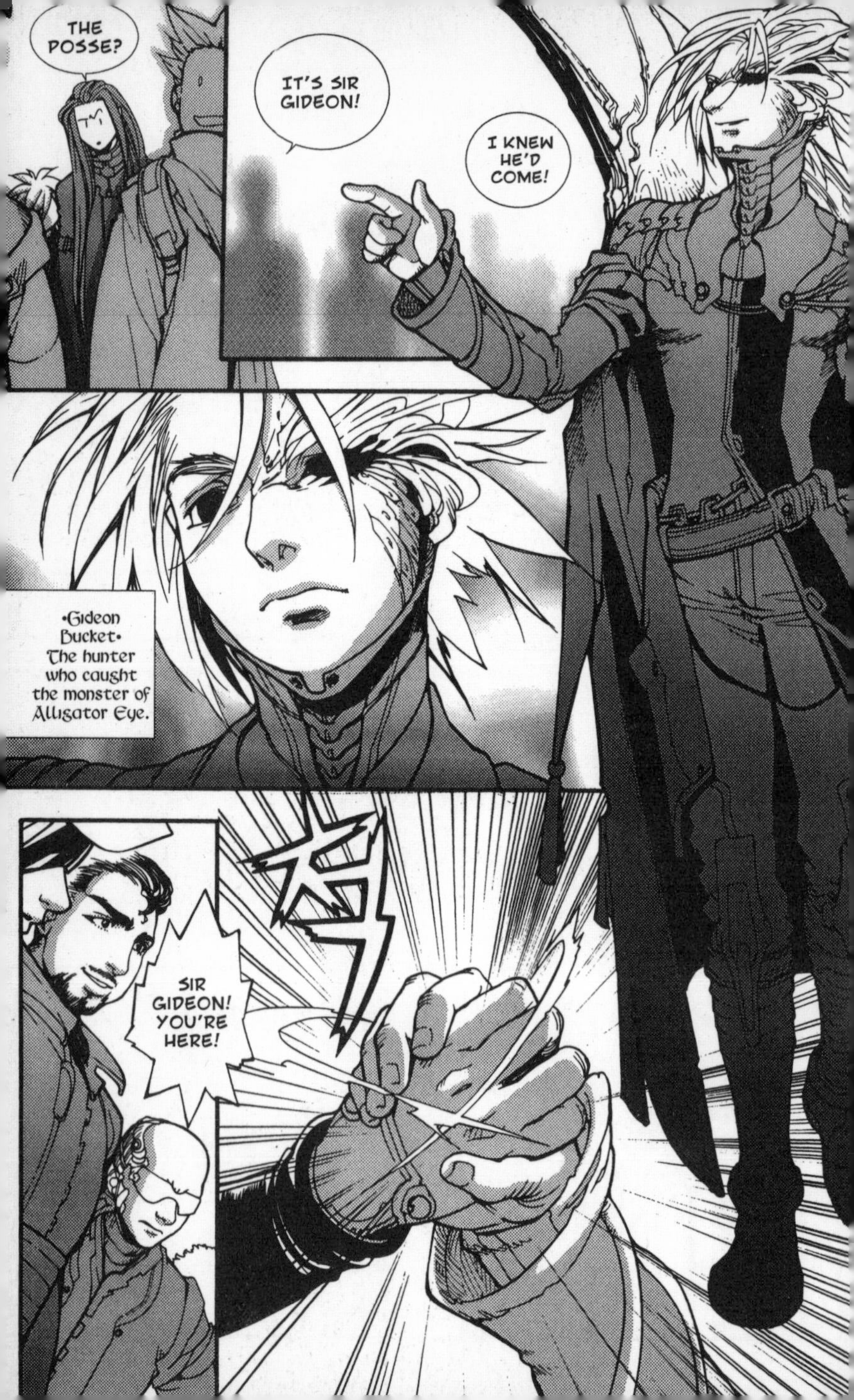
THE POSSE?
IT'S SIR GIDEON!
I KNEW HE'D COME!
•Gideon Bucket• The hunter who caught the monster of Alligator Eye.
SIR GIDEON! YOU'RE HERE!

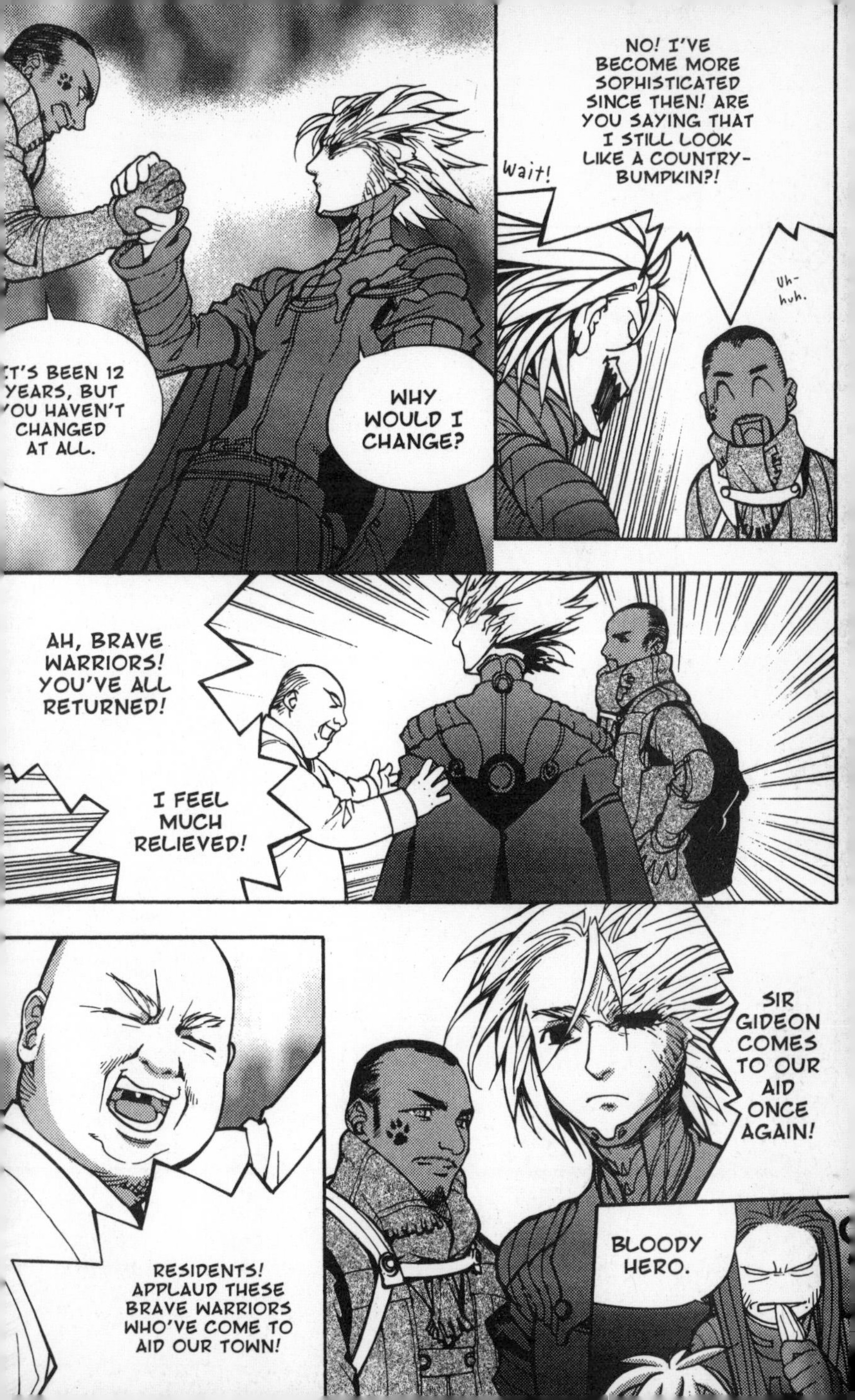
IT'S BEEN 12 YEARS, BUT YOU HAVEN'T CHANGED AT ALL.
WHY WOULD I CHANGE?
Wait!
NO! I'VE BECOME MORE SOPHISTICATED SINCE THEN! ARE YOU SAYING THAT I STILL LOOK LIKE A COUNTRY-BUMPKIN?!
Uh-huh.
AH, BRAVE WARRIORS! YOU'VE ALL RETURNED!
I FEEL MUCH RELIEVED!
RESIDENTS! APPLAUD THESE BRAVE WARRIORS WHO'VE COME TO AID OUR TOWN!
SIR GIDEON COMES TO OUR AID ONCE AGAIN!
BLOODY HERO.

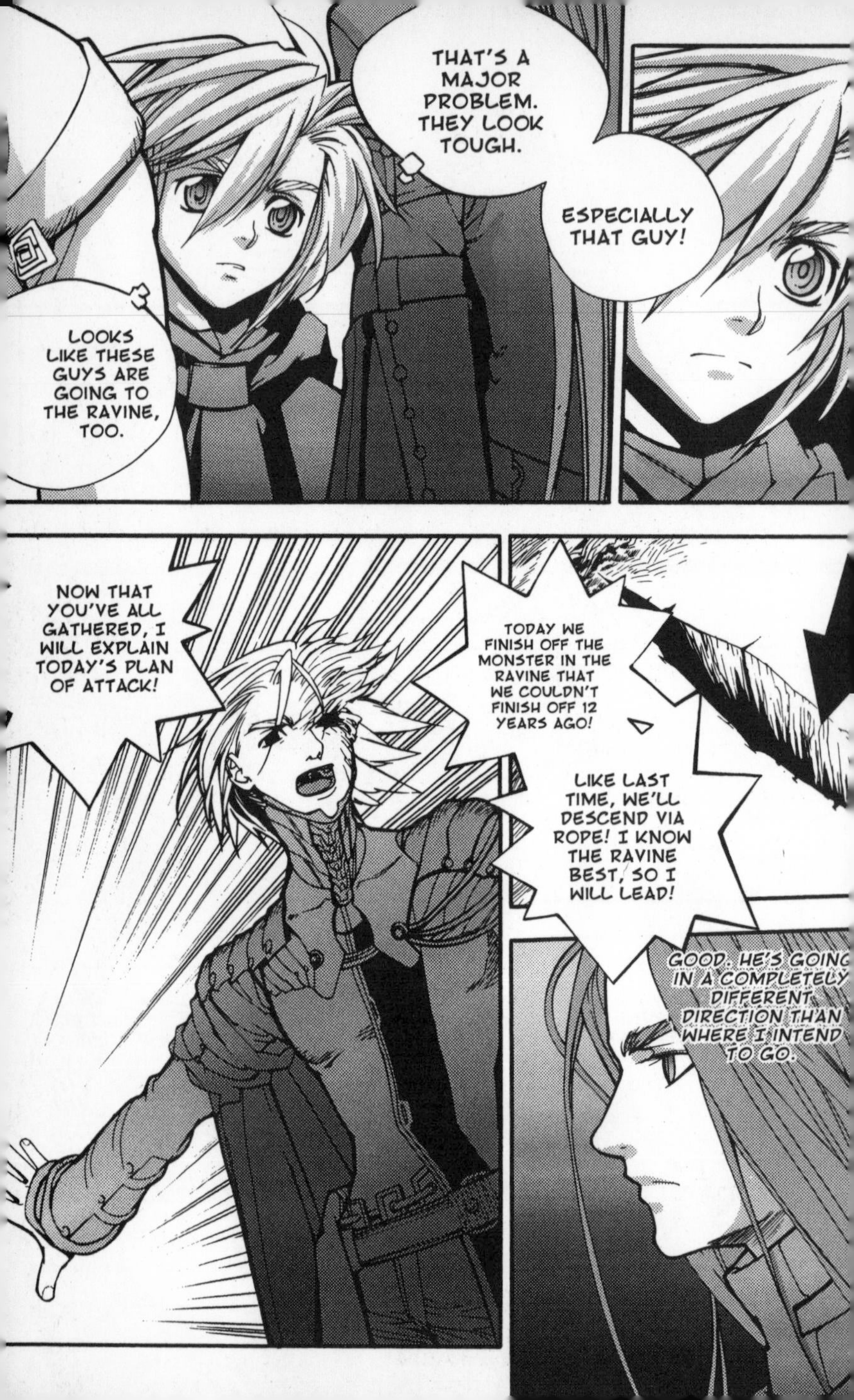
LOOKS LIKE THESE GUYS ARE GOING TO THE RAVINE, TOO.
THAT'S A MAJOR PROBLEM. THEY LOOK TOUGH.
ESPECIALLY THAT GUY!
NOW THAT YOU'VE ALL GATHERED, I WILL EXPLAIN TODAY'S PLAN OF ATTACK!
TODAY WE FINISH OFF THE MONSTER IN THE RAVINE THAT WE COULDN'T FINISH OFF 12 YEARS AGO!
LIKE LAST TIME, WE'LL DESCEND VIA ROPE! I KNOW THE RAVINE BEST, SO I WILL LEAD!
GOOD. HE'S GOING IN A COMPLETELY DIFFERENT DIRECTION THAN WHERE I INTEND TO GO.

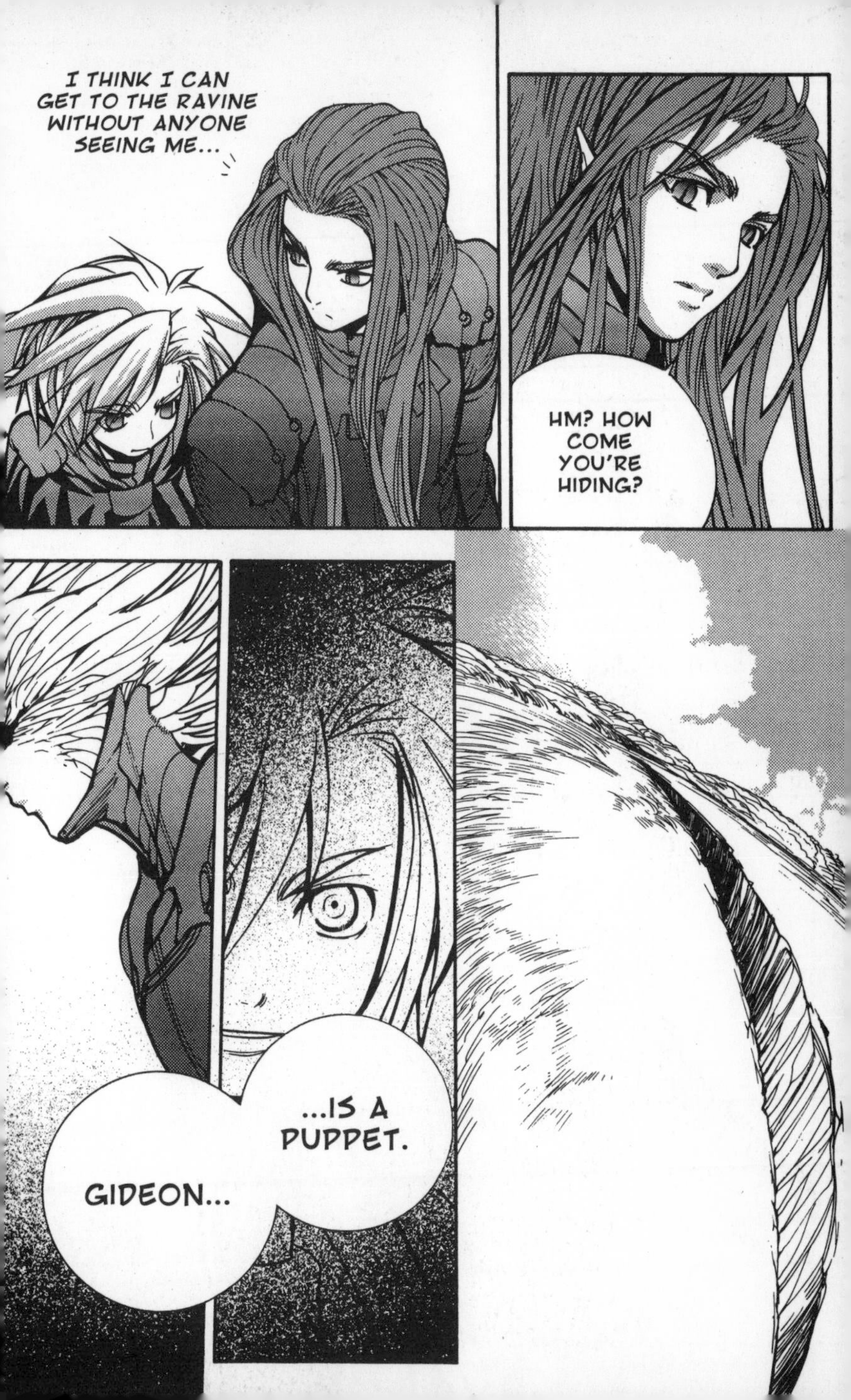

I THINK I CAN GET TO THE RAVINE WITHOUT ANYONE SEEING ME...
HM? HOW COME YOU'RE HIDING?
GIDEON...
...IS A PUPPET.

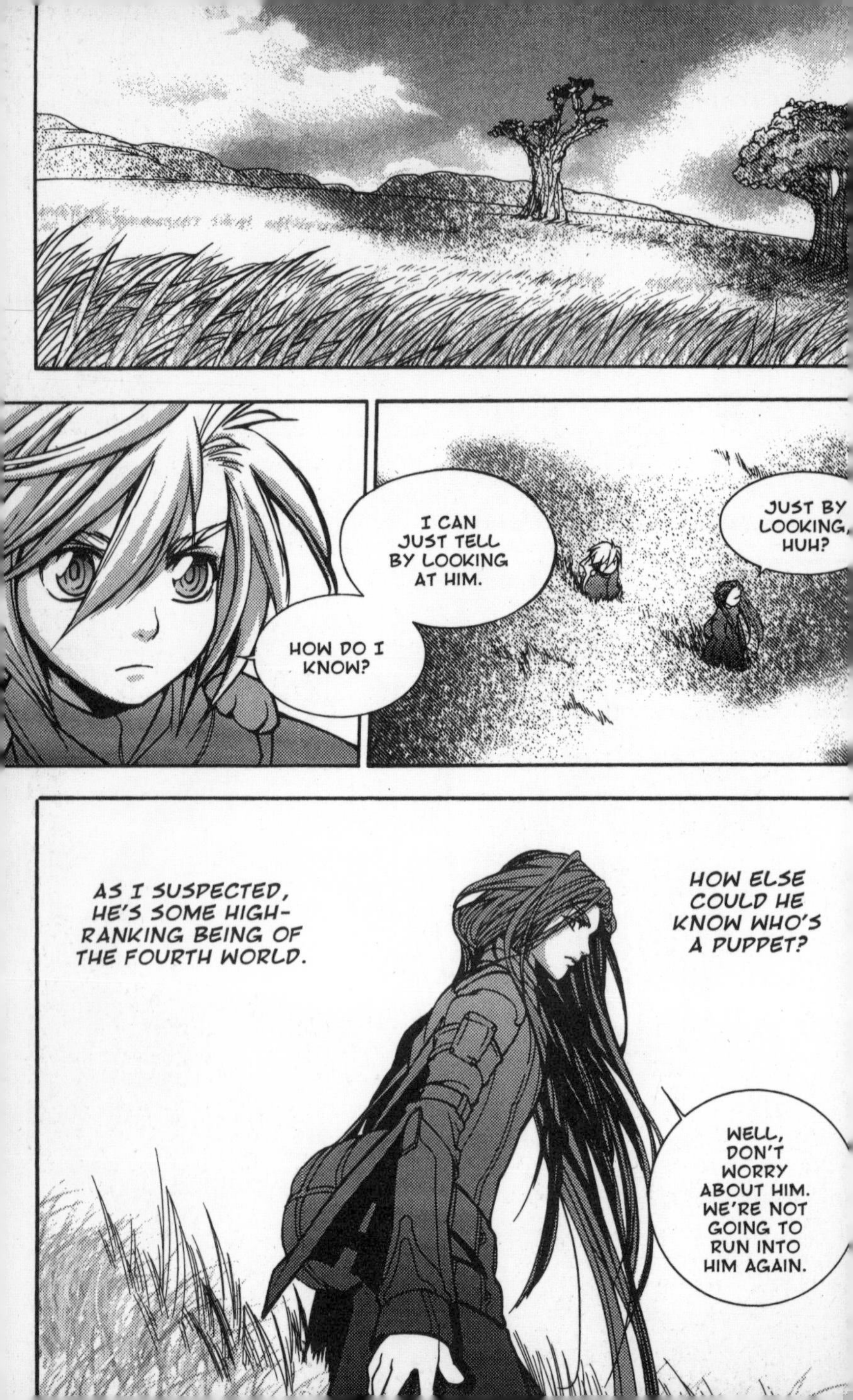
HOW DO I KNOW?
I CAN JUST TELL BY LOOKING AT HIM.
JUST BY LOOKING, HUH?
AS I SUSPECTED, HE'S SOME HIGH-RANKING BEING OF THE FOURTH WORLD.
HOW ELSE COULD HE KNOW WHO'S A PUPPET?
WELL, DON'T WORRY ABOUT HIM. WE'RE NOT GOING TO RUN INTO HIM AGAIN.

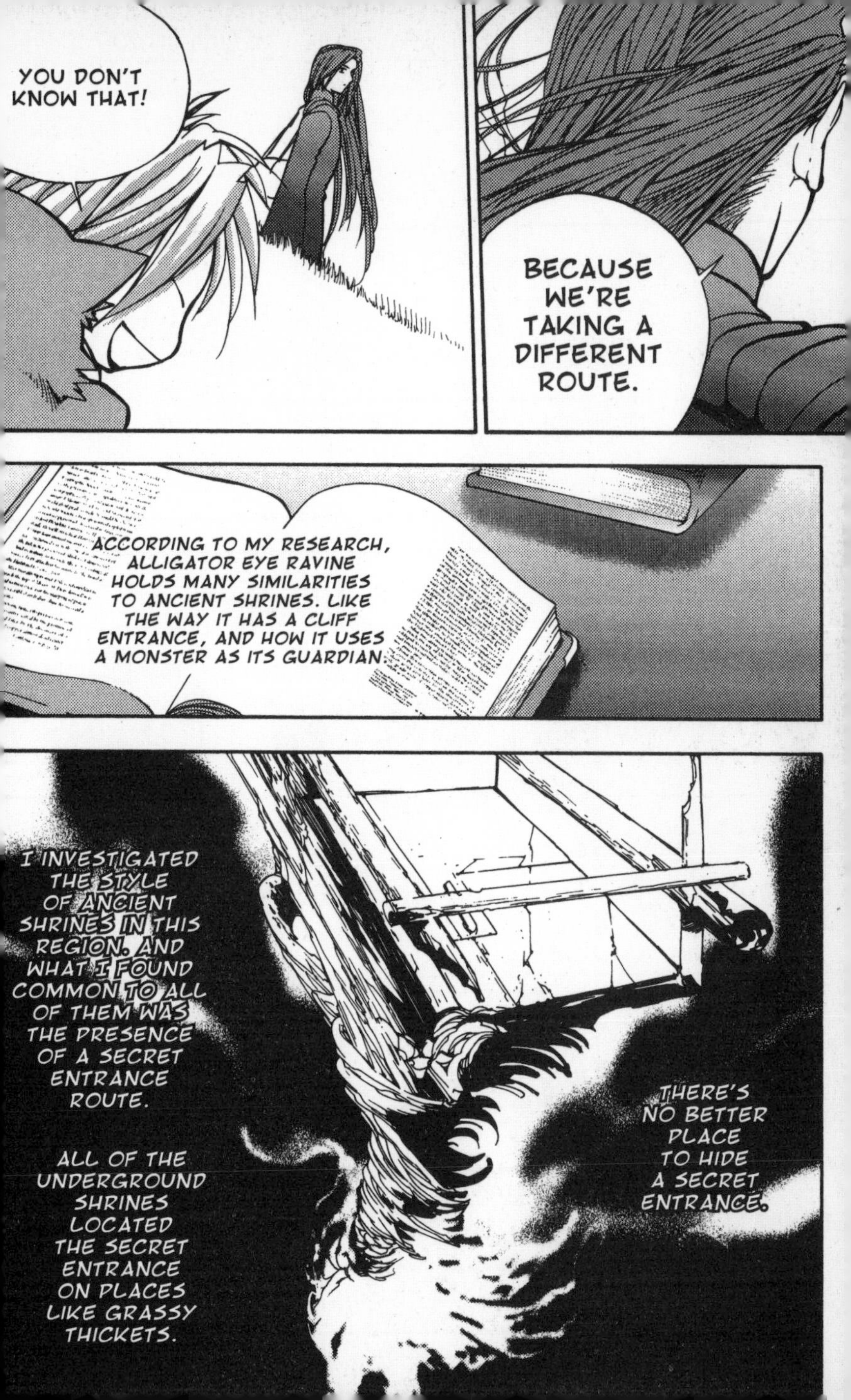
YOU DON'T KNOW THAT!
BECAUSE WE'RE TAKING A DIFFERENT ROUTE.
ACCORDING TO MY RESEARCH, ALLIGATOR EYE RAVINE HOLDS MANY SIMILARITIES TO ANCIENT SHRINES. LIKE THE WAY IT HAS A CLIFF ENTRANCE, AND HOW IT USES A MONSTER AS ITS GUARDIAN.
I INVESTIGATED THE STYLE OF ANCIENT SHRINES IN THIS REGION. AND WHAT I FOUND COMMON TO ALL OF THEM WAS THE PRESENCE OF A SECRET ENTRANCE ROUTE.
ALL OF THE UNDERGROUND SHRINES LOCATED THE SECRET ENTRANCE ON PLACES LIKE GRASSY THICKETS.
THERE'S NO BETTER PLACE TO HIDE A SECRET ENTRANCE.

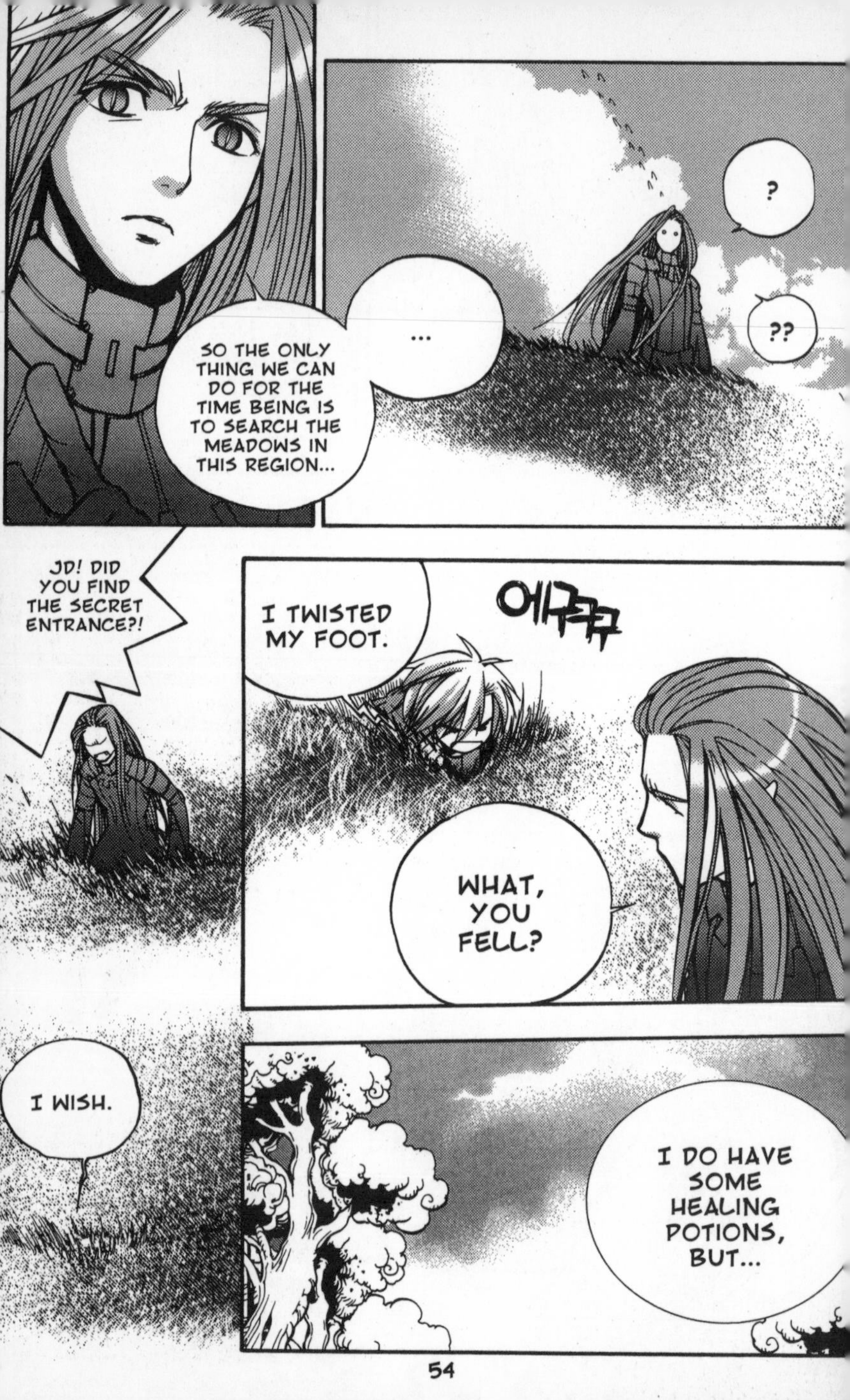
SO THE ONLY THING WE CAN DO FOR THE TIME BEING IS TO SEARCH THE MEADOWS IN THIS REGION...
...
?
??
JD! DID YOU FIND THE SECRET ENTRANCE?!
I TWISTED MY FOOT.
WHAT, YOU FELL?
I WISH.
I DO HAVE SOME HEALING POTIONS, BUT...

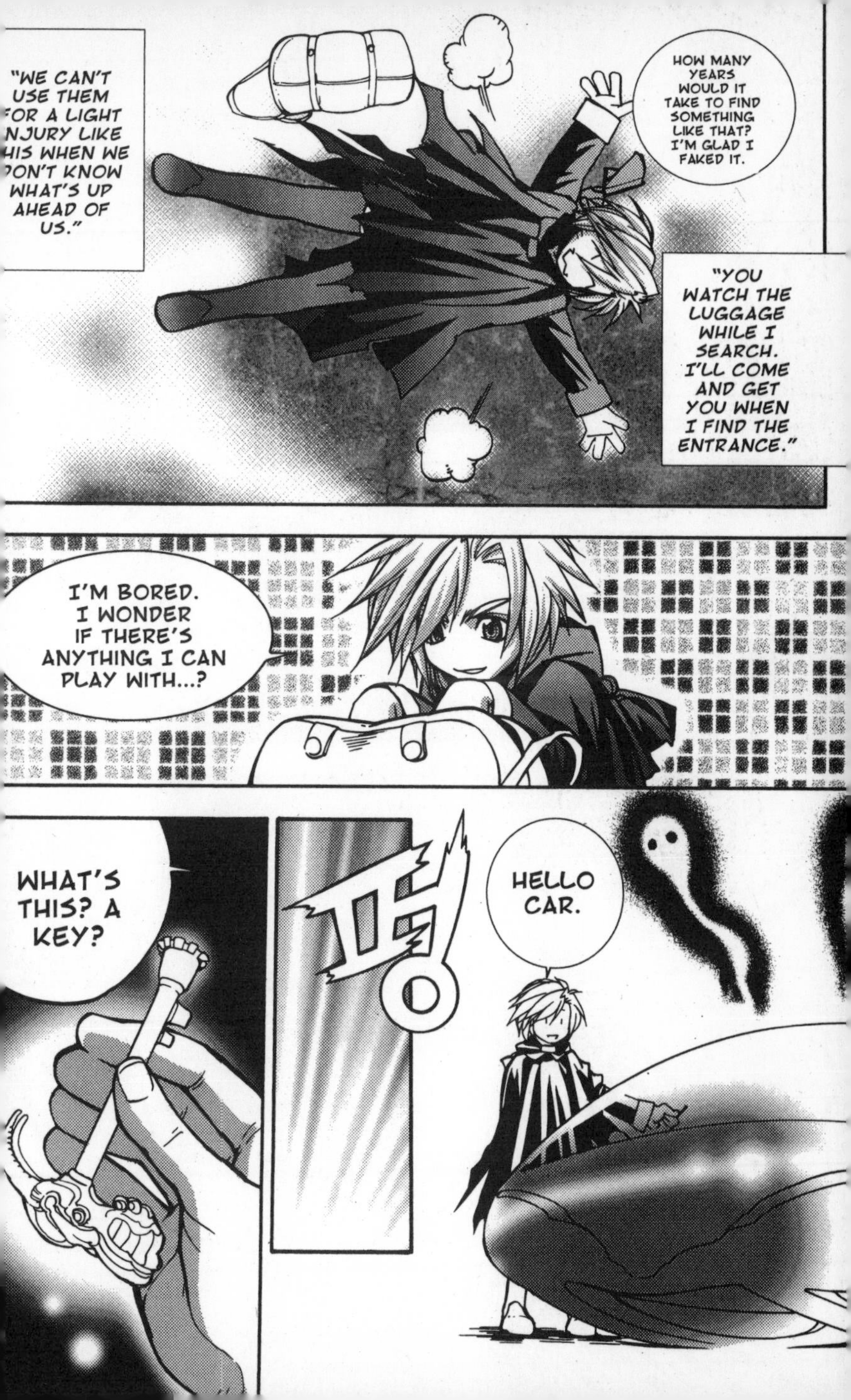
"WE CAN'T USE THEM OR A LIGHT NJURY LIKE HIS WHEN WE ON'T KNOW WHAT'S UP AHEAD OF US."
HOW MANY YEARS WOULD IT TAKE TO FIND SOMETHING LIKE THAT? I'M GLAD I FAKED IT.
"YOU WATCH THE LUGGAGE WHILE I SEARCH. I'LL COME AND GET YOU WHEN I FIND THE ENTRANCE."
I'M BORED. I WONDER IF THERE'S ANYTHING I CAN PLAY WITH...?
WHAT'S THIS? A KEY?
HELLO CAR.

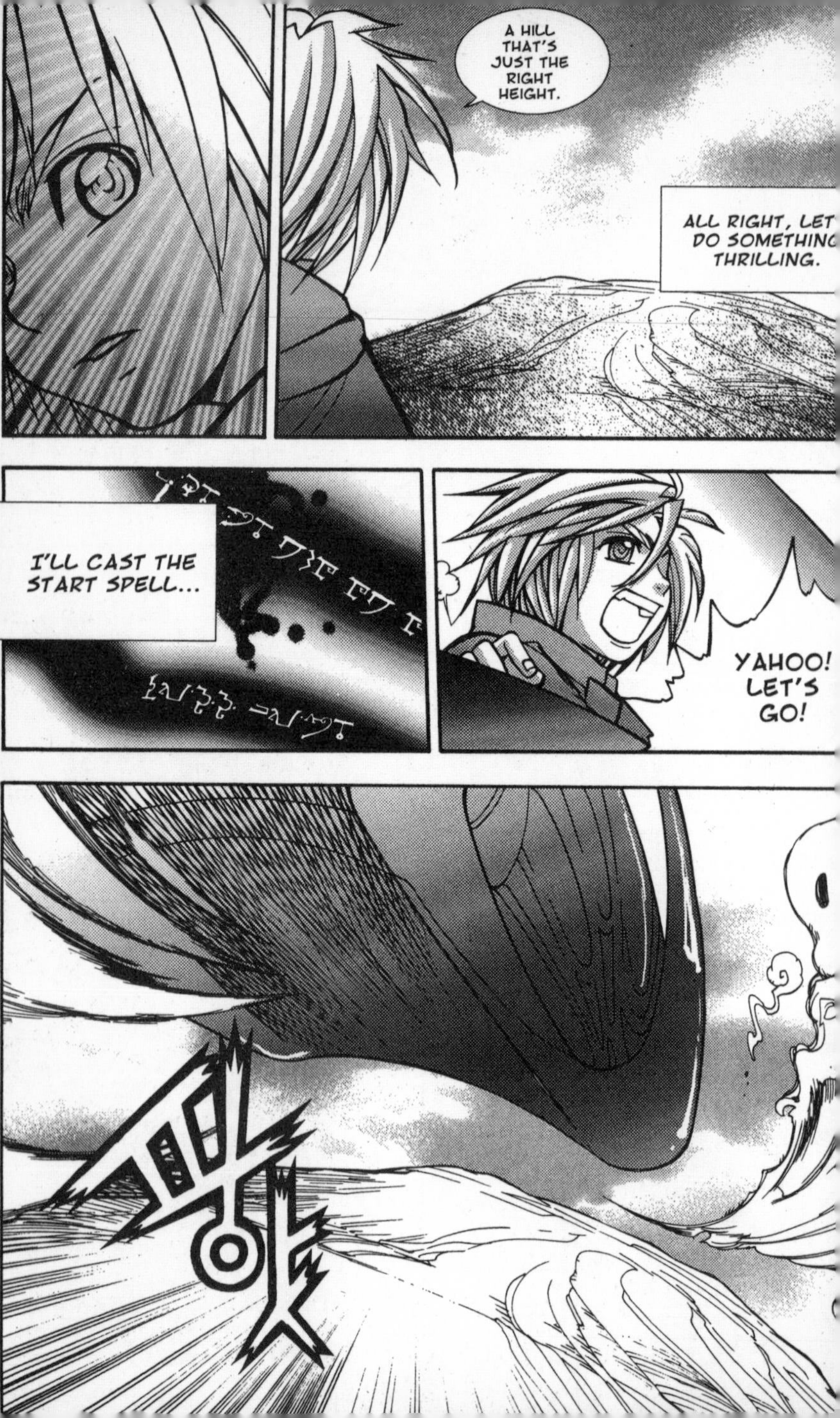
A HILL THAT'S JUST THE RIGHT HEIGHT.
ALL RIGHT, LET DO SOMETHING THRILLING.
I'LL CAST THE START SPELL...
YAHOO! LET'S GO!

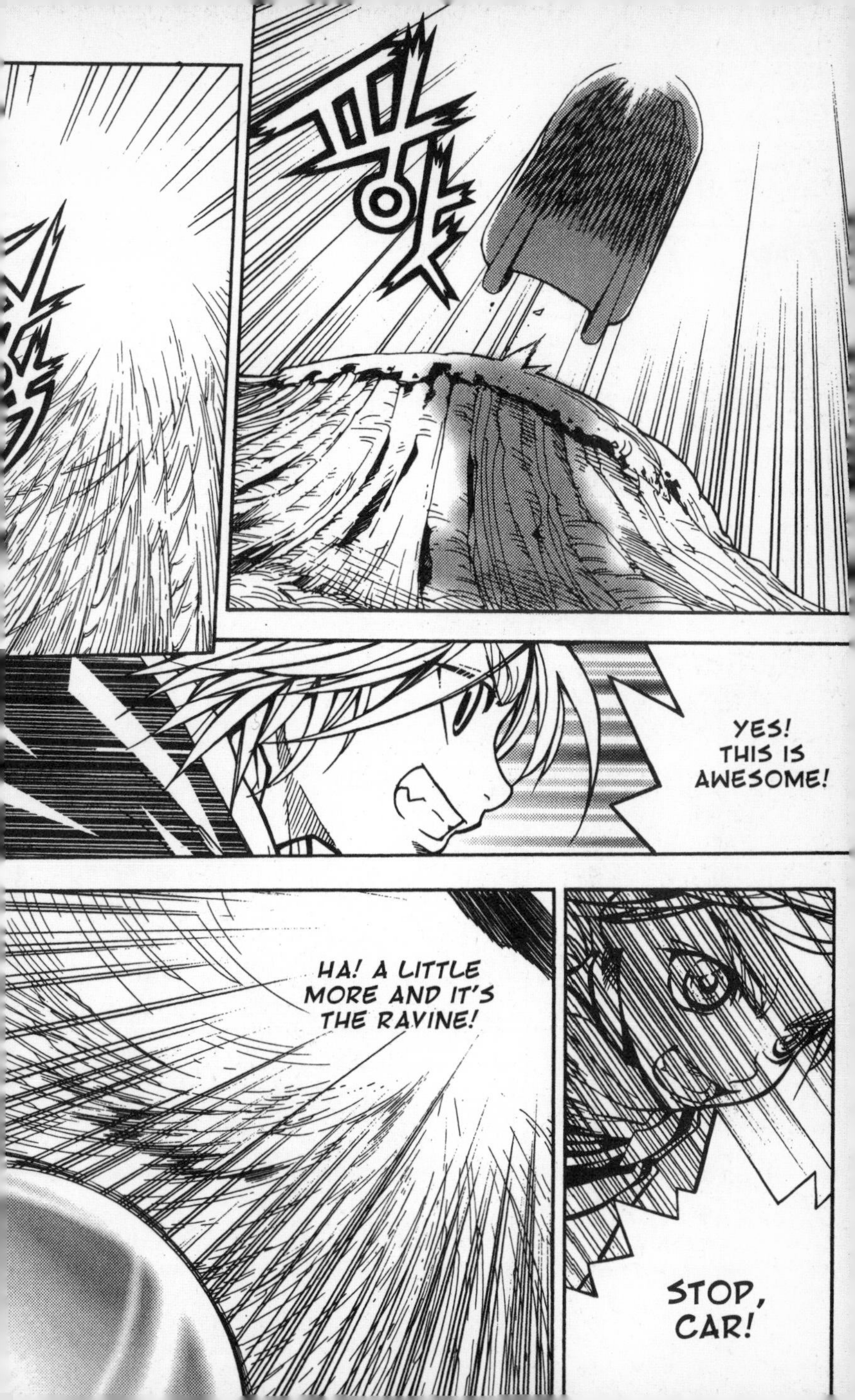
YES! THIS IS AWESOME!
HA! A LITTLE MORE AND IT'S THE RAVINE!
STOP, CAR!

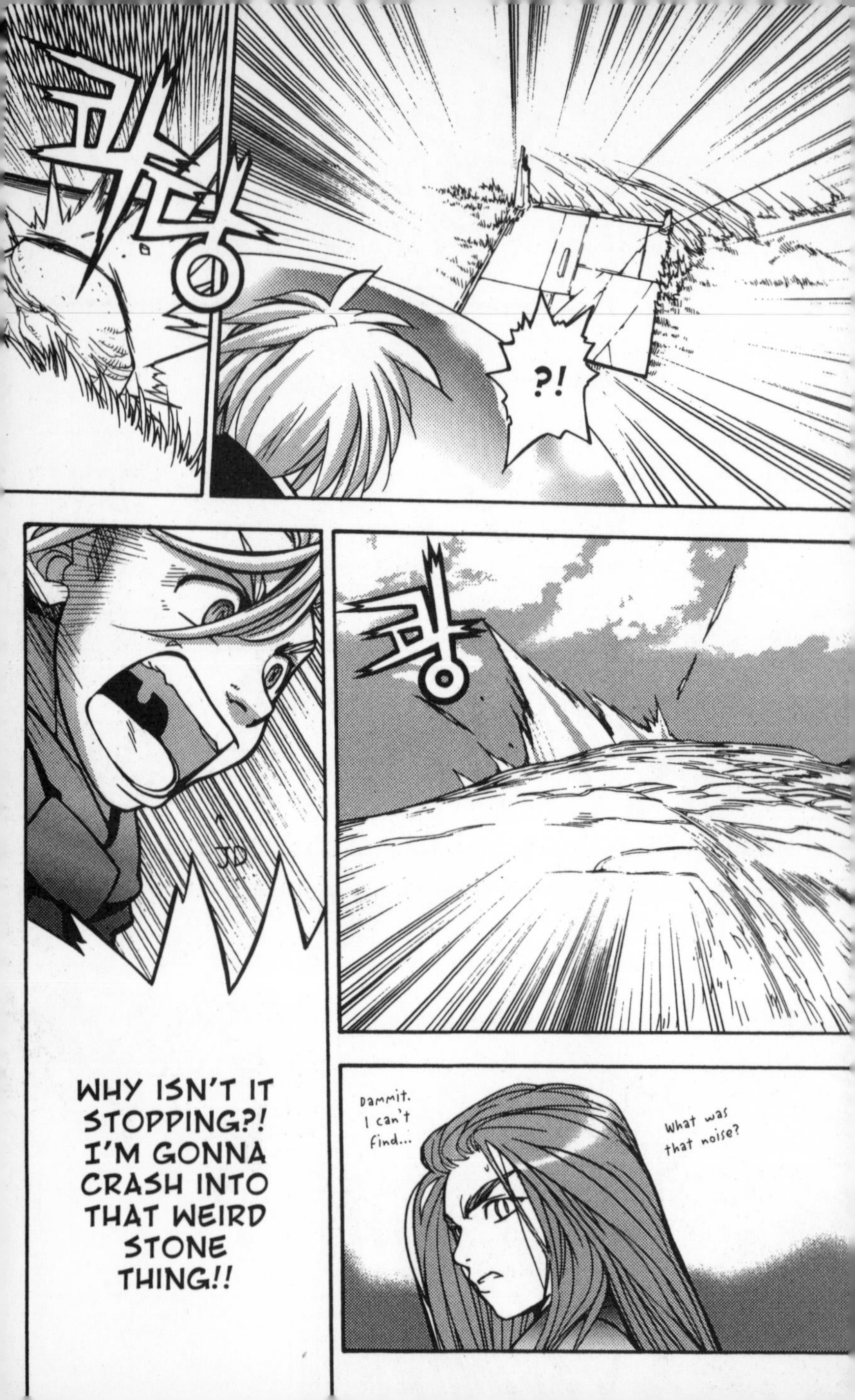
콰당
?!
WHY ISN'T IT STOPPING?! I'M GONNA CRASH INTO THAT WEIRD STONE THING!!
쾅
Dammit. I can't find...
What was that noise?

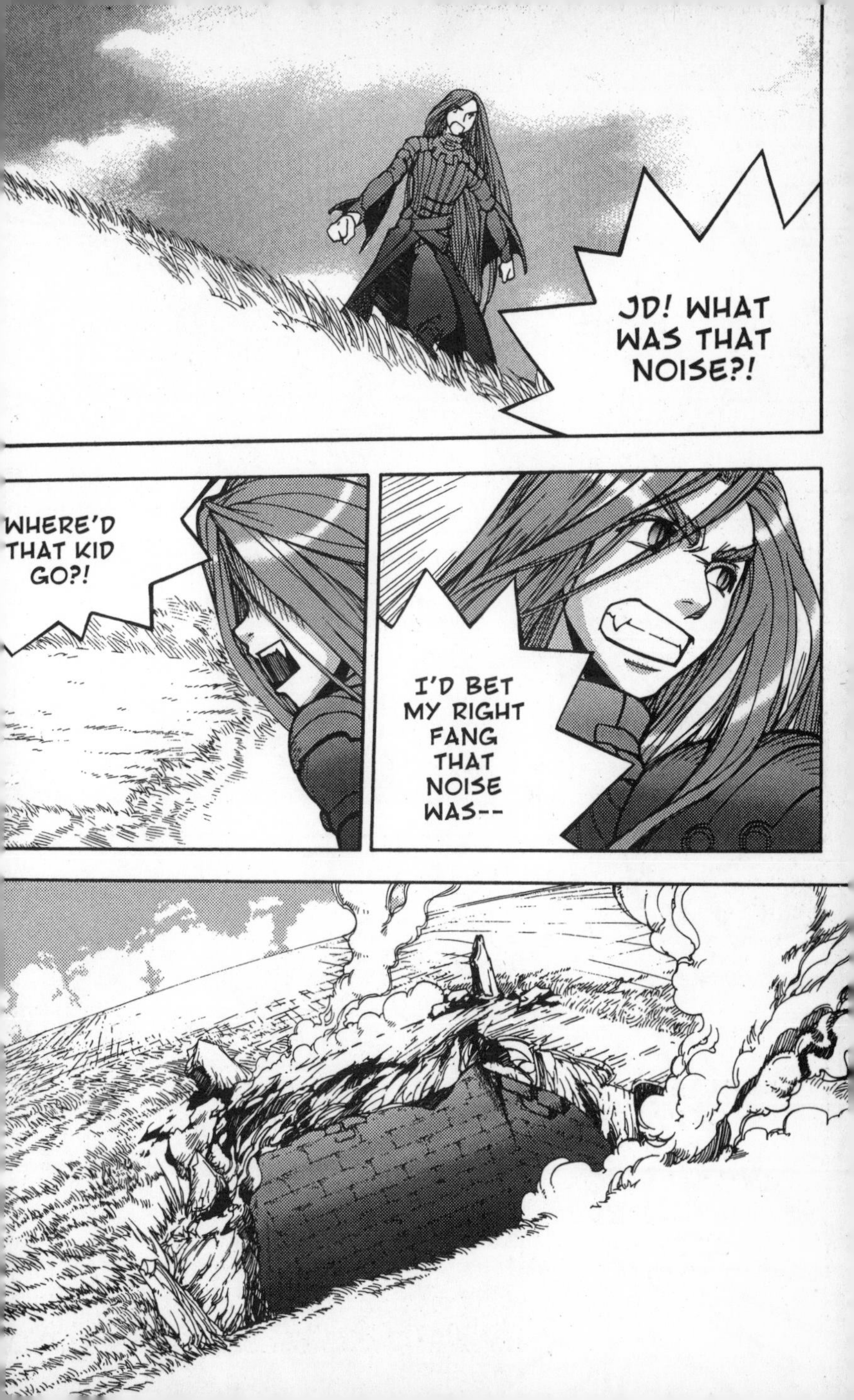
JD! WHAT WAS THAT NOISE?!
WHERE'D THAT KID GO?!
I'D BET MY RIGHT FANG THAT NOISE WAS--

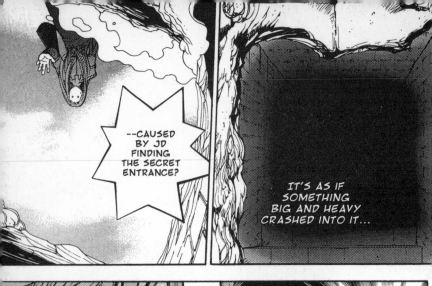

--CAUSED BY JD FINDING THE SECRET ENTRANCE?

IT'S AS IF SOMETHING BIG AND HEAVY CRASHED INTO IT...

MY SPIRIT CAR! (AND FAMILY HEIRLOOM!)

AAAAARGH!

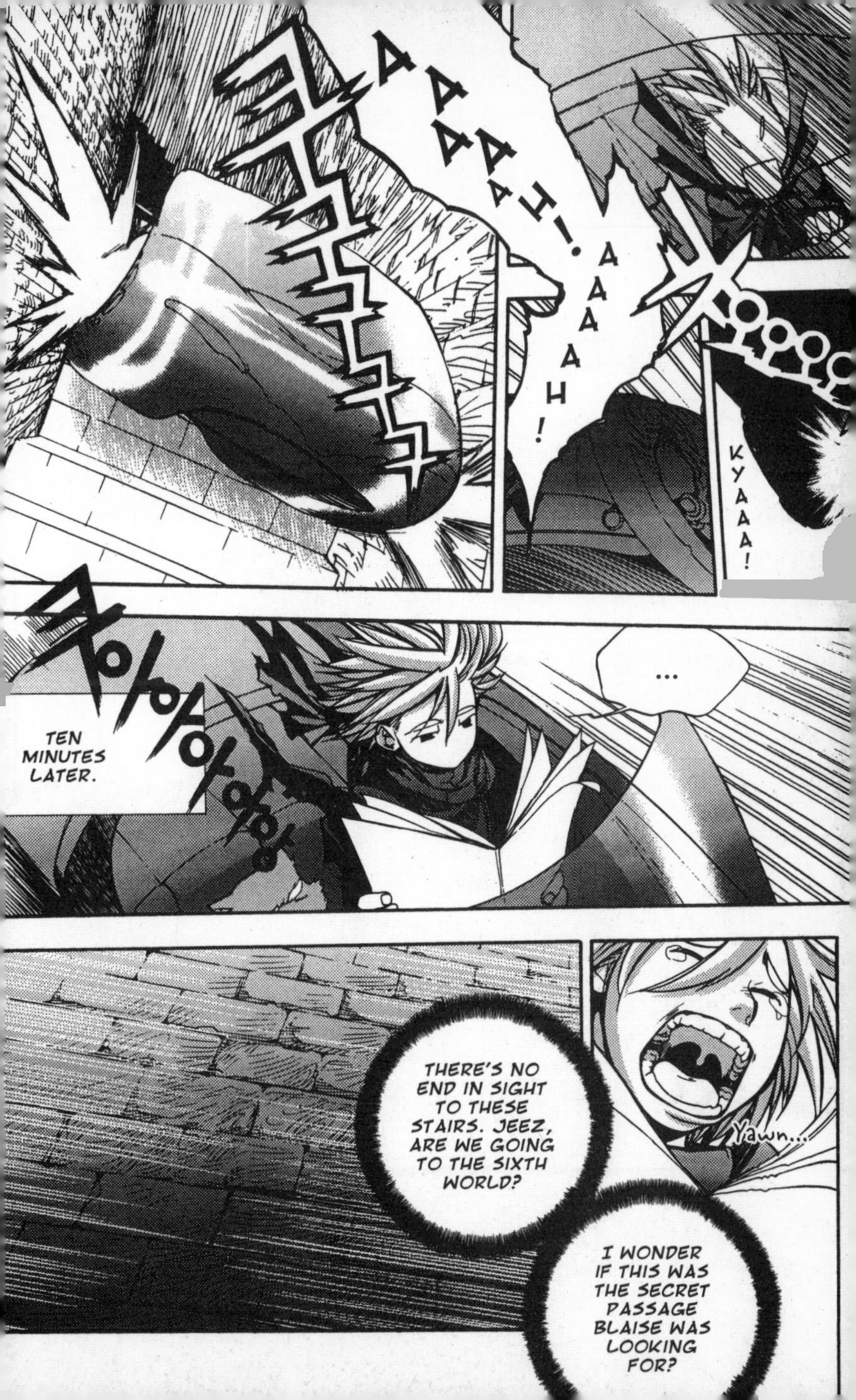
AAAAH!!
AAAAH!
KYAAAA!
TEN MINUTES LATER.
...
THERE'S NO END IN SIGHT TO THESE STAIRS. JEEZ, ARE WE GOING TO THE SIXTH WORLD?
Yawn...
I WONDER IF THIS WAS THE SECRET PASSAGE BLAISE WAS LOOKING FOR?

Ahh!

IT WAS JUST A HUNK OF JUNK ANYWAY...

THE CAR IS THE LEAST OF MY WORRIES...

IT TOOK MORE THAN TEN MINUTES TO GET DOWN HERE BY CAR, SO IT'S GOING TO TAKE A LONG TIME TO GET BACK ON FOOT. NOT TO MENTION IT'S GOING UP. BUT I DON'T KNOW IF I SHOULD GO DOWN FURTHER WHEN I DON'T EVEN KNOW WHERE I AM...

!!

WATER?

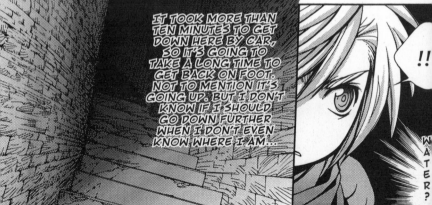

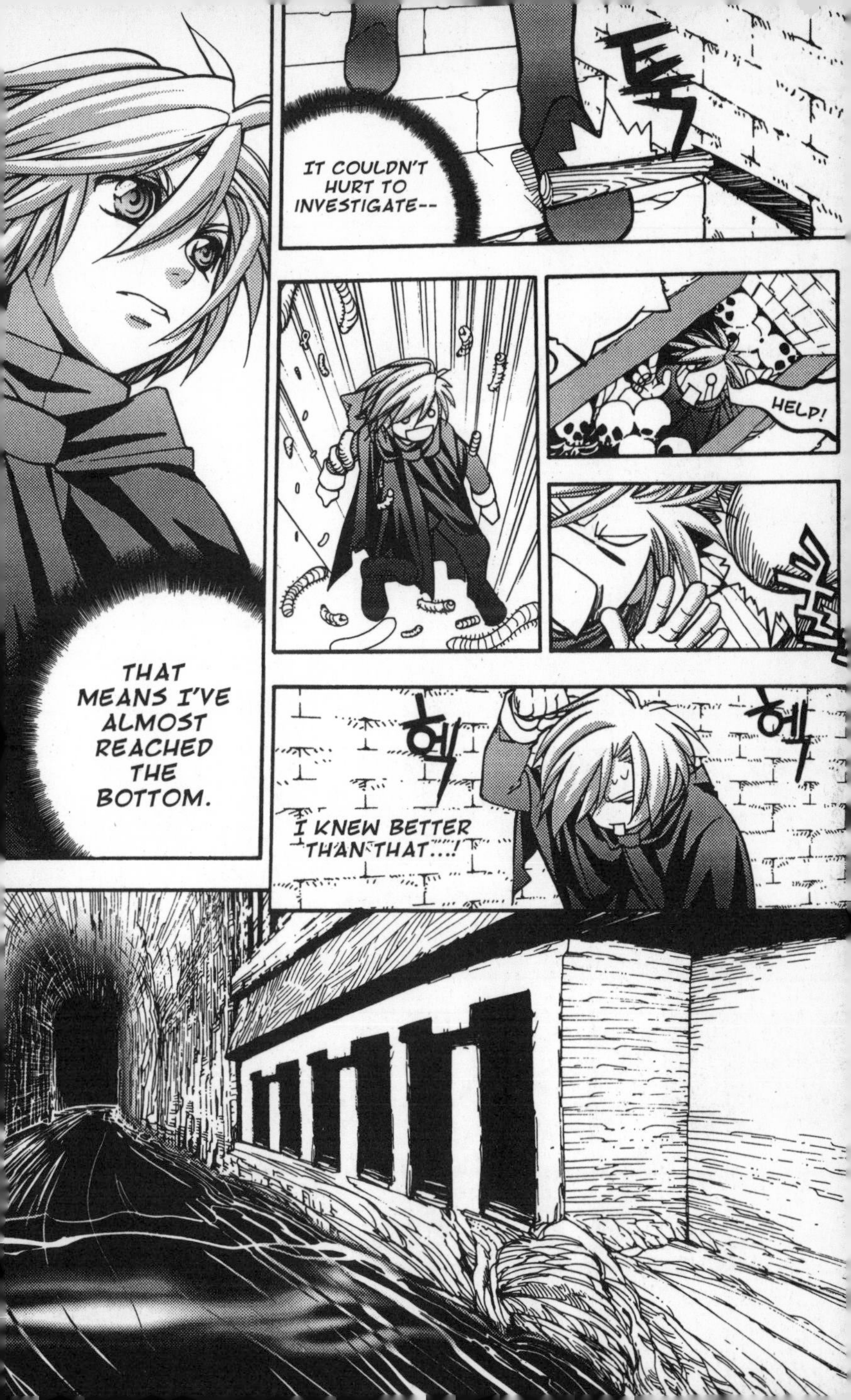
THAT MEANS I'VE ALMOST REACHED THE BOTTOM.
IT COULDN'T HURT TO INVESTIGATE--
HELP!
I KNEW BETTER THAN THAT...!

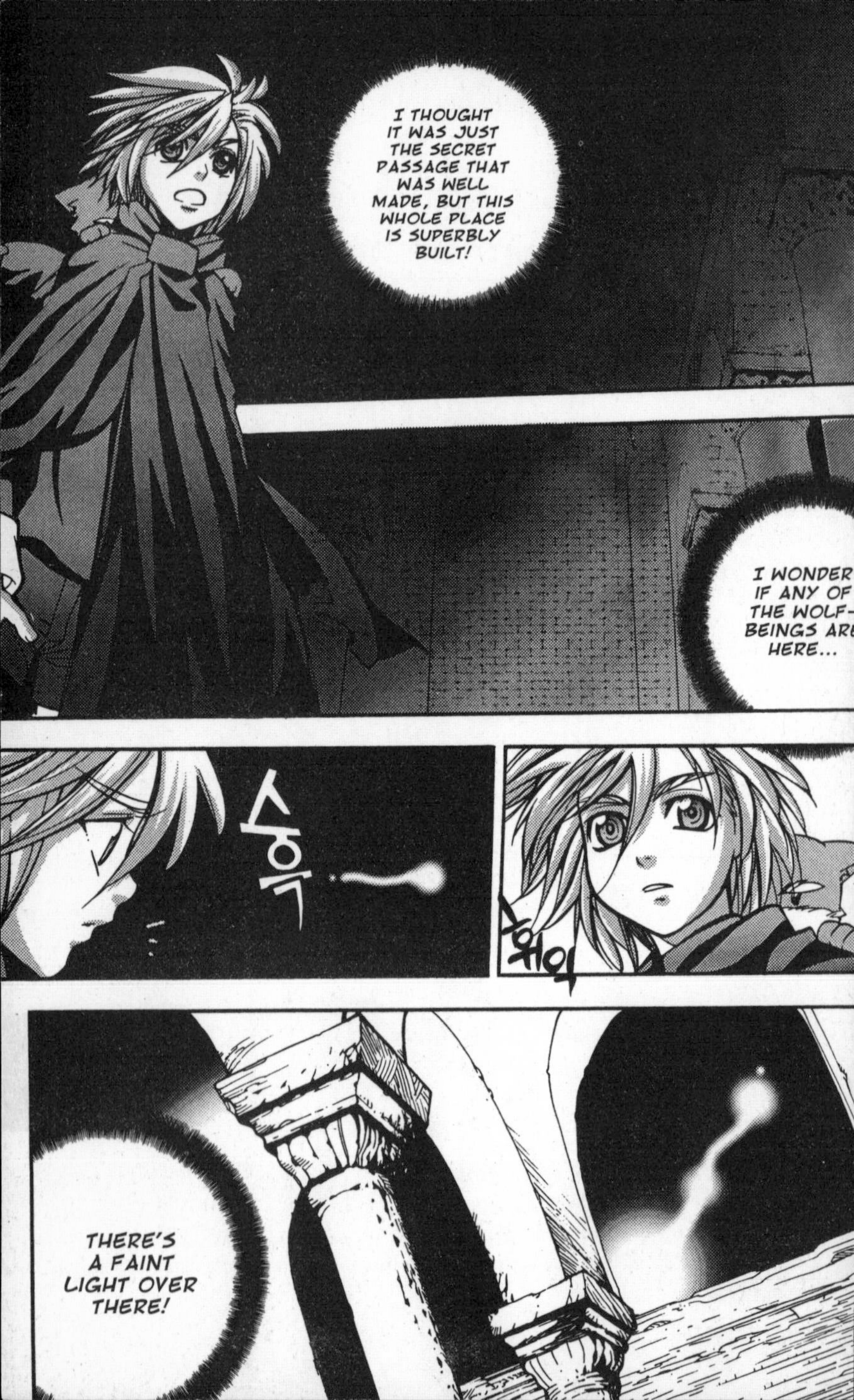
I THOUGHT IT WAS JUST THE SECRET PASSAGE THAT WAS WELL MADE, BUT THIS WHOLE PLACE IS SUPERBLY BUILT!
I WONDER IF ANY OF THE WOLF-BEINGS ARE HERE...
THERE'S A FAINT LIGHT OVER THERE!

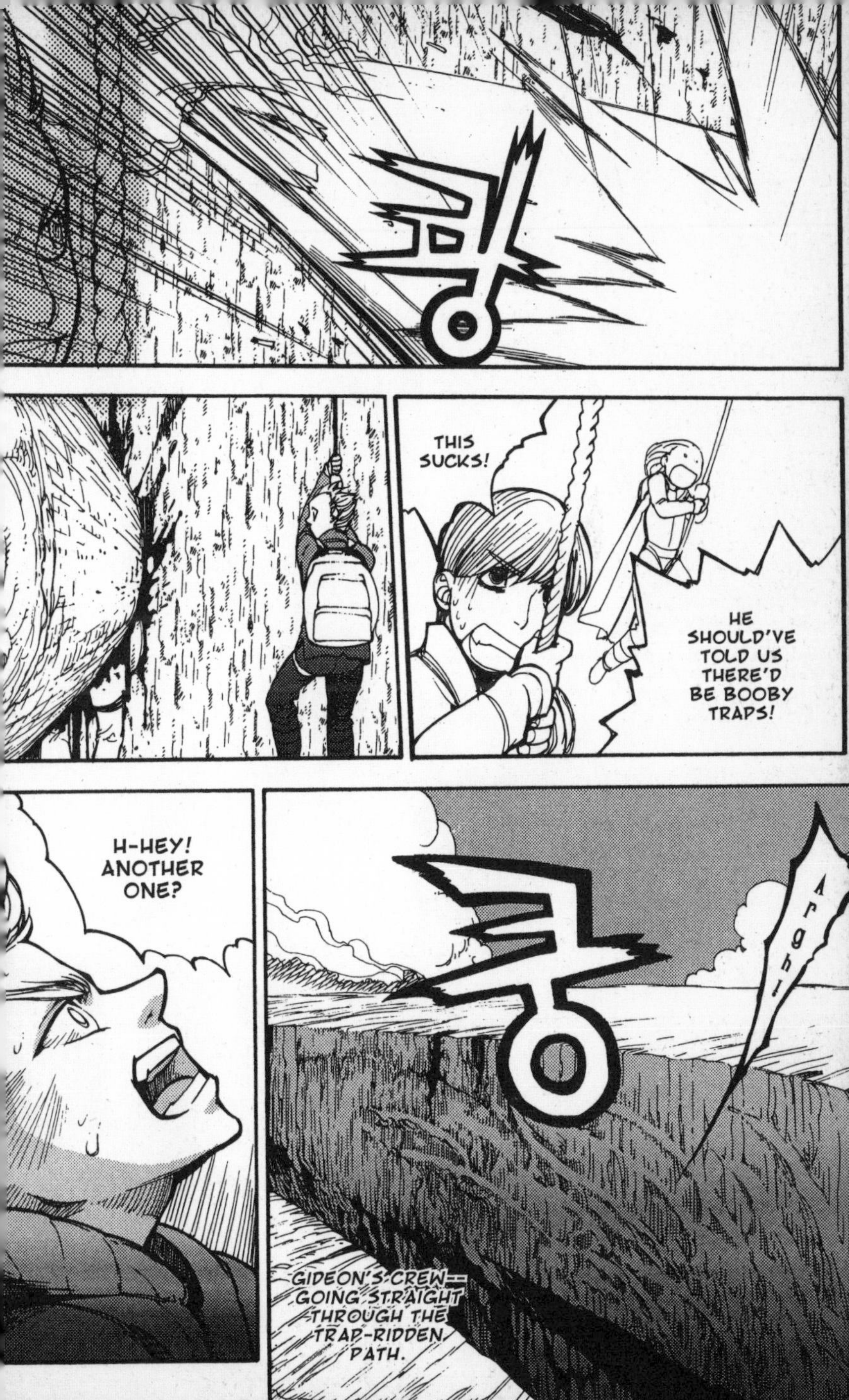
THIS SUCKS!
HE SHOULD'VE TOLD US THERE'D BE BOOBY TRAPS!
H-HEY! ANOTHER ONE?
Argh!
GIDEON'S CREW-- GOING STRAIGHT THROUGH THE TRAP-RIDDEN PATH.

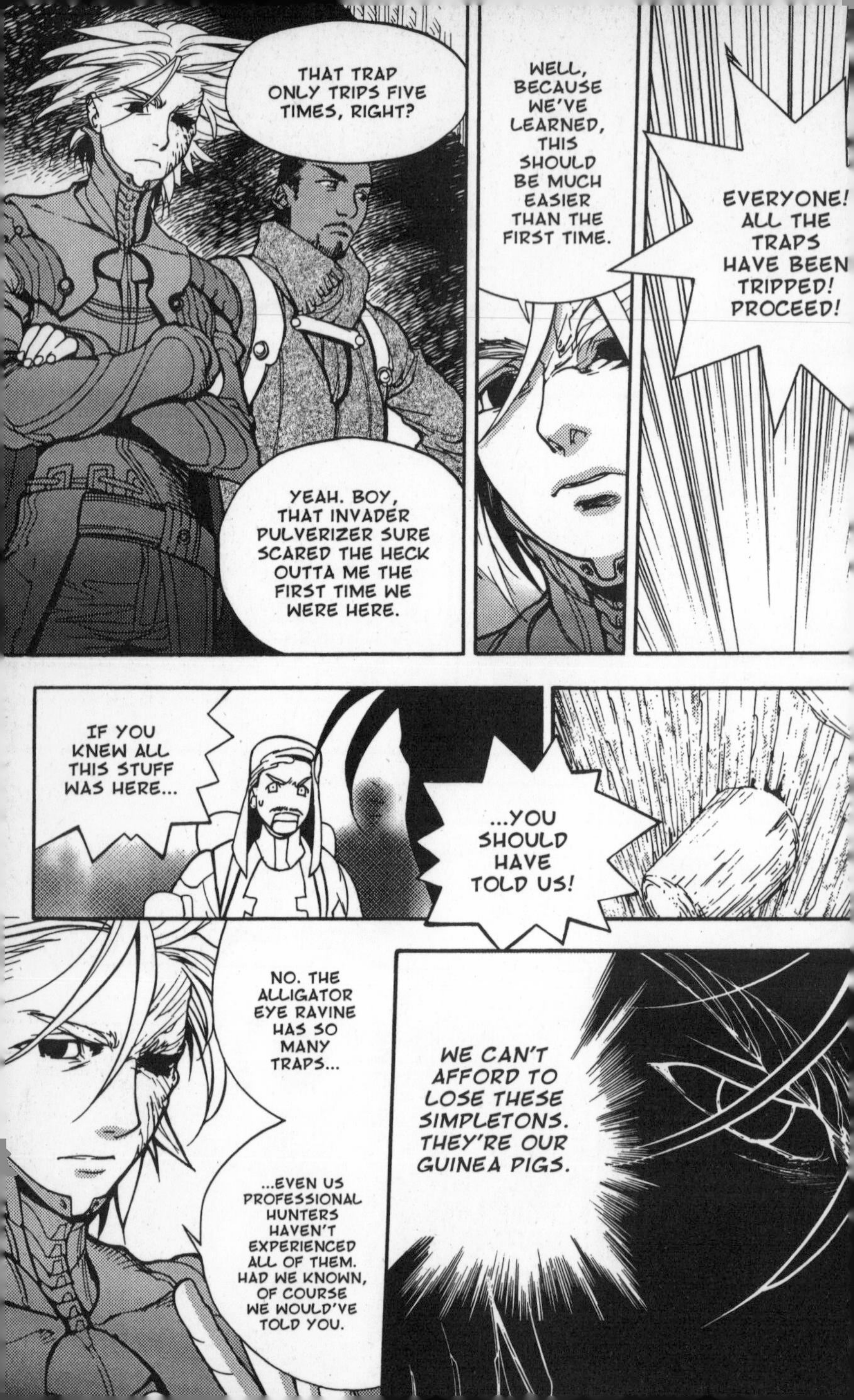
THAT TRAP ONLY TRIPS FIVE TIMES, RIGHT?
YEAH. BOY, THAT INVADER PULVERIZER SURE SCARED THE HECK OUTTA ME THE FIRST TIME WE WERE HERE.
WELL, BECAUSE WE'VE LEARNED, THIS SHOULD BE MUCH EASIER THAN THE FIRST TIME.
EVERYONE! ALL THE TRAPS HAVE BEEN TRIPPED! PROCEED!
IF YOU KNEW ALL THIS STUFF WAS HERE...
...YOU SHOULD HAVE TOLD US!
NO. THE ALLIGATOR EYE RAVINE HAS SO MANY TRAPS...
...EVEN US PROFESSIONAL HUNTERS HAVEN'T EXPERIENCED ALL OF THEM. HAD WE KNOWN, OF COURSE WE WOULD'VE TOLD YOU.
WE CAN'T AFFORD TO LOSE THESE SIMPLETONS. THEY'RE OUR GUINEA PIGS.

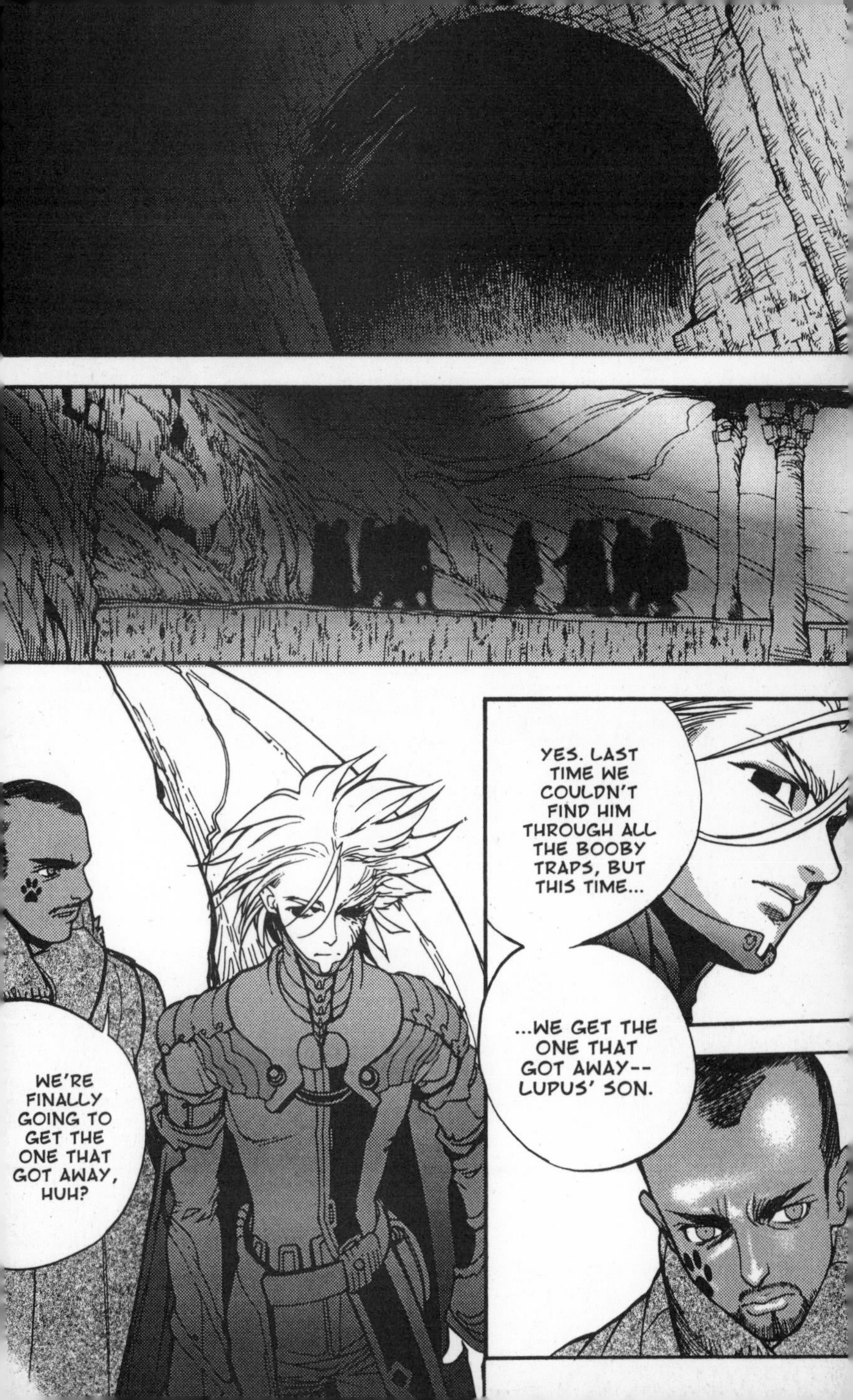
WE'RE FINALLY GOING TO GET THE ONE THAT GOT AWAY, HUH?
YES. LAST TIME WE COULDN'T FIND HIM THROUGH ALL THE BOOBY TRAPS, BUT THIS TIME...
...WE GET THE ONE THAT GOT AWAY--LUPUS' SON.

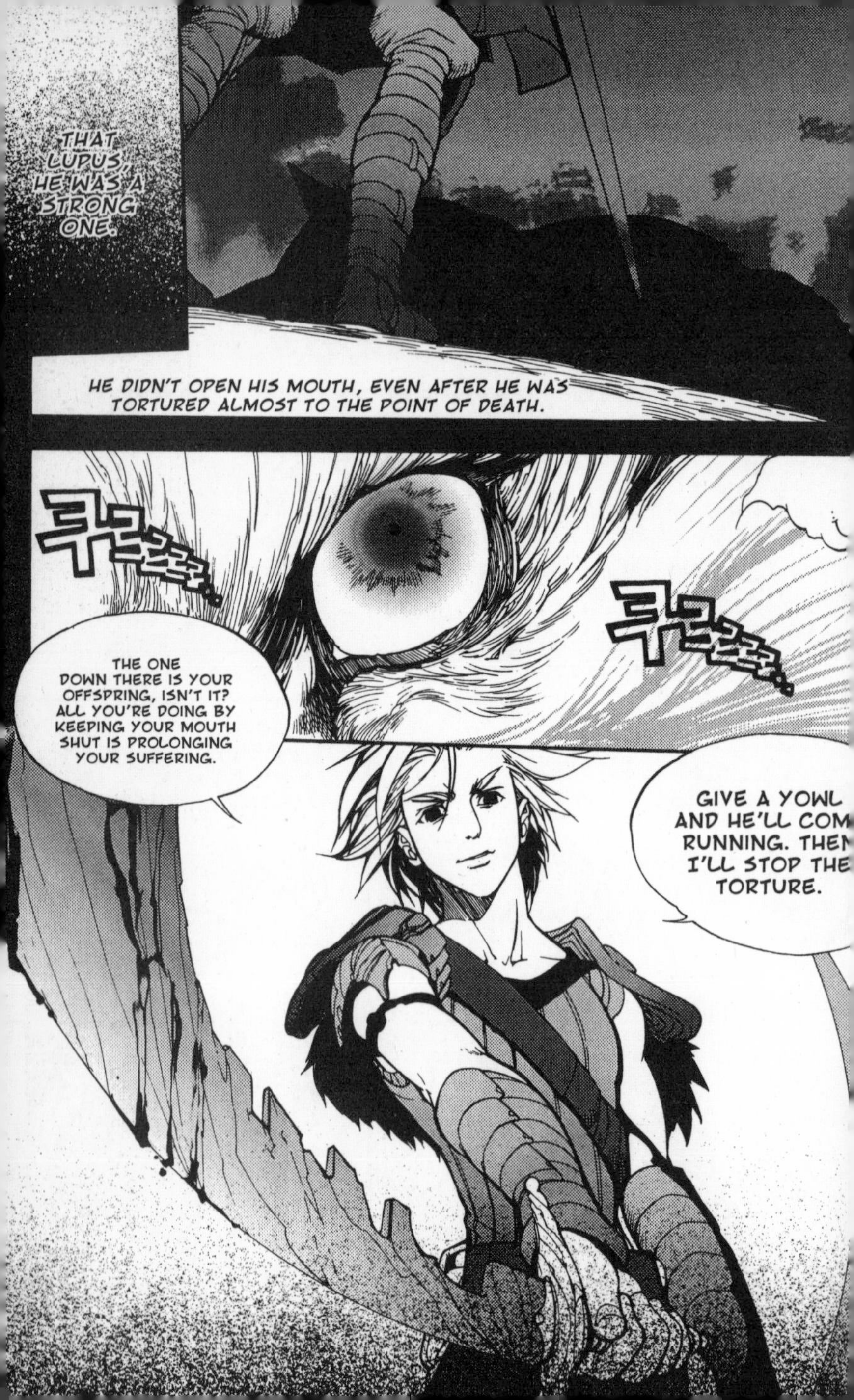
THAT LUPUS, HE WAS A STRONG ONE.
HE DIDN'T OPEN HIS MOUTH, EVEN AFTER HE WAS TORTURED ALMOST TO THE POINT OF DEATH.
쿠그그그...
쿠그그그...
THE ONE DOWN THERE IS YOUR OFFSPRING, ISN'T IT? ALL YOU'RE DOING BY KEEPING YOUR MOUTH SHUT IS PROLONGING YOUR SUFFERING.
GIVE A YOWL AND HE'LL COM RUNNING. THEN I'LL STOP THE TORTURE.

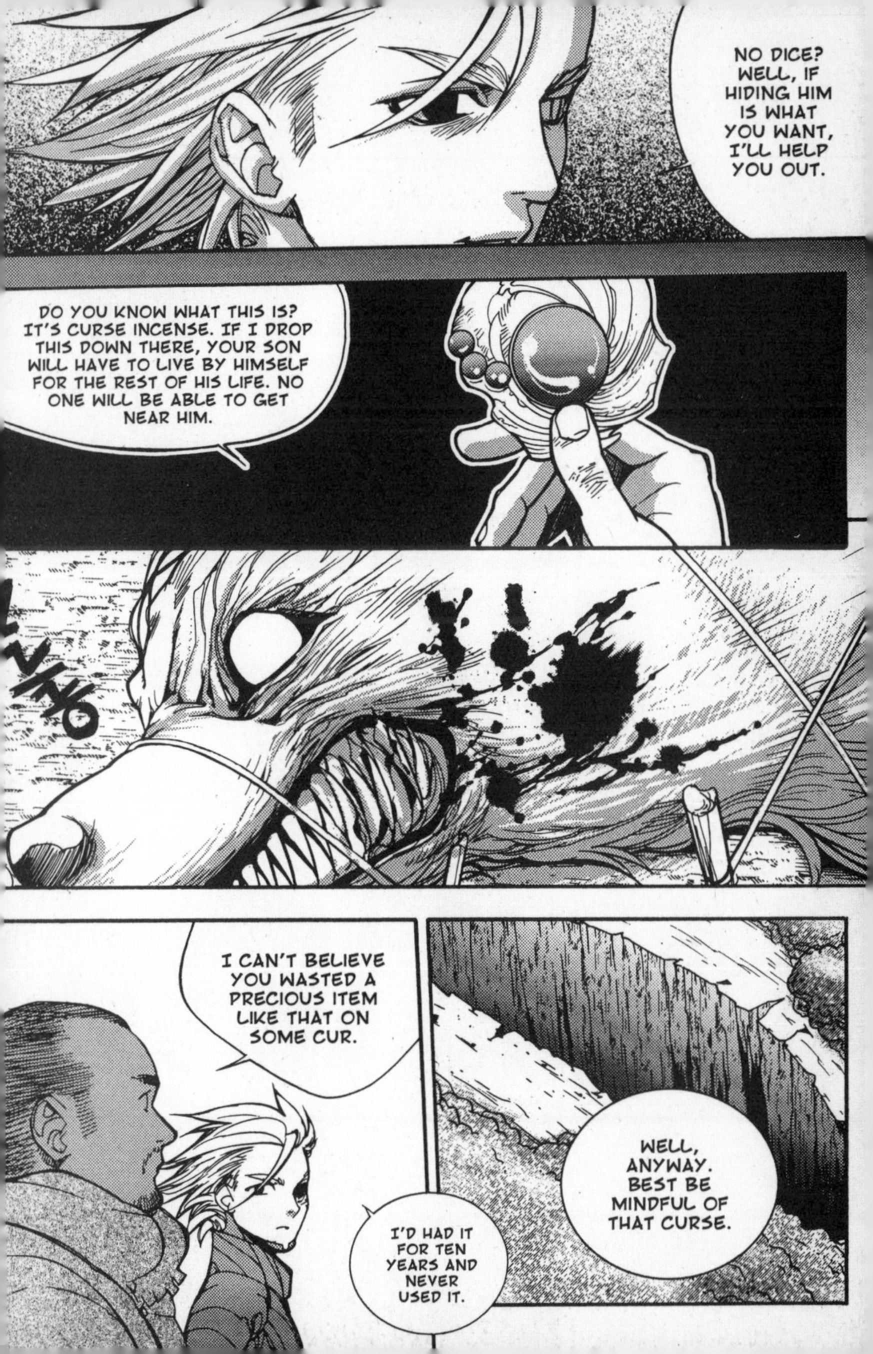

NO DICE? WELL, IF HIDING HIM IS WHAT YOU WANT, I'LL HELP YOU OUT.
DO YOU KNOW WHAT THIS IS? IT'S CURSE INCENSE. IF I DROP THIS DOWN THERE, YOUR SON WILL HAVE TO LIVE BY HIMSELF FOR THE REST OF HIS LIFE. NO ONE WILL BE ABLE TO GET NEAR HIM.
I CAN'T BELIEVE YOU WASTED A PRECIOUS ITEM LIKE THAT ON SOME CUR.
I'D HAD IT FOR TEN YEARS AND NEVER USED IT.
WELL, ANYWAY. BEST BE MINDFUL OF THAT CURSE.

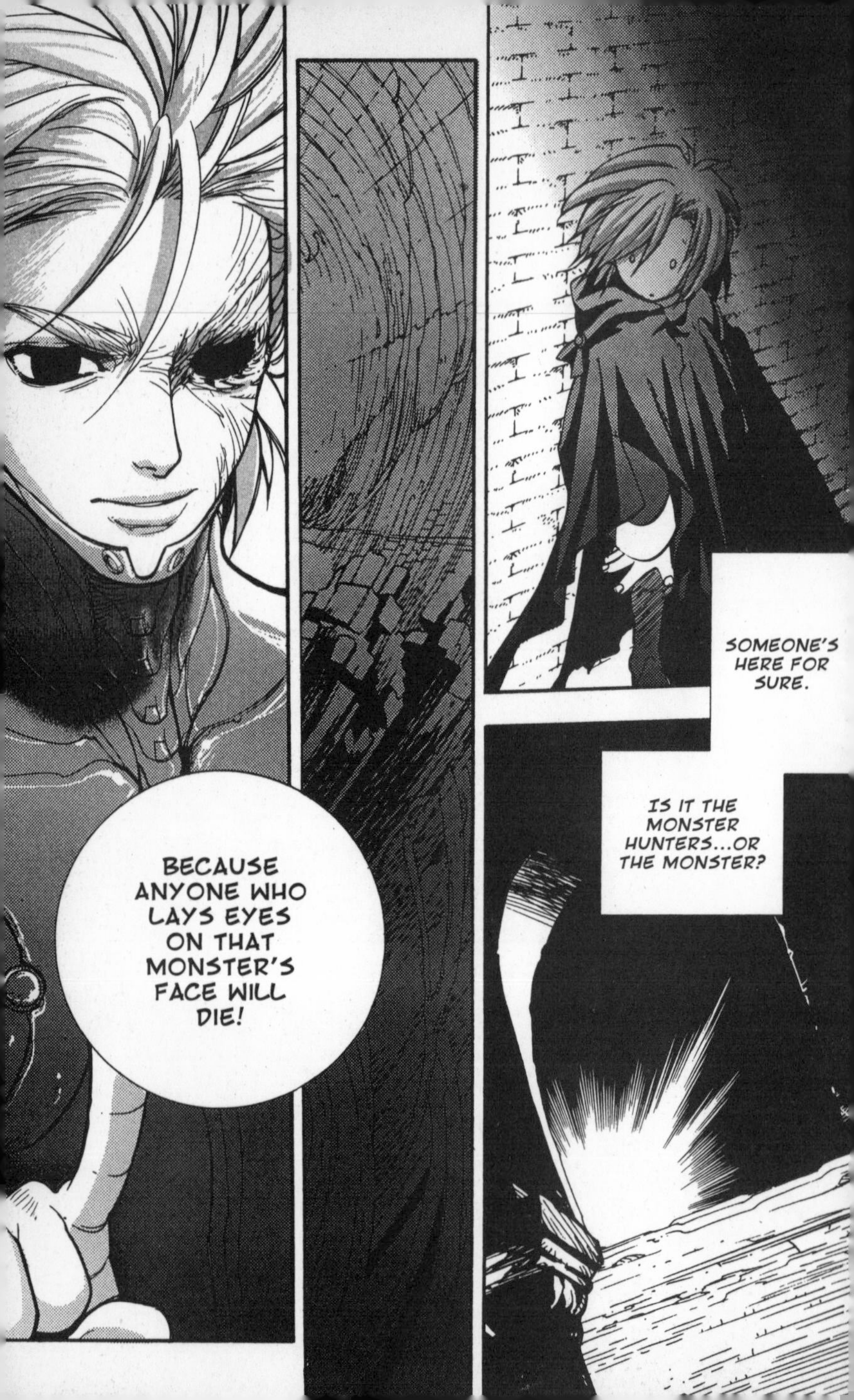
BECAUSE ANYONE WHO LAYS EYES ON THAT MONSTER'S FACE WILL DIE!
SOMEONE'S HERE FOR SURE.
IS IT THE MONSTER HUNTERS...OR THE MONSTER?

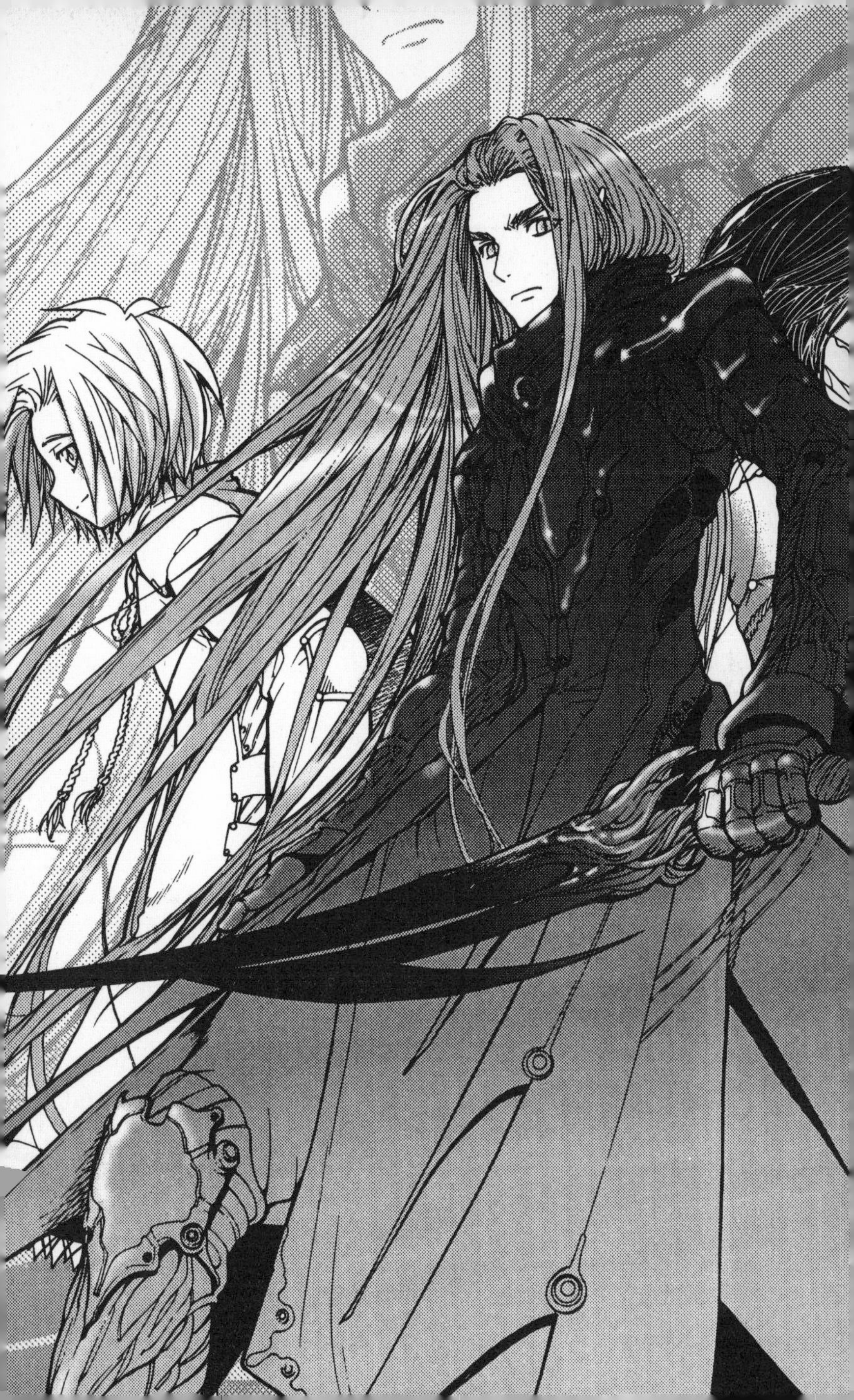

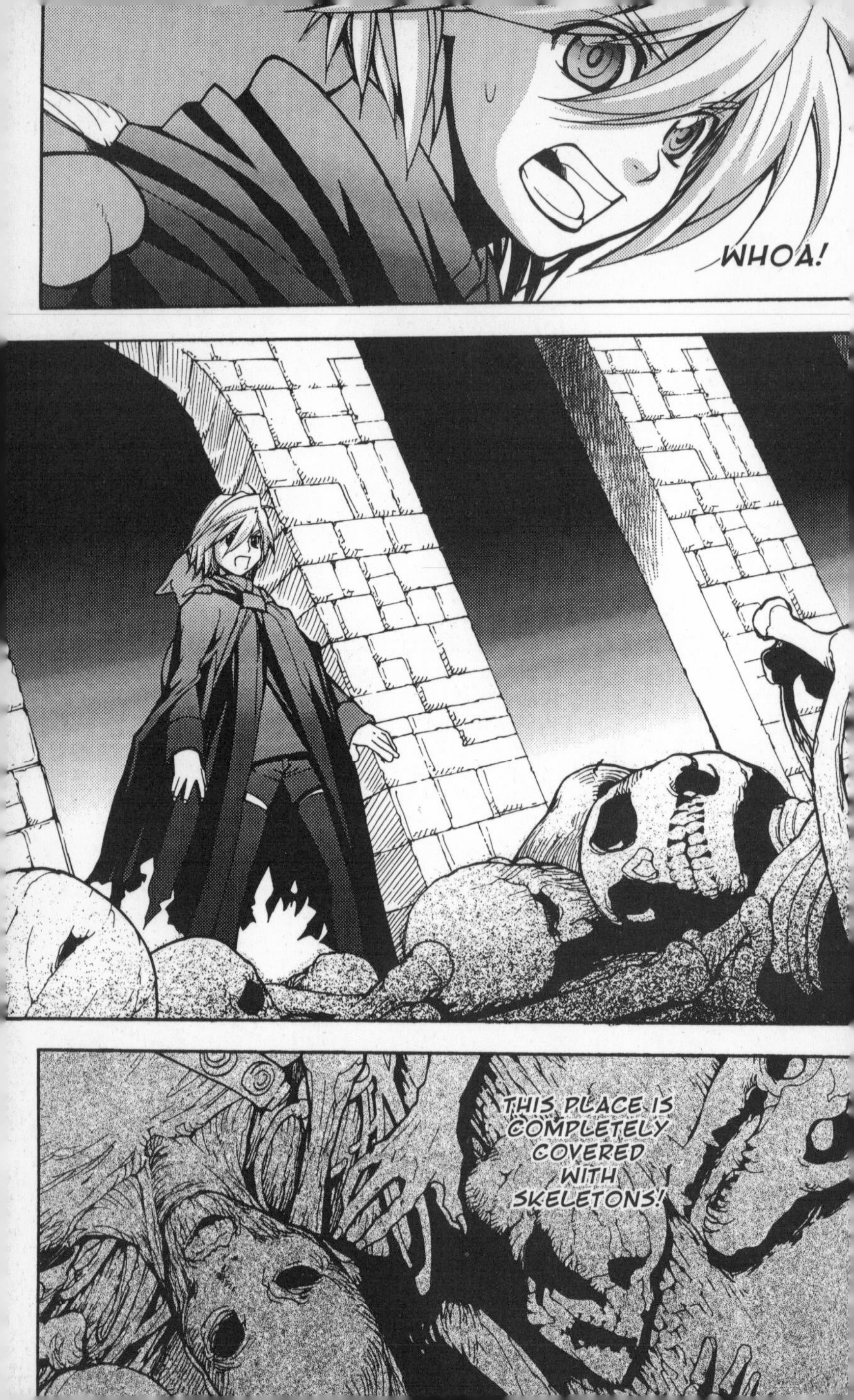
WHOA!
THIS PLACE IS COMPLETELY COVERED WITH SKELETONS!

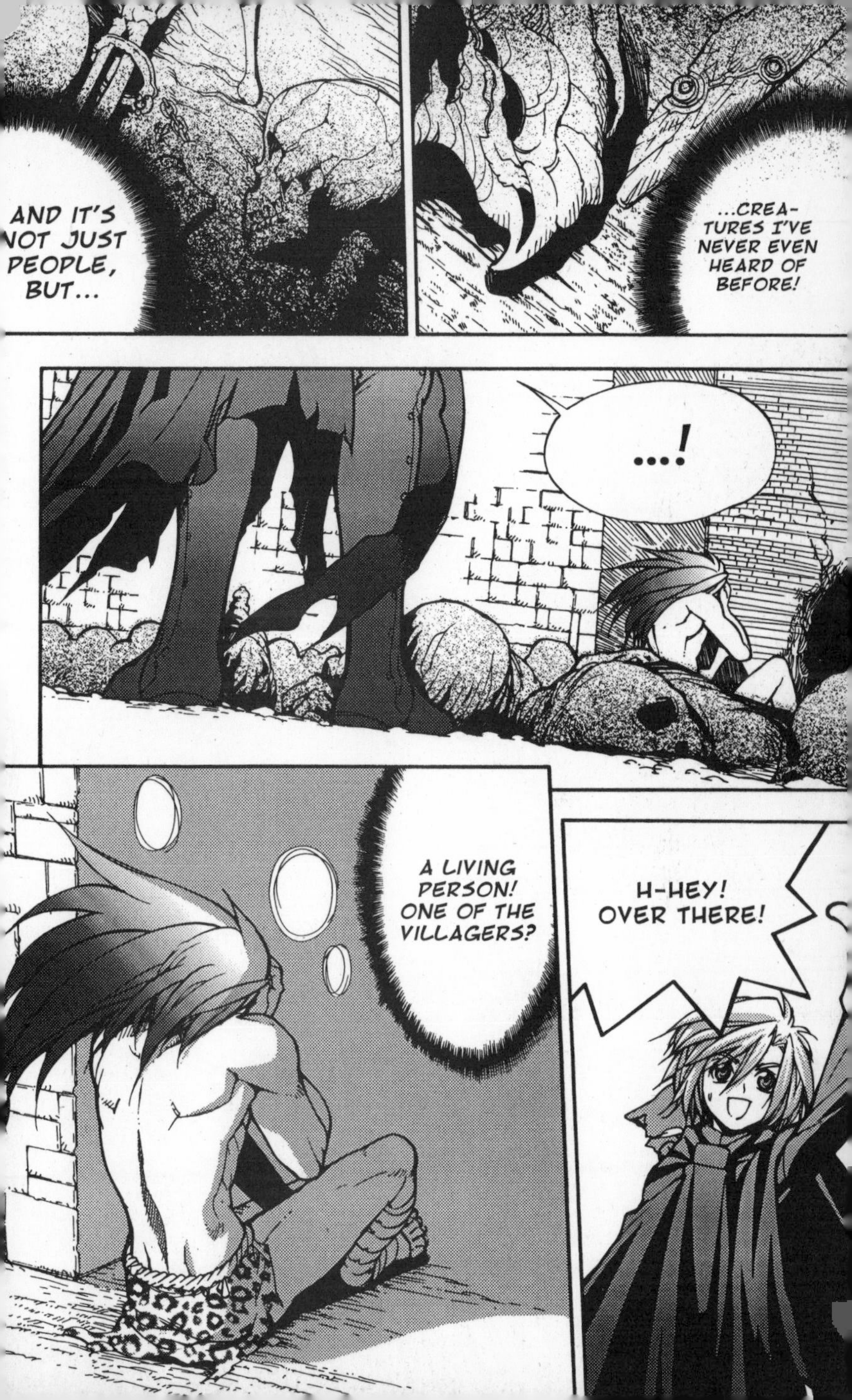
AND IT'S NOT JUST PEOPLE, BUT...
...CREA-TURES I'VE NEVER EVEN HEARD OF BEFORE!
...!
A LIVING PERSON! ONE OF THE VILLAGERS?
H-HEY! OVER THERE!

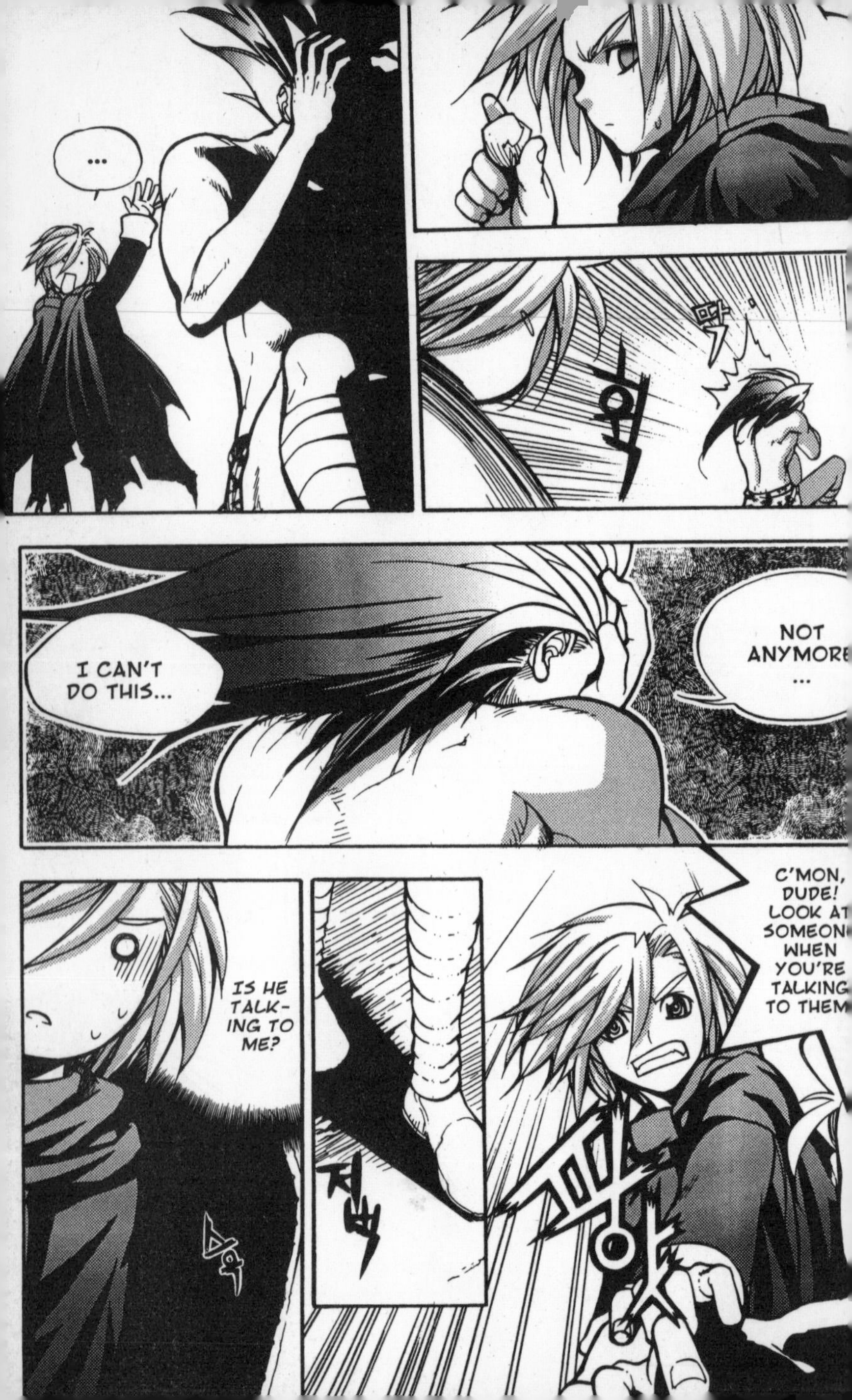
...
I CAN'T DO THIS...
NOT ANYMORE ...
IS HE TALK-ING TO ME?
C'MON, DUDE! LOOK AT SOMEON WHEN YOU'RE TALKING TO THEM

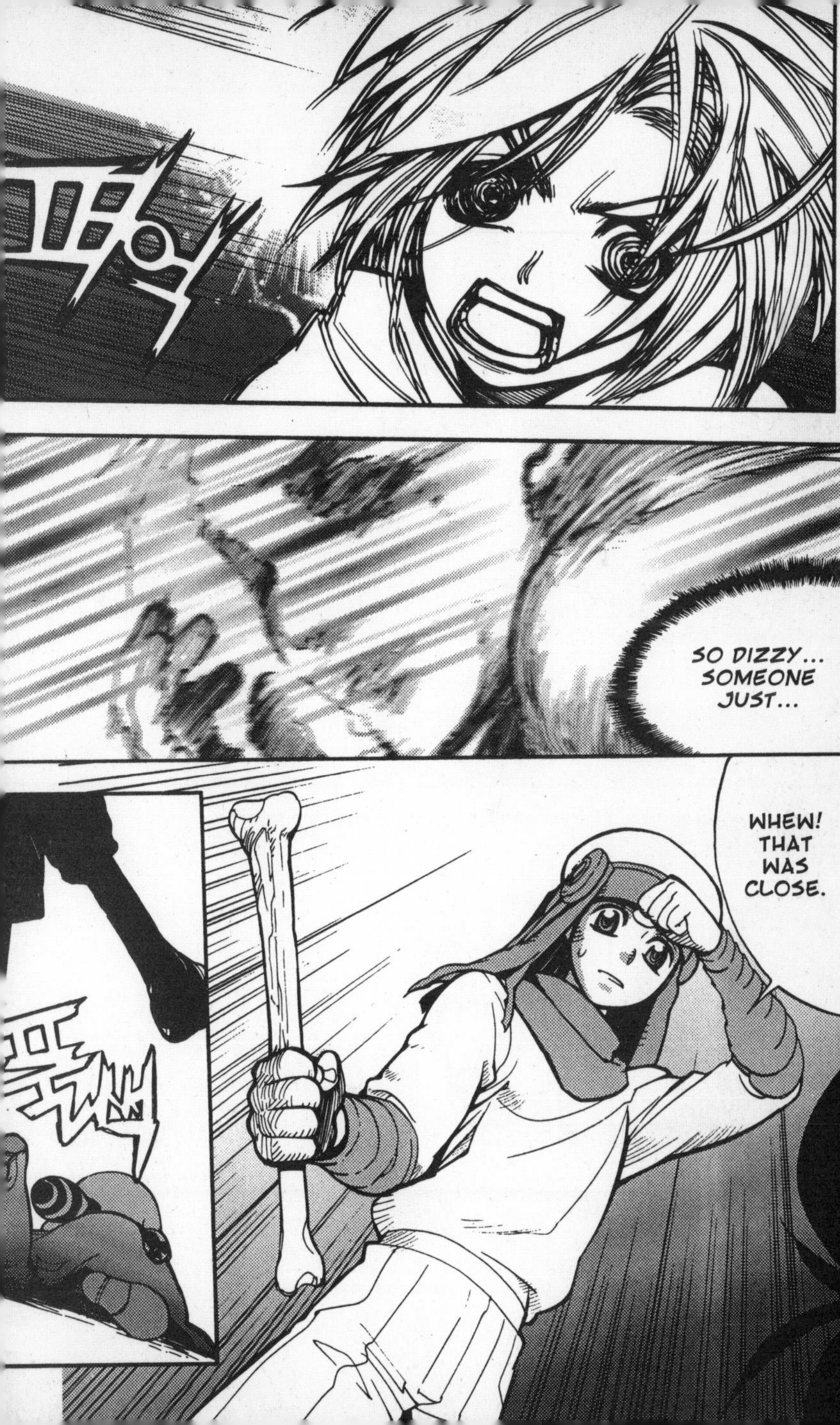
SO DIZZY... SOMEONE JUST...
WHEW! THAT WAS CLOSE.

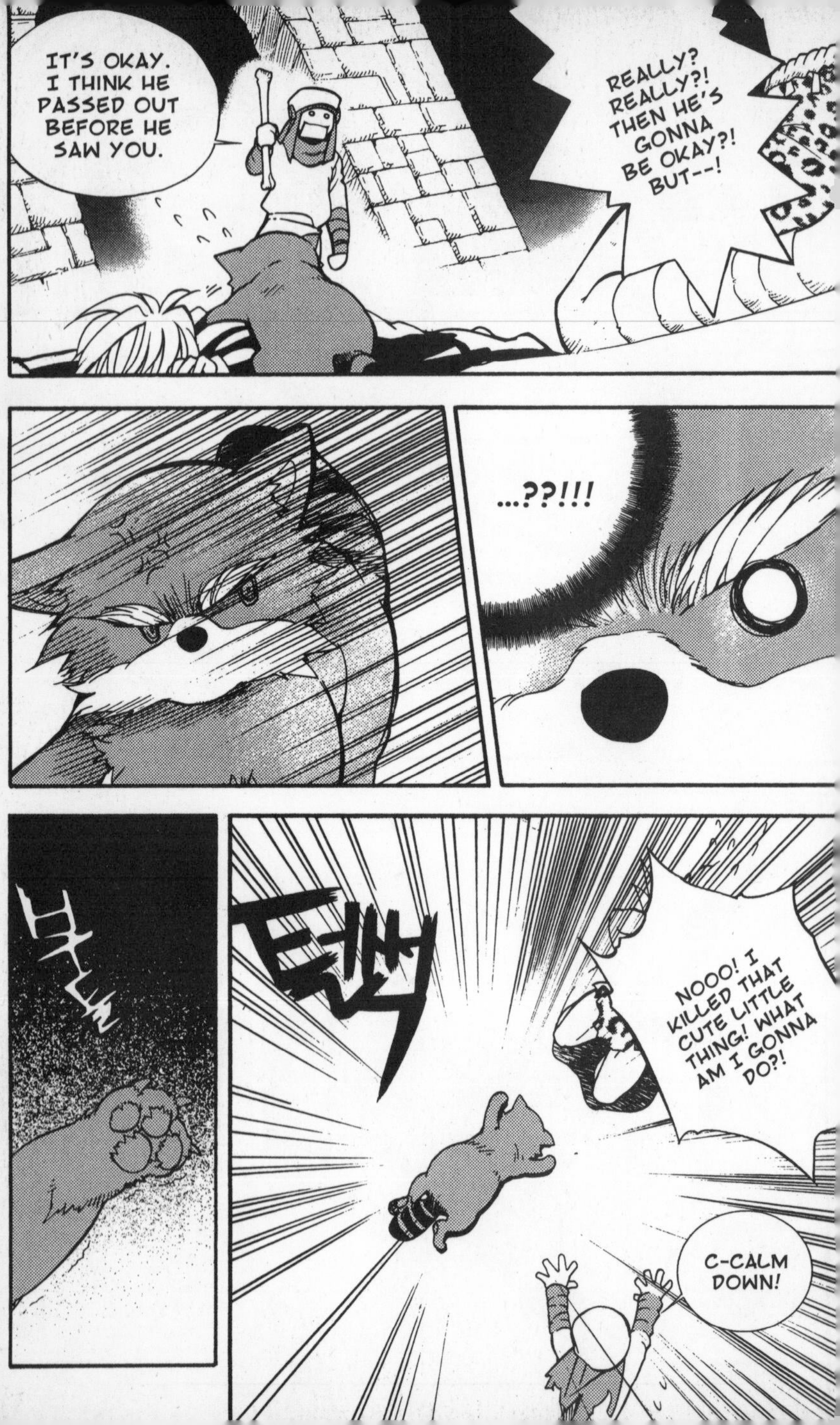
IT'S OKAY. I THINK HE PASSED OUT BEFORE HE SAW YOU.
REALLY? REALLY?! THEN HE'S GONNA BE OKAY?! BUT--!
...??!!!
NOOO! I KILLED THAT CUTE LITTLE THING! WHAT AM I GONNA DO?!
C-CALM DOWN!

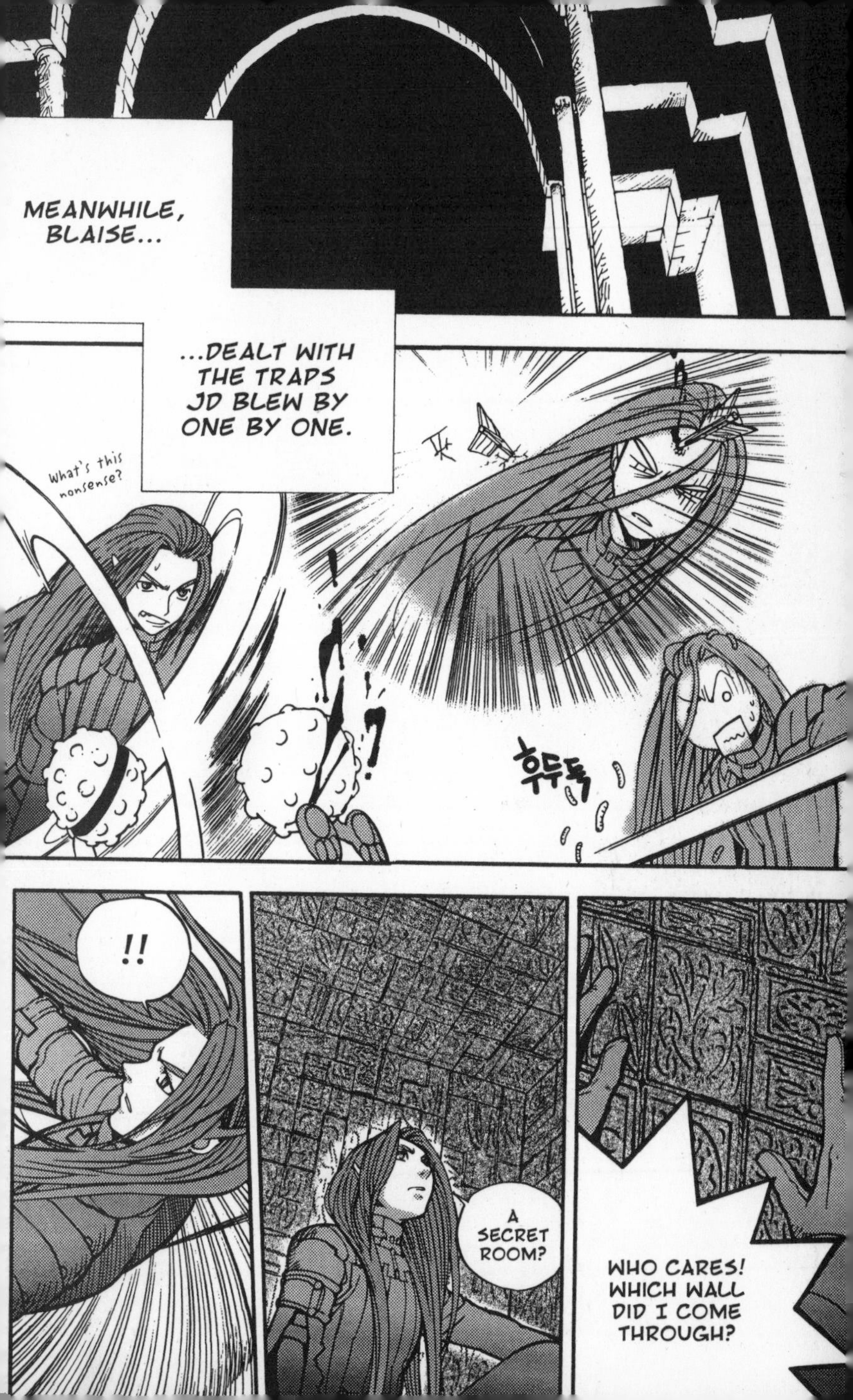
MEANWHILE, BLAISE...
...DEALT WITH THE TRAPS JD BLEW BY ONE BY ONE.
What's this nonsense?
!
후두둑
!!
A SECRET ROOM?
WHO CARES! WHICH WALL DID I COME THROUGH?

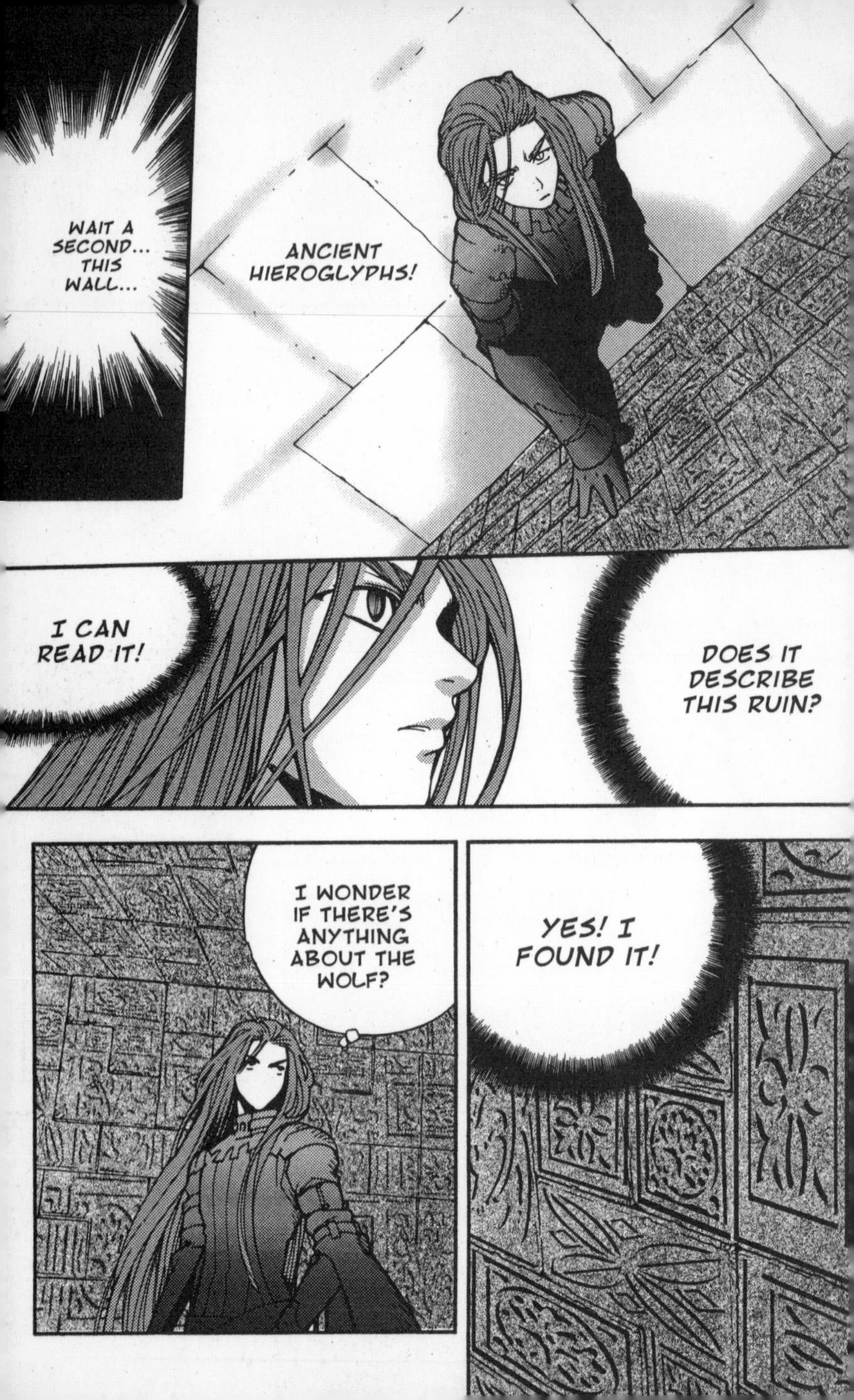
WAIT A SECOND... THIS WALL...
ANCIENT HIEROGLYPHS!
I CAN READ IT!
DOES IT DESCRIBE THIS RUIN?
I WONDER IF THERE'S ANYTHING ABOUT THE WOLF?
YES! I FOUND IT!

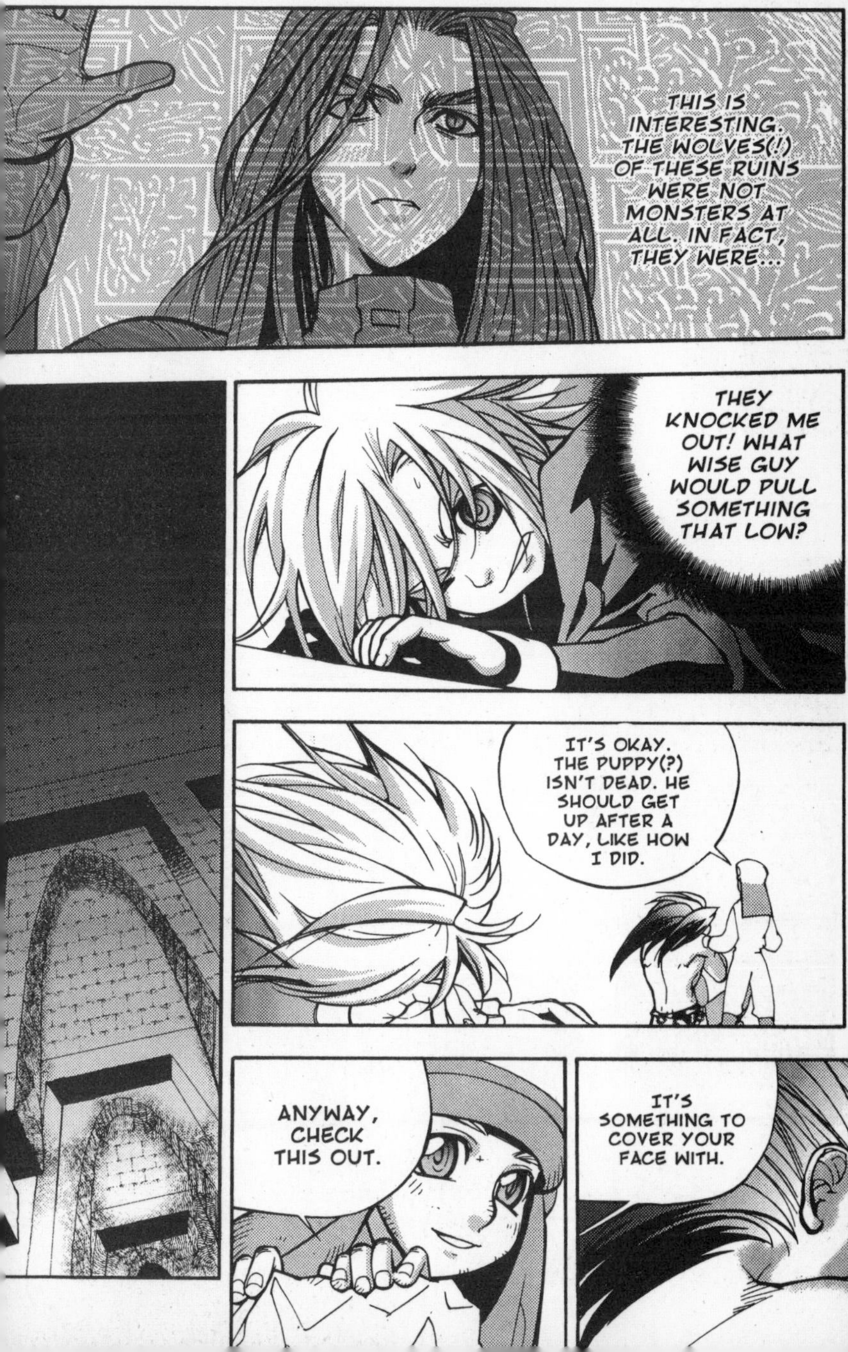
THIS IS INTERESTING. THE WOLVES(!) OF THESE RUINS WERE NOT MONSTERS AT ALL. IN FACT, THEY WERE...
THEY KNOCKED ME OUT! WHAT WISE GUY WOULD PULL SOMETHING THAT LOW?
IT'S OKAY. THE PUPPY(?) ISN'T DEAD. HE SHOULD GET UP AFTER A DAY, LIKE HOW I DID.
ANYWAY, CHECK THIS OUT.
IT'S SOMETHING TO COVER YOUR FACE WITH.

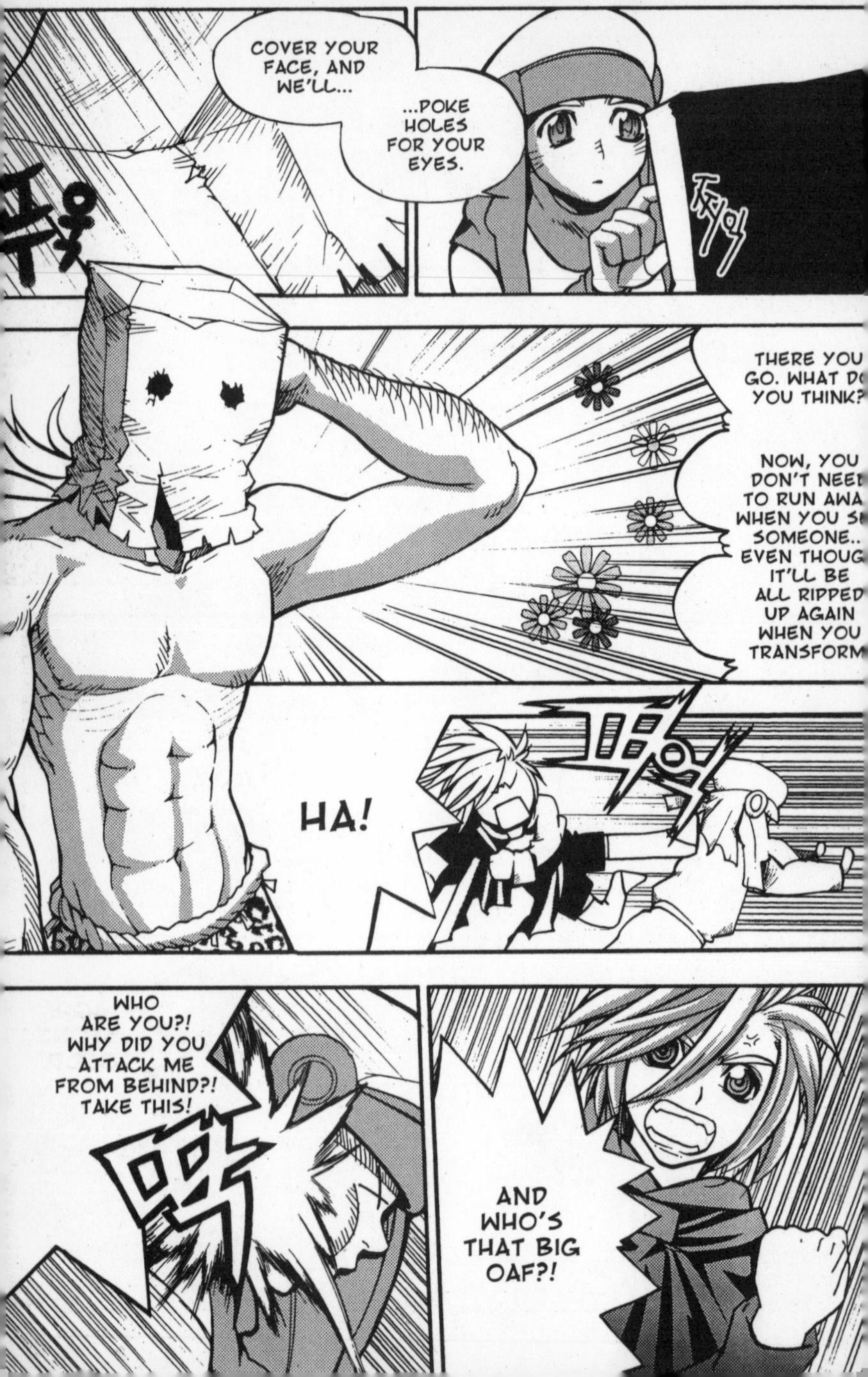
COVER YOUR FACE, AND WE'LL...
...POKE HOLES FOR YOUR EYES.
THERE YOU GO. WHAT D
YOU THINK?
NOW, YOU DON'T NEE
TO RUN AWA
WHEN YOU S
SOMEONE..
EVEN THOUG
IT'LL BE ALL RIPPED UP AGAIN WHEN YOU TRANSFORM
HA!
WHO ARE YOU?! WHY DID YOU ATTACK ME FROM BEHIND?! TAKE THIS!
AND WHO'S THAT BIG OAF?!

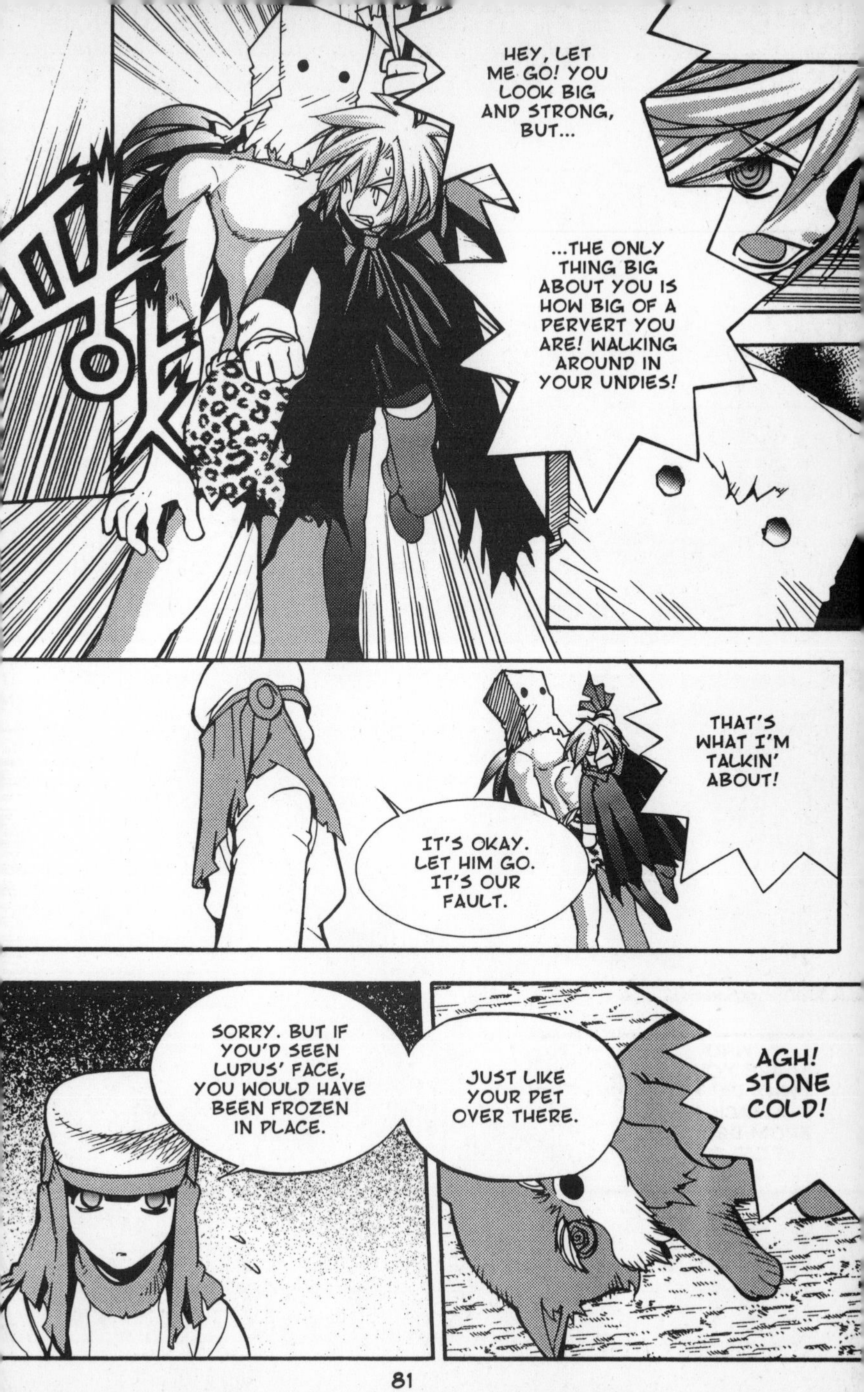
HEY, LET ME GO! YOU LOOK BIG AND STRONG, BUT...
...THE ONLY THING BIG ABOUT YOU IS HOW BIG OF A PERVERT YOU ARE! WALKING AROUND IN YOUR UNDIES!
THAT'S WHAT I'M TALKIN' ABOUT!
IT'S OKAY. LET HIM GO. IT'S OUR FAULT.
SORRY. BUT IF YOU'D SEEN LUPUS' FACE, YOU WOULD HAVE BEEN FROZEN IN PLACE.
JUST LIKE YOUR PET OVER THERE.
AGH! STONE COLD!

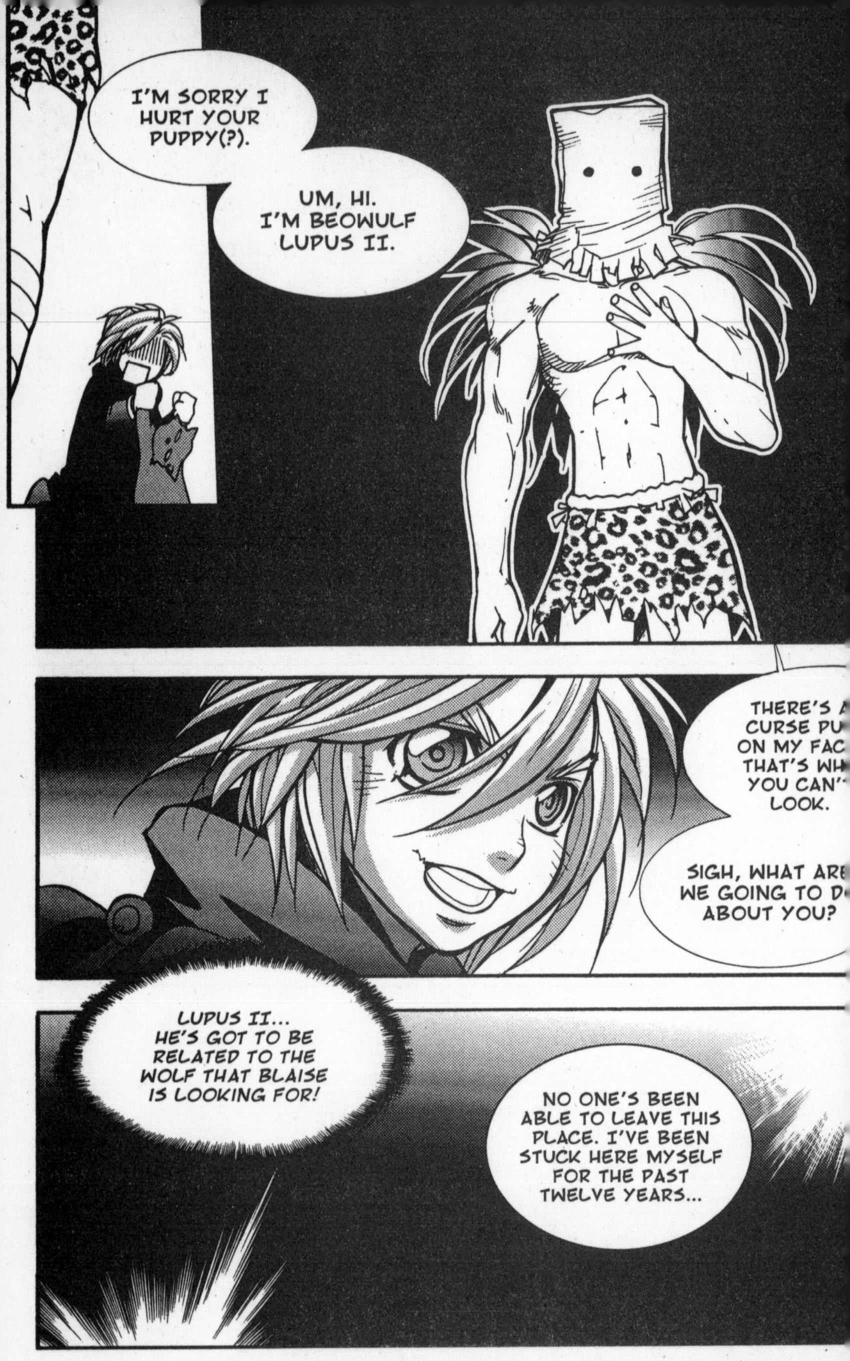
I'M SORRY I HURT YOUR PUPPY(?).
UM, HI. I'M BEOWULF LUPUS II.
THERE'S A CURSE PU ON MY FAC THAT'S WH YOU CAN' LOOK.
SIGH, WHAT ARE WE GOING TO D ABOUT YOU?
LUPUS II... HE'S GOT TO BE RELATED TO THE WOLF THAT BLAISE IS LOOKING FOR!
NO ONE'S BEEN ABLE TO LEAVE THIS PLACE. I'VE BEEN STUCK HERE MYSELF FOR THE PAST TWELVE YEARS...

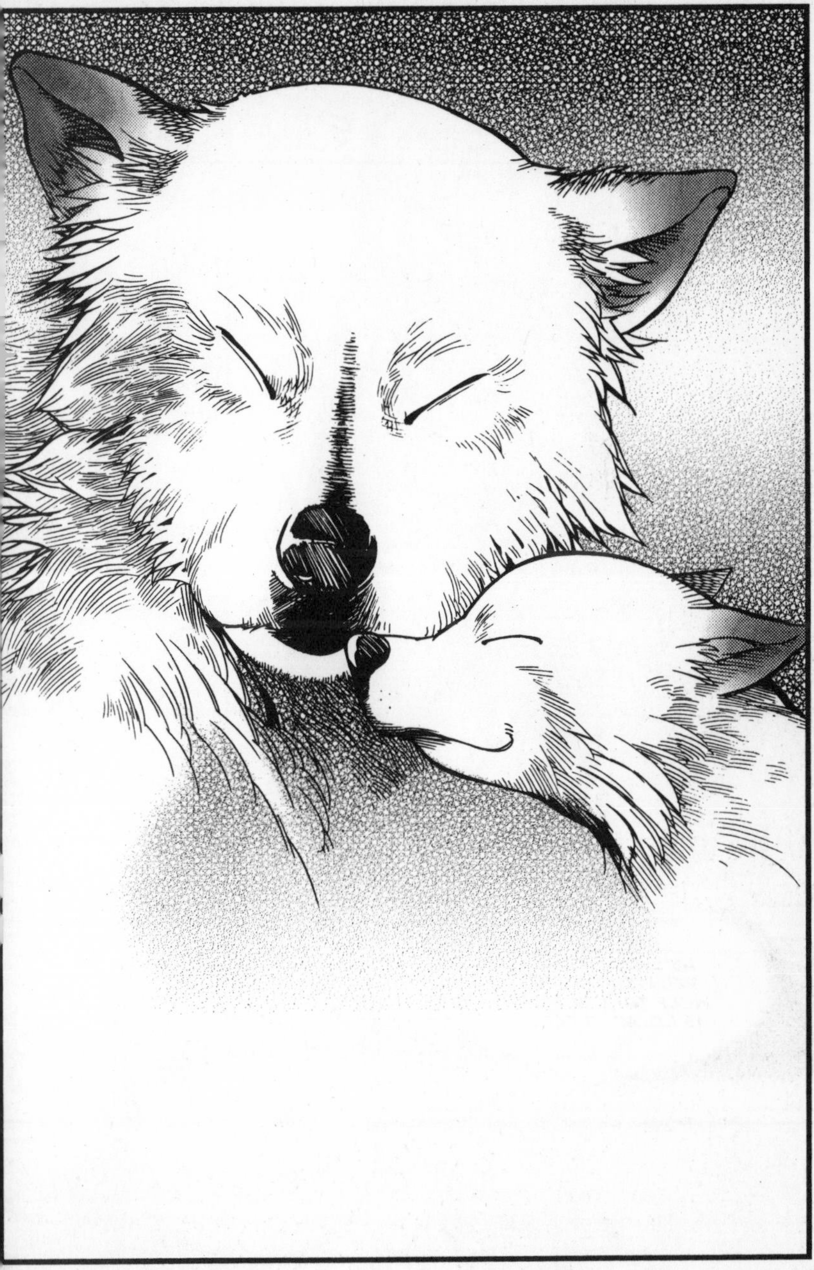

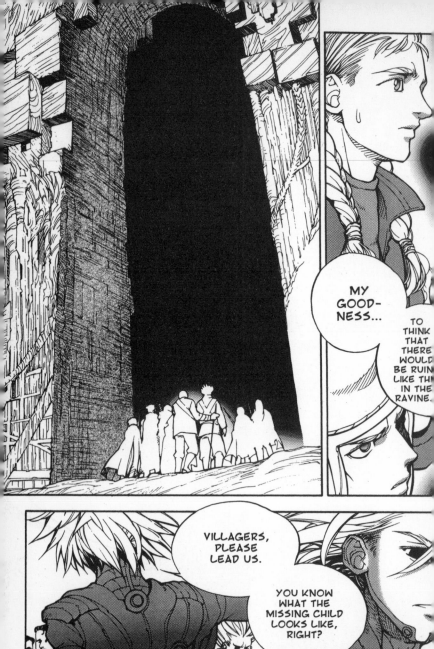

MY GOOD-NESS...

TO THINK THAT THERE WOULD BE RUIN LIKE TH IN THE RAVINE.

VILLAGERS, PLEASE LEAD US.

YOU KNOW WHAT THE MISSING CHILD LOOKS LIKE, RIGHT?

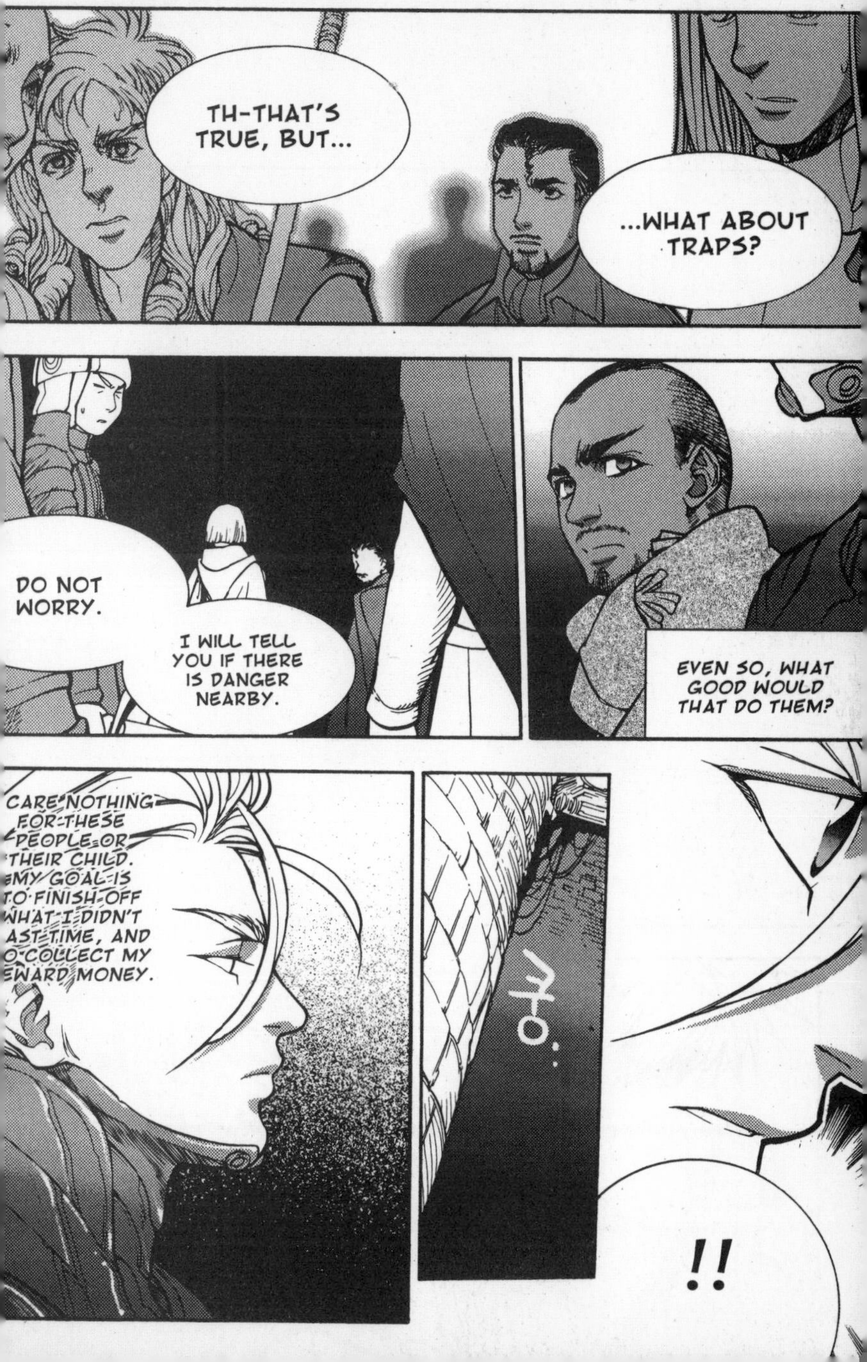
TH-THAT'S TRUE, BUT...
...WHAT ABOUT TRAPS?
DO NOT WORRY.
I WILL TELL YOU IF THERE IS DANGER NEARBY.
EVEN SO, WHAT GOOD WOULD THAT DO THEM?
CARE NOTHING FOR THESE PEOPLE OR THEIR CHILD. MY GOAL IS TO FINISH OFF WHAT I DIDN'T AST TIME, AND O COLLECT MY EWARD MONEY.
쿵..
!!

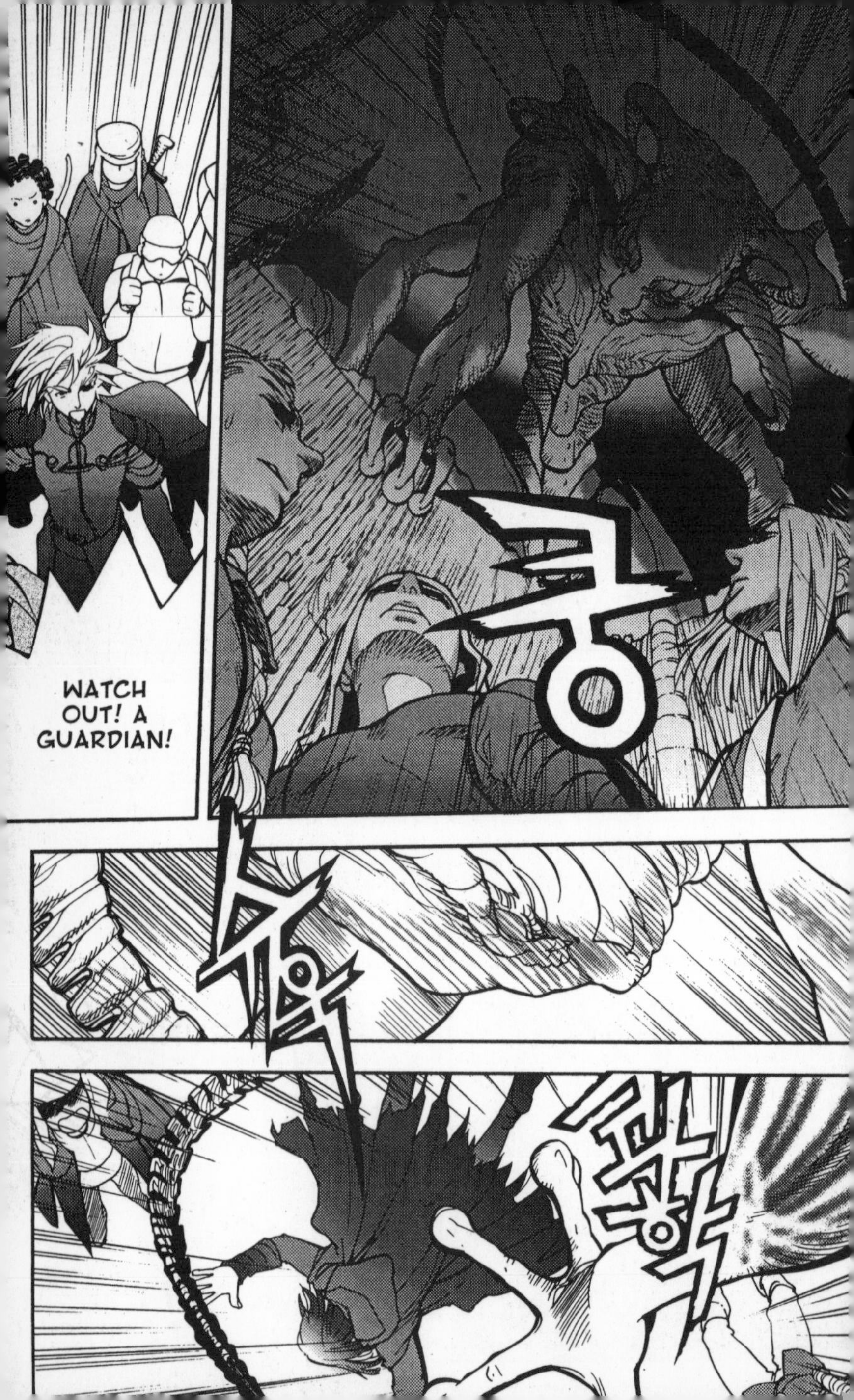
WATCH OUT! A GUARDIAN!

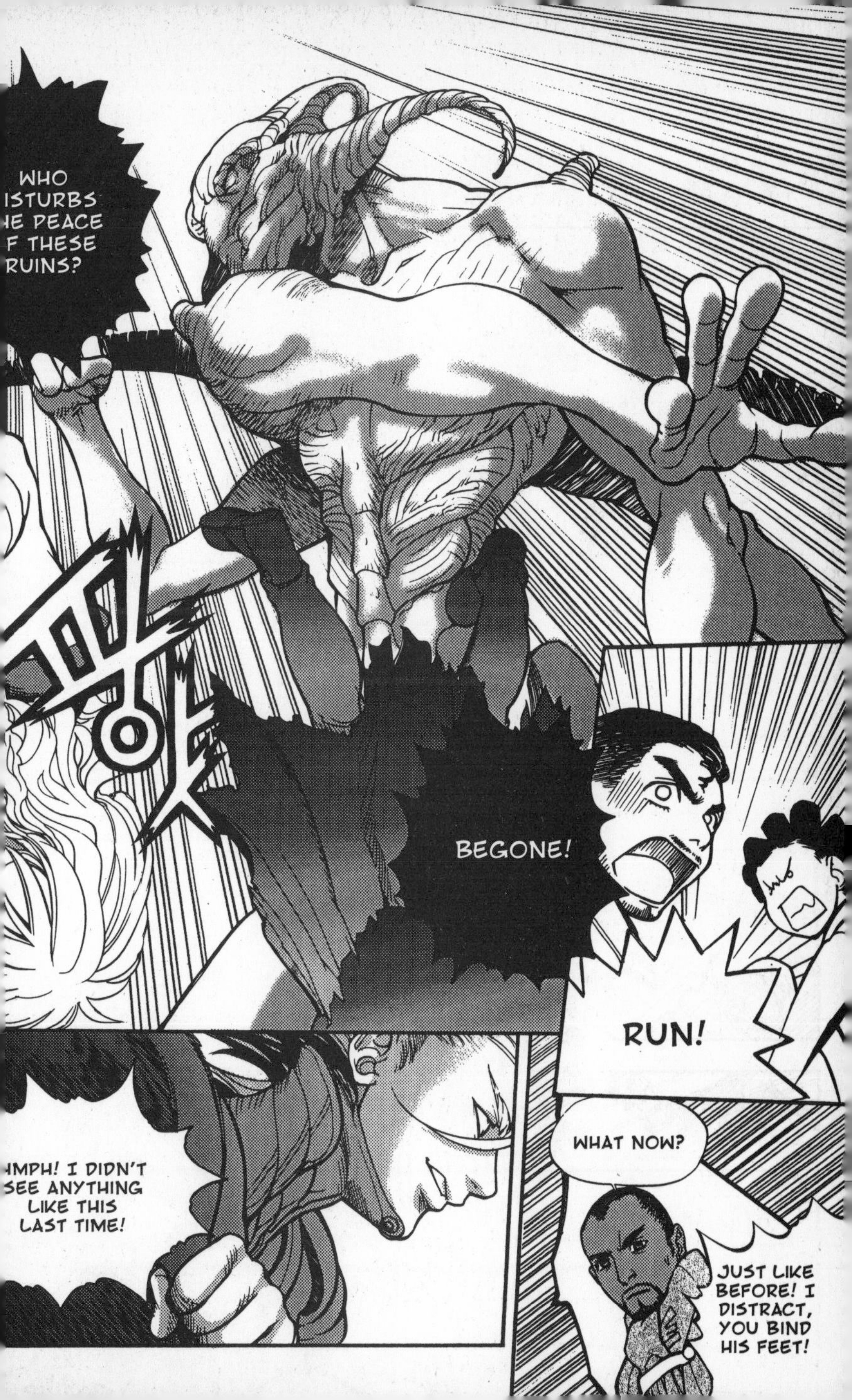
WHO ISTURBS HE PEACE F THESE RUINS?
BEGONE!
RUN!
HMPH! I DIDN'T SEE ANYTHING LIKE THIS LAST TIME!
WHAT NOW?
JUST LIKE BEFORE! I DISTRACT, YOU BIND HIS FEET!

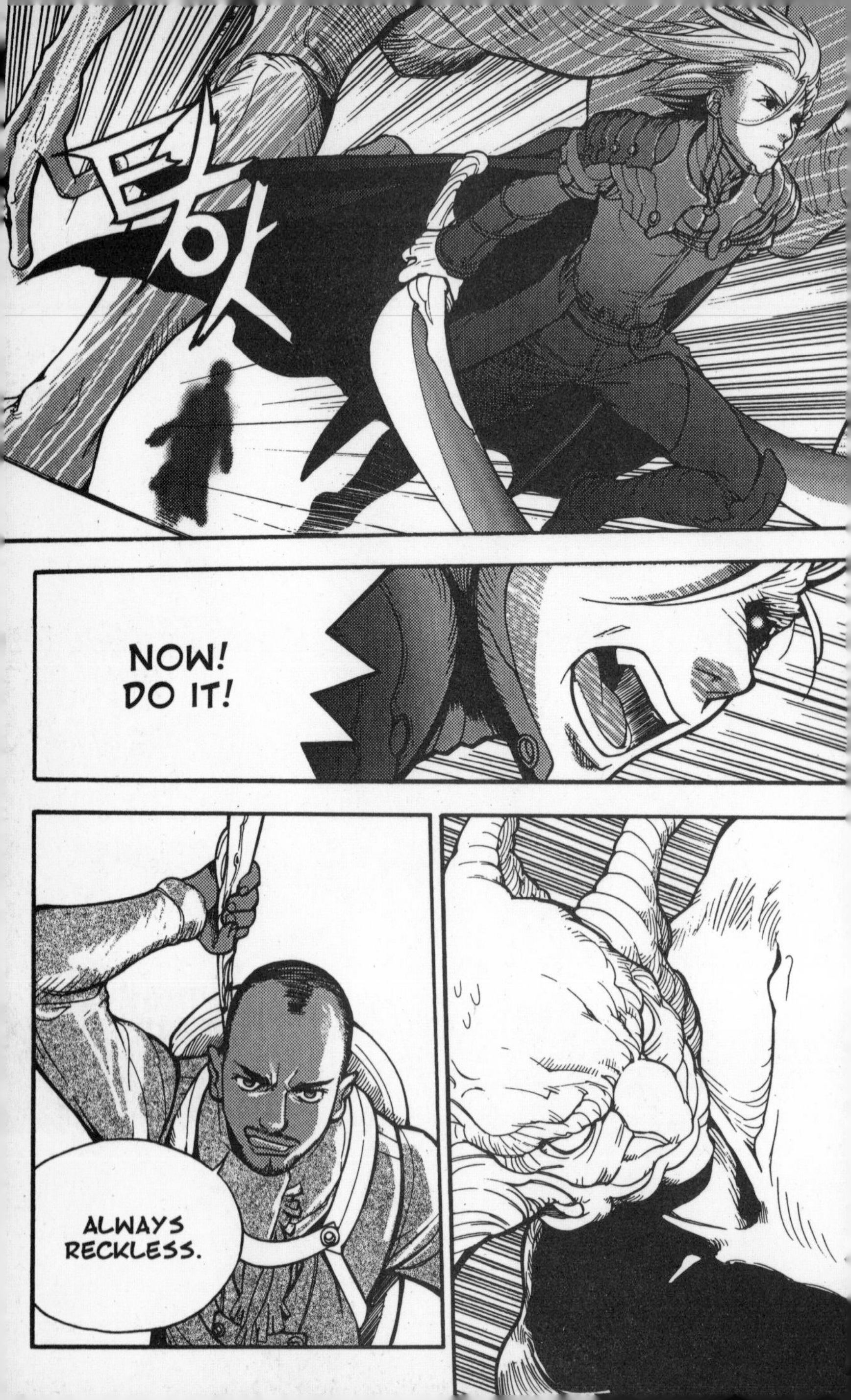
NOW!
DO IT!
ALWAYS
RECKLESS.

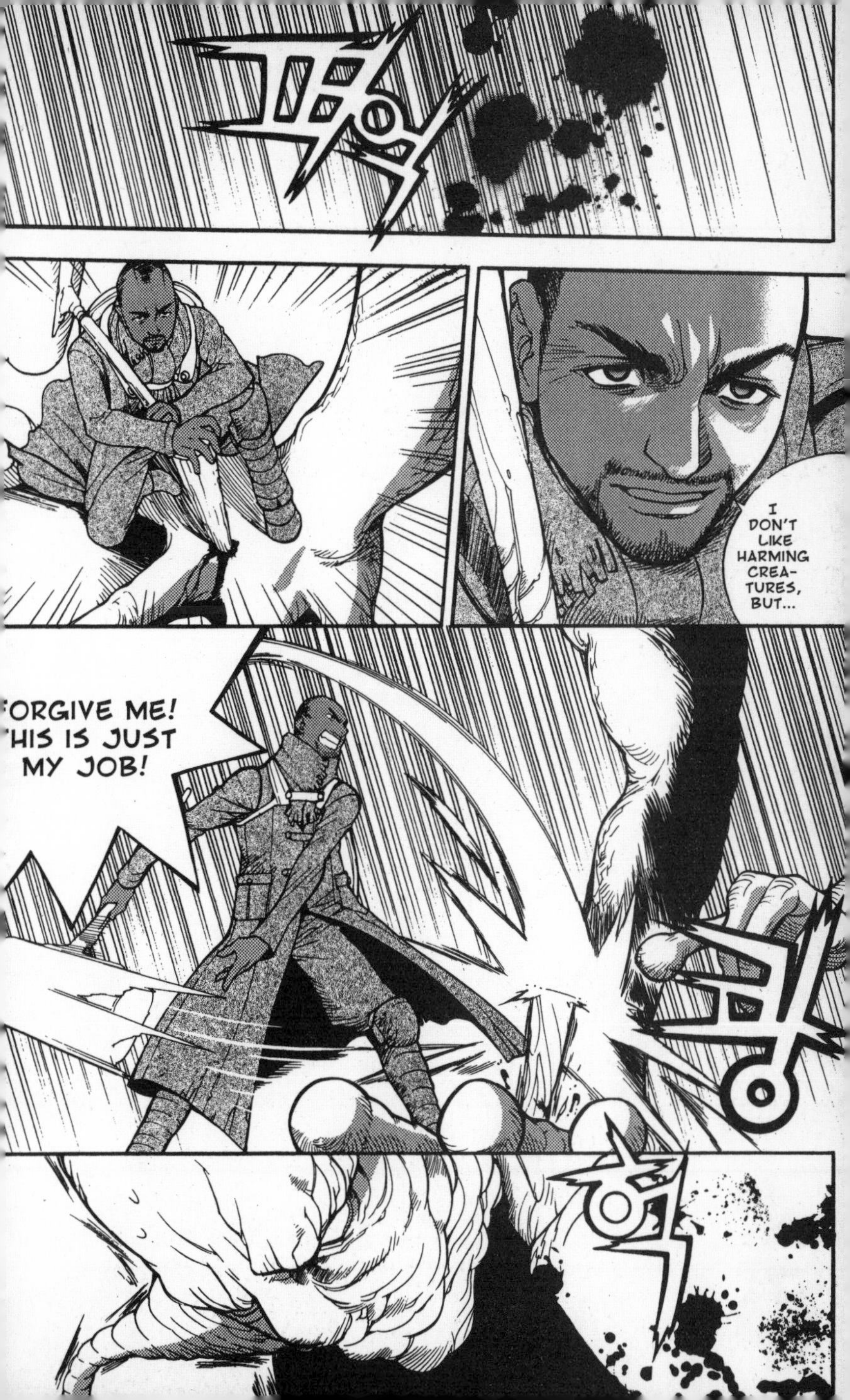
I DON'T LIKE HARMING CREA-TURES, BUT...
FORGIVE ME! THIS IS JUST MY JOB!

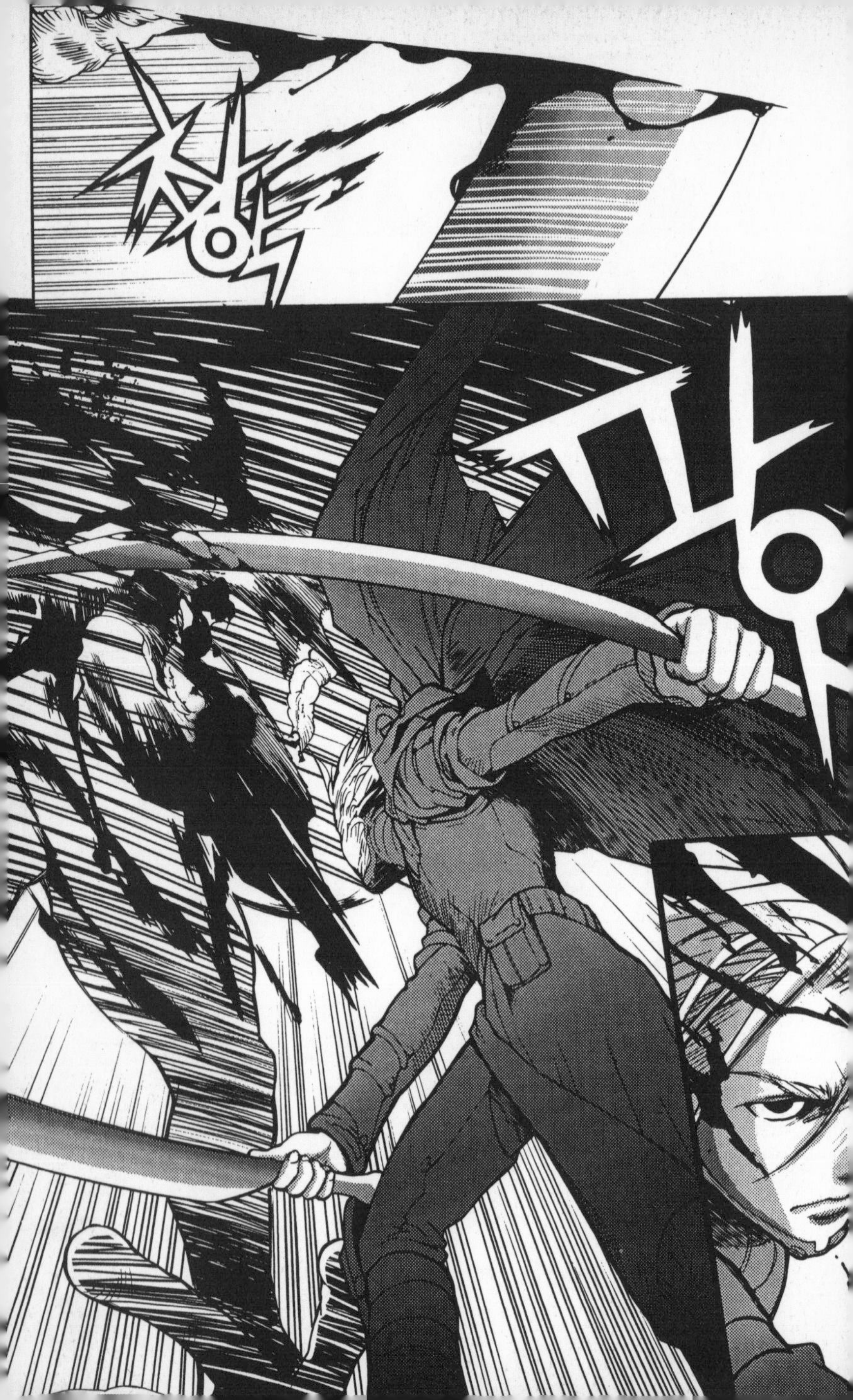

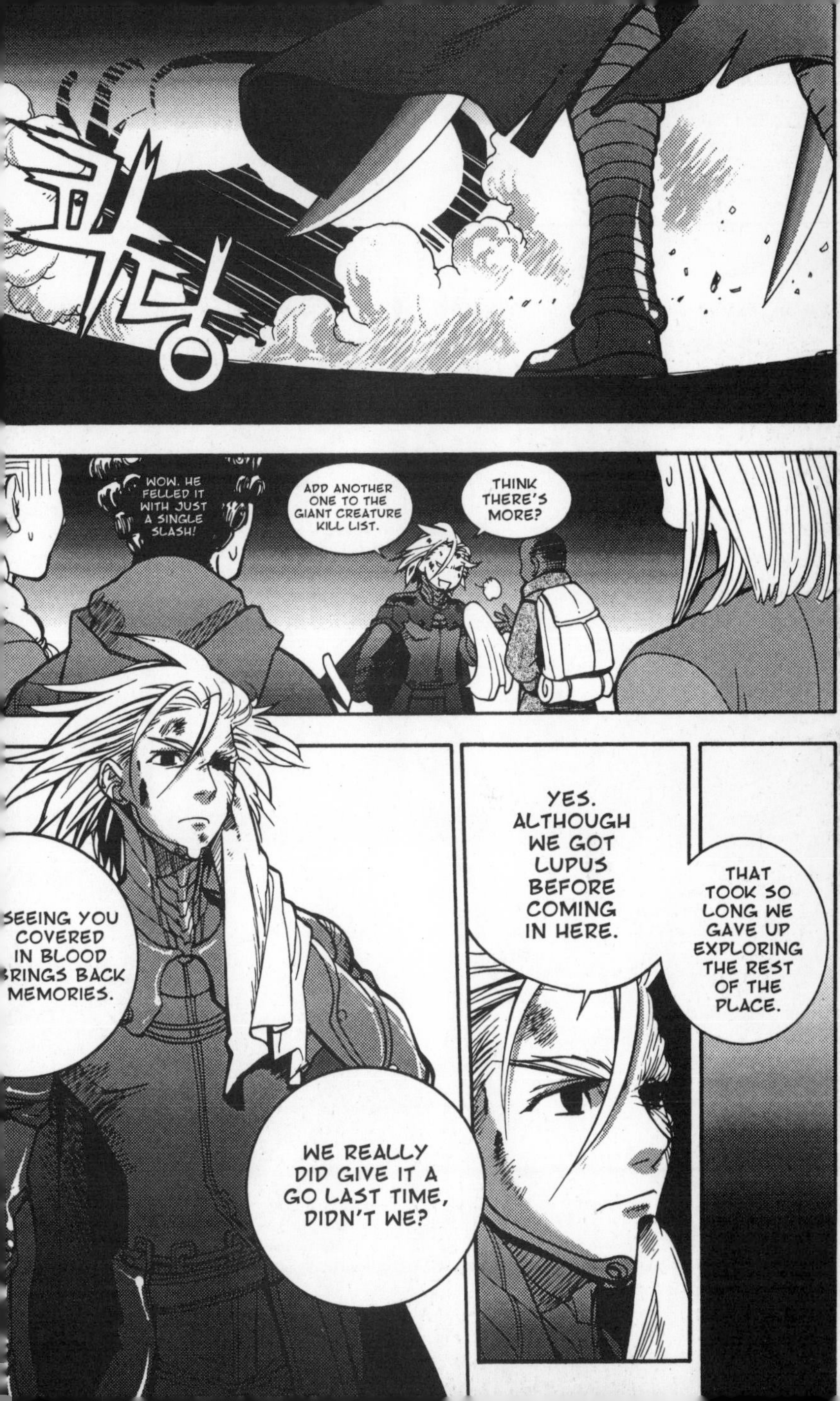
WOW. HE FELLED IT WITH JUST A SINGLE SLASH!
ADD ANOTHER ONE TO THE GIANT CREATURE KILL LIST.
THINK THERE'S MORE?
SEEING YOU COVERED IN BLOOD BRINGS BACK MEMORIES.
WE REALLY DID GIVE IT A GO LAST TIME, DIDN'T WE?
YES. ALTHOUGH WE GOT LUPUS BEFORE COMING IN HERE.
THAT TOOK SO LONG WE GAVE UP EXPLORING THE REST OF THE PLACE.

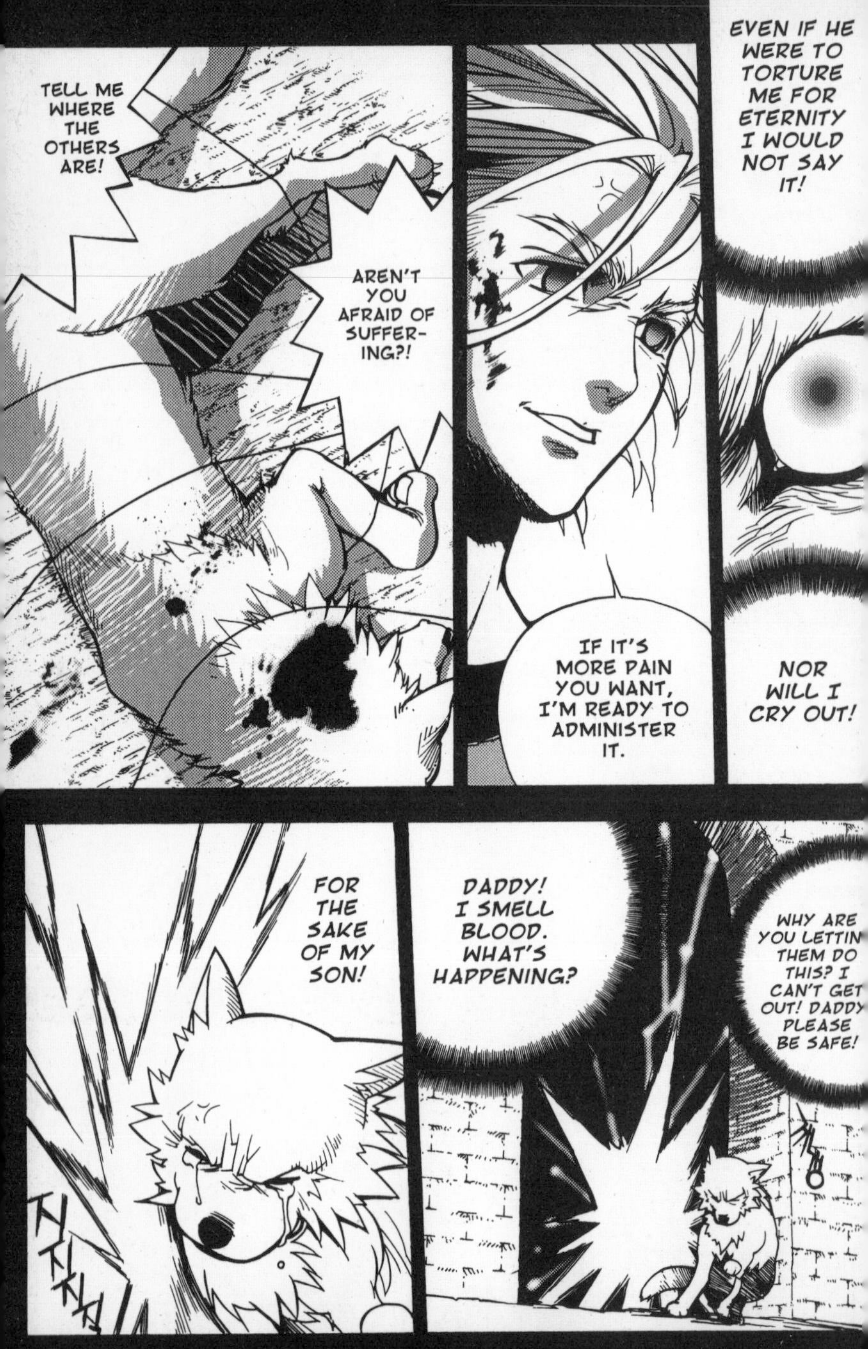
TELL ME WHERE THE OTHERS ARE!
AREN'T YOU AFRAID OF SUFFER-ING?!
IF IT'S MORE PAIN YOU WANT, I'M READY TO ADMINISTER IT.
EVEN IF HE WERE TO TORTURE ME FOR ETERNITY I WOULD NOT SAY IT!
NOR WILL I CRY OUT!
FOR THE SAKE OF MY SON!
DADDY! I SMELL BLOOD. WHAT'S HAPPENING?
WHY ARE YOU LETTIN THEM DO THIS? I CAN'T GET OUT! DADDY PLEASE BE SAFE!

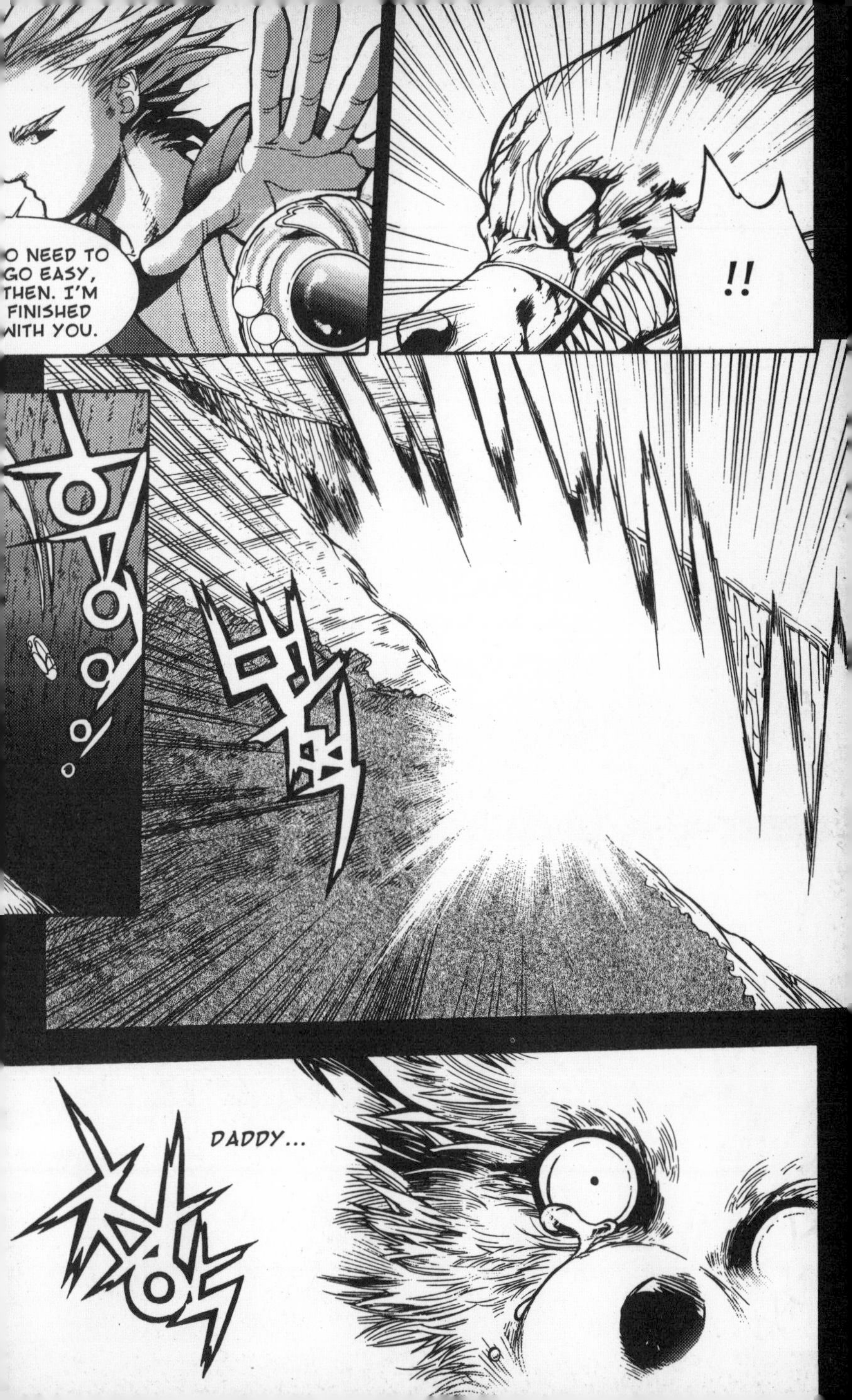
O NEED TO GO EASY, THEN. I'M FINISHED WITH YOU.
!!
DADDY...

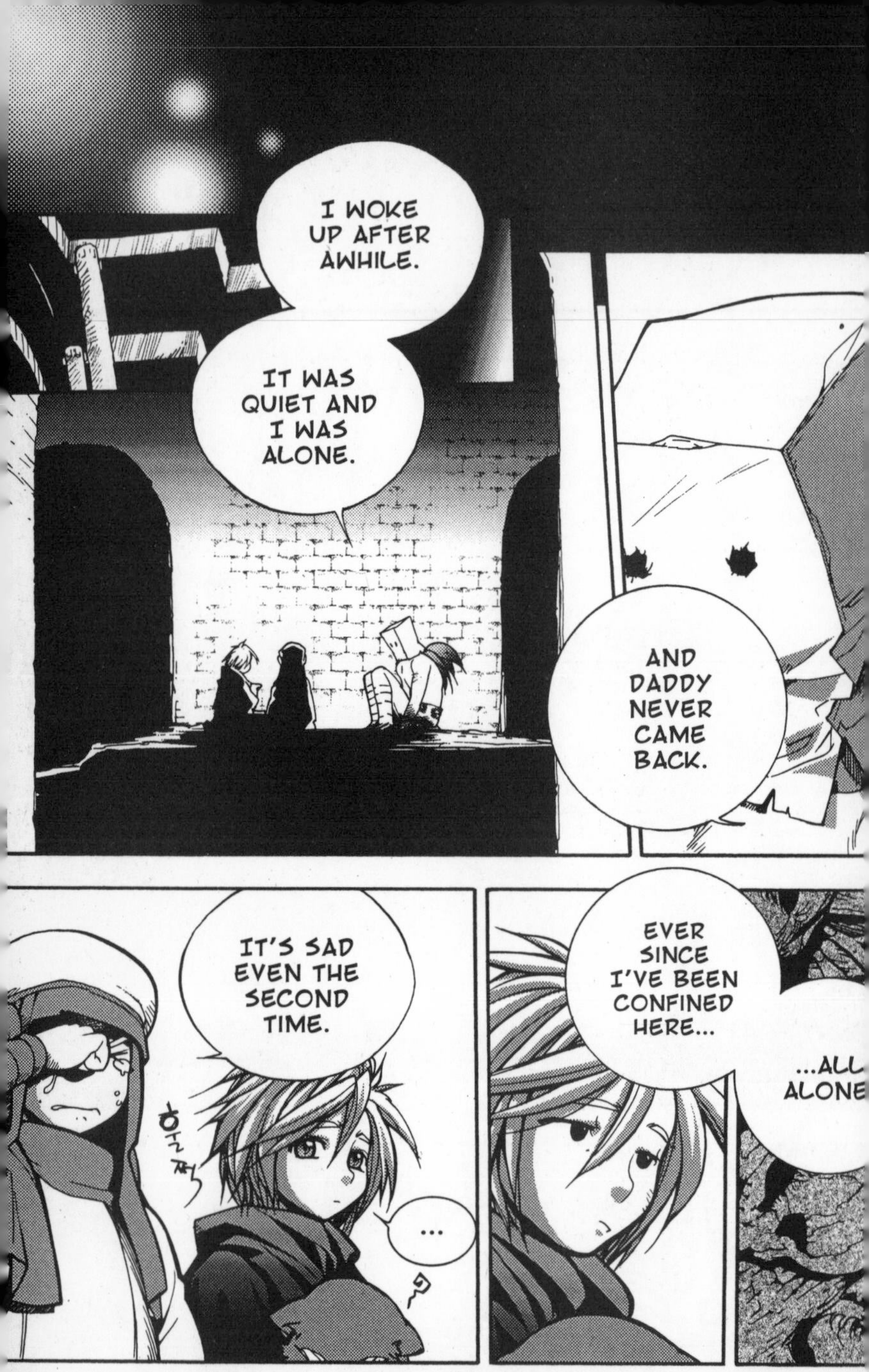
I WOKE UP AFTER AWHILE.
IT WAS QUIET AND I WAS ALONE.
AND DADDY NEVER CAME BACK.
IT'S SAD EVEN THE SECOND TIME.
...
EVER SINCE I'VE BEEN CONFINED HERE...
...ALL ALONE

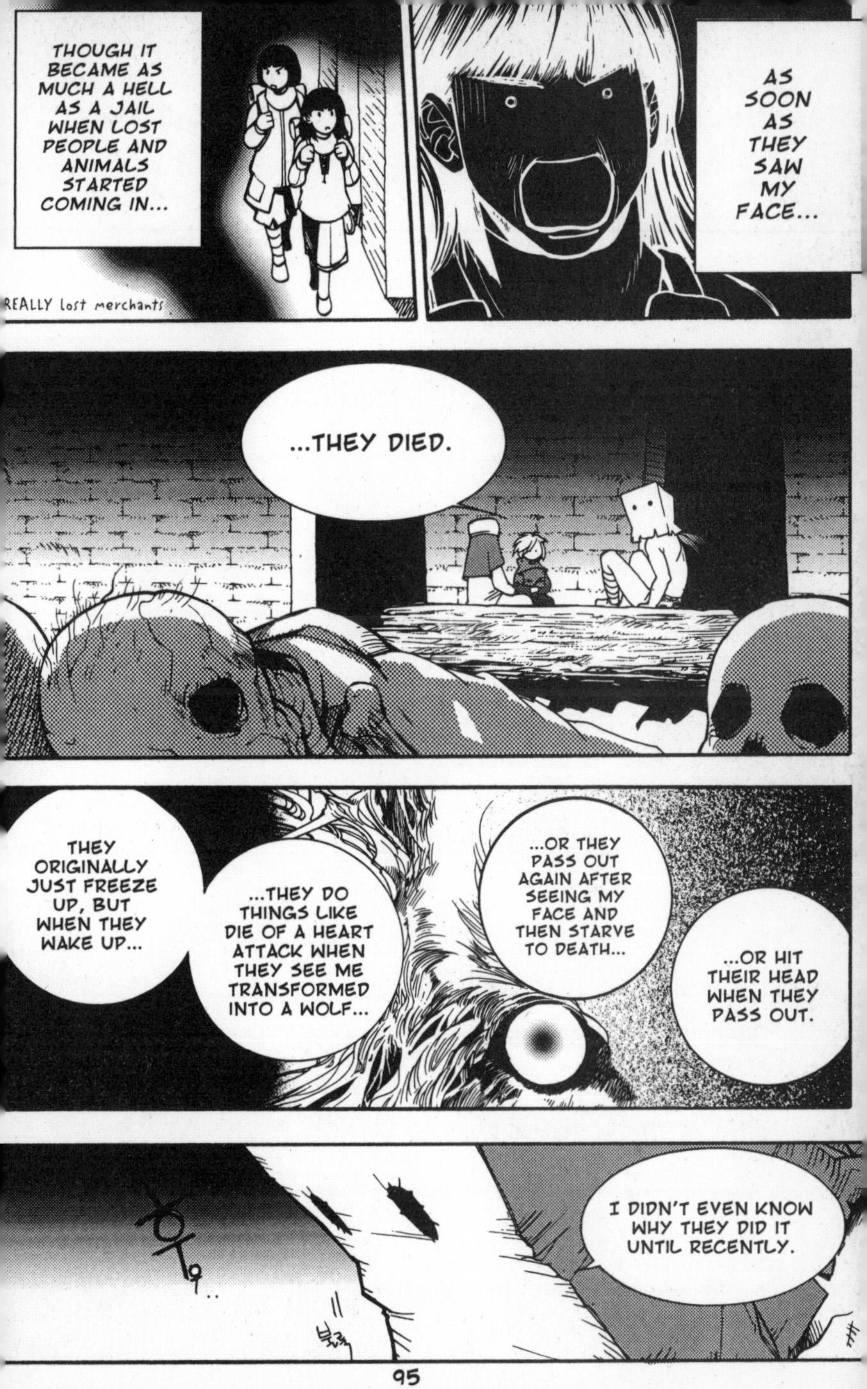
THOUGH IT BECAME AS MUCH A HELL AS A JAIL WHEN LOST PEOPLE AND ANIMALS STARTED COMING IN...
REALLY lost merchants
AS SOON AS THEY SAW MY FACE...
...THEY DIED.
THEY ORIGINALLY JUST FREEZE UP, BUT WHEN THEY WAKE UP...
...THEY DO THINGS LIKE DIE OF A HEART ATTACK WHEN THEY SEE ME TRANSFORMED INTO A WOLF...
...OR THEY PASS OUT AGAIN AFTER SEEING MY FACE AND THEN STARVE TO DEATH...
...OR HIT THEIR HEAD WHEN THEY PASS OUT.
I DIDN'T EVEN KNOW WHY THEY DID IT UNTIL RECENTLY.

BUT THEN, AFTER LOOKING AT MY OWN FACE IN A MIRROR THAT I FOUND IN A DEAD PERSON'S BAG, I FOUND OUT.

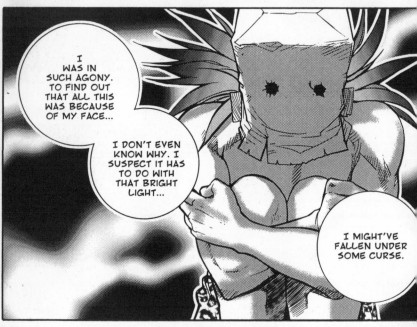

I WAS IN SUCH AGONY. TO FIND OUT THAT ALL THIS WAS BECAUSE OF MY FACE...

I DON'T EVEN KNOW WHY. I SUSPECT IT HAS TO DO WITH THAT BRIGHT LIGHT...

I MIGHT'VE FALLEN UNDER SOME CURSE.

I DON'T WANT ANY MORE PEOPLE DYING IN FRONT OF ME.

A CURSE?
WHAT
CURSE?

Ha ha!

JUST EXACTLY
HOW UGLY
ARE YOU THAT
PEOPLE DIE OF
SHOCK WHEN
THEY SEE YOU?!

I MEAN,
YOUR
FACE IS
ACTUALLY
A WEAPON!

WHAT DO
YOU KNOW?!
DO YOU HAVE
ANY IDEA HOW
PAINFUL MY LIFE
HAS BEEN?!

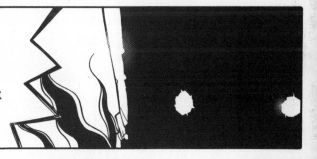

YOU
HAVEN'T
EVEN SEEN
MY FACE!

WHY DON'T YOU
TAKE A LOOK AND
TELL ME WHAT
YOU THINK?!

I'LL PASS.

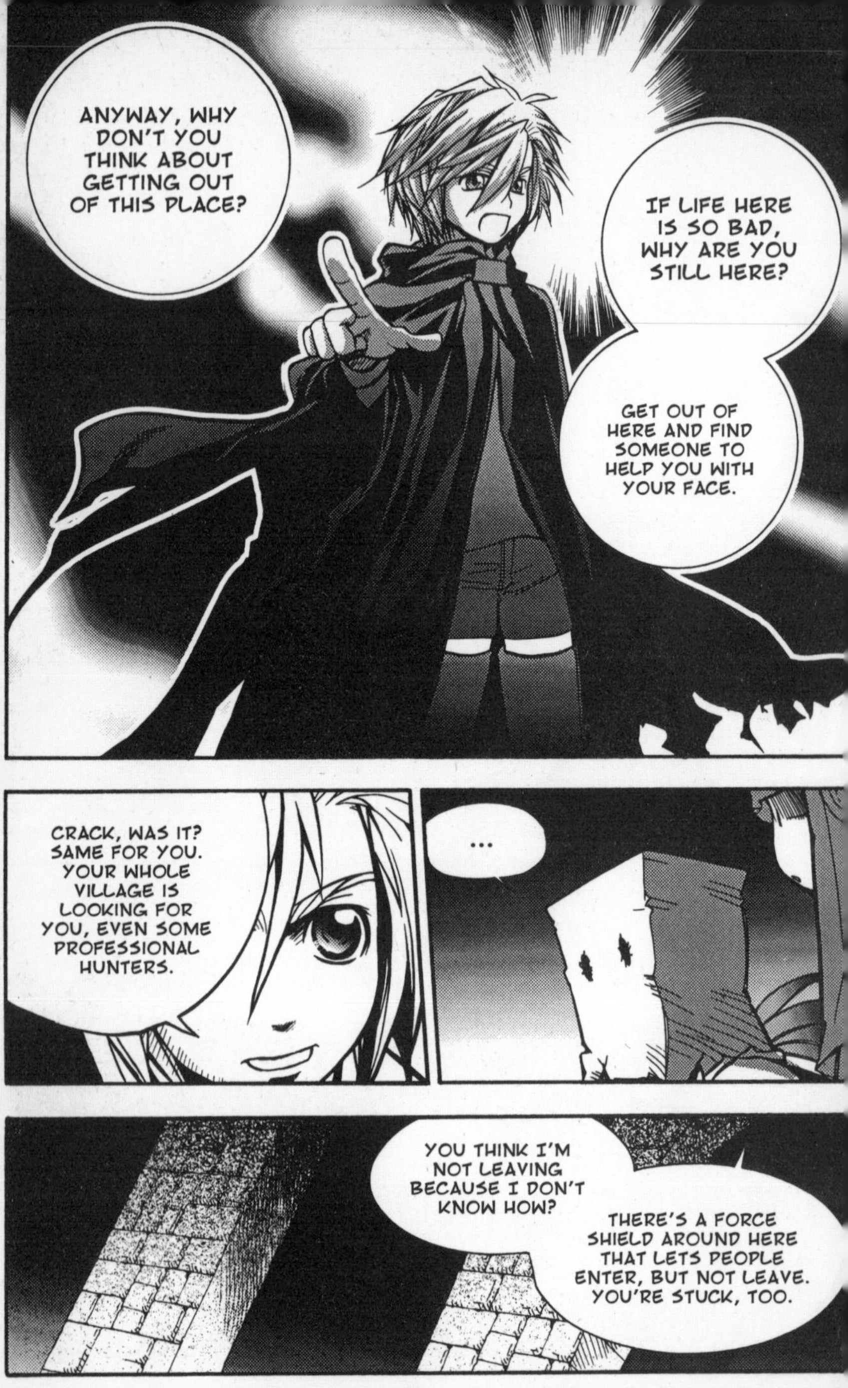
ANYWAY, WHY DON'T YOU THINK ABOUT GETTING OUT OF THIS PLACE?
IF LIFE HERE IS SO BAD, WHY ARE YOU STILL HERE?
GET OUT OF HERE AND FIND SOMEONE TO HELP YOU WITH YOUR FACE.
CRACK, WAS IT? SAME FOR YOU. YOUR WHOLE VILLAGE IS LOOKING FOR YOU, EVEN SOME PROFESSIONAL HUNTERS.
...
YOU THINK I'M NOT LEAVING BECAUSE I DON'T KNOW HOW?
THERE'S A FORCE SHIELD AROUND HERE THAT LETS PEOPLE ENTER, BUT NOT LEAVE. YOU'RE STUCK, TOO.

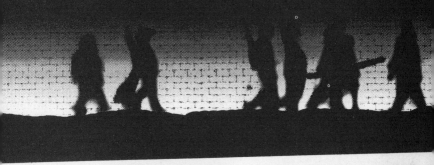

HEY, EVERYONE'S STILL IN ONE PIECE, RIGHT?

GOOD.

I FEEL LIKE I JUST LOST TEN YEARS OF MY LIFE, THOUGH!

I DON'T EVEN TRUST THE GUYS LEADING US!

HEY, THEY'RE NOT LEADING, WE ARE!

YEAH, IN A DANGEROUS PLACE LIKE THIS...

IF HE WASN'T OUR VILLAGE HERO, THEN I'D JUST LEAVE!

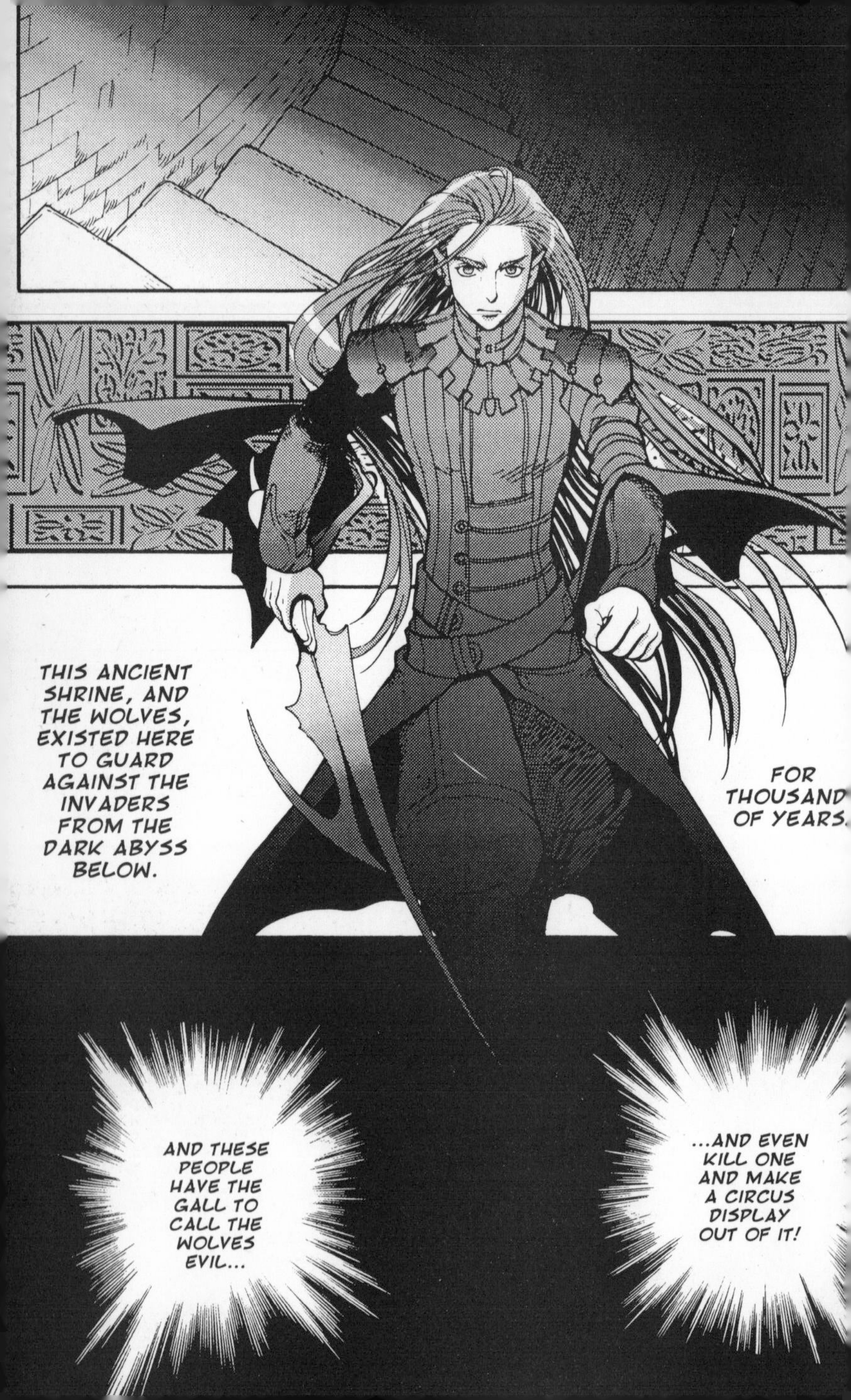
THIS ANCIENT SHRINE, AND THE WOLVES, EXISTED HERE TO GUARD AGAINST THE INVADERS FROM THE DARK ABYSS BELOW.
FOR THOUSAND OF YEARS.
AND THESE PEOPLE HAVE THE GALL TO CALL THE WOLVES EVIL...
...AND EVEN KILL ONE AND MAKE A CIRCUS DISPLAY OUT OF IT!

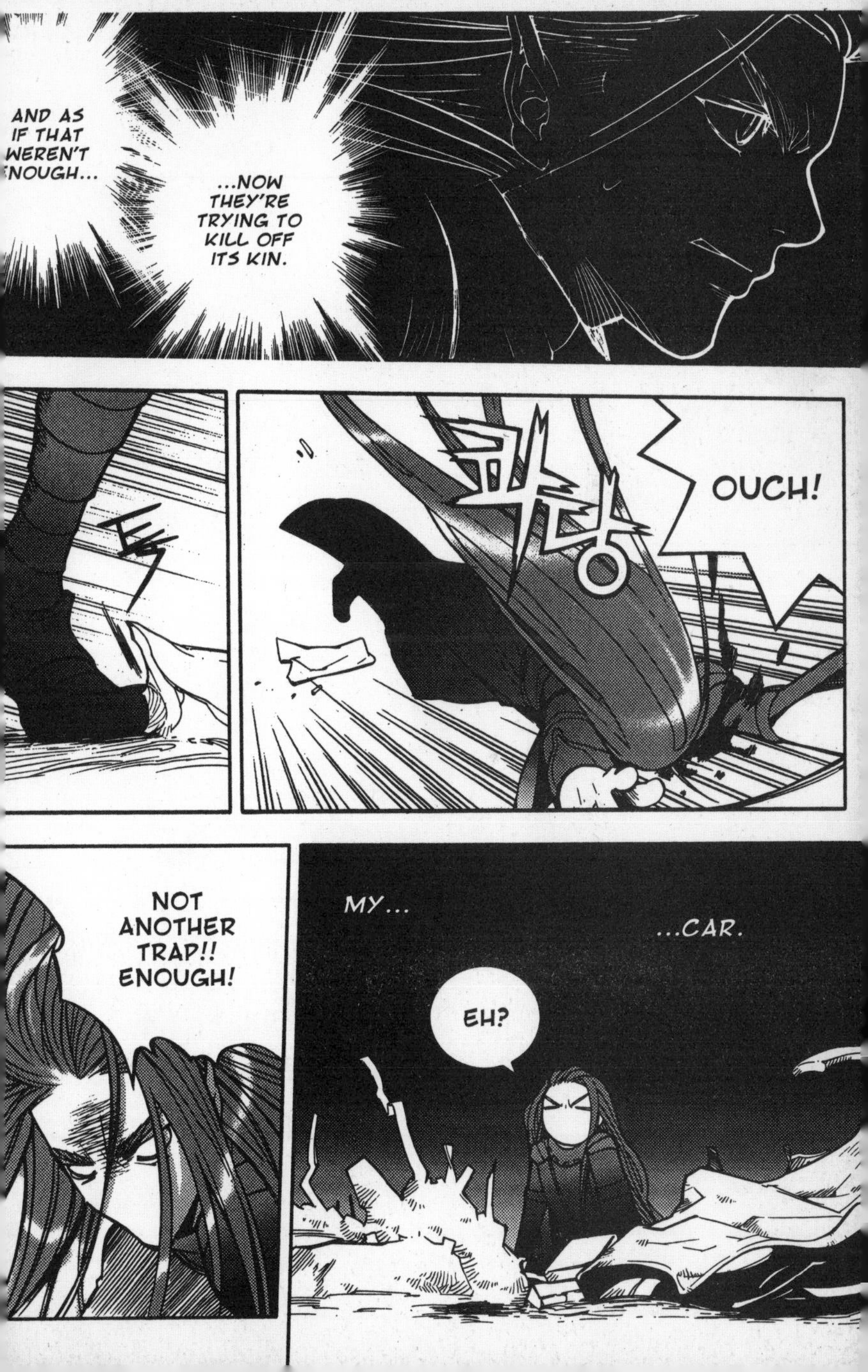
AND AS
IF THAT
WEREN'T
ENOUGH...
...NOW THEY'RE TRYING TO KILL OFF ITS KIN.
OUCH!
NOT ANOTHER TRAP!! ENOUGH!
MY...
...CAR.
EH?

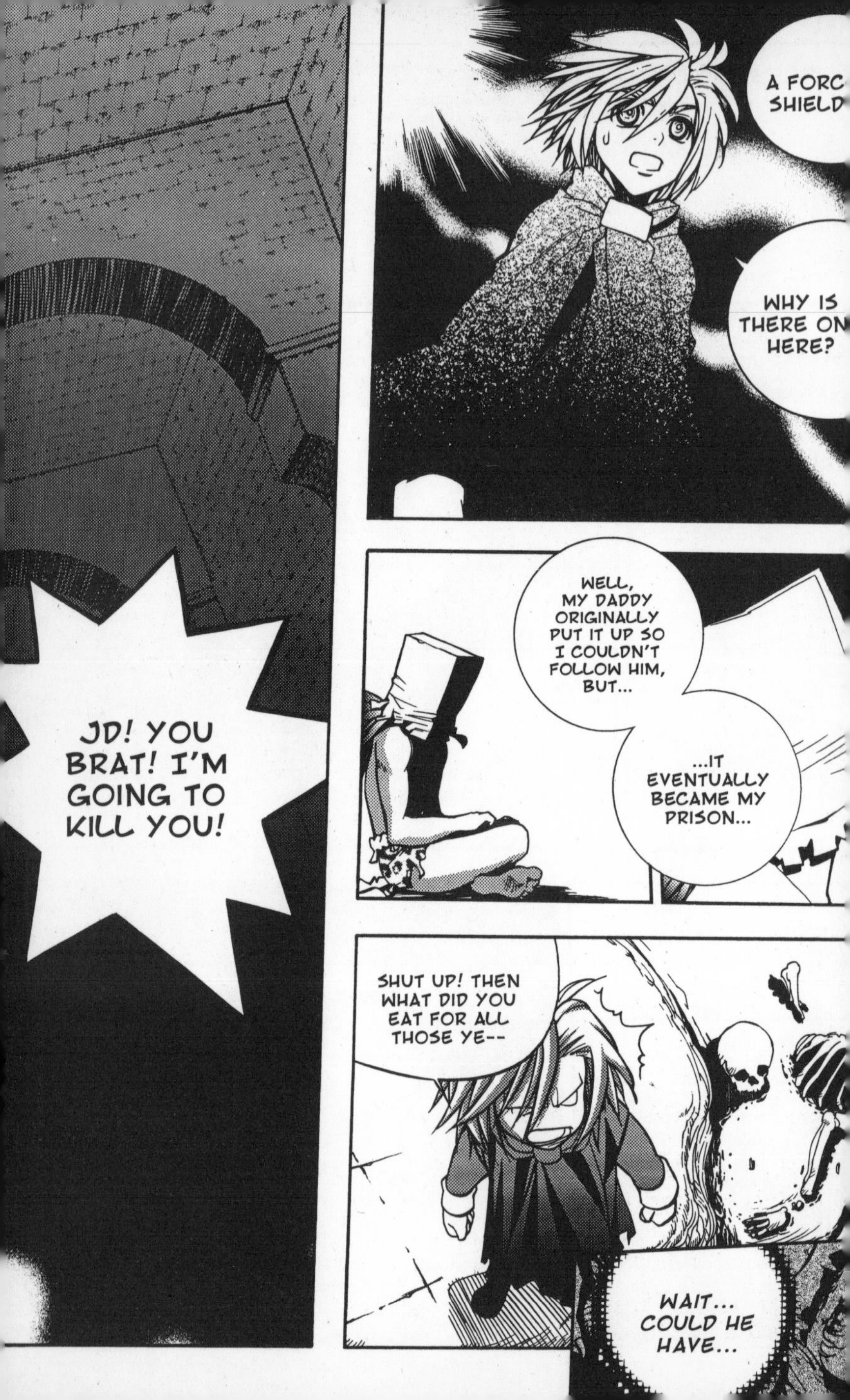
JD! YOU BRAT! I'M GOING TO KILL YOU!
A FORC SHIELD
WHY IS THERE ON HERE?
WELL, MY DADDY ORIGINALLY PUT IT UP SO I COULDN'T FOLLOW HIM, BUT...
...IT EVENTUALLY BECAME MY PRISON...
SHUT UP! THEN WHAT DID YOU EAT FOR ALL THOSE YE--
WAIT... COULD HE HAVE...

...EATEN THE FLESH FROM ALL THE SKELETONS IN HERE?!

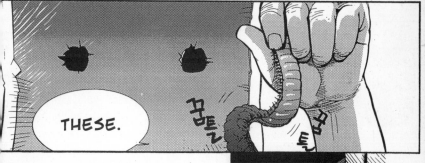

THESE.

THEY'RE ALL THERE IS TO EAT AROUND HERE.

EVEN IF THEY'RE JUST BUGS, THEY'RE STILL ALIVE, SO THEY CAN'T GO BACK OUT ONCE THEY COME IN.

IT DOESN'T TAKE MUCH TIME TO GATHER ENOUGH FOR A MEAL.

ONE DAY, WHEN I WOKE UP, THIS PLACE WAS FULL OF BUGS THAT HAD CRAWLED IN.

I HAD TO TAKE CARE OF IT BY EATING THEM. I MEAN, I WAS HUNGRY AND ALL, TOO.

HAVEN'T YOU CONSIDERED ANY OTHER WAYS OUT?

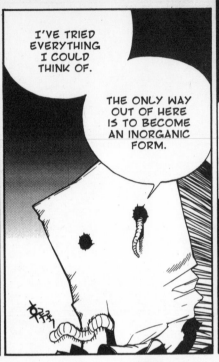

I'VE TRIED EVERYTHING I COULD THINK OF.

THE ONLY WAY OUT OF HERE IS TO BECOME AN INORGANIC FORM.

IN OTHER WORDS, YOU HAVE TO DIE.

THEN WHAT KIND OF SICKO ARE YOU TO STILL KEEP ALL THIS AROUND?!

HM? A GRADE REPORT RECORDER? WHY IS THIS HERE?

UH... THAT'S MINE...

MAYBE I CAN USE THIS TO INFORM BLAISE OF MY SITUATION!

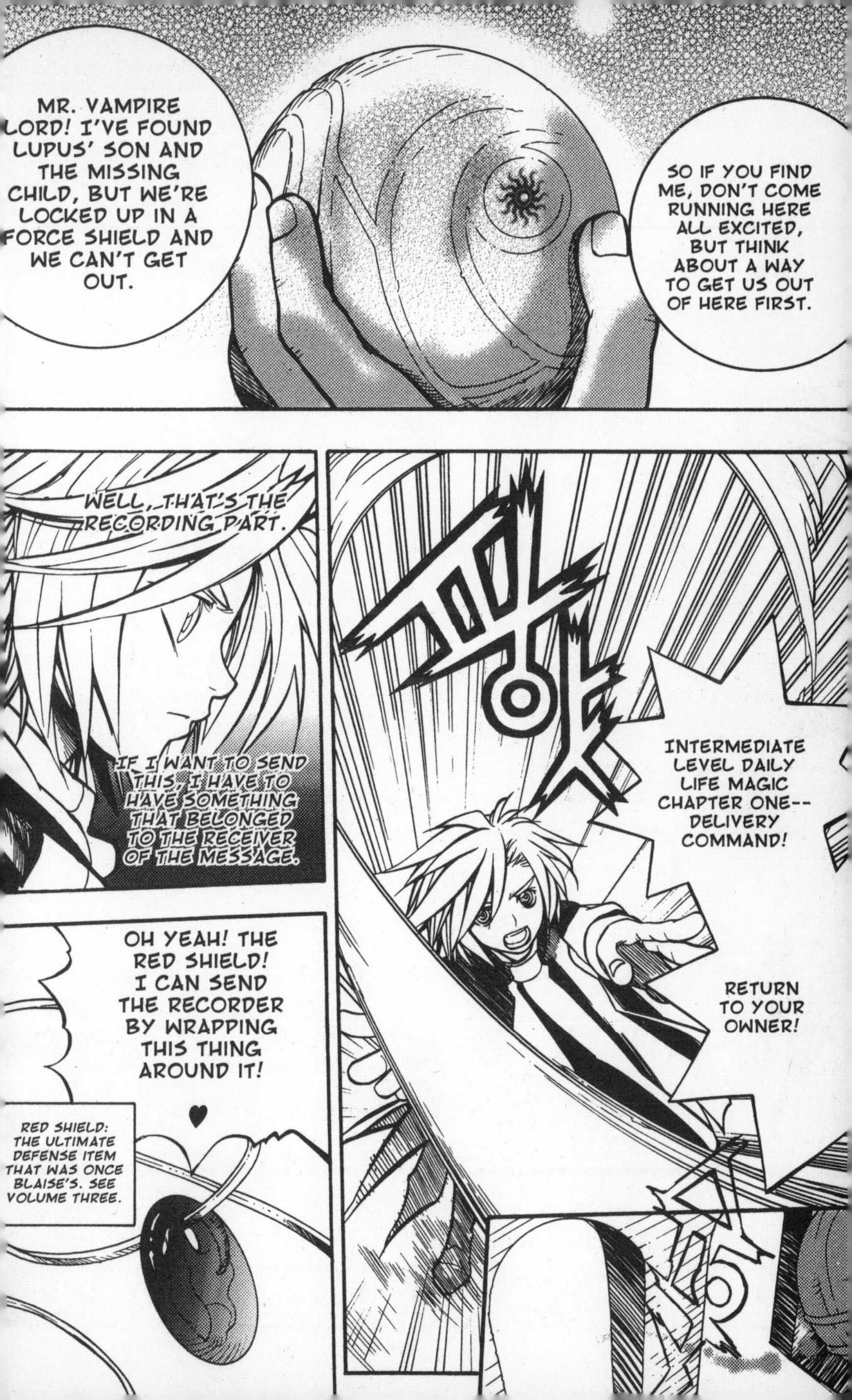
MR. VAMPIRE LORD! I'VE FOUND LUPUS' SON AND THE MISSING CHILD, BUT WE'RE LOCKED UP IN A FORCE SHIELD AND WE CAN'T GET OUT.
SO IF YOU FIND ME, DON'T COME RUNNING HERE ALL EXCITED, BUT THINK ABOUT A WAY TO GET US OUT OF HERE FIRST.
WELL, THAT'S THE RECORDING PART.
IF I WANT TO SEND THIS, I HAVE TO HAVE SOMETHING THAT BELONGED TO THE RECEIVER OF THE MESSAGE.
OH YEAH! THE RED SHIELD! I CAN SEND THE RECORDER BY WRAPPING THIS THING AROUND IT!
RED SHIELD: THE ULTIMATE DEFENSE ITEM THAT WAS ONCE BLAISE'S. SEE VOLUME THREE.
INTERMEDIATE LEVEL DAILY LIFE MAGIC CHAPTER ONE-- DELIVERY COMMAND!
RETURN TO YOUR OWNER!

WHAT DID YOU DO?

NOT MUCH. I JUST TOLD MY COMPANION ABOUT OUR SITUATION.

YOU'RE WITH SOMEONE ELSE? I'VE BEEN CURIOUS. WHO ARE YOU, EXACTLY?

AH, I FORGOT TO INTRODUCE MYSELF.

MY NAME IS JD. I CAME HERE TO ASK A FAVOR FROM YOUR FATHER ON BEHALF OF THE LORD OF THE JADE REGION.

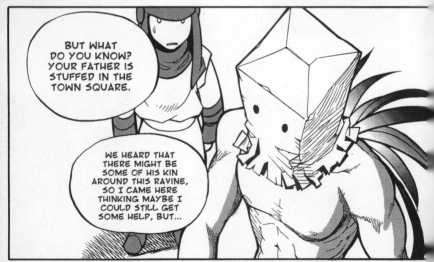

BUT WHAT DO YOU KNOW? YOUR FATHER IS STUFFED IN THE TOWN SQUARE.

WE HEARD THAT THERE MIGHT BE SOME OF HIS KIN AROUND THIS RAVINE, SO I CAME HERE THINKING MAYBE I COULD STILL GET SOME HELP, BUT...

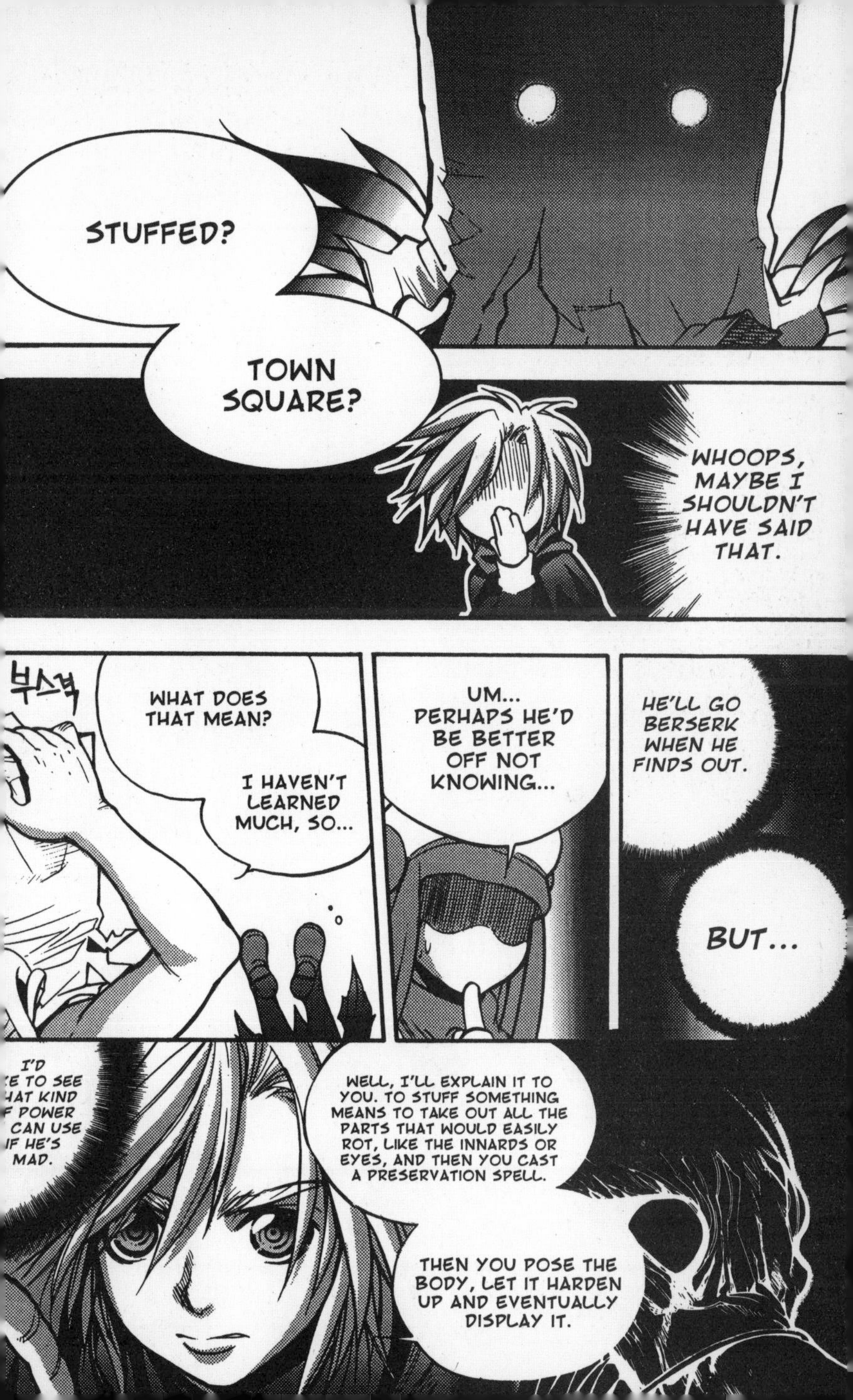
STUFFED?
TOWN SQUARE?
WHOOPS, MAYBE I SHOULDN'T HAVE SAID THAT.
부스럭
WHAT DOES THAT MEAN?
I HAVEN'T LEARNED MUCH, SO...
UM... PERHAPS HE'D BE BETTER OFF NOT KNOWING...
HE'LL GO BERSERK WHEN HE FINDS OUT.
BUT...
I'D E TO SEE HAT KIND F POWER CAN USE IF HE'S MAD.
WELL, I'LL EXPLAIN IT TO YOU. TO STUFF SOMETHING MEANS TO TAKE OUT ALL THE PARTS THAT WOULD EASILY ROT, LIKE THE INNARDS OR EYES, AND THEN YOU CAST A PRESERVATION SPELL.
THEN YOU POSE THE BODY, LET IT HARDEN UP AND EVENTUALLY DISPLAY IT.

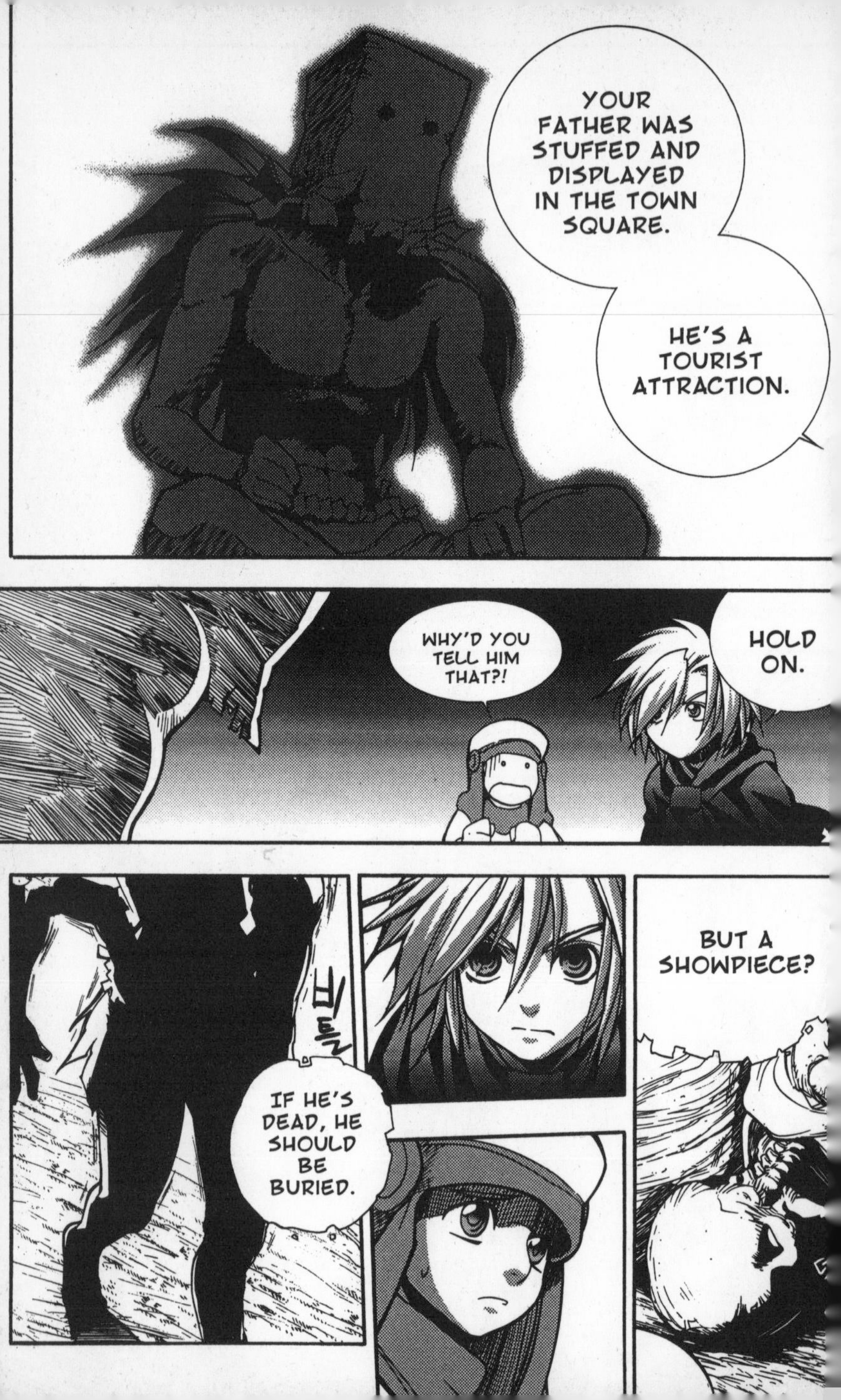
YOUR FATHER WAS STUFFED AND DISPLAYED IN THE TOWN SQUARE.
HE'S A TOURIST ATTRACTION.
WHY'D YOU TELL HIM THAT?!
HOLD ON.
IF HE'S DEAD, HE SHOULD BE BURIED.
BUT A SHOWPIECE?

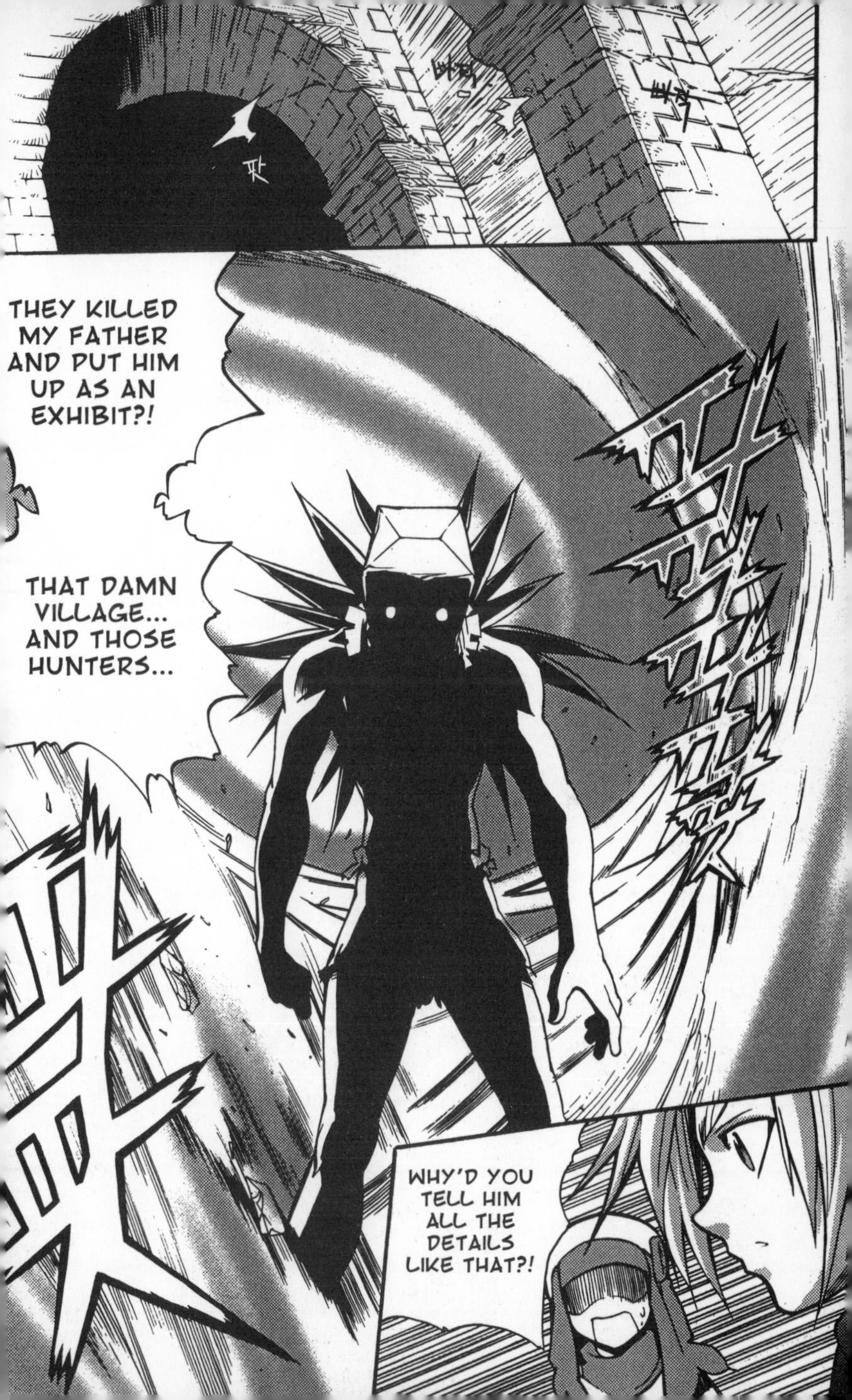
THEY KILLED MY FATHER AND PUT HIM UP AS AN EXHIBIT?!
THAT DAMN VILLAGE... AND THOSE HUNTERS...
WHY'D YOU TELL HIM ALL THE DETAILS LIKE THAT?!

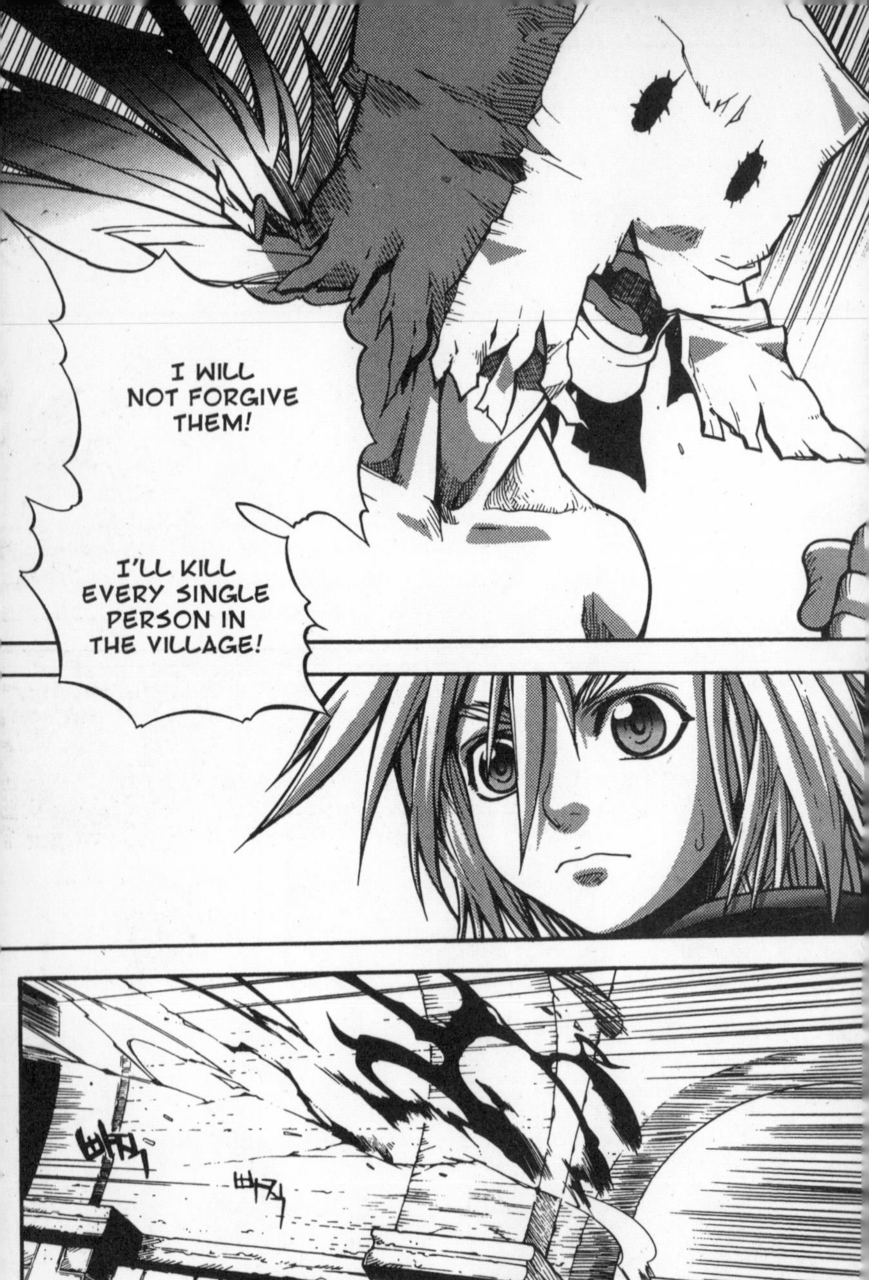
I WILL NOT FORGIVE THEM!
I'LL KILL EVERY SINGLE PERSON IN THE VILLAGE!

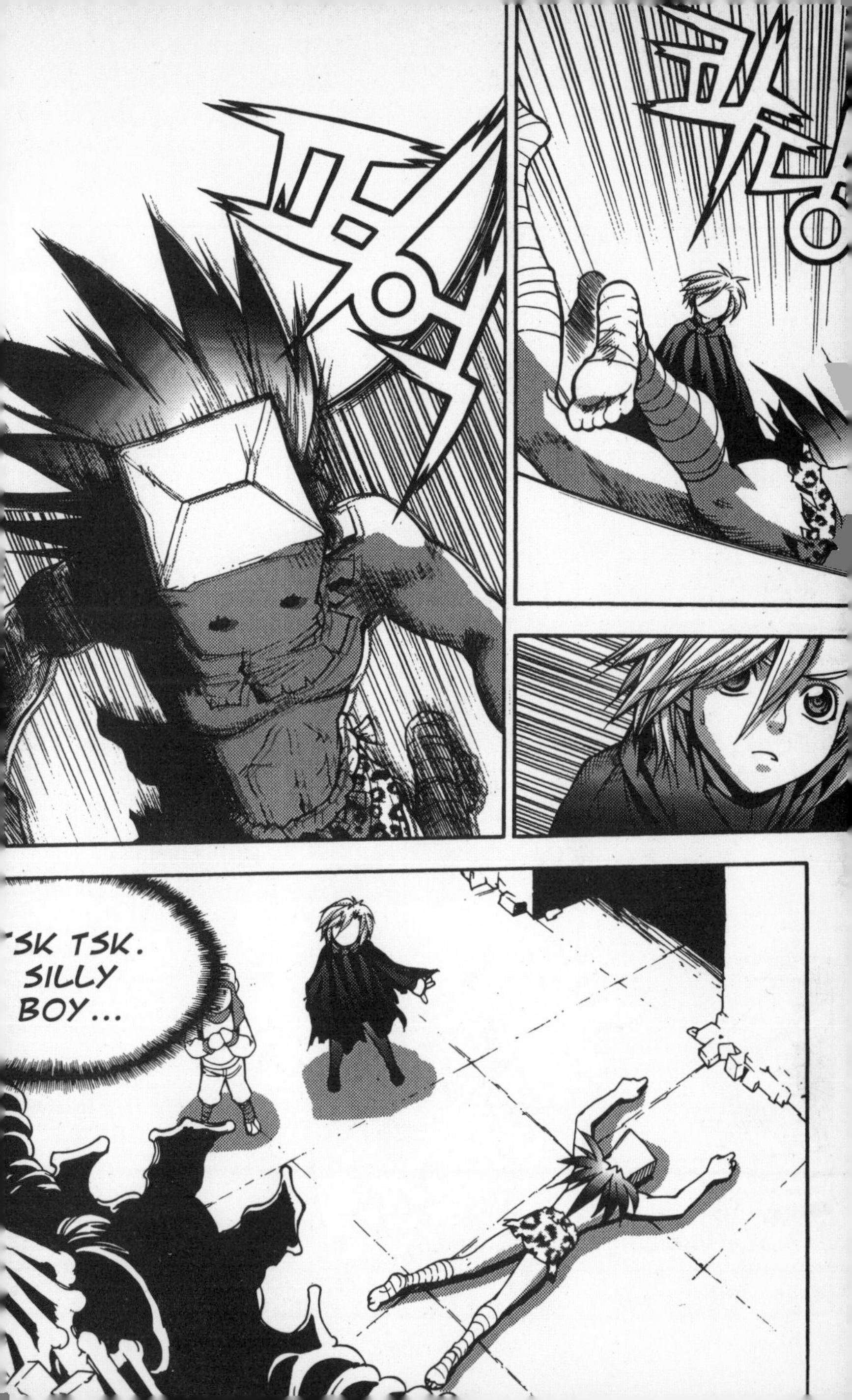
SK TSK. SILLY BOY...

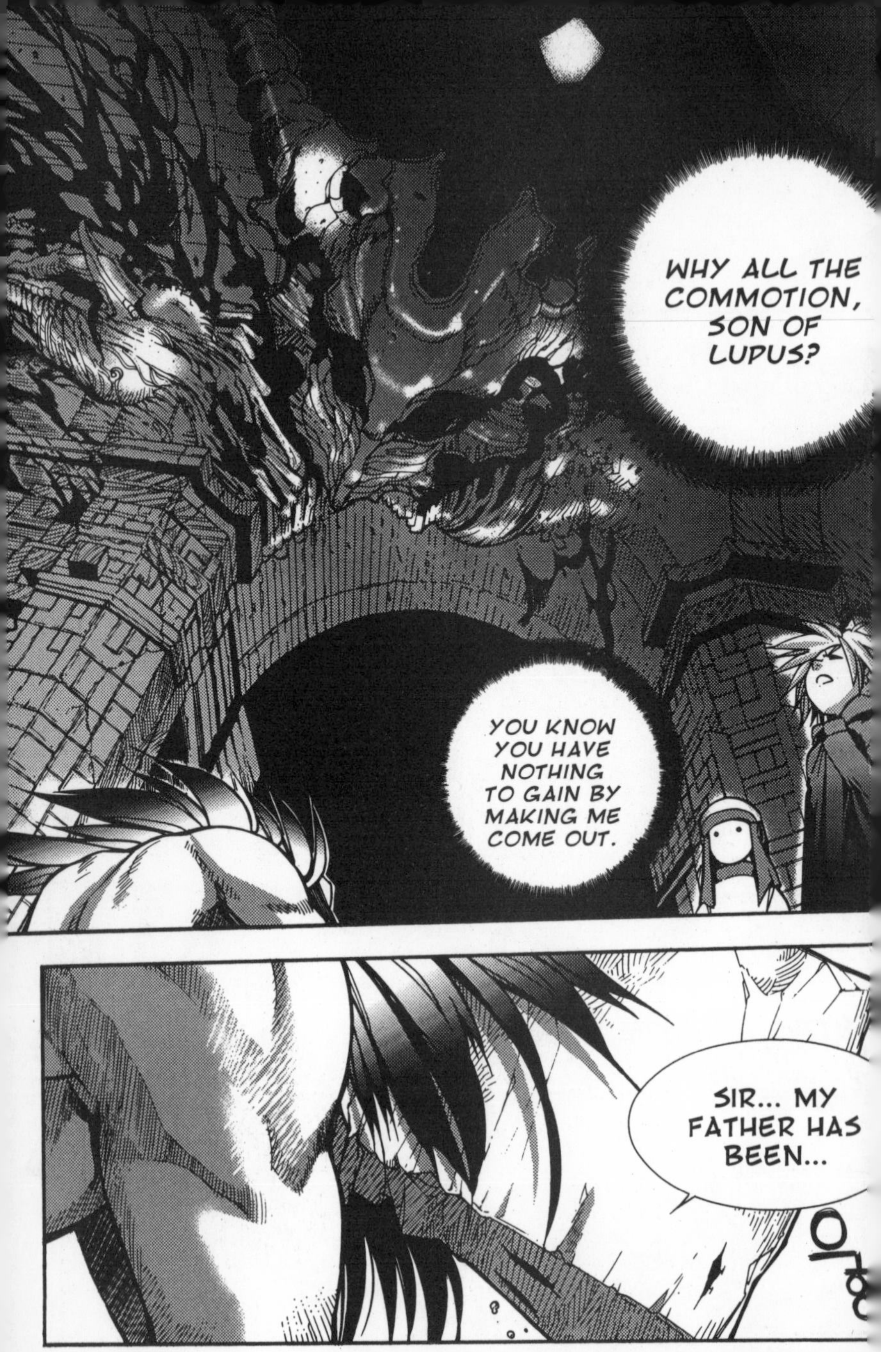
WHY ALL THE COMMOTION, SON OF LUPUS?
YOU KNOW YOU HAVE NOTHING TO GAIN BY MAKING ME COME OUT.
SIR... MY FATHER HAS BEEN...

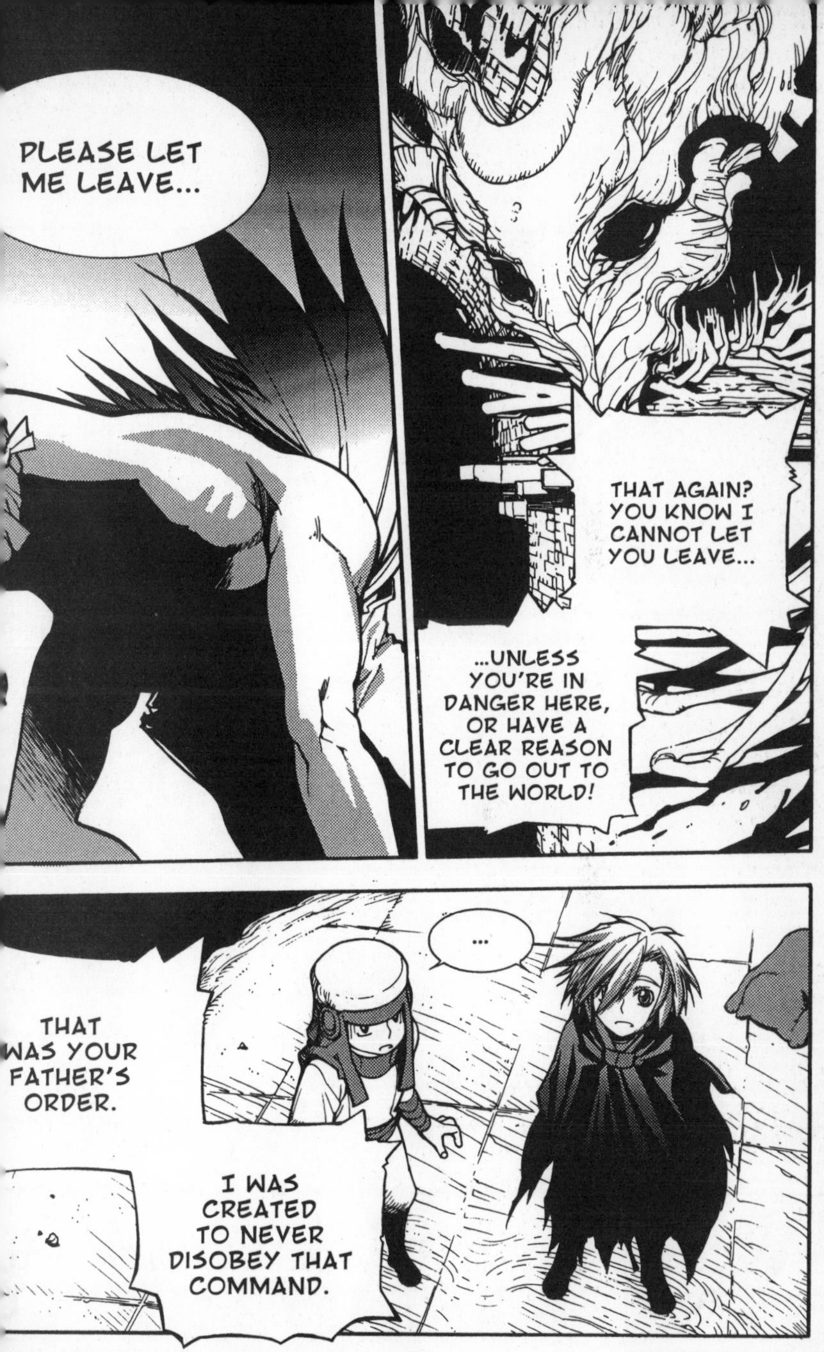
PLEASE LET ME LEAVE...
THAT AGAIN? YOU KNOW I CANNOT LET YOU LEAVE...
...UNLESS YOU'RE IN DANGER HERE, OR HAVE A CLEAR REASON TO GO OUT TO THE WORLD!
...
THAT WAS YOUR FATHER'S ORDER.
I WAS CREATED TO NEVER DISOBEY THAT COMMAND.

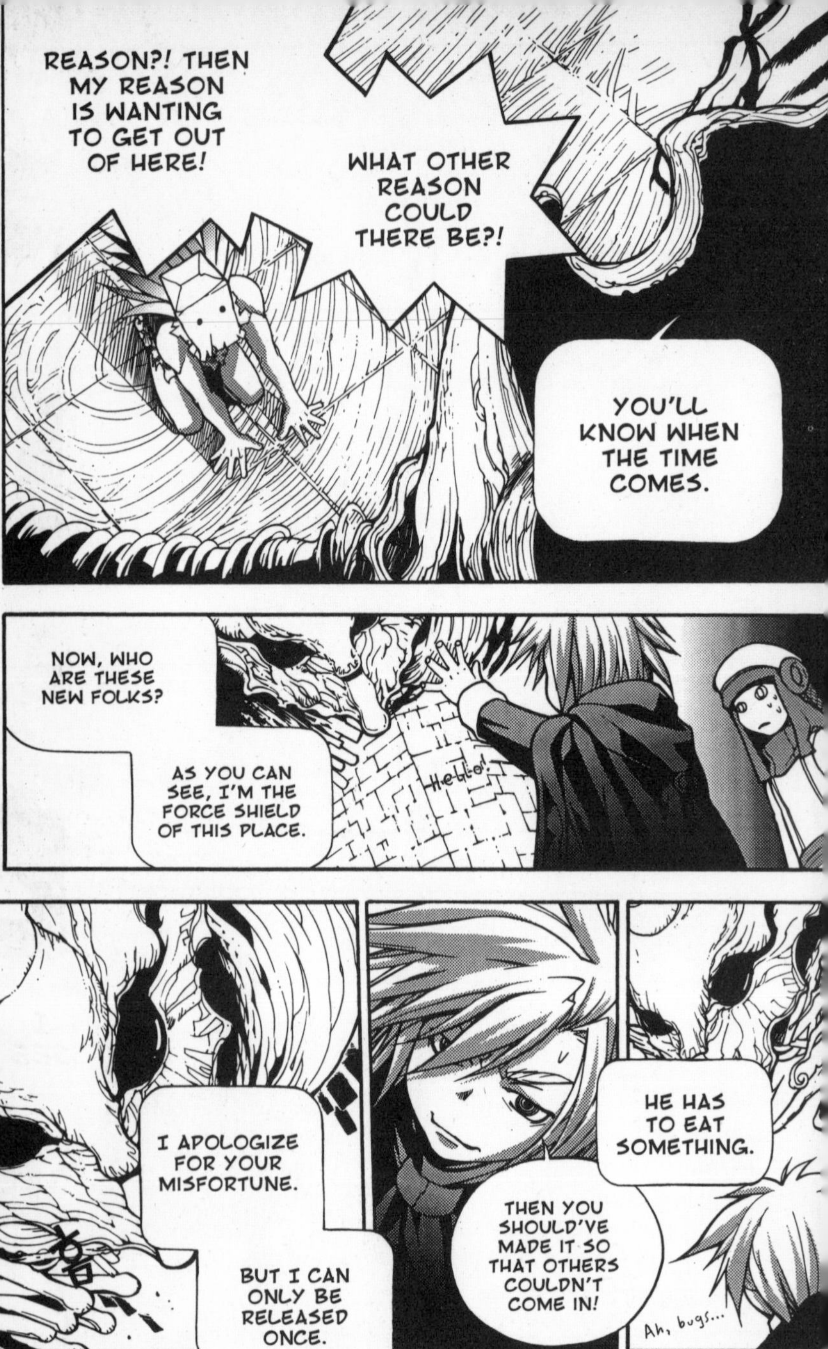
REASON?! THEN MY REASON IS WANTING TO GET OUT OF HERE!
WHAT OTHER REASON COULD THERE BE?!
YOU'LL KNOW WHEN THE TIME COMES.
NOW, WHO ARE THESE NEW FOLKS?
AS YOU CAN SEE, I'M THE FORCE SHIELD OF THIS PLACE.
Hello!
I APOLOGIZE FOR YOUR MISFORTUNE.
BUT I CAN ONLY BE RELEASED ONCE.
THEN YOU SHOULD'VE MADE IT SO THAT OTHERS COULDN'T COME IN!
HE HAS TO EAT SOMETHING.
Ah, bugs...

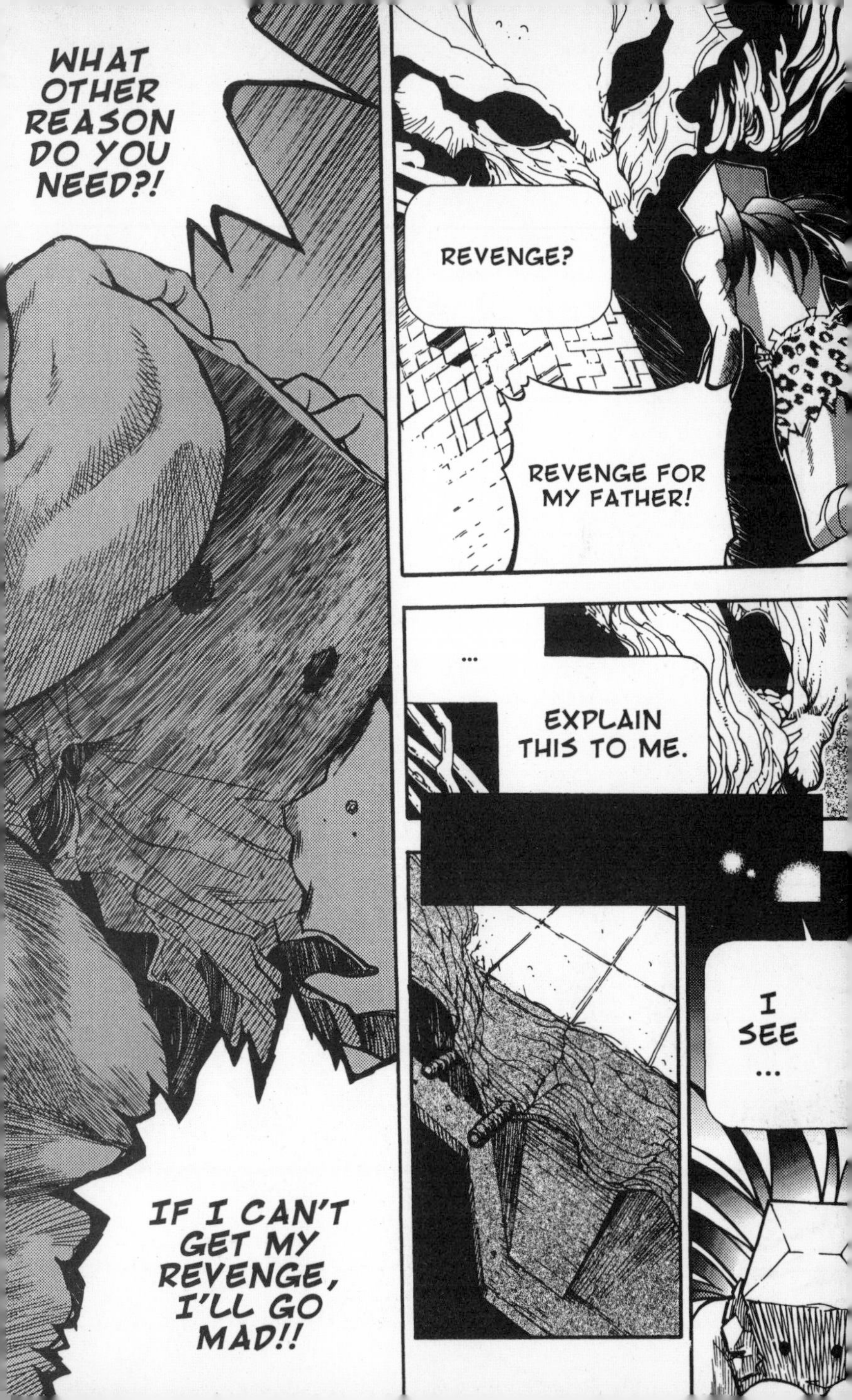
WHAT OTHER REASON DO YOU NEED?!
IF I CAN'T GET MY REVENGE, I'LL GO MAD!!
REVENGE?
REVENGE FOR MY FATHER!
...
EXPLAIN THIS TO ME.
I SEE ...

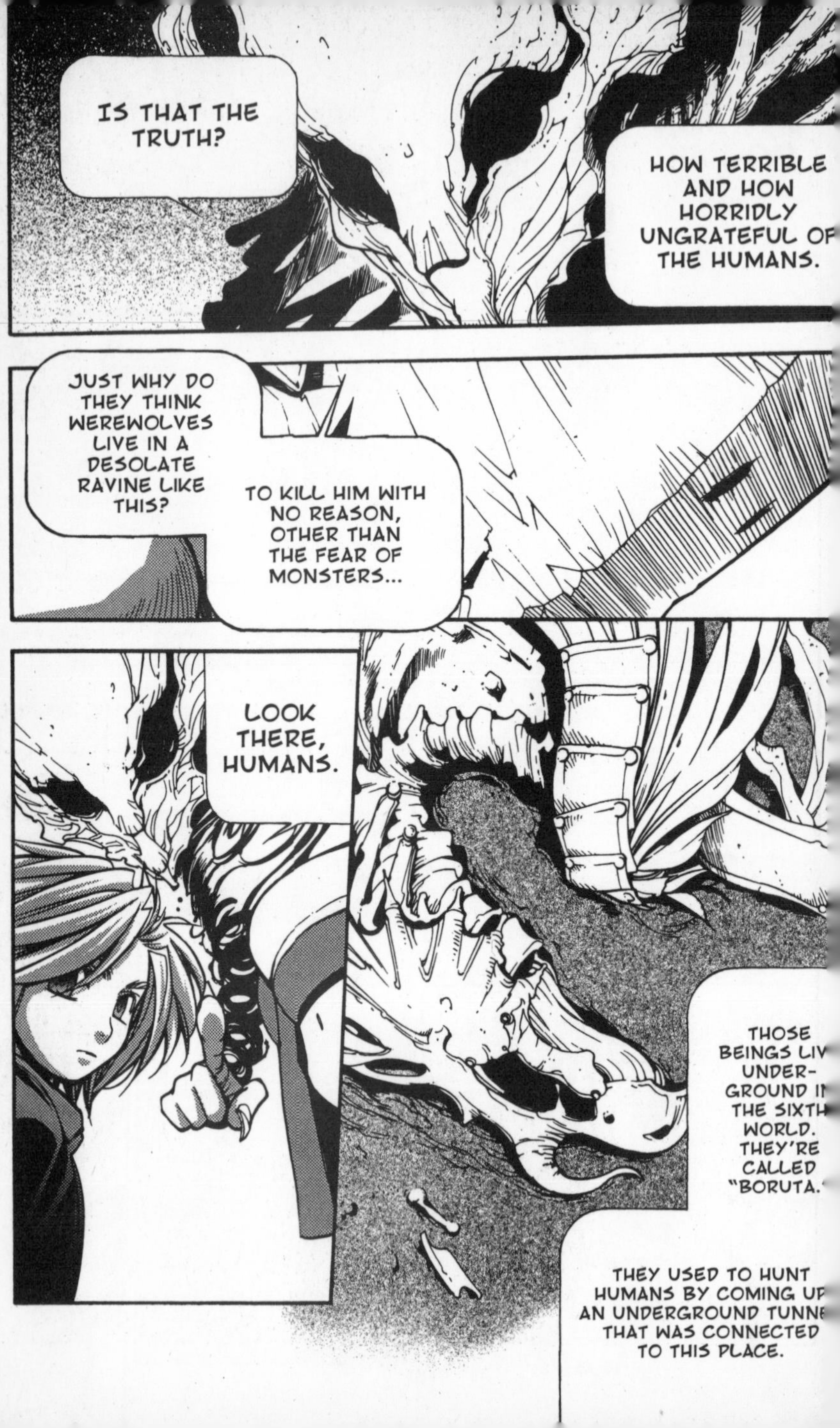
IS THAT THE TRUTH?
HOW TERRIBLE AND HOW HORRIDLY UNGRATEFUL OF THE HUMANS.
JUST WHY DO THEY THINK WEREWOLVES LIVE IN A DESOLATE RAVINE LIKE THIS?
TO KILL HIM WITH NO REASON, OTHER THAN THE FEAR OF MONSTERS...
LOOK THERE, HUMANS.
THOSE BEINGS LIV UNDER-GROUND I THE SIXTH WORLD. THEY'RE CALLED "BORUTA.
THEY USED TO HUNT HUMANS BY COMING UP AN UNDERGROUND TUNN THAT WAS CONNECTED TO THIS PLACE.

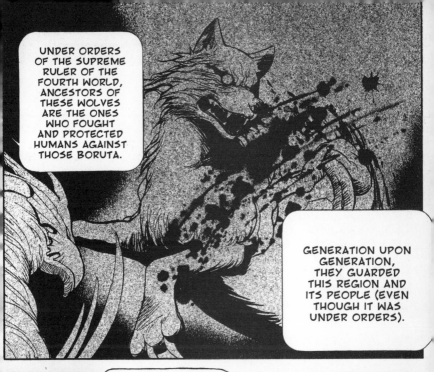

UNDER ORDERS OF THE SUPREME RULER OF THE FOURTH WORLD, ANCESTORS OF THESE WOLVES ARE THE ONES WHO FOUGHT AND PROTECTED HUMANS AGAINST THOSE BORUTA.

GENERATION UPON GENERATION, THEY GUARDED THIS REGION AND ITS PEOPLE (EVEN THOUGH IT WAS UNDER ORDERS).

BUT THE HUMANS' IGNORANCE IS ABSOLUTE.

SO THEN THEY KILLED LUPUS...

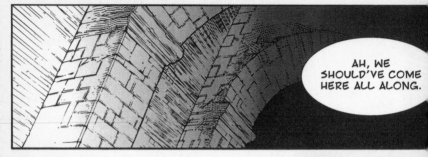

AH, WE SHOULD'VE COME HERE ALL ALONG.

I DON'T KNOW WHY I SPENT YEARS TRYING TO CATCH THAT DUMB GORGON.

Tch!

AND I NEVER CAUGHT HIM.

AT LEAST I KNOW THAT IF I CAN'T CATCH IT...

...THEN NO ONE CAN.

THAT'S ONE WAY TO FEEL BETTER ABOUT IT.

I'M STILL SURPRISED THAT YOU'RE STILL KICKING...

...AFTER LUPUS' FINAL ATTACK HIT YOU.

STOP THERE. I'D RATHER NOT RELIVE THAT MEMORY.

IT WAS THE WORST MOMENT IN MY LIFE.

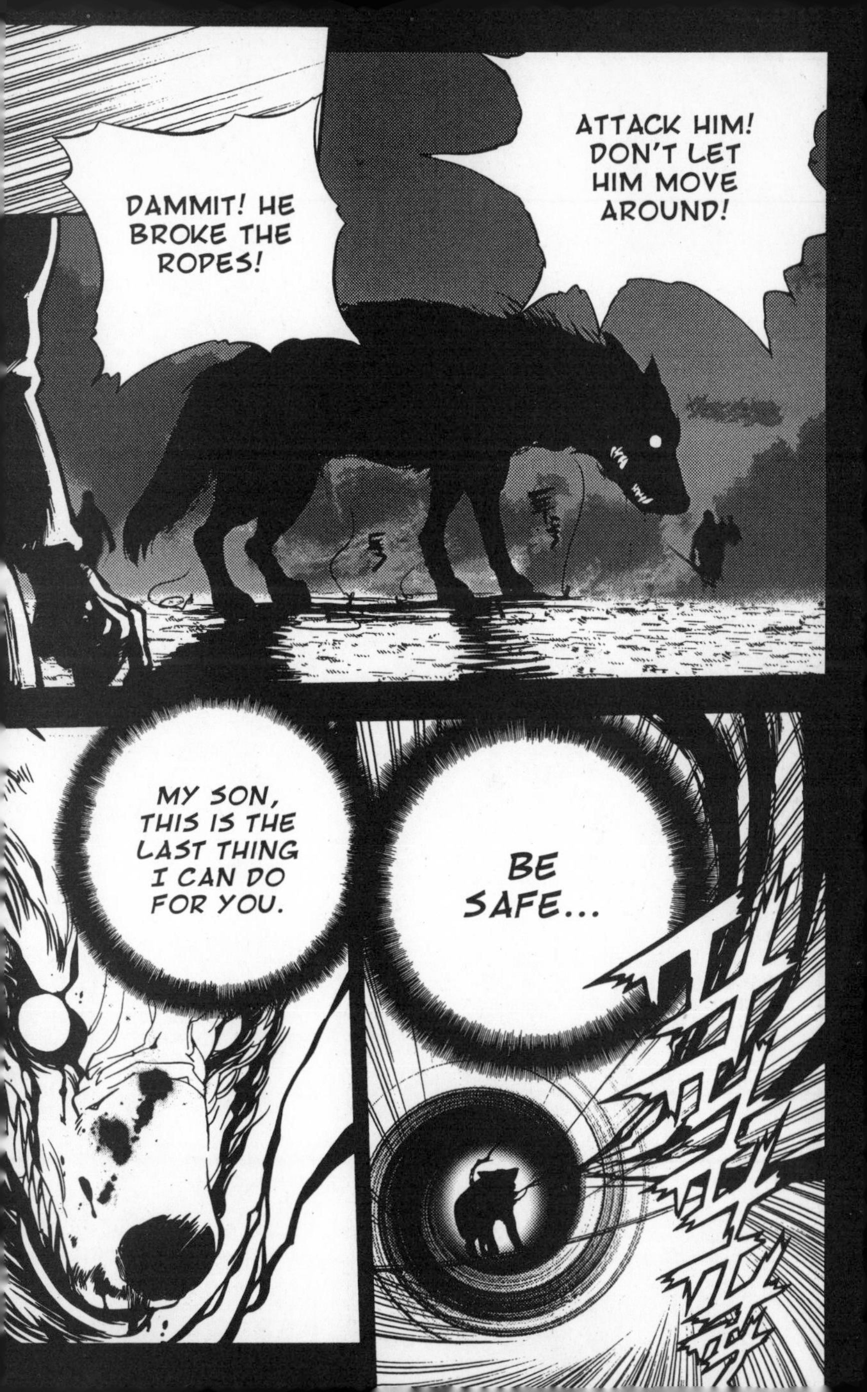
DAMMIT! HE BROKE THE ROPES!
ATTACK HIM! DON'T LET HIM MOVE AROUND!
MY SON, THIS IS THE LAST THING I CAN DO FOR YOU.
BE SAFE...

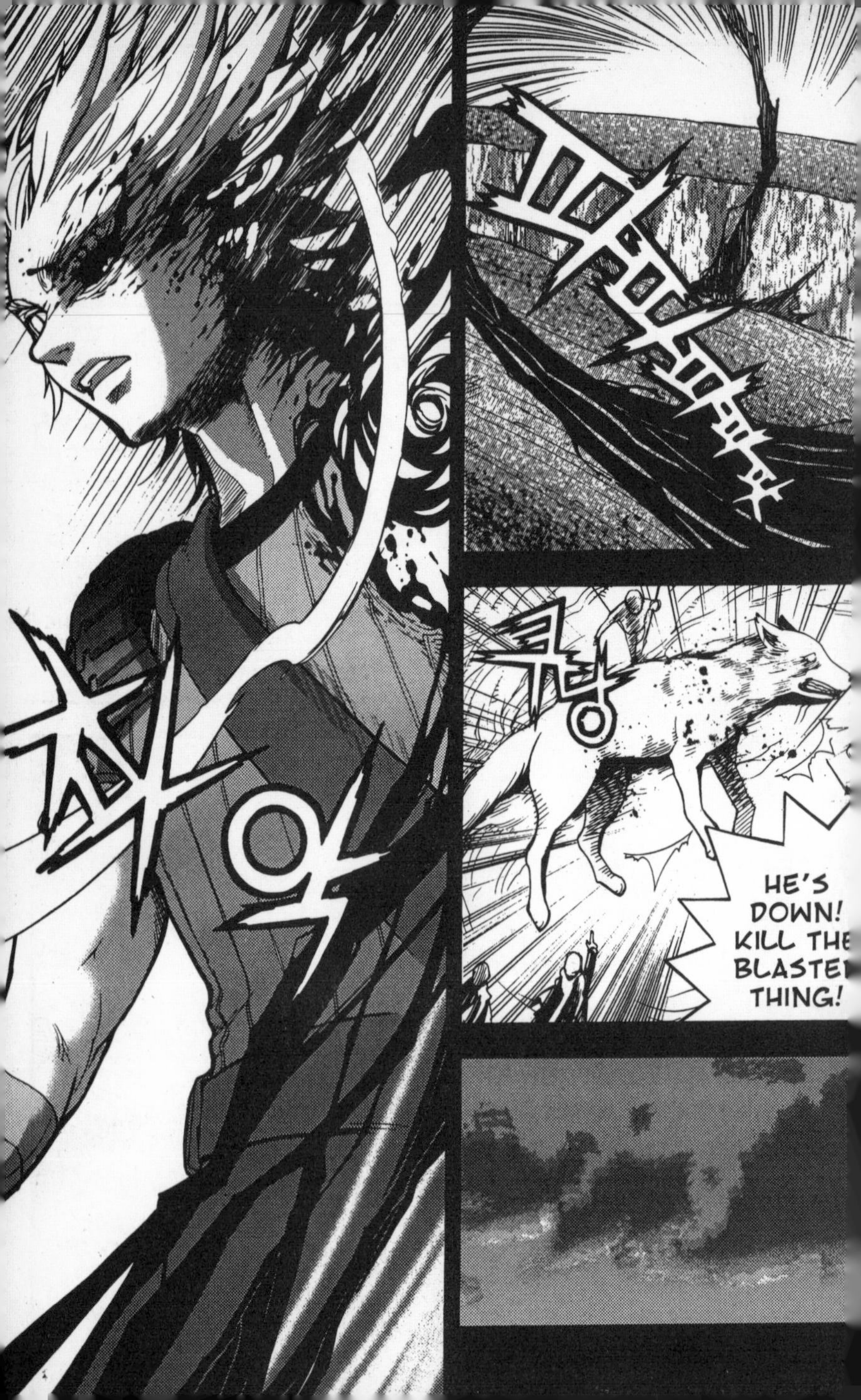
HE'S DOWN! KILL THE BLASTER THING!

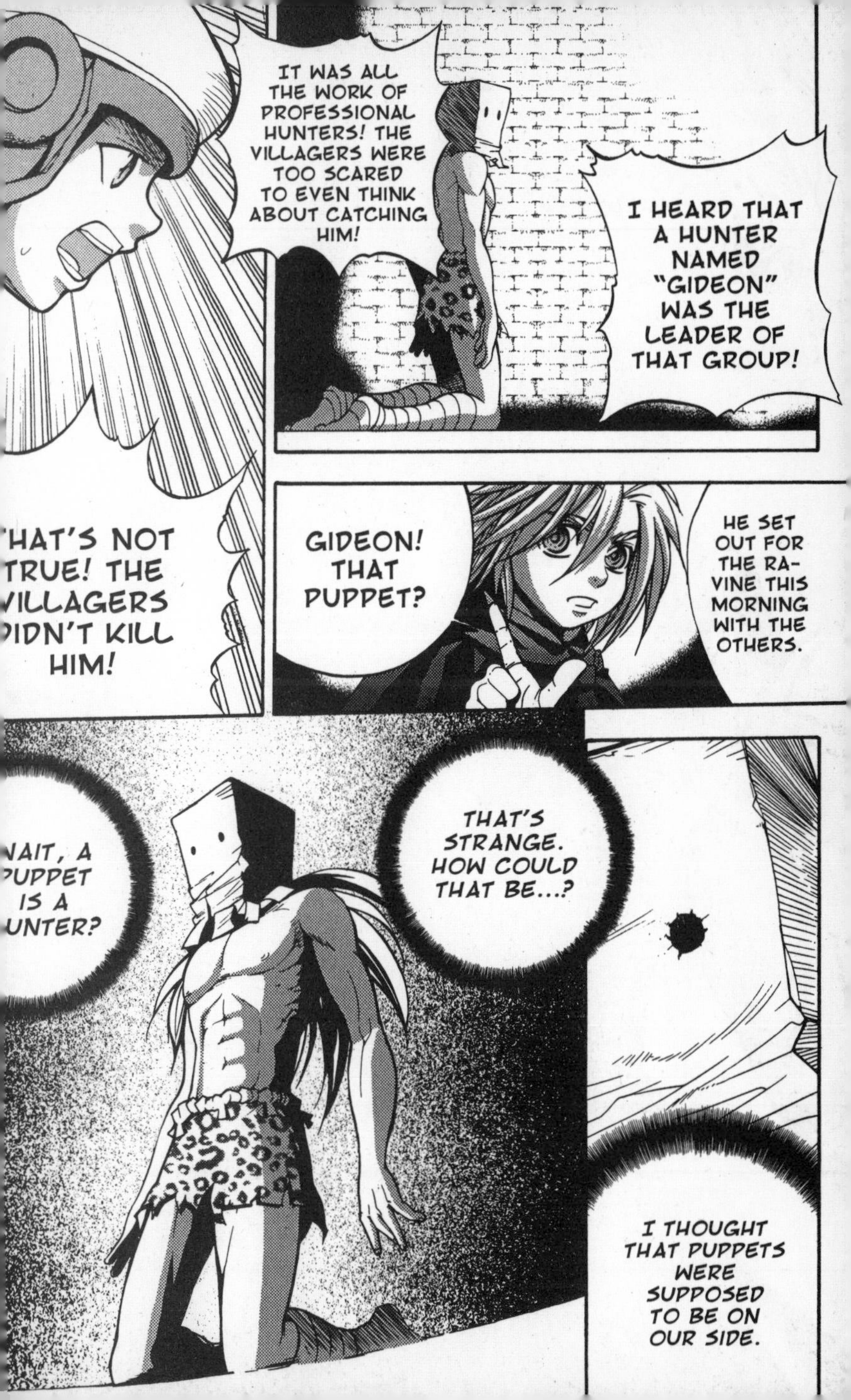
HAT'S NOT TRUE! THE ILLAGERS IDN'T KILL HIM!
IT WAS ALL THE WORK OF PROFESSIONAL HUNTERS! THE VILLAGERS WERE TOO SCARED TO EVEN THINK ABOUT CATCHING HIM!
I HEARD THAT A HUNTER NAMED "GIDEON" WAS THE LEADER OF THAT GROUP!
GIDEON! THAT PUPPET?
HE SET OUT FOR THE RA-VINE THIS MORNING WITH THE OTHERS.
AIT, A UPPET IS A UNTER?
THAT'S STRANGE. HOW COULD THAT BE...?
I THOUGHT THAT PUPPETS WERE SUPPOSED TO BE ON OUR SIDE.

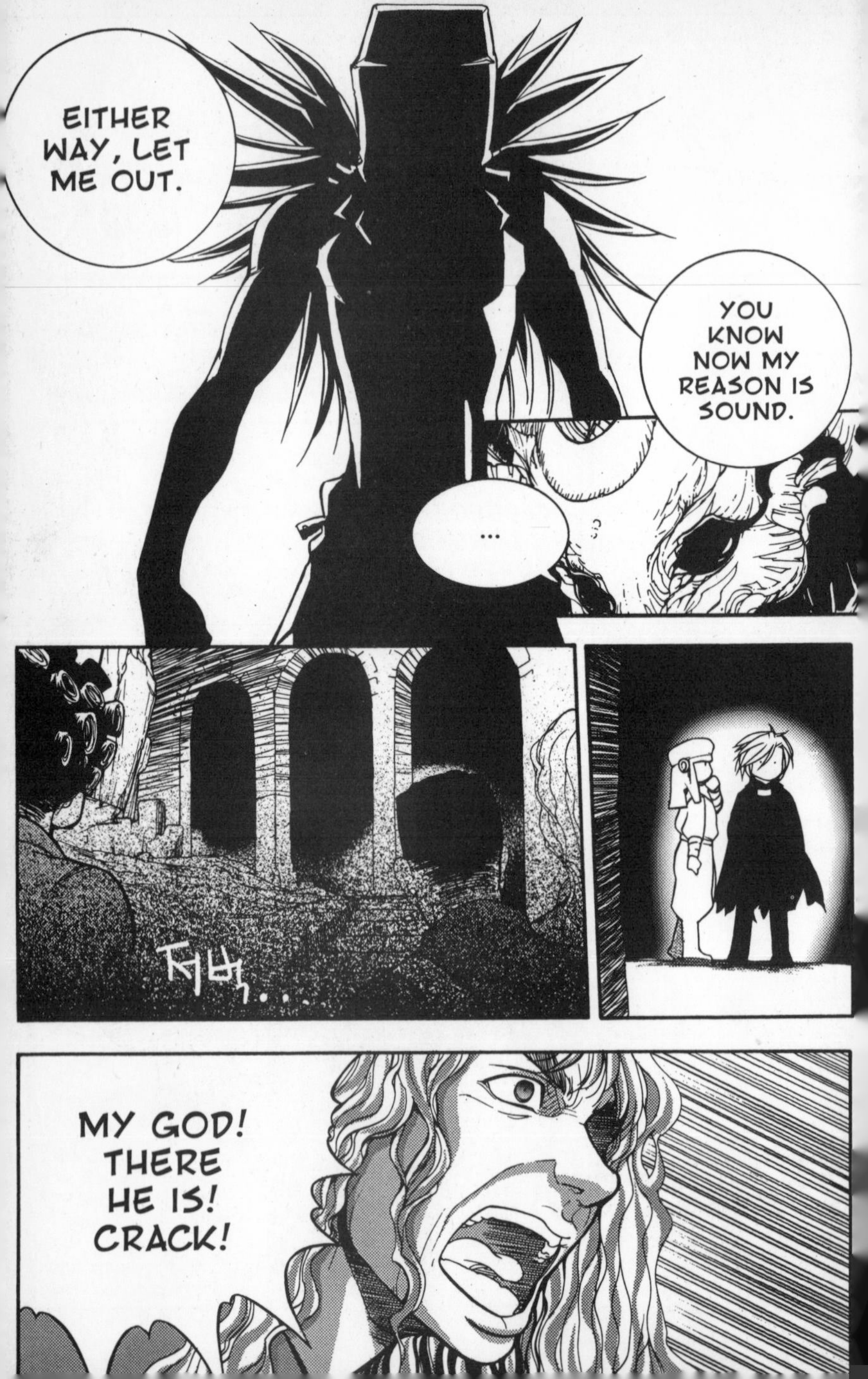
EITHER WAY, LET ME OUT.
YOU KNOW NOW MY REASON IS SOUND.
...
저벅....
MY GOD! THERE HE IS! CRACK!

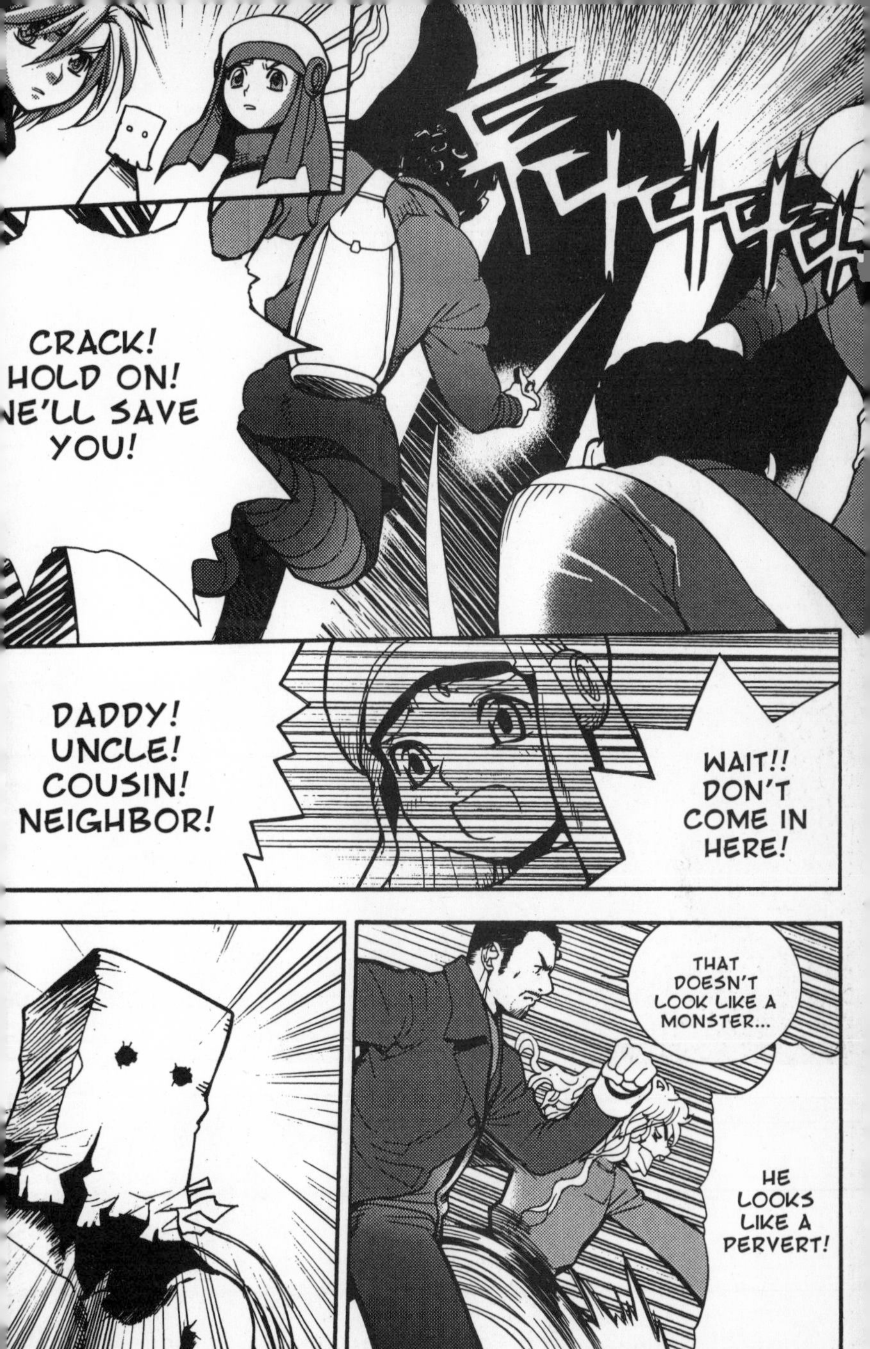
CRACK! HOLD ON! WE'LL SAVE YOU!
DADDY! UNCLE! COUSIN! NEIGHBOR!
WAIT!! DON'T COME IN HERE!
THAT DOESN'T LOOK LIKE A MONSTER...
HE LOOKS LIKE A PERVERT!

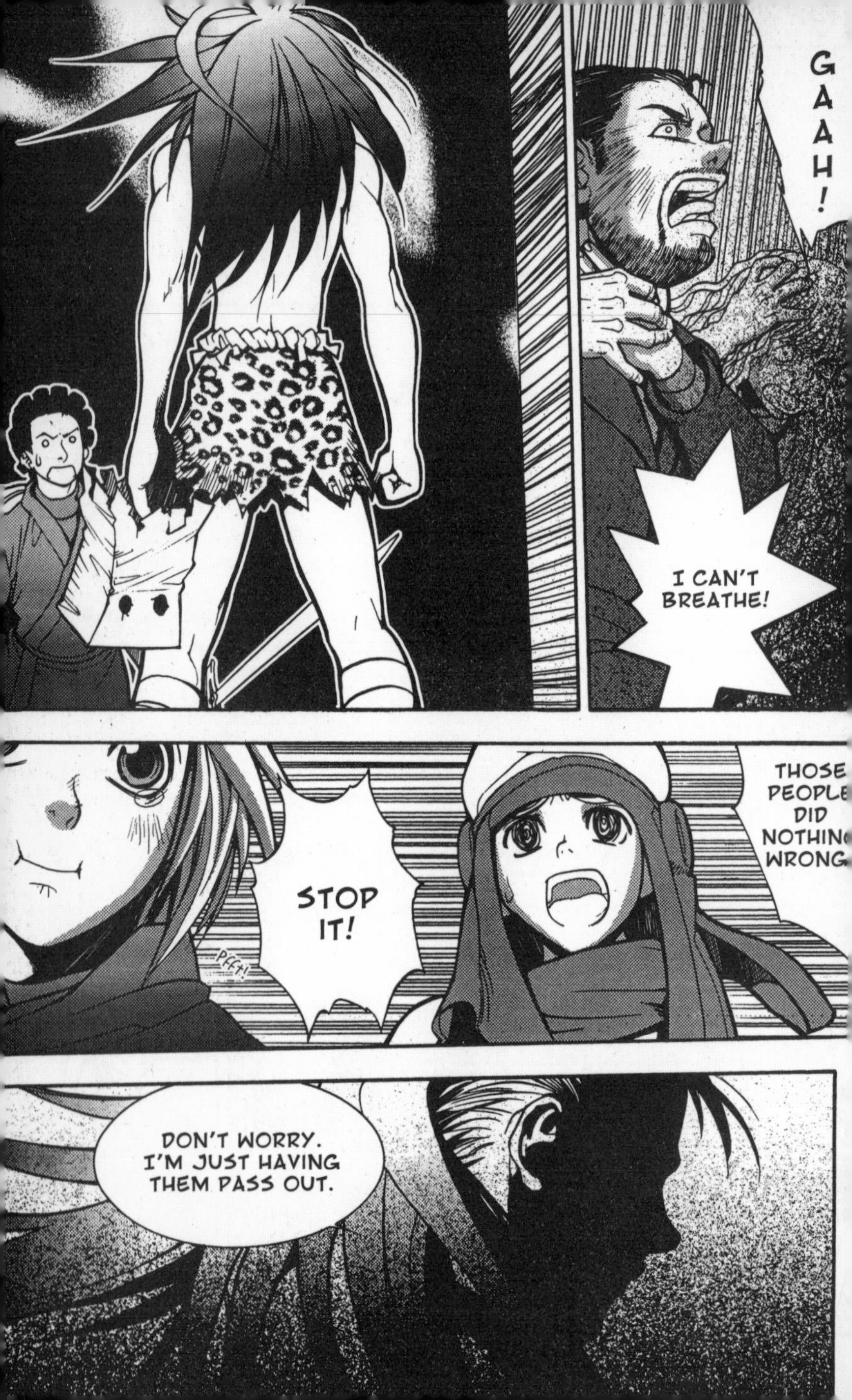
GAAH!
I CAN'T BREATHE!
PFFT!
STOP IT!
THOSE PEOPLE DID NOTHING WRONG
DON'T WORRY. I'M JUST HAVING THEM PASS OUT.

IT WAS MY GREATEST SHAME TO LET PREY THAT I HAD IN THE BAG GET ME LIKE THAT.

SHIELD! TAKE THE KIDS TO SOMEWHERE SAFE!

NATURALLY.

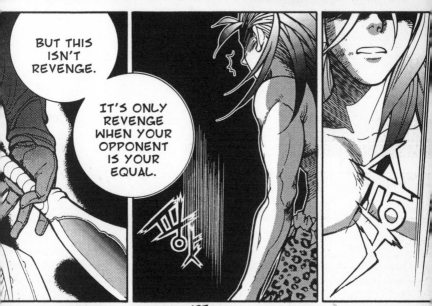

BUT THIS ISN'T REVENGE.

IT'S ONLY REVENGE WHEN YOUR OPPONENT IS YOUR EQUAL.

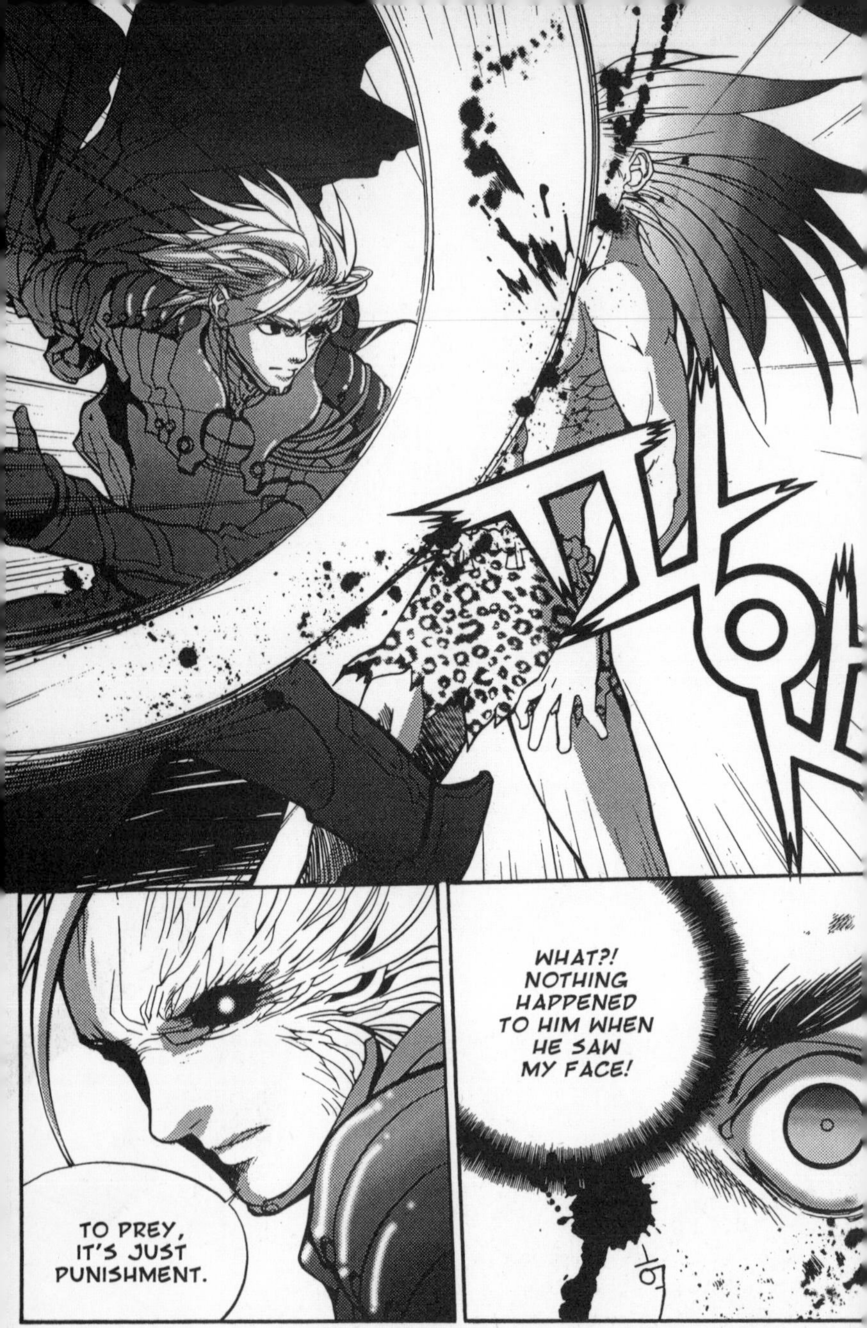
TO PREY, IT'S JUST PUNISHMENT.
WHAT?! NOTHING HAPPENED TO HIM WHEN HE SAW MY FACE!

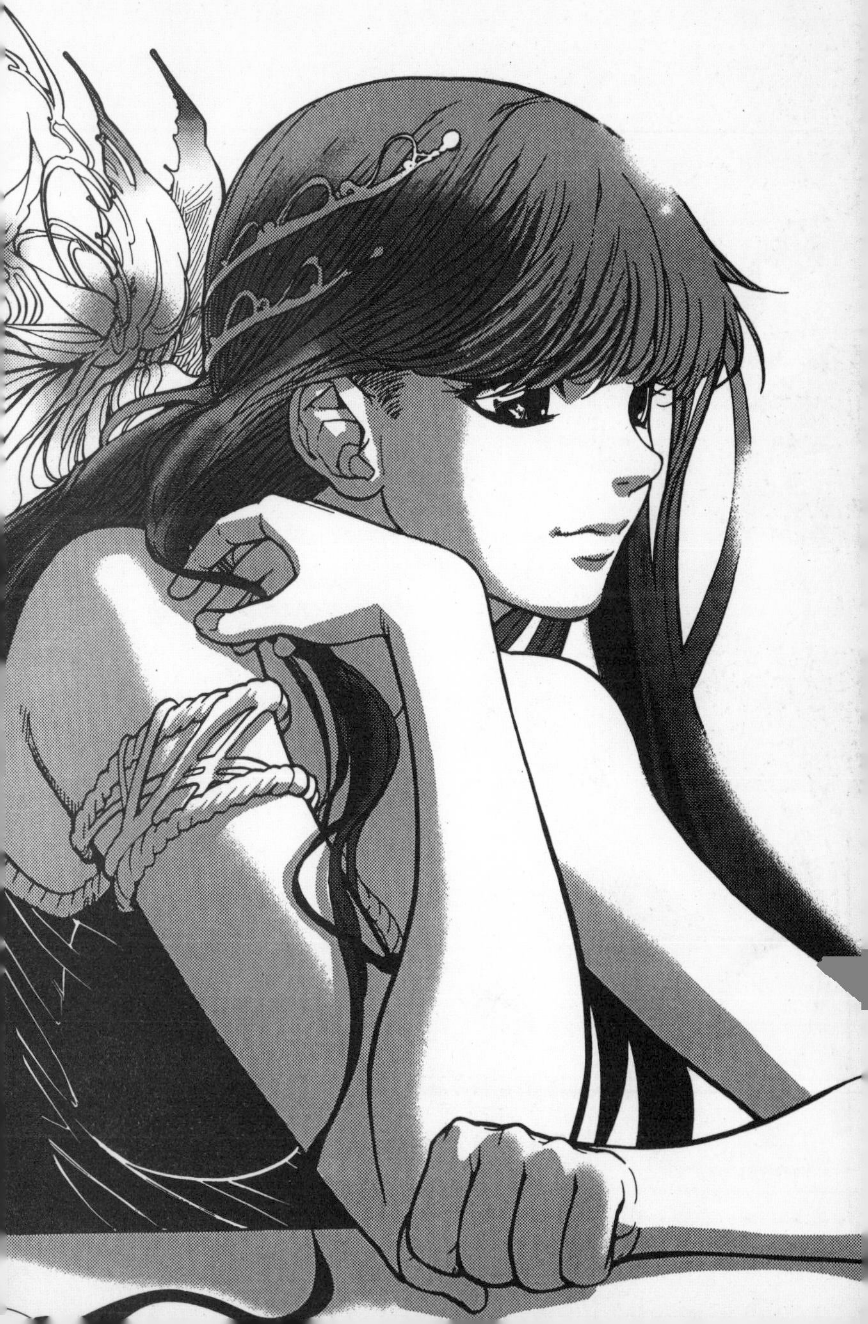

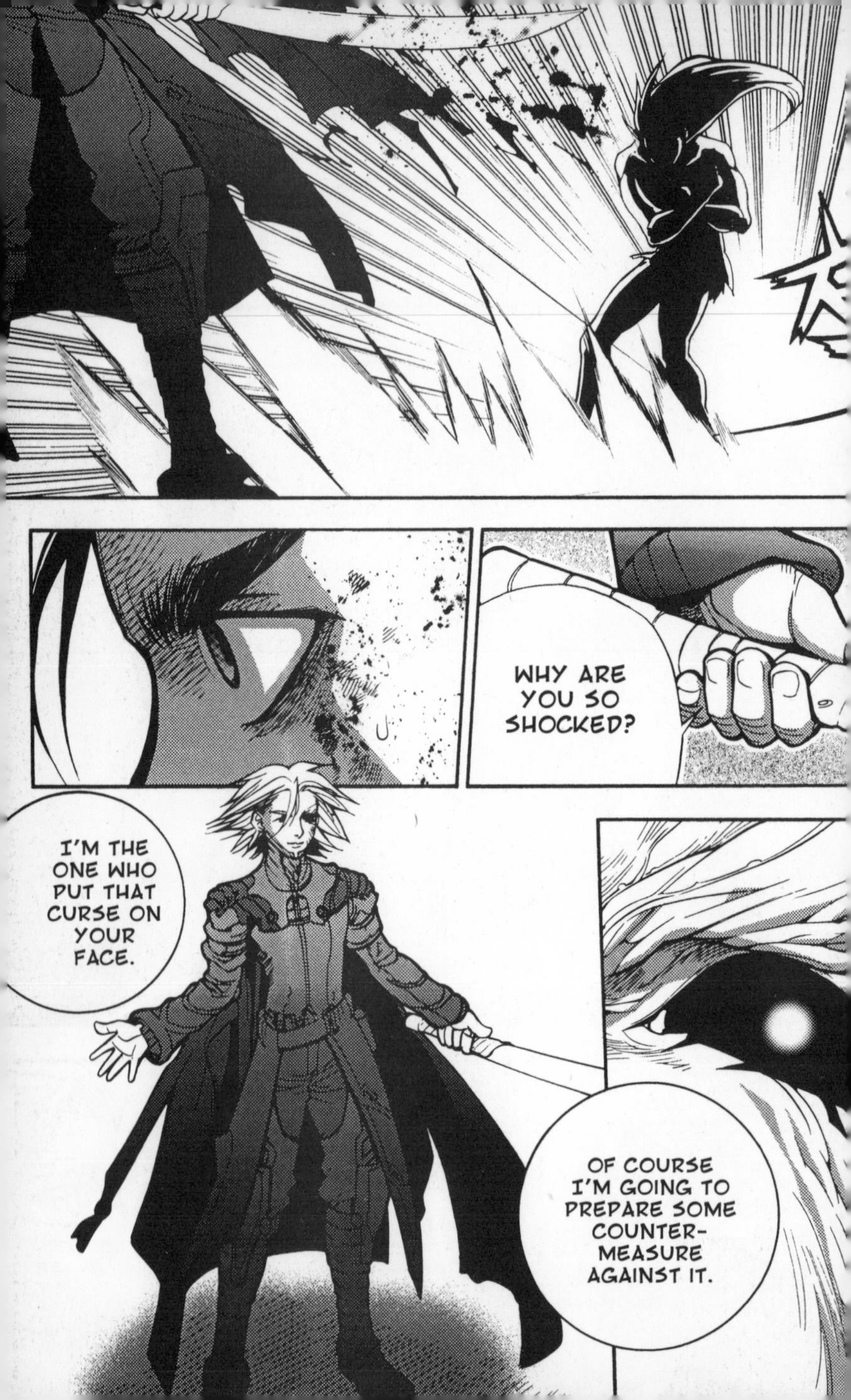
WHY ARE YOU SO SHOCKED?
I'M THE ONE WHO PUT THAT CURSE ON YOUR FACE.
OF COURSE I'M GOING TO PREPARE SOME COUNTER-MEASURE AGAINST IT.

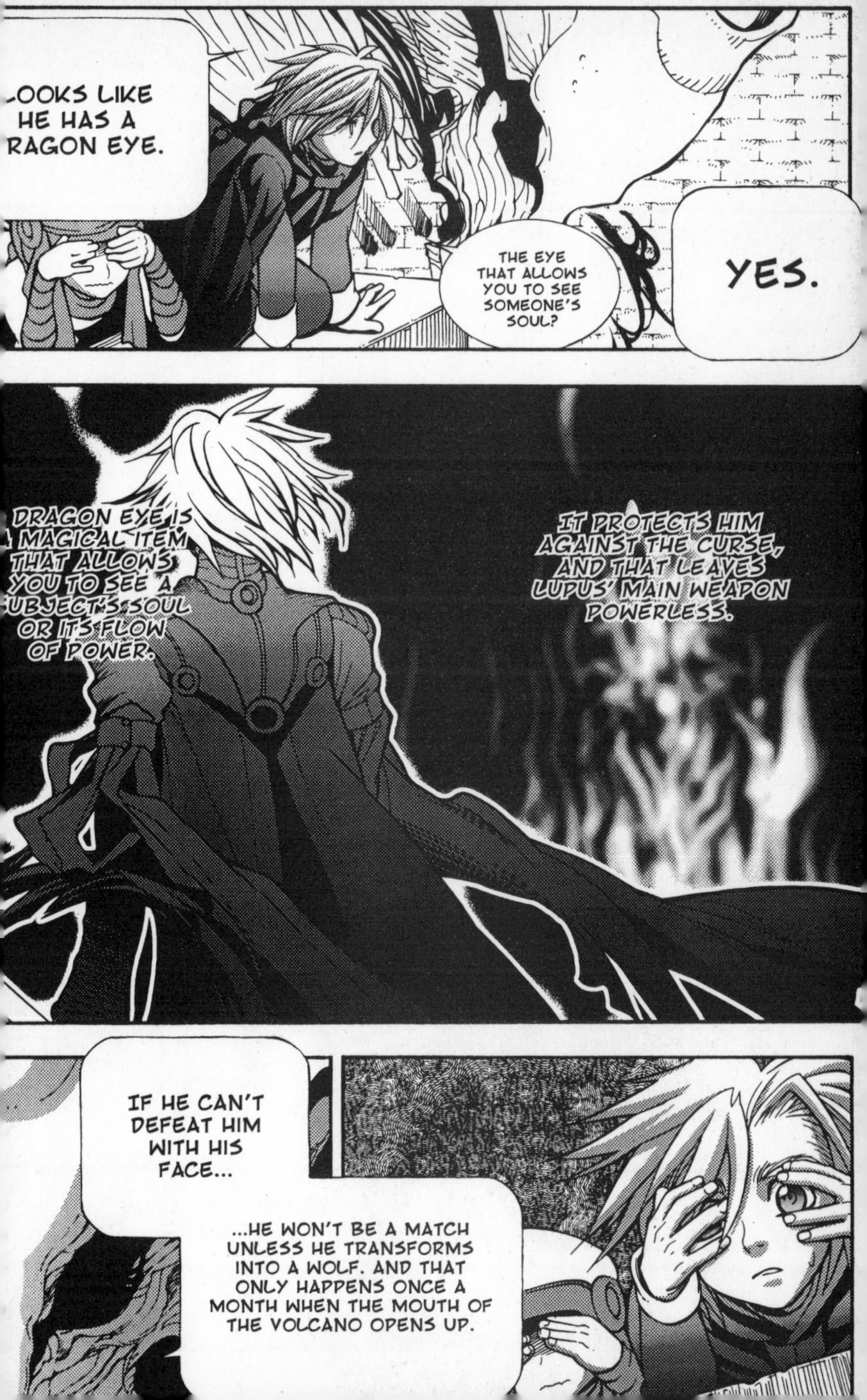

-OOKS LIKE HE HAS A RAGON EYE.
THE EYE THAT ALLOWS YOU TO SEE SOMEONE'S SOUL?
YES.
DRAGON EYE IS A MAGICAL ITEM THAT ALLOWS YOU TO SEE A UBJECT'S SOUL OR ITS FLOW OF POWER.
IT PROTECTS HIM AGAINST THE CURSE, AND THAT LEAVES LUPUS' MAIN WEAPON POWERLESS.
IF HE CAN'T DEFEAT HIM WITH HIS FACE...
...HE WON'T BE A MATCH UNLESS HE TRANSFORMS INTO A WOLF. AND THAT ONLY HAPPENS ONCE A MONTH WHEN THE MOUTH OF THE VOLCANO OPENS UP.

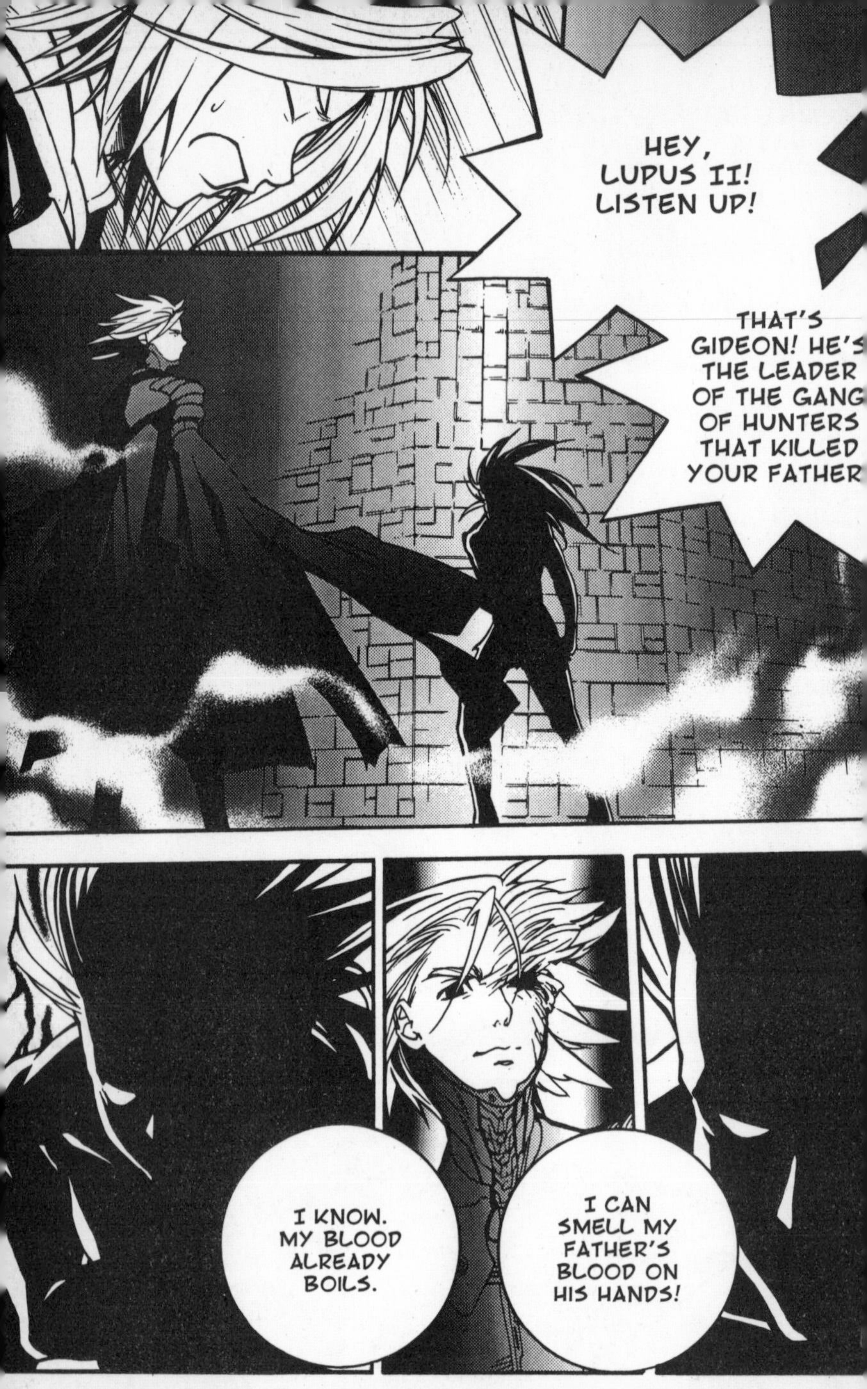
HEY, LUPUS II! LISTEN UP!
THAT'S GIDEON! HE'S THE LEADER OF THE GANG OF HUNTERS THAT KILLED YOUR FATHER
I KNOW. MY BLOOD ALREADY BOILS.
I CAN SMELL MY FATHER'S BLOOD ON HIS HANDS!

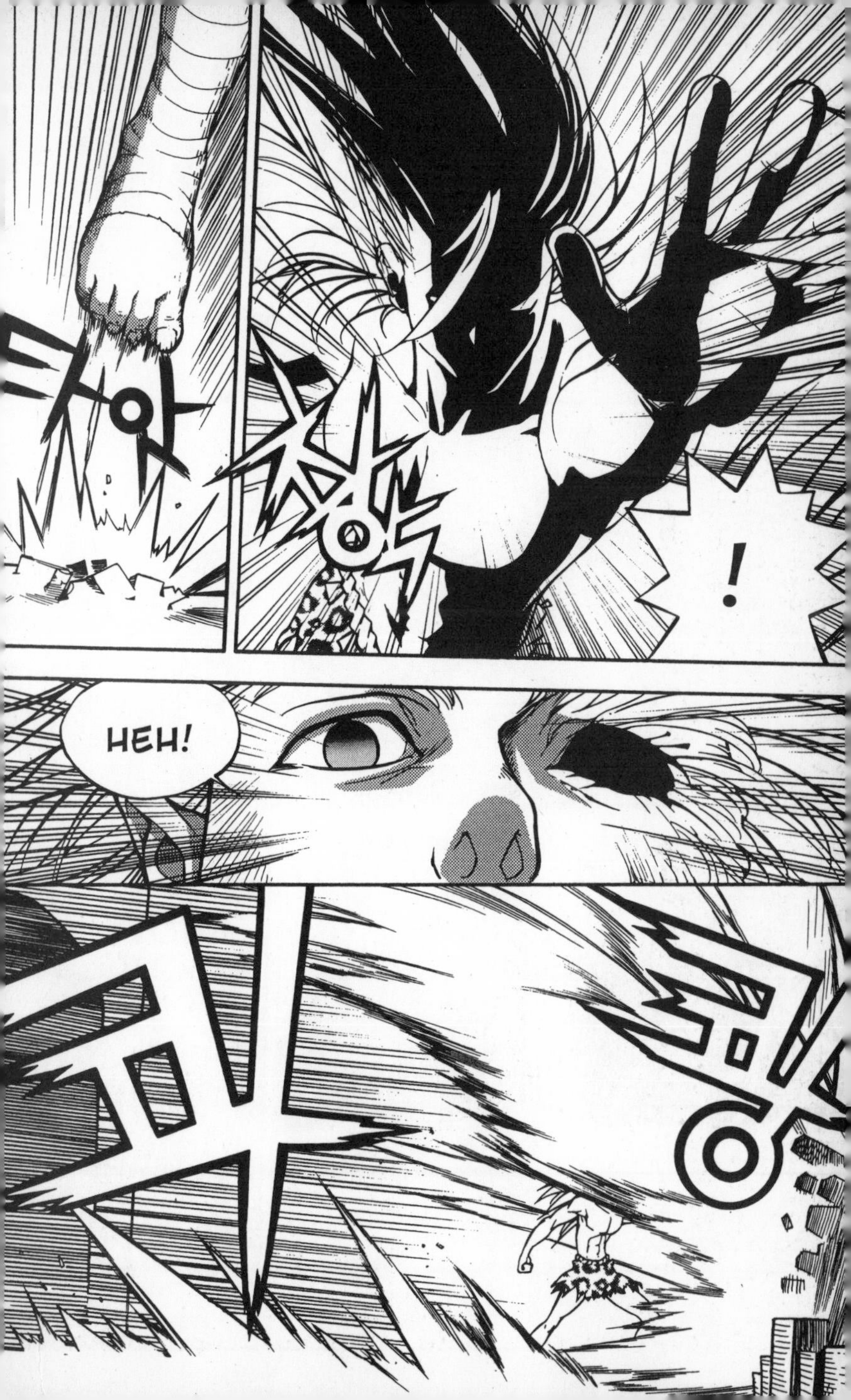
!
HEH!

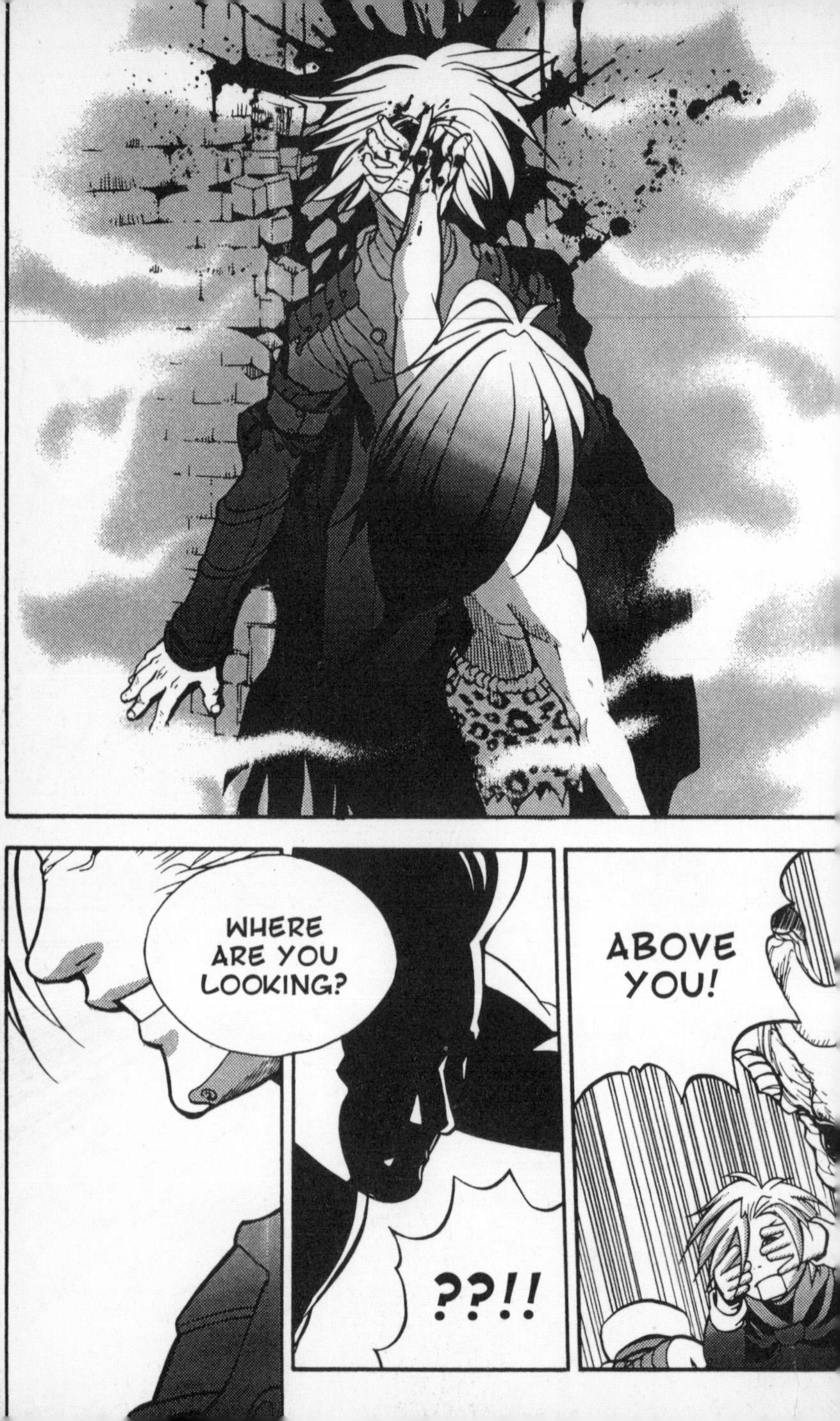
WHERE ARE YOU LOOKING?
??!!
ABOVE YOU!

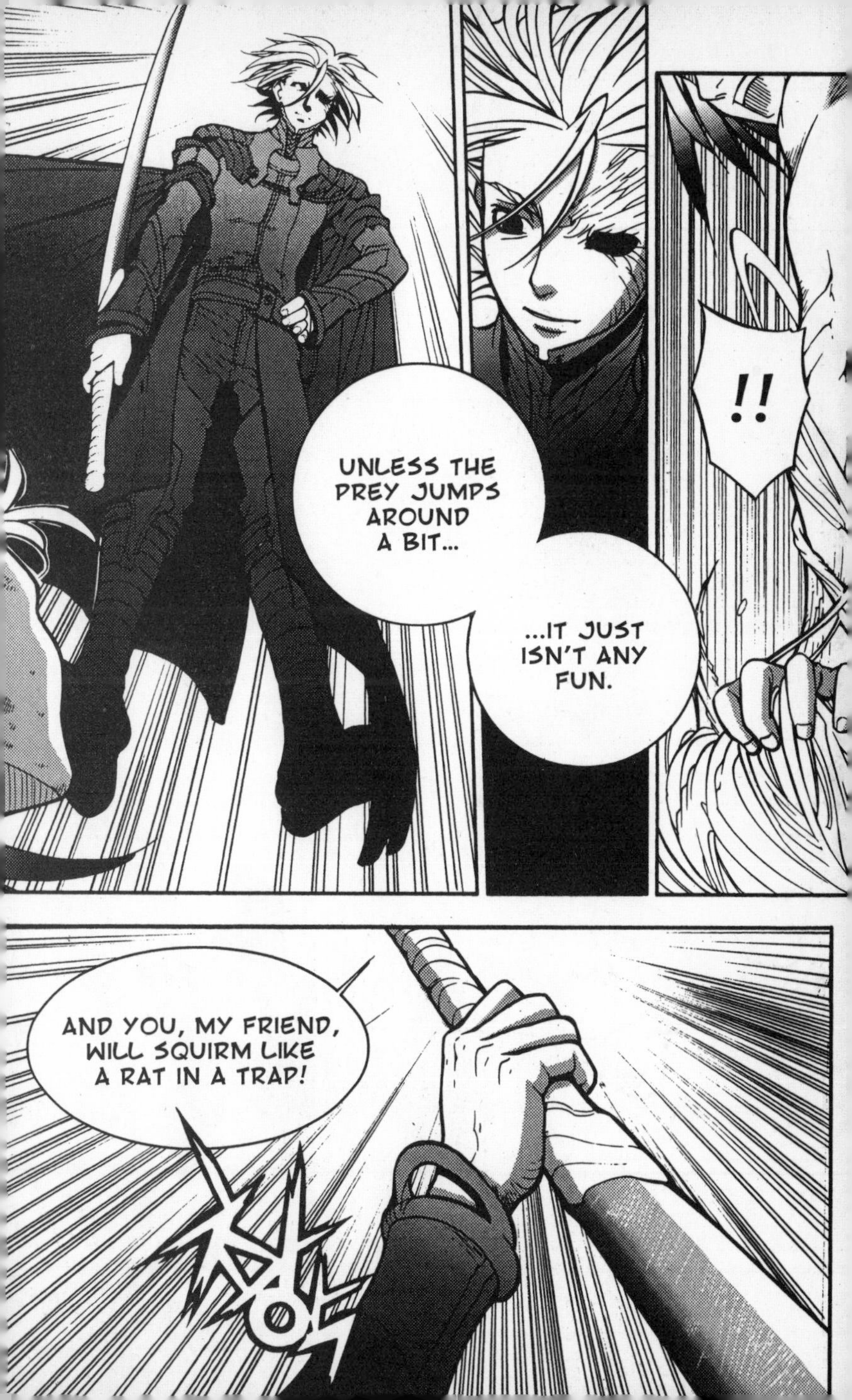
UNLESS THE PREY JUMPS AROUND A BIT...
...IT JUST ISN'T ANY FUN.
!!
AND YOU, MY FRIEND, WILL SQUIRM LIKE A RAT IN A TRAP!

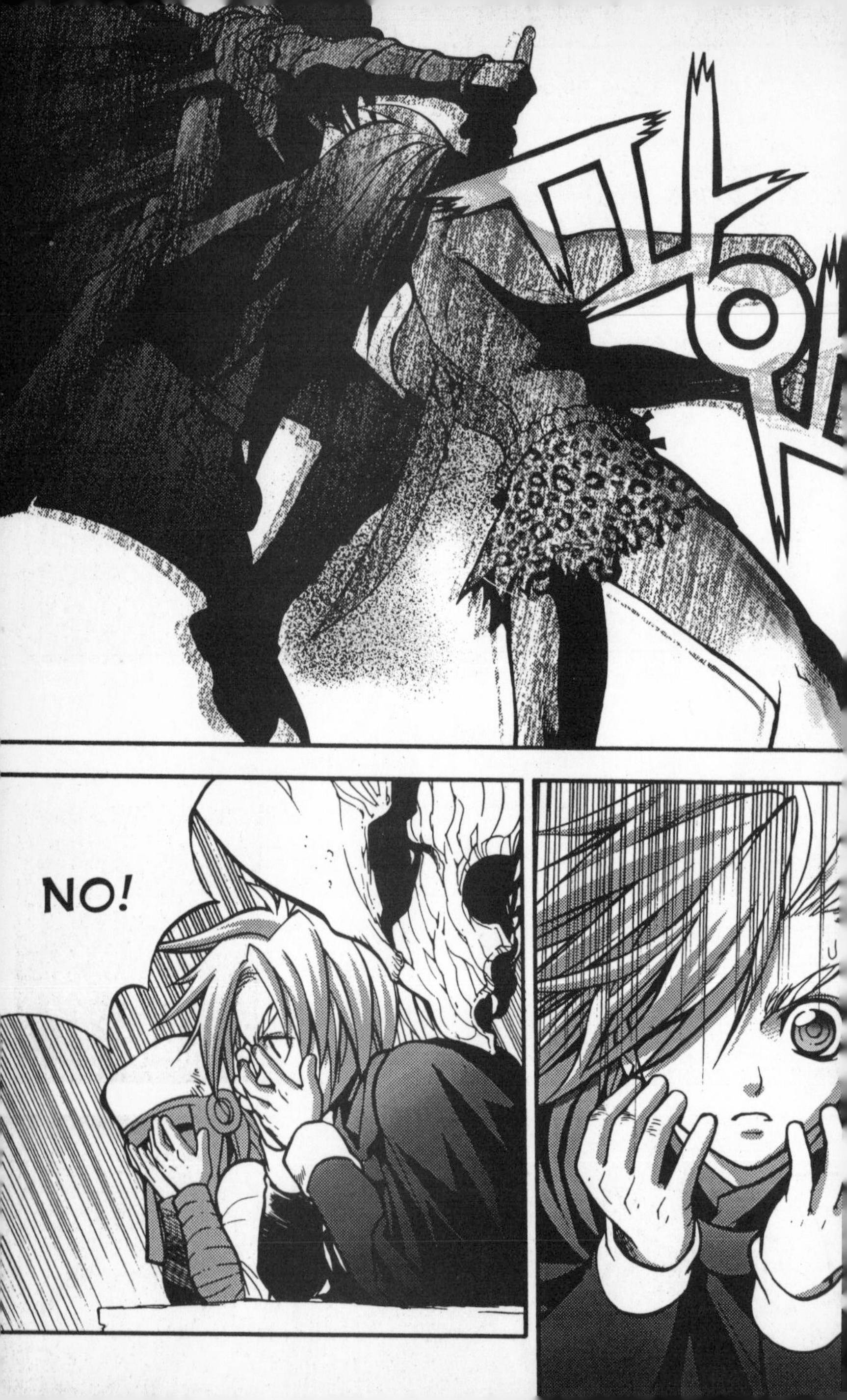
NO!

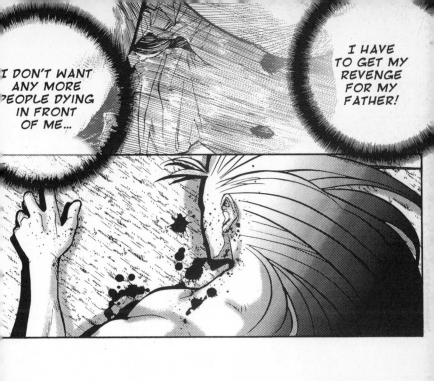

I DON'T WANT ANY MORE PEOPLE DYING IN FRONT OF ME...

I HAVE TO GET MY REVENGE FOR MY FATHER!

IN THE END...

...HE WASN'T ABLE TO DO A THING...?

HE SO BADLY WANTED TO GET OUT OF THIS HELLISH PLACE AND GET HIS REVENGE...

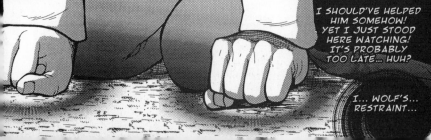

I SHOULD'VE HELPED HIM SOMEHOW! YET I JUST STOOD HERE WATCHING! IT'S PROBABLY TOO LATE... HUH?

I... WOLF'S... RESTRAINT...

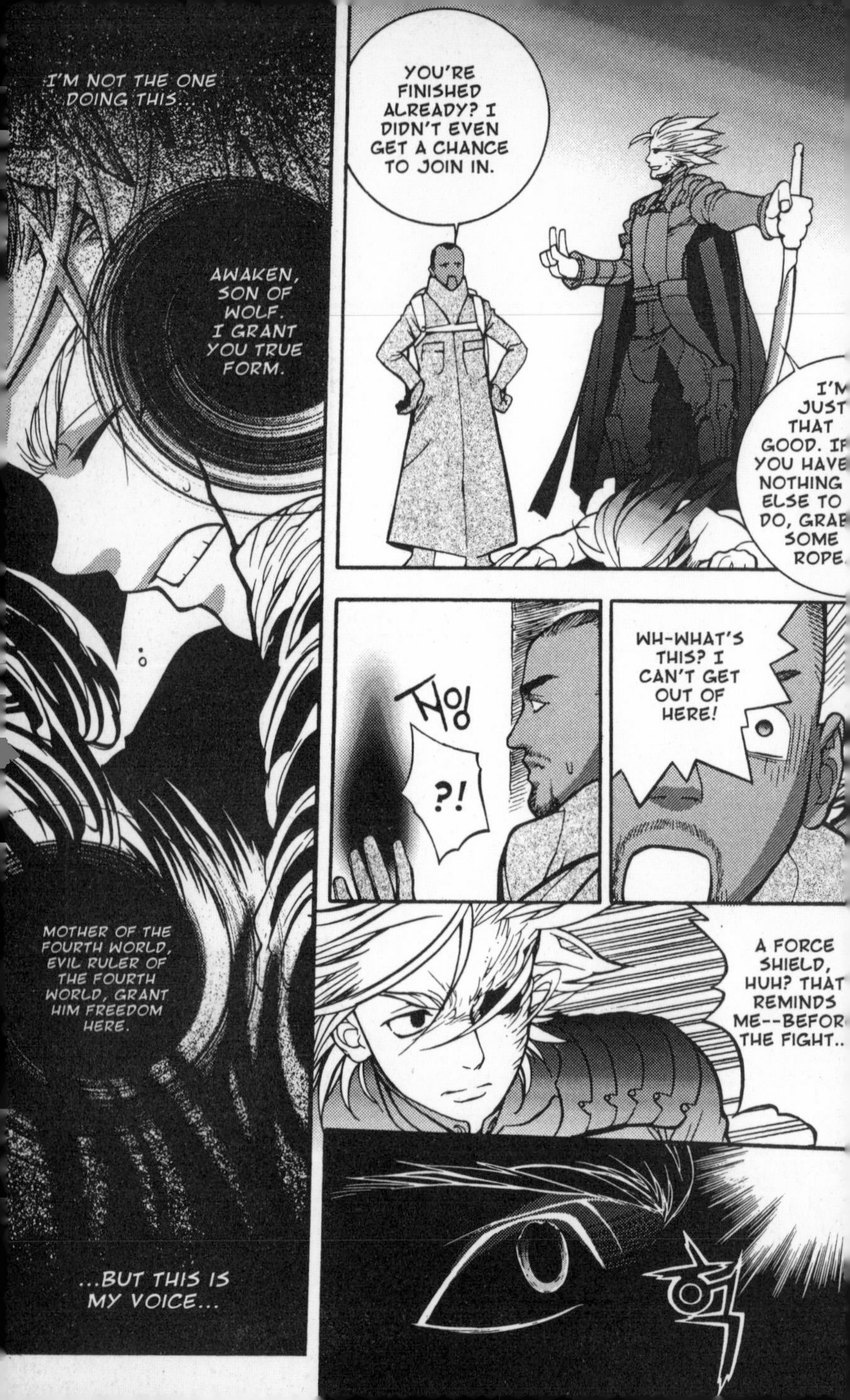
I'M NOT THE ONE DOING THIS...
AWAKEN, SON OF WOLF. I GRANT YOU TRUE FORM.
MOTHER OF THE FOURTH WORLD, EVIL RULER OF THE FOURTH WORLD, GRANT HIM FREEDOM HERE.
...BUT THIS IS MY VOICE...
YOU'RE FINISHED ALREADY? I DIDN'T EVEN GET A CHANCE TO JOIN IN.
I'M JUST THAT GOOD. IF YOU HAVE NOTHING ELSE TO DO, GRAB SOME ROPE.
?!
WH-WHAT'S THIS? I CAN'T GET OUT OF HERE!
A FORCE SHIELD, HUH? THAT REMINDS ME--BEFORE THE FIGHT..

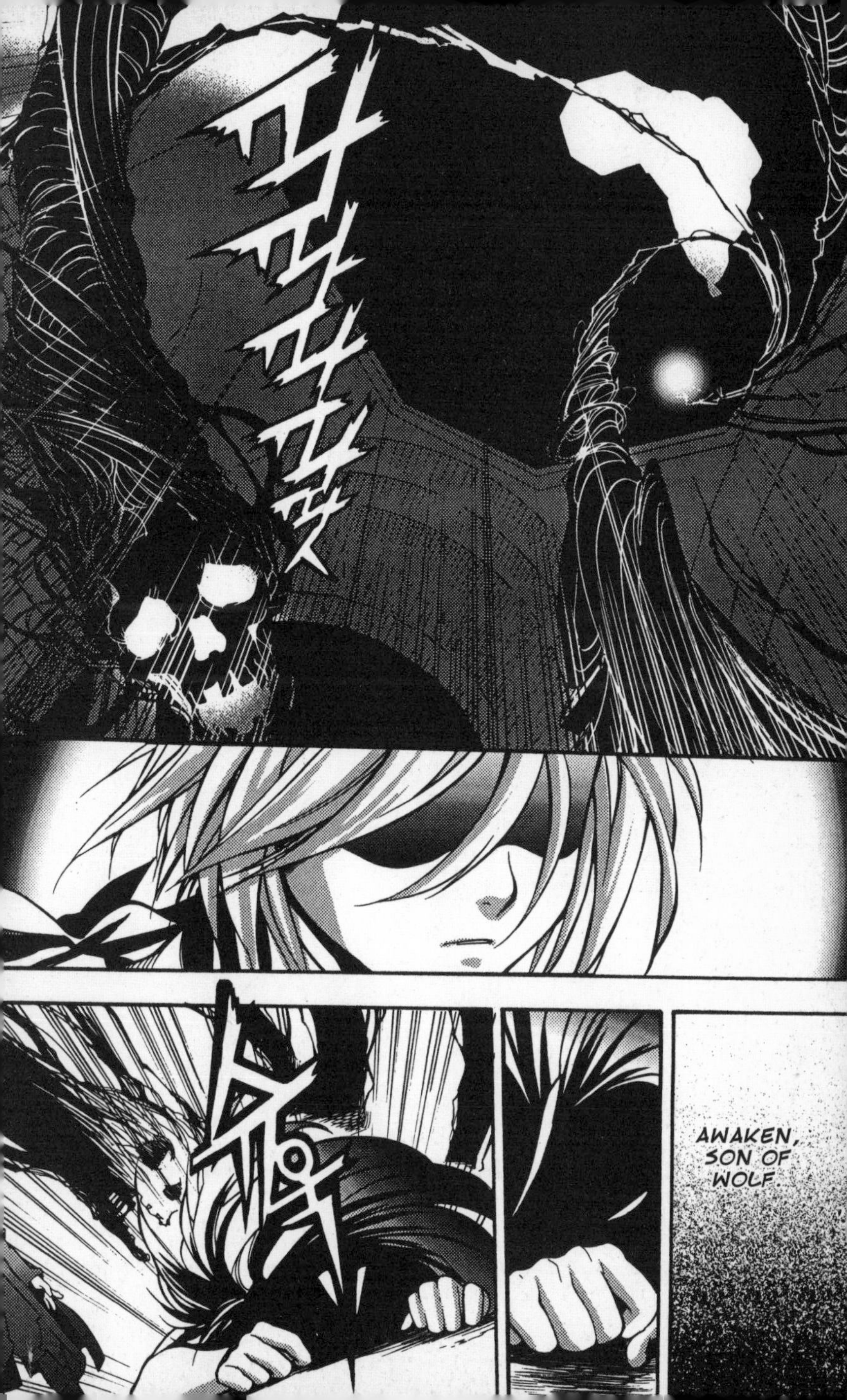
AWAKEN, SON OF WOLF.

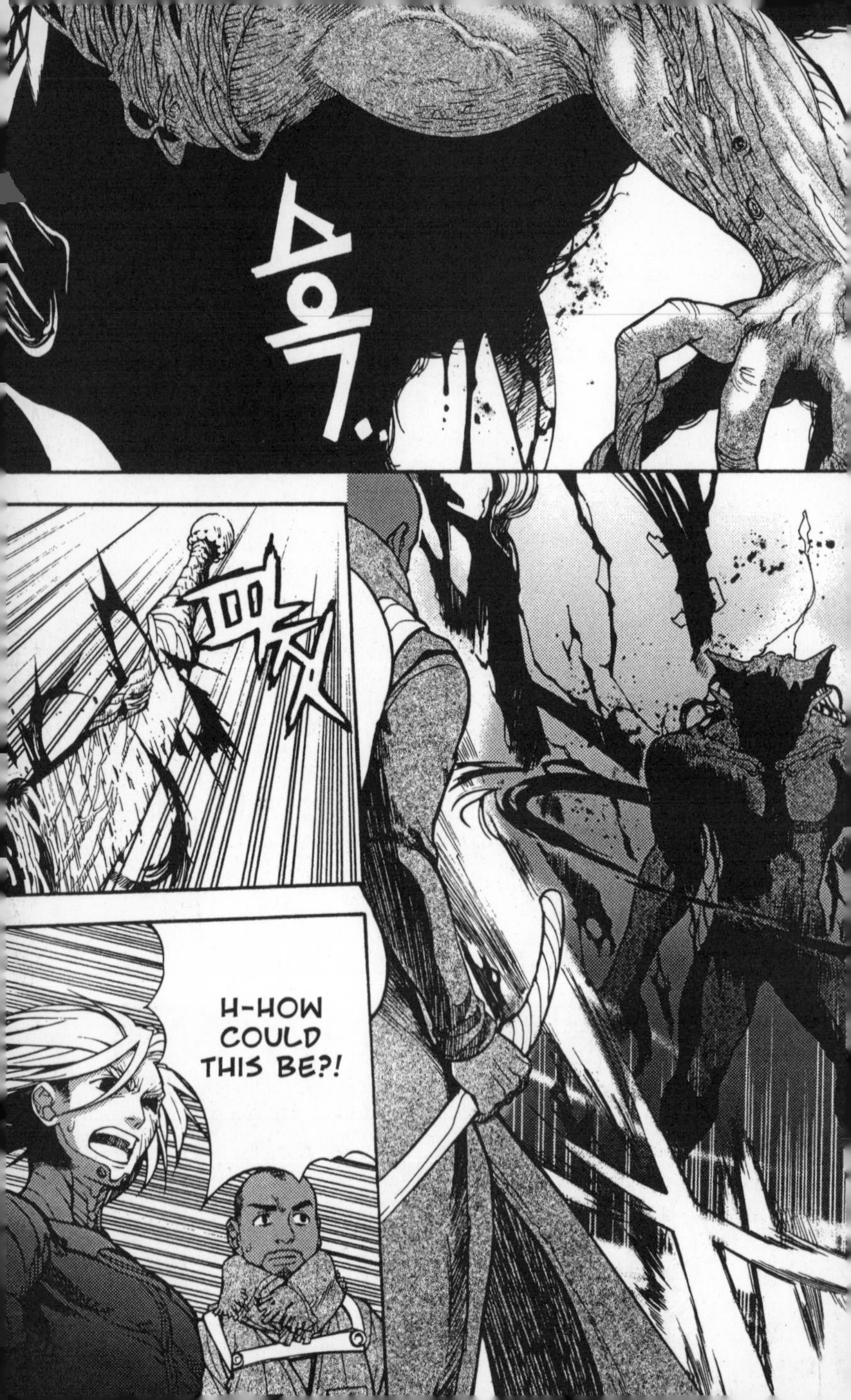
H-HOW COULD THIS BE?!

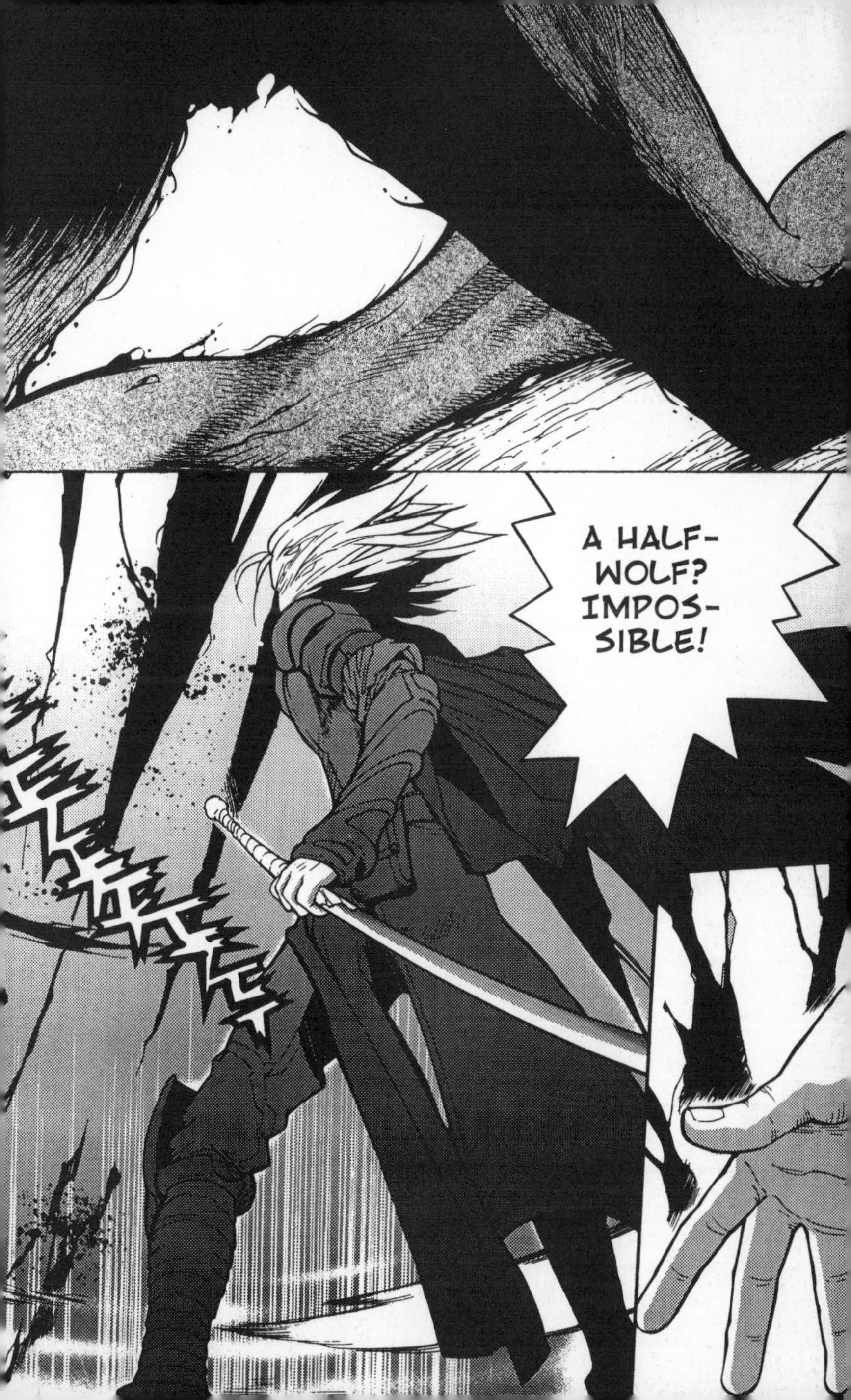
A HALF-WOLF? IMPOSSIBLE!

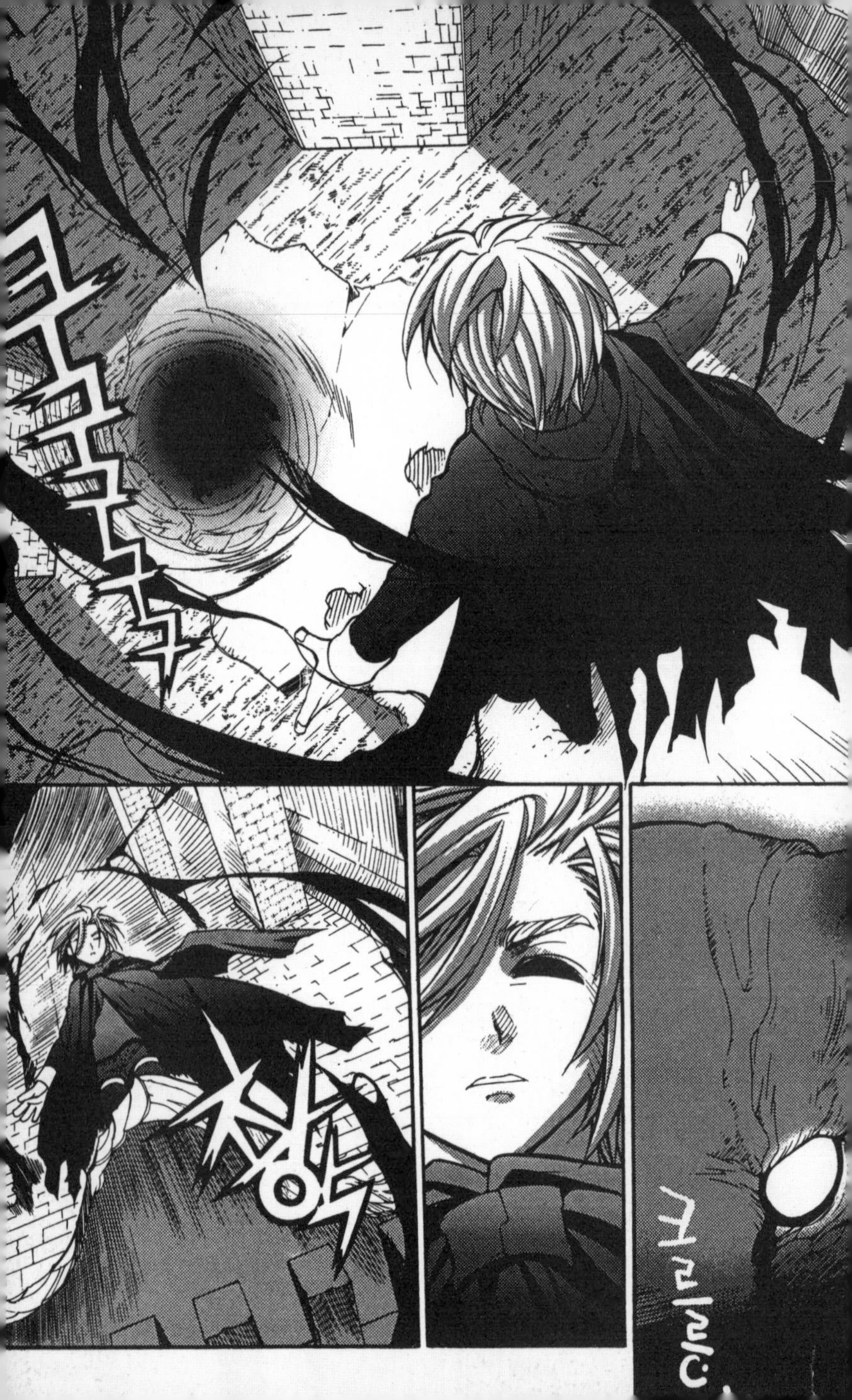

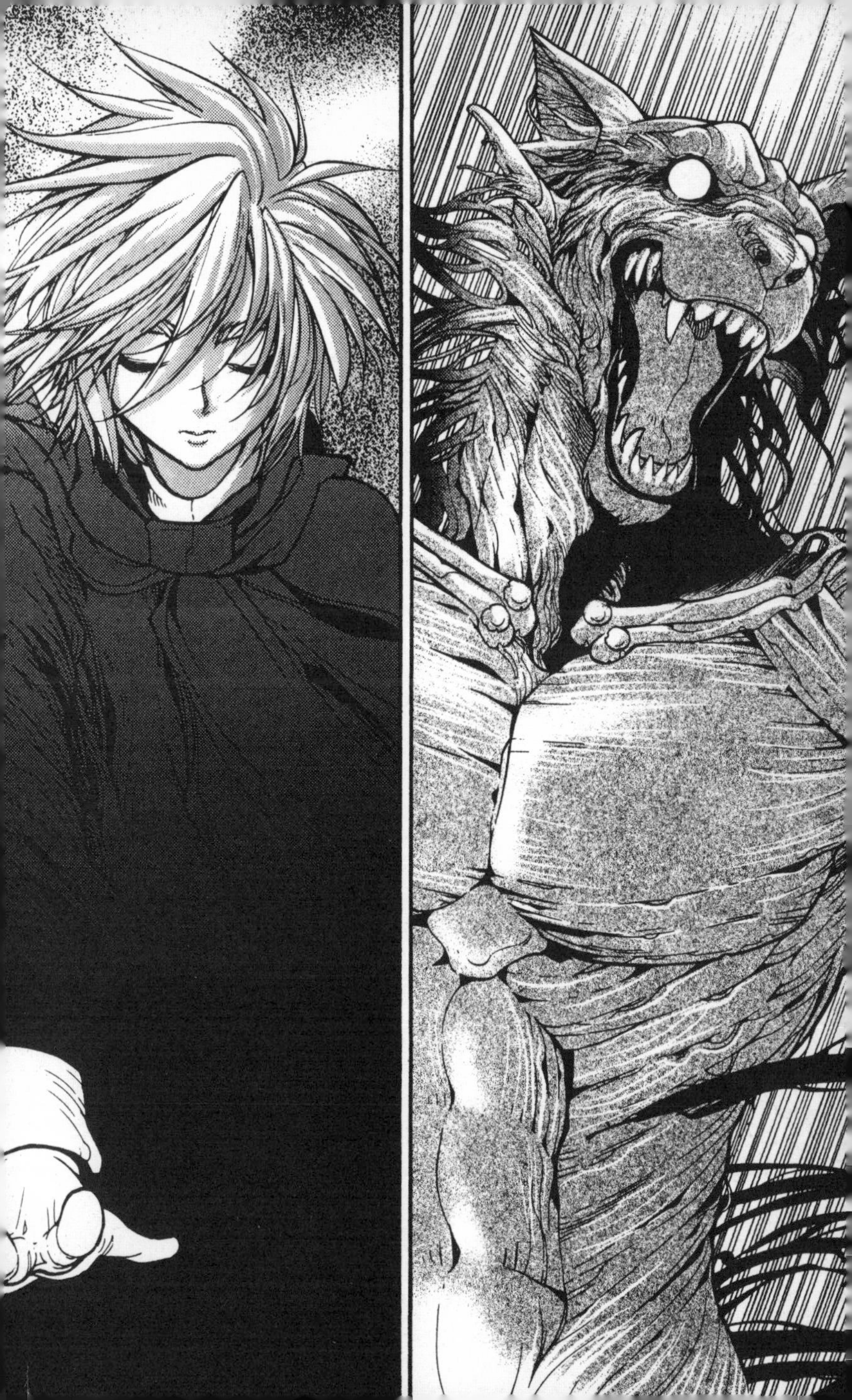

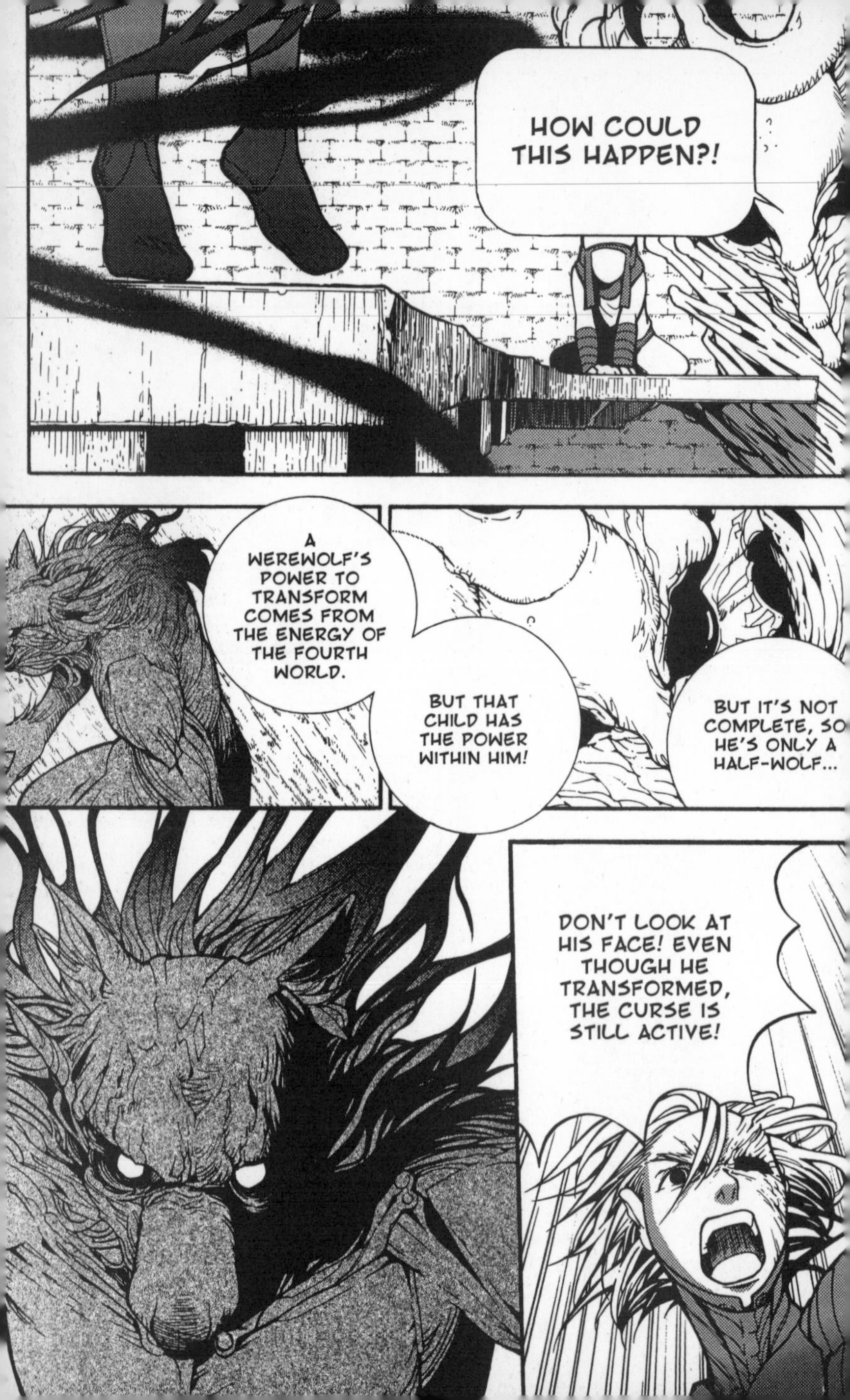
HOW COULD THIS HAPPEN?!
A WEREWOLF'S POWER TO TRANSFORM COMES FROM THE ENERGY OF THE FOURTH WORLD.
BUT THAT CHILD HAS THE POWER WITHIN HIM!
BUT IT'S NOT COMPLETE, SO HE'S ONLY A HALF-WOLF...
DON'T LOOK AT HIS FACE! EVEN THOUGH HE TRANSFORMED, THE CURSE IS STILL ACTIVE!

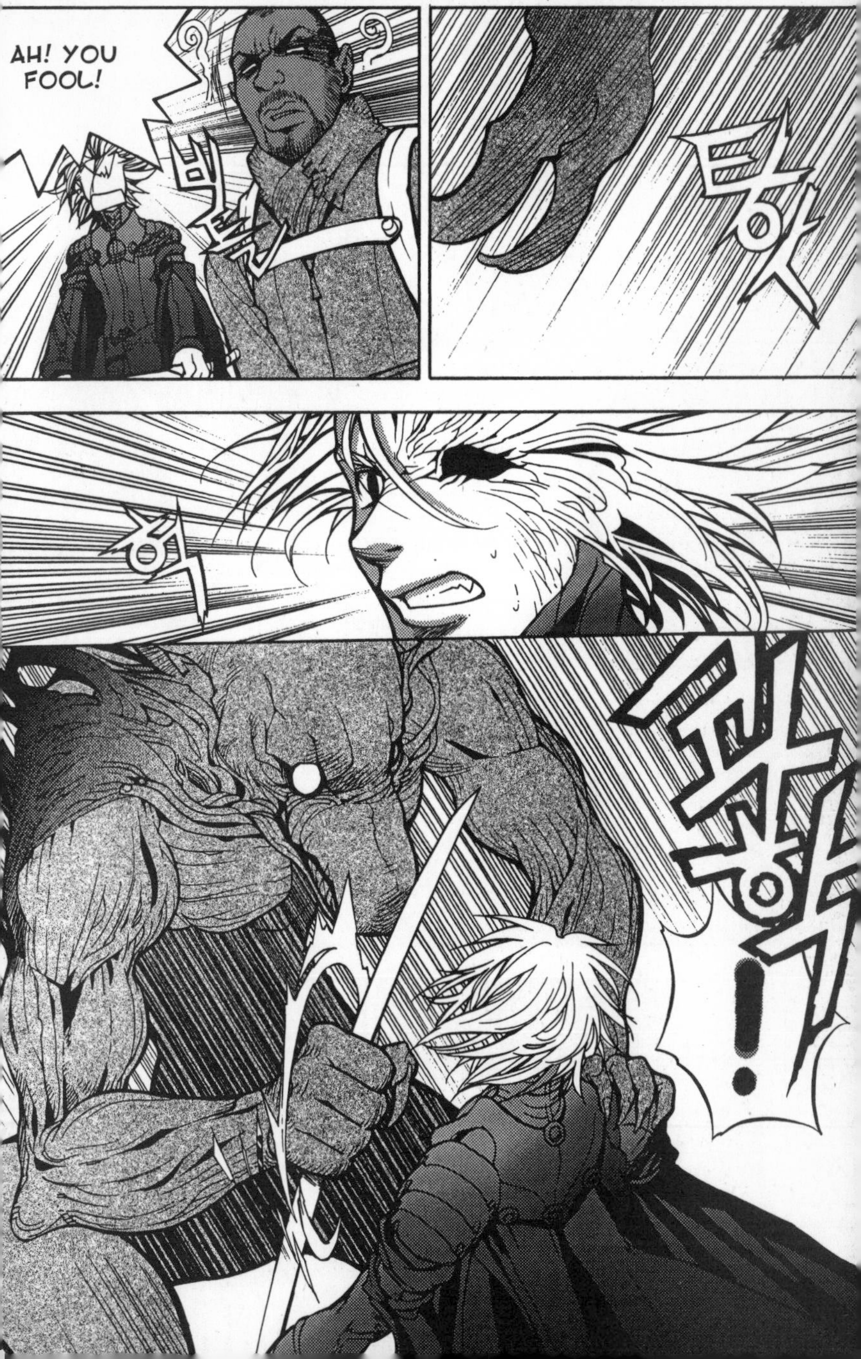
AH! YOU FOOL!

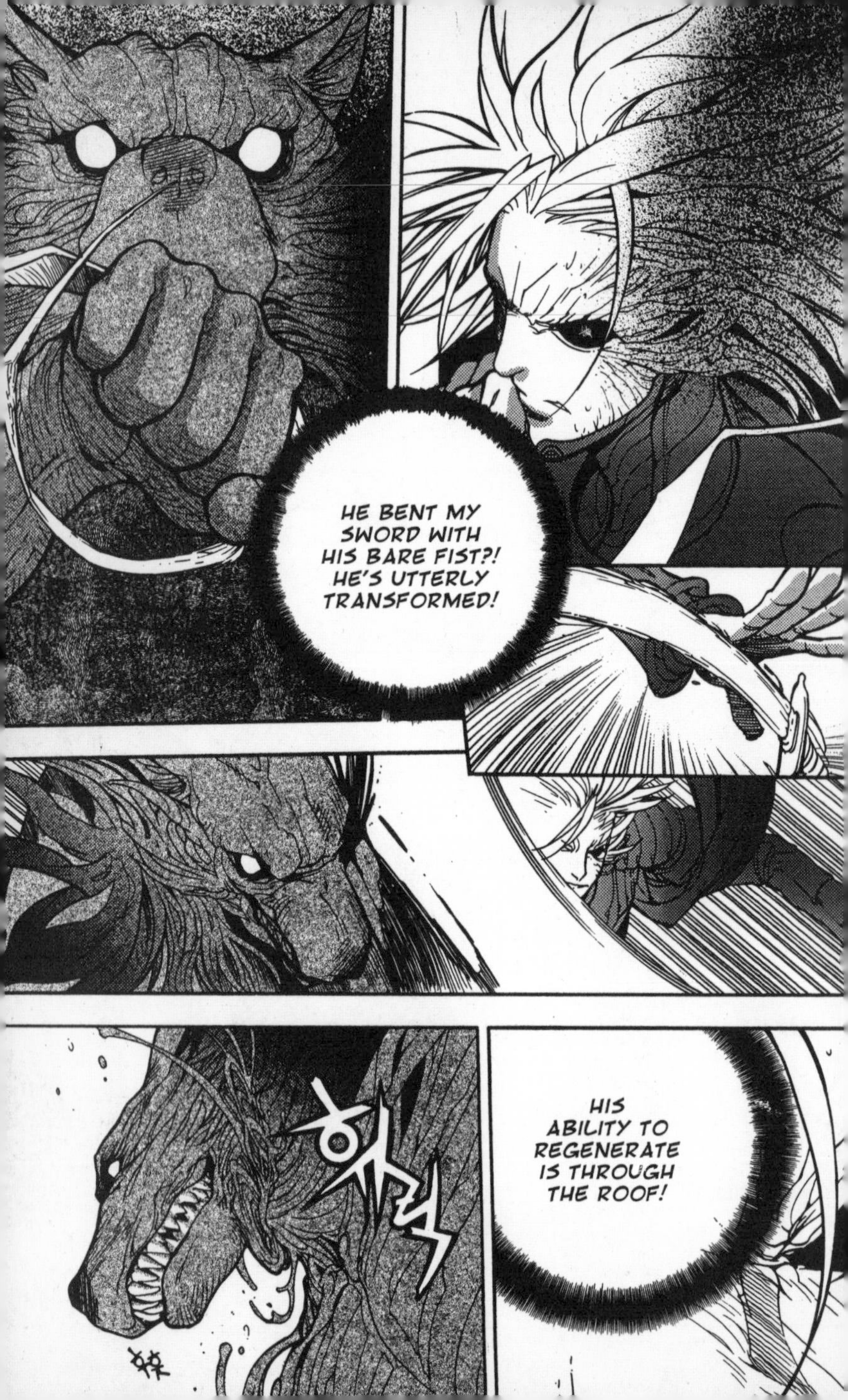
HE BENT MY SWORD WITH HIS BARE FIST?! HE'S UTTERLY TRANSFORMED!
HIS ABILITY TO REGENERATE IS THROUGH THE ROOF!

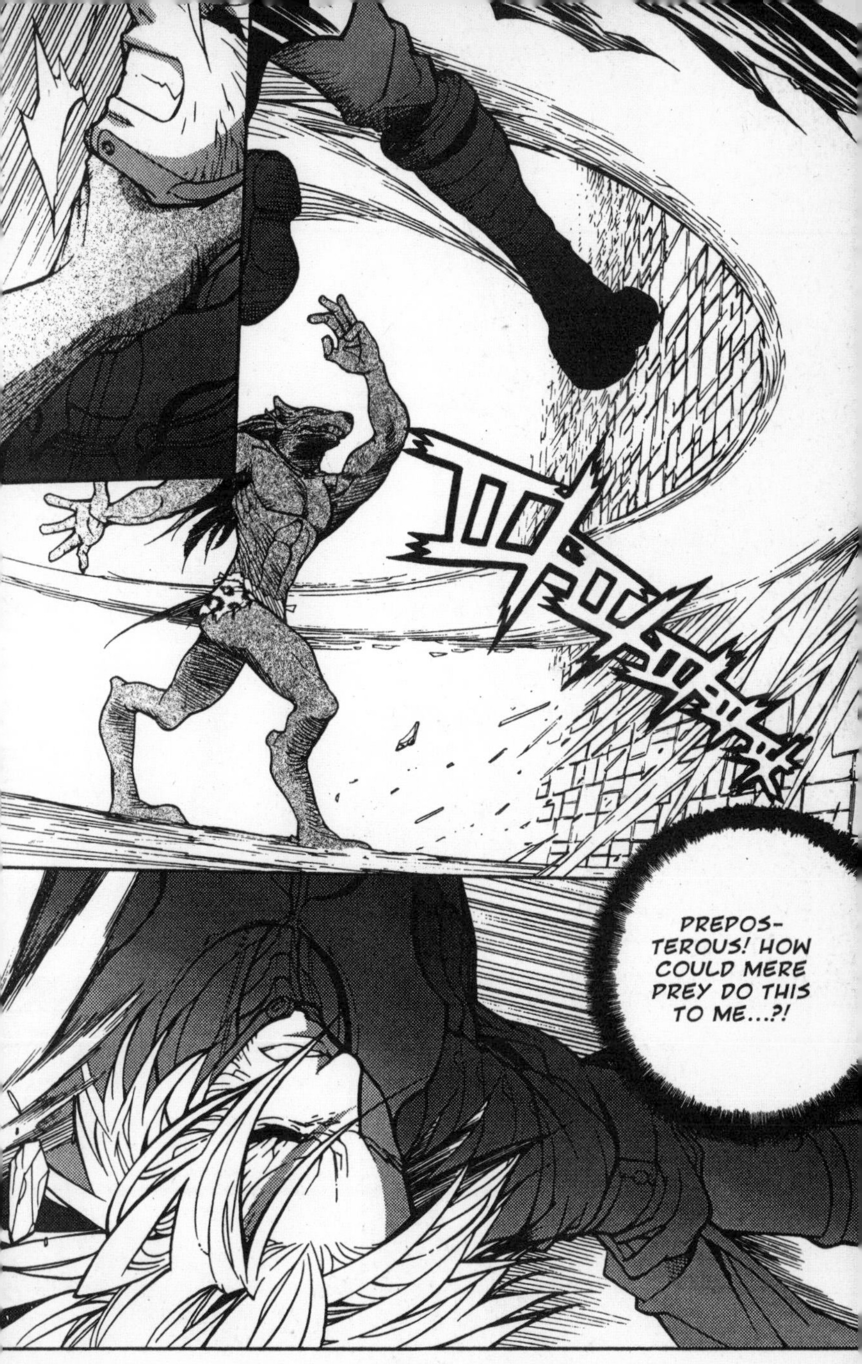
PREPOS-
TEROUS! HOW
COULD MERE
PREY DO THIS
TO ME...?!

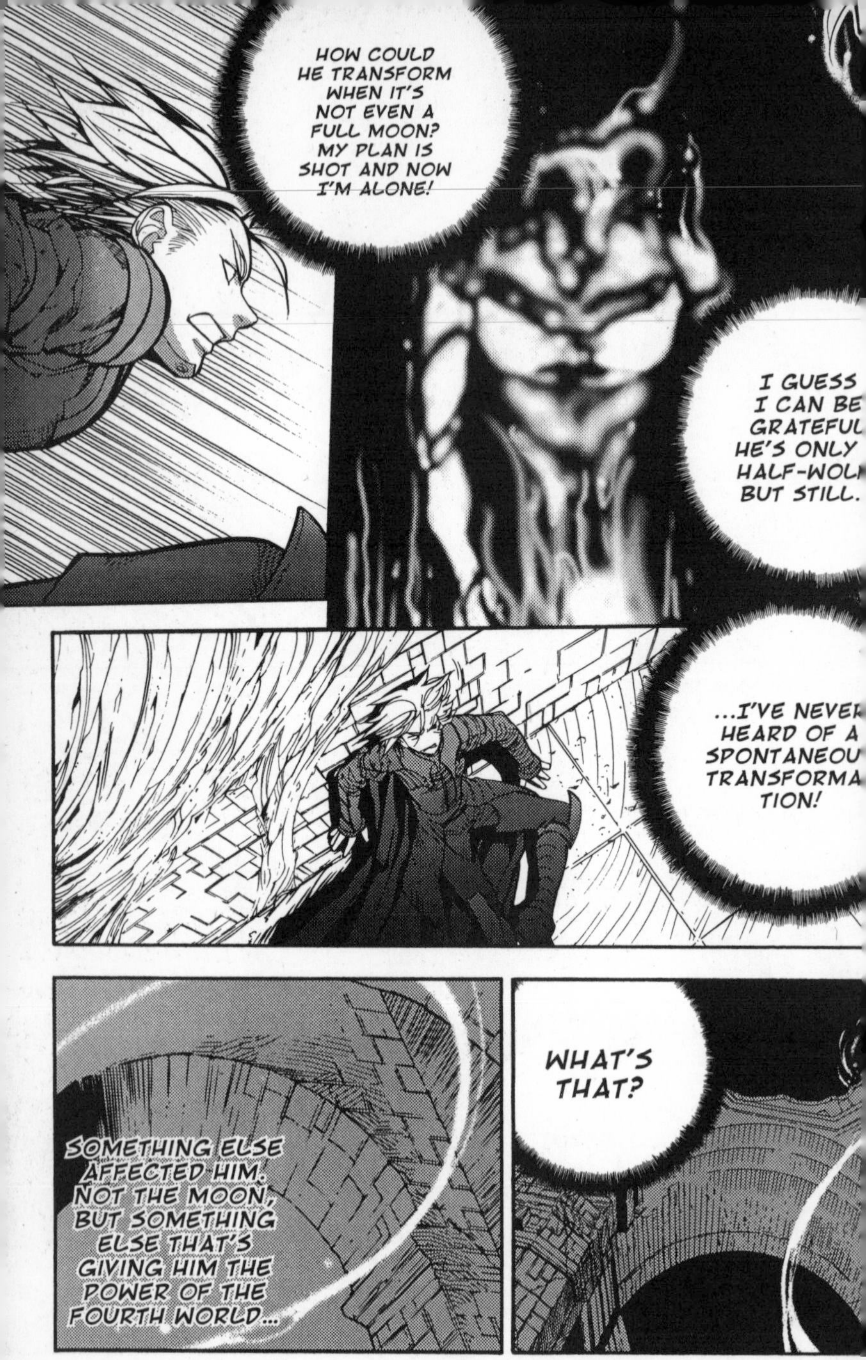
HOW COULD HE TRANSFORM WHEN IT'S NOT EVEN A FULL MOON? MY PLAN IS SHOT AND NOW I'M ALONE!
I GUESS I CAN BE GRATEFUL HE'S ONLY HALF-WOL BUT STILL.
...I'VE NEVER HEARD OF A SPONTANEOU TRANSFORMA TION!
SOMETHING ELSE AFFECTED HIM. NOT THE MOON, BUT SOMETHING ELSE THAT'S GIVING HIM THE POWER OF THE FOURTH WORLD...
WHAT'S THAT?

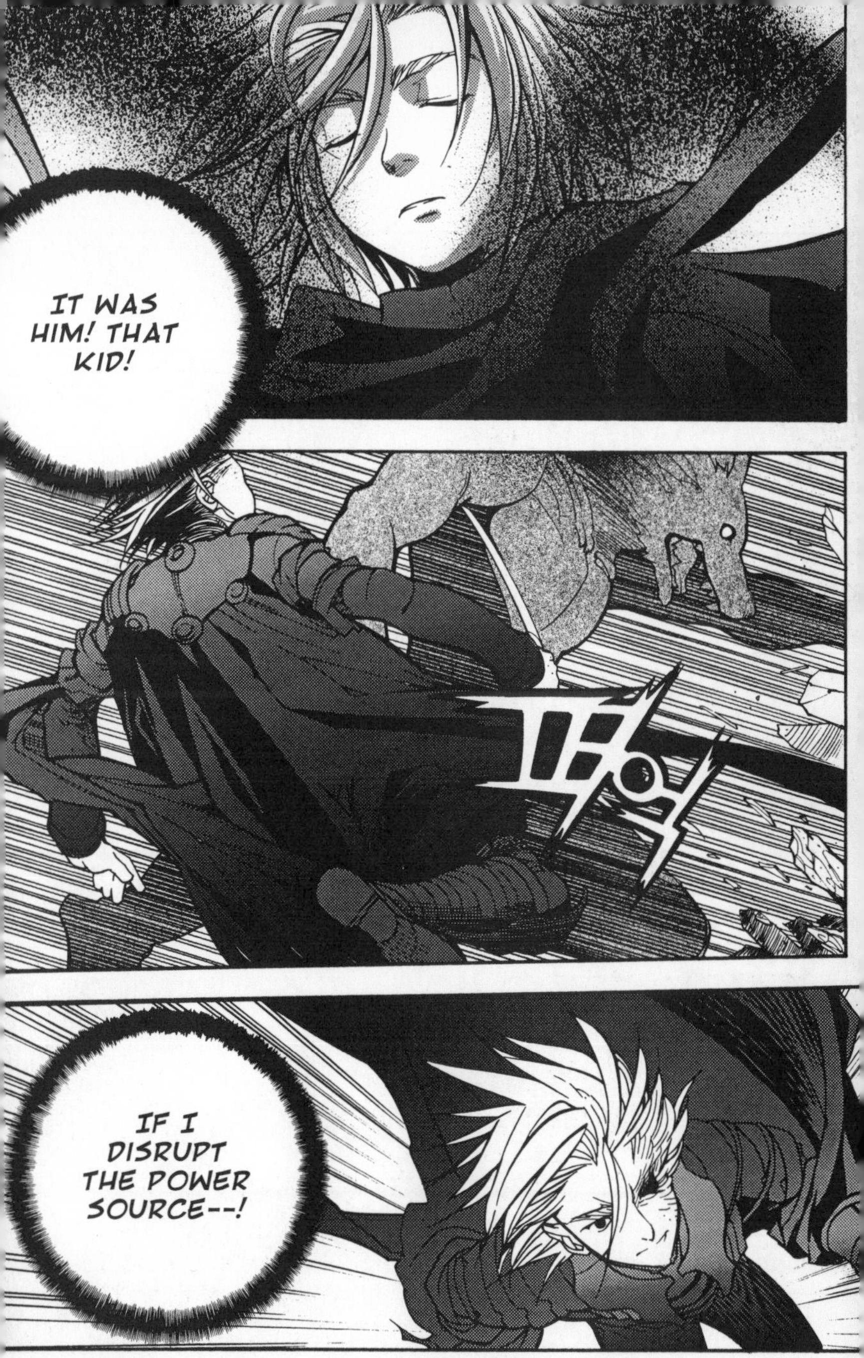
IT WAS HIM! THAT KID!
IF I DISRUPT THE POWER SOURCE--!

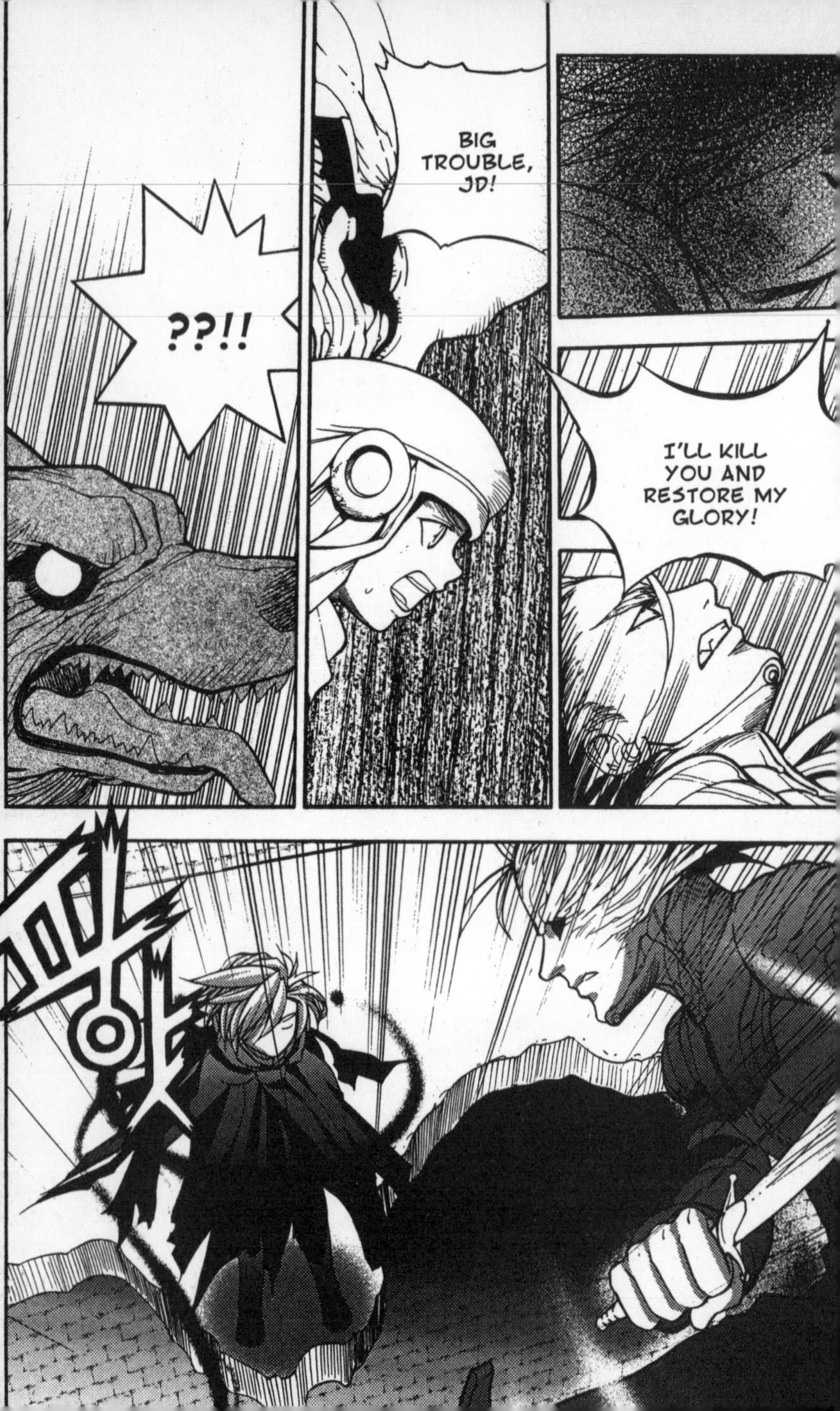
??!!
BIG TROUBLE, JD!
I'LL KILL YOU AND RESTORE MY GLORY!

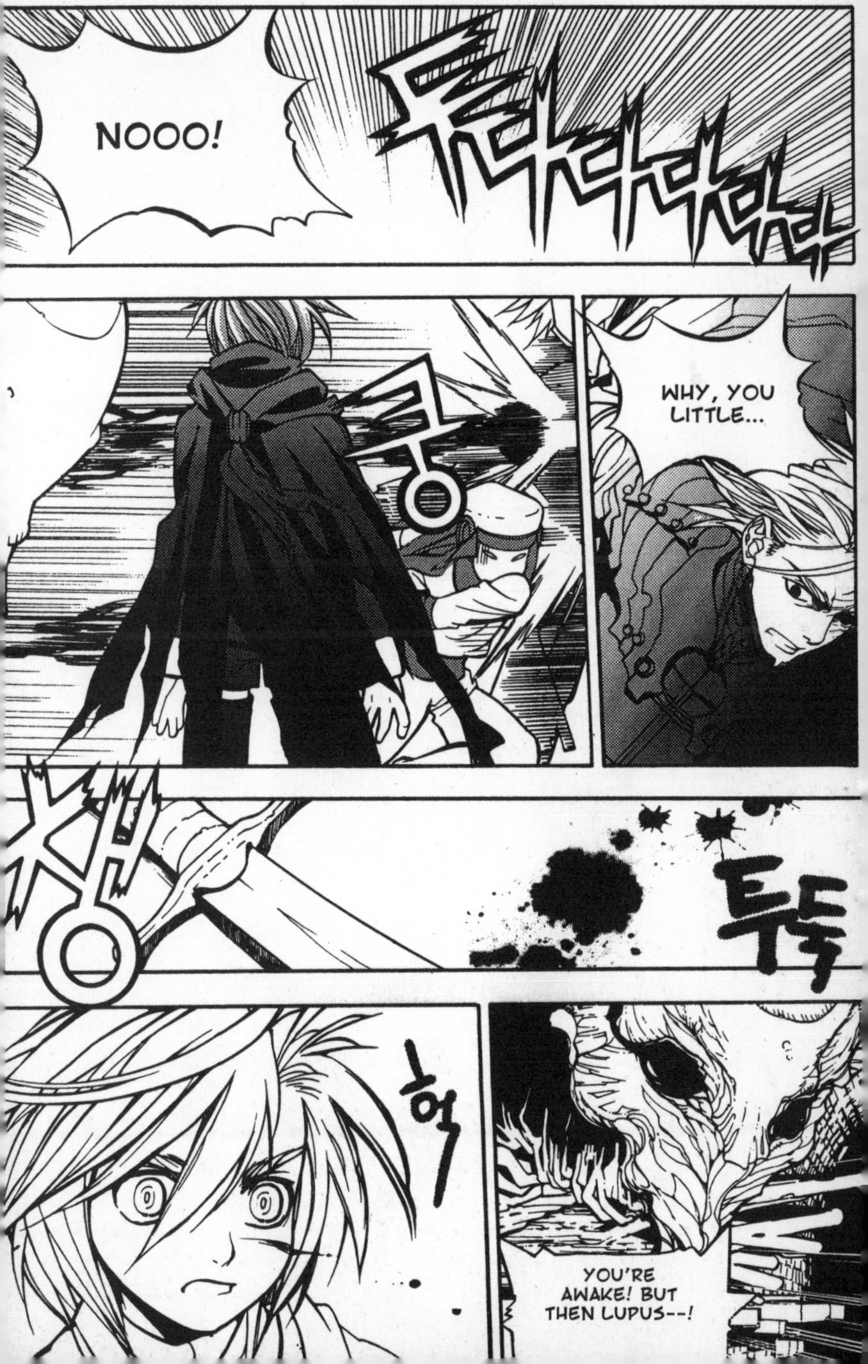
NOOO!
WHY, YOU LITTLE...
YOU'RE AWAKE! BUT THEN LUPUS--!

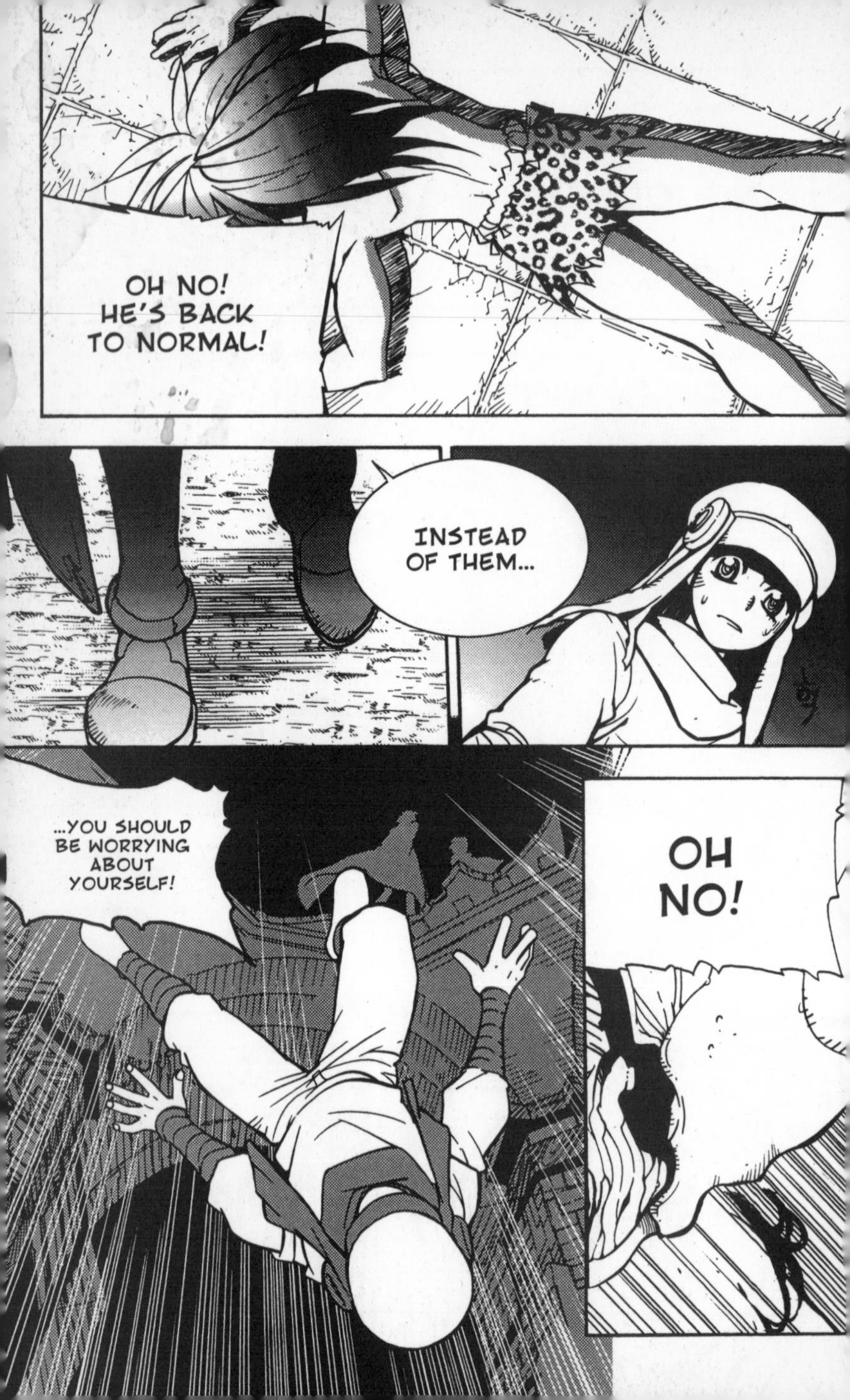
OH NO! HE'S BACK TO NORMAL!
INSTEAD OF THEM...
...YOU SHOULD BE WORRYING ABOUT YOURSELF!
OH NO!

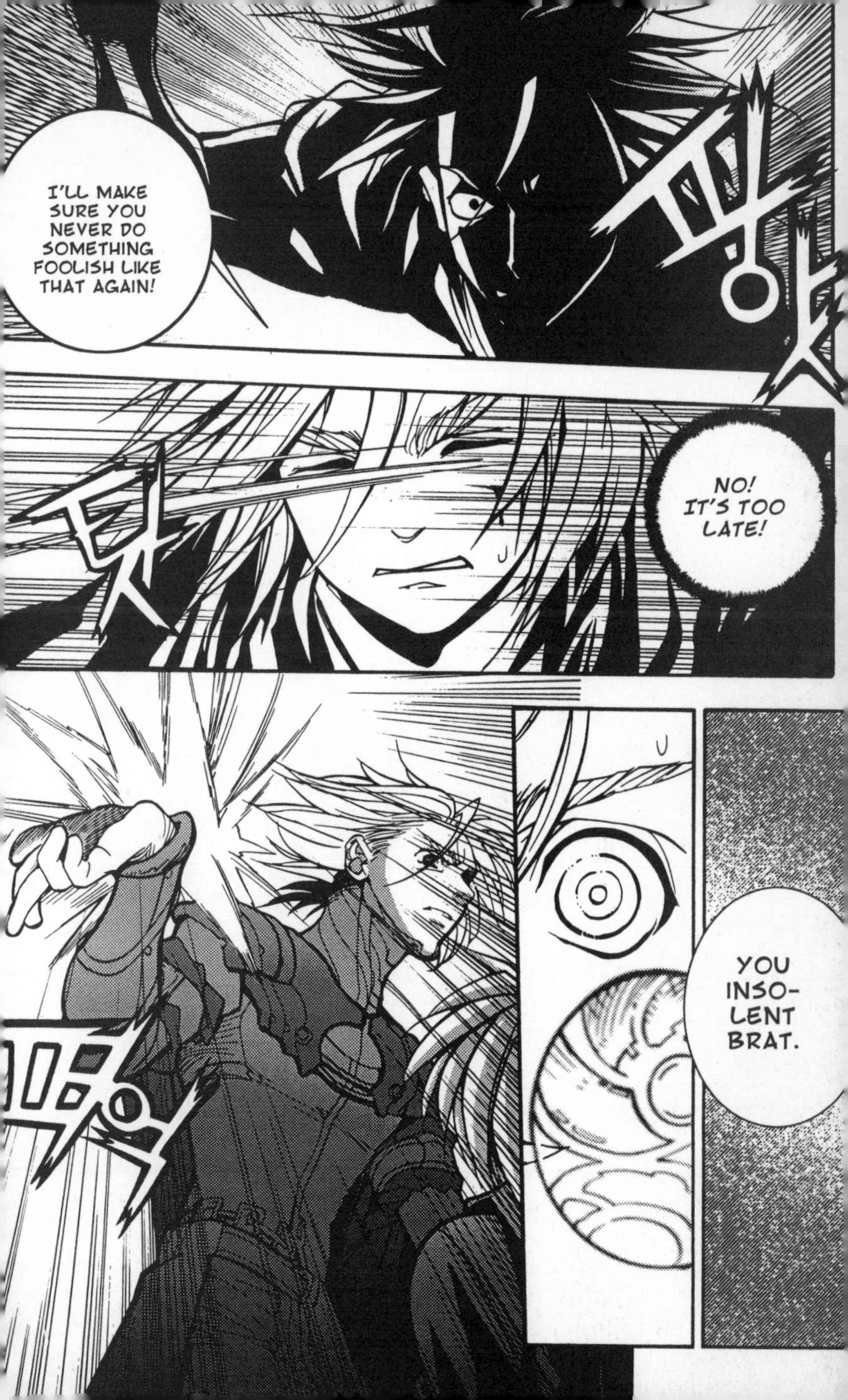
I'LL MAKE SURE YOU NEVER DO SOMETHING FOOLISH LIKE THAT AGAIN!
NO! IT'S TOO LATE!
YOU INSO-LENT BRAT.

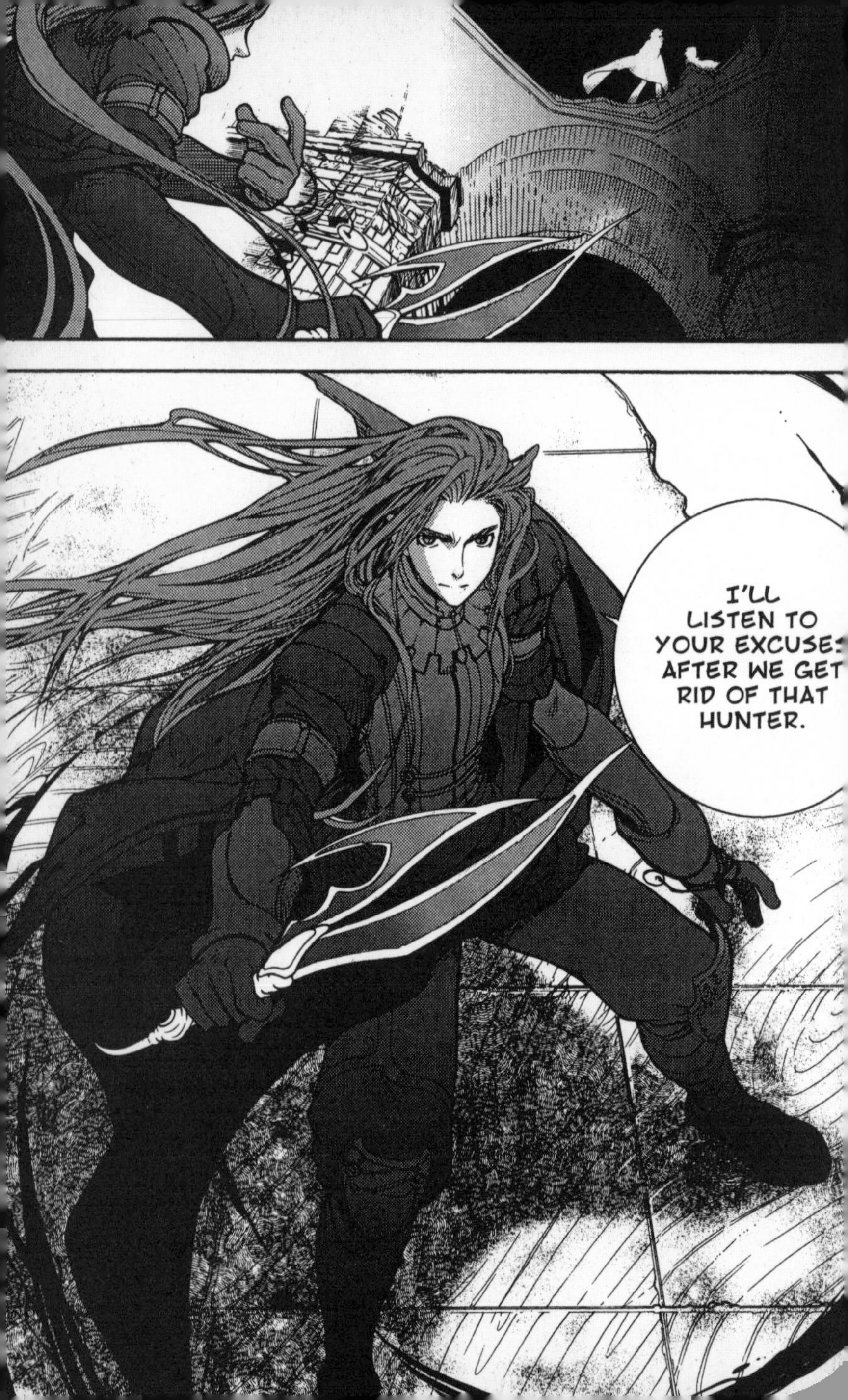
I'LL LISTEN TO YOUR EXCUSE AFTER WE GET RID OF THAT HUNTER.

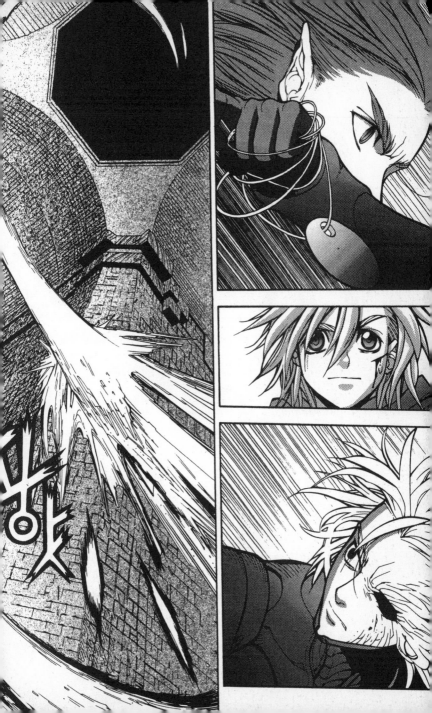

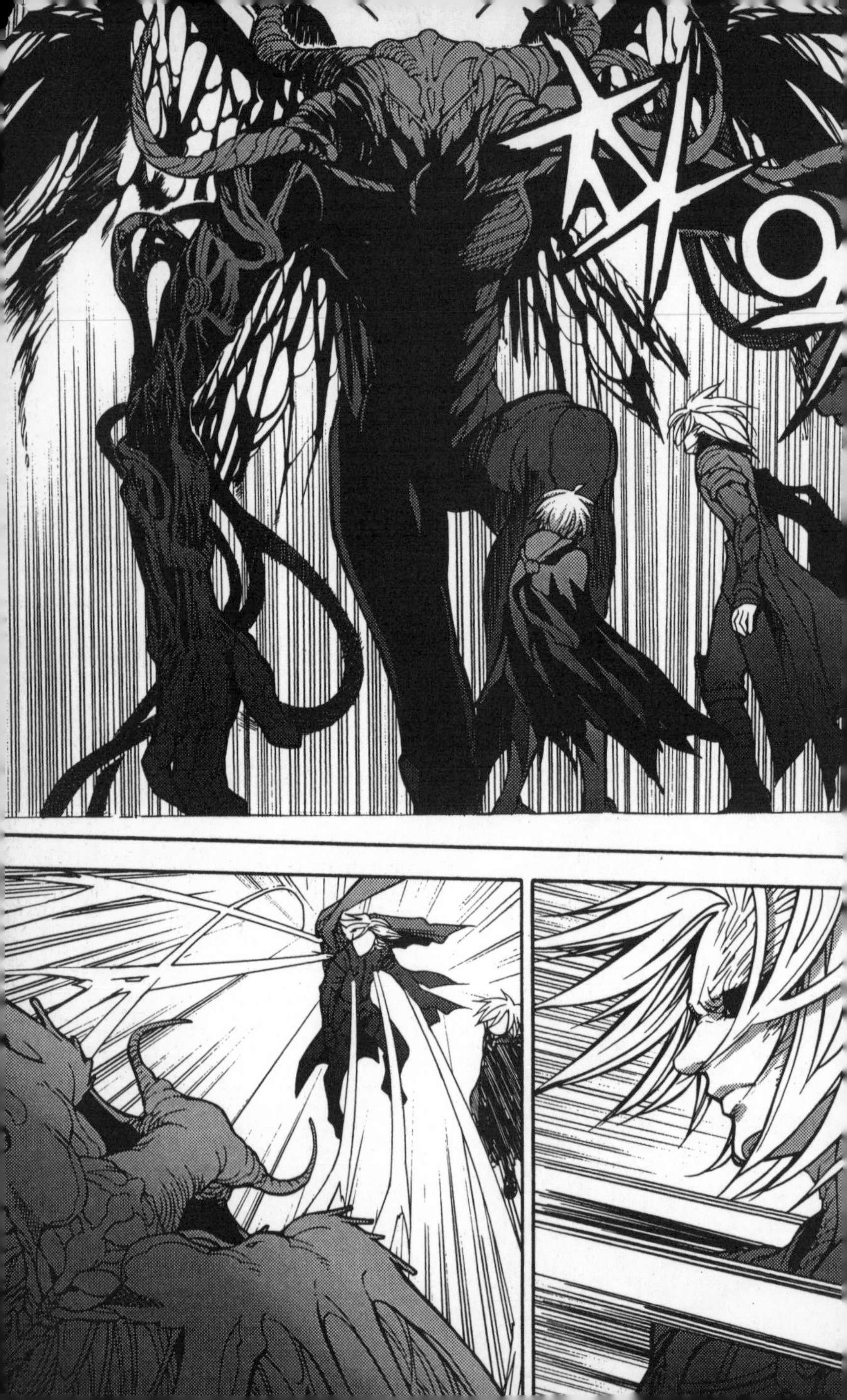

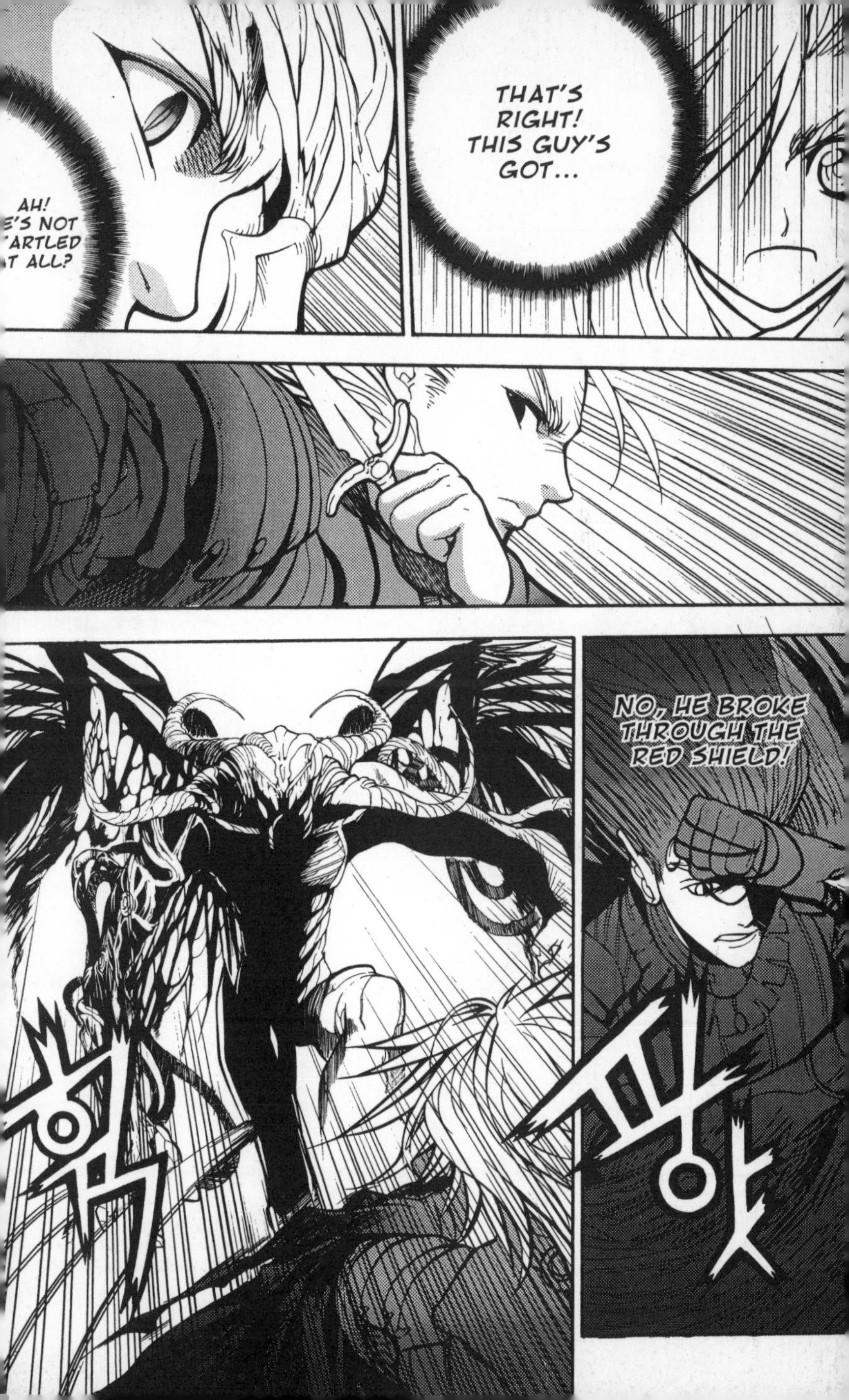
AH! E'S NOT ARTLED T ALL?
THAT'S RIGHT! THIS GUY'S GOT...
NO, HE BROKE THROUGH THE RED SHIELD!

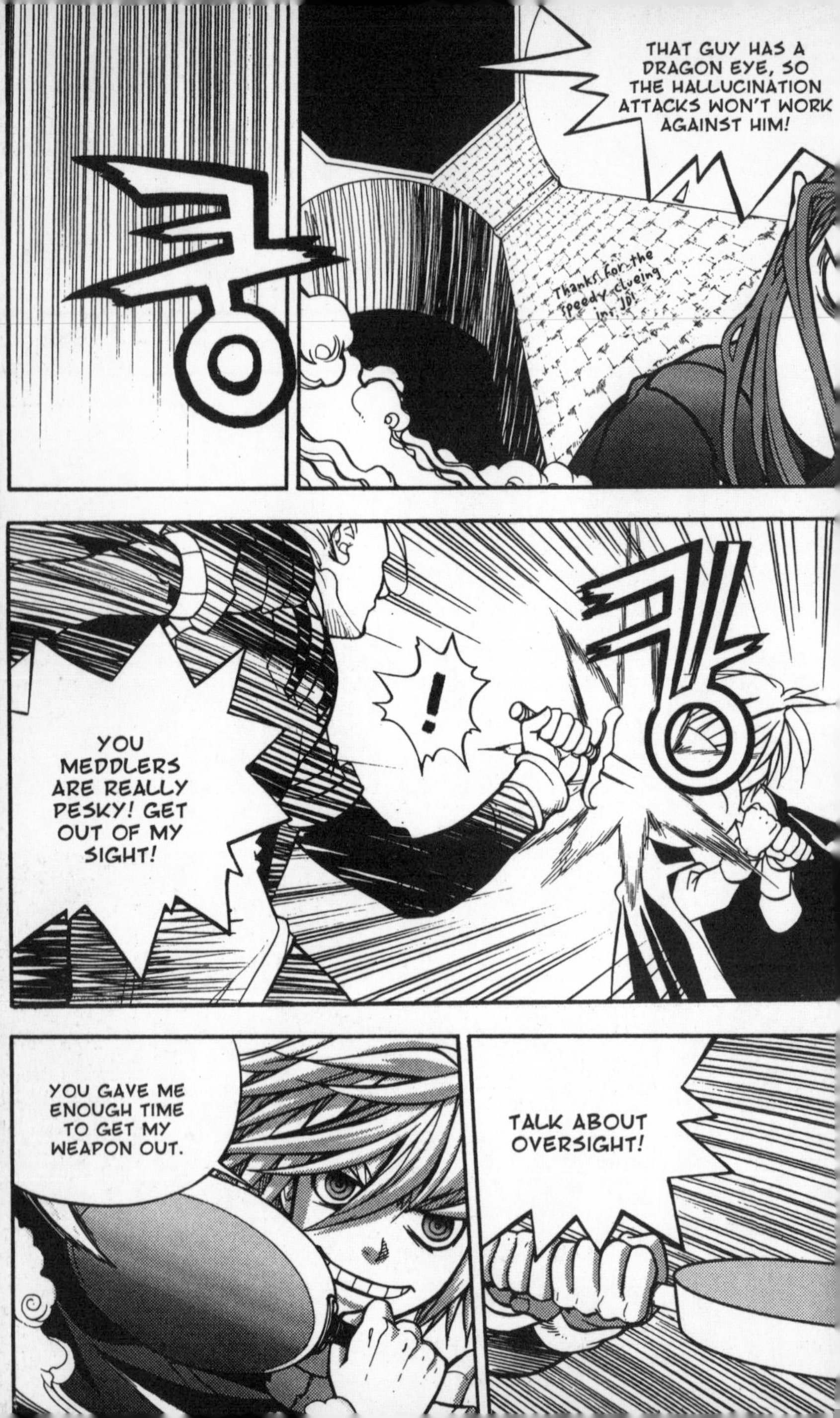
THAT GUY HAS A DRAGON EYE, SO THE HALLUCINATION ATTACKS WON'T WORK AGAINST HIM!
Thanks for the speedy clueing in, JD!
YOU MEDDLERS ARE REALLY PESKY! GET OUT OF MY SIGHT!
!
YOU GAVE ME ENOUGH TIME TO GET MY WEAPON OUT.
TALK ABOUT OVERSIGHT!

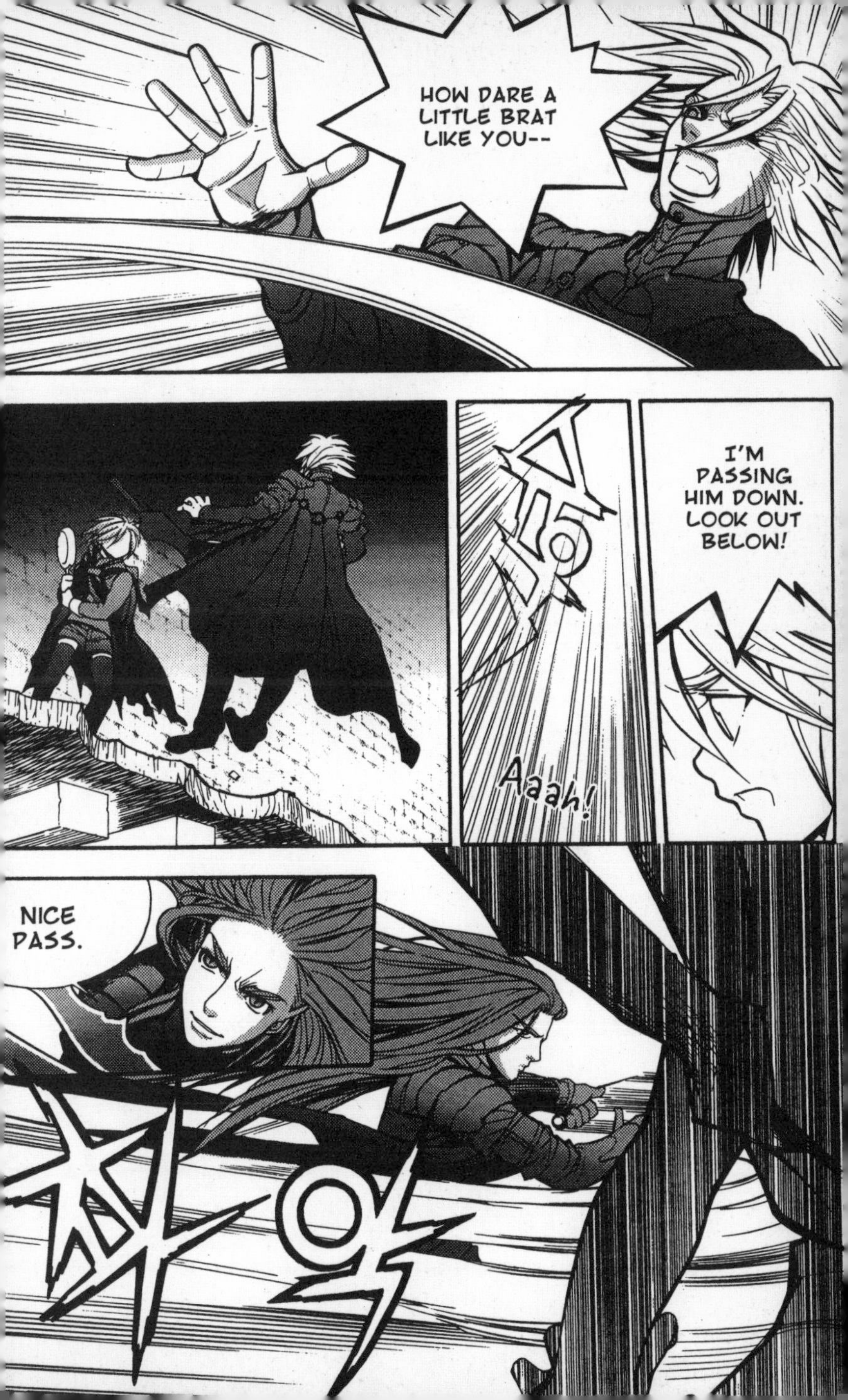
HOW DARE A LITTLE BRAT LIKE YOU--
Aaah!
I'M PASSING HIM DOWN. LOOK OUT BELOW!
NICE PASS.

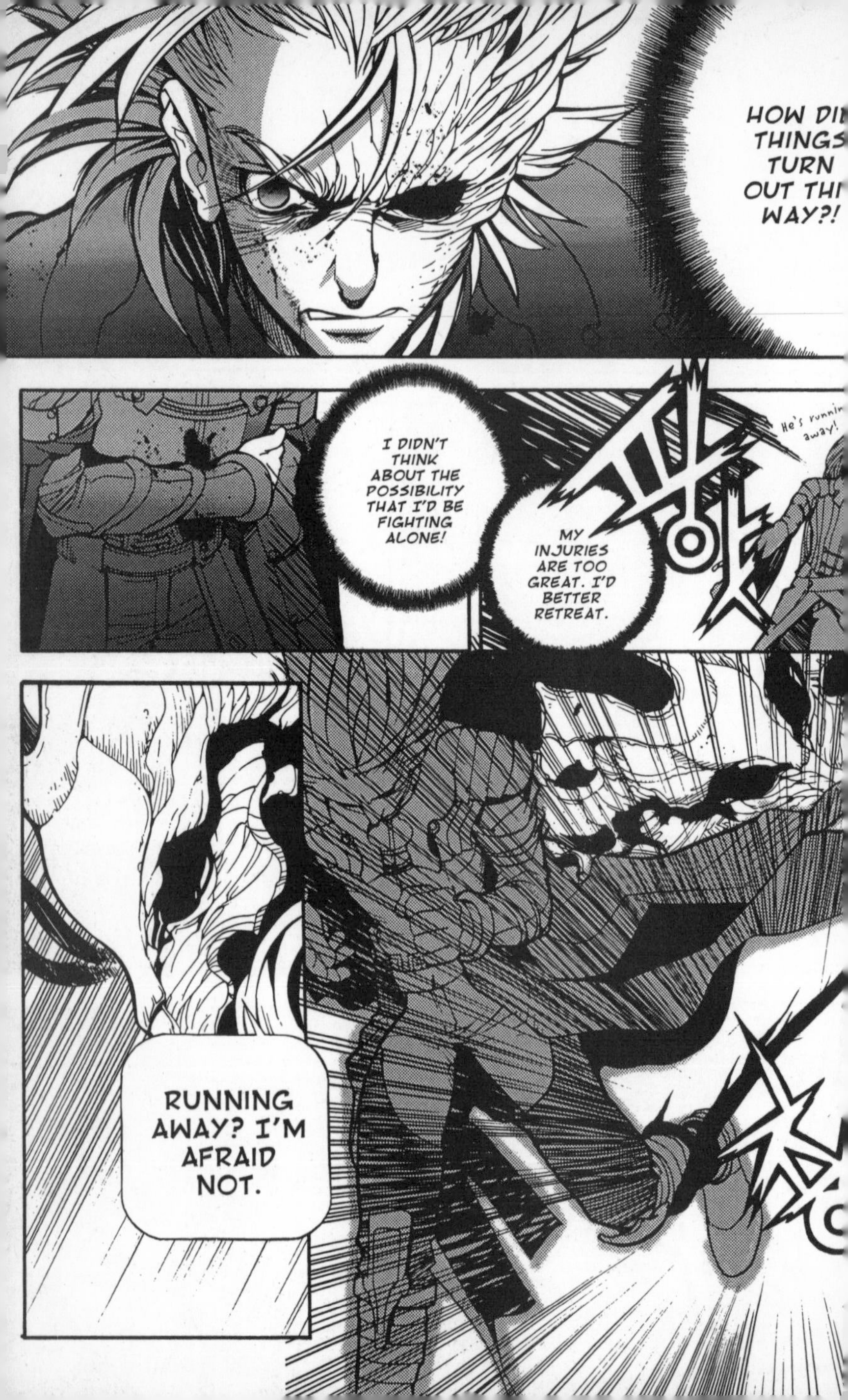
HOW DI THINGS TURN OUT THI WAY?!
I DIDN'T THINK ABOUT THE POSSIBILITY THAT I'D BE FIGHTING ALONE!
MY INJURIES ARE TOO GREAT. I'D BETTER RETREAT.
He's runnin away!
RUNNING AWAY? I'M AFRAID NOT.

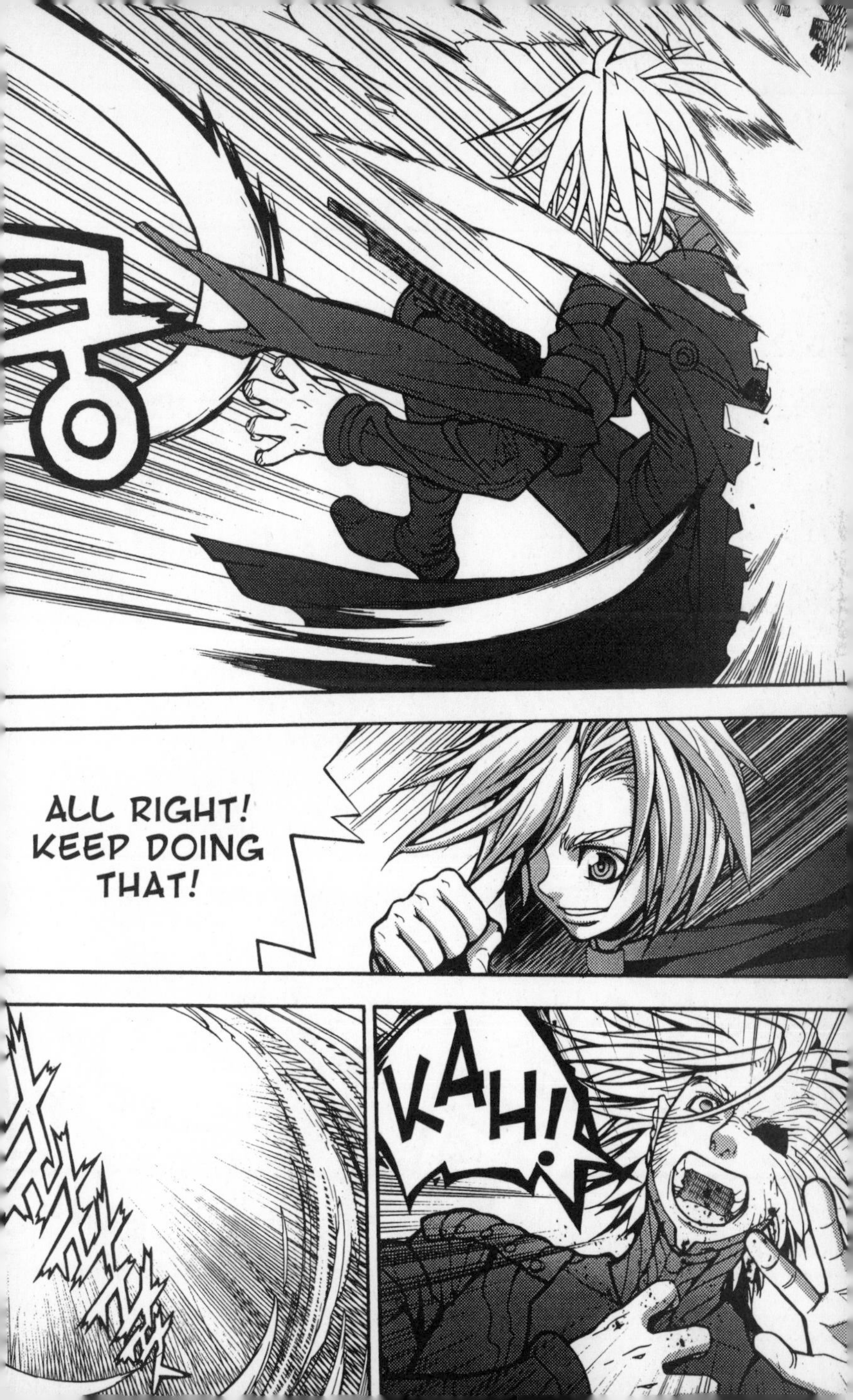
ALL RIGHT! KEEP DOING THAT!
KAHI!

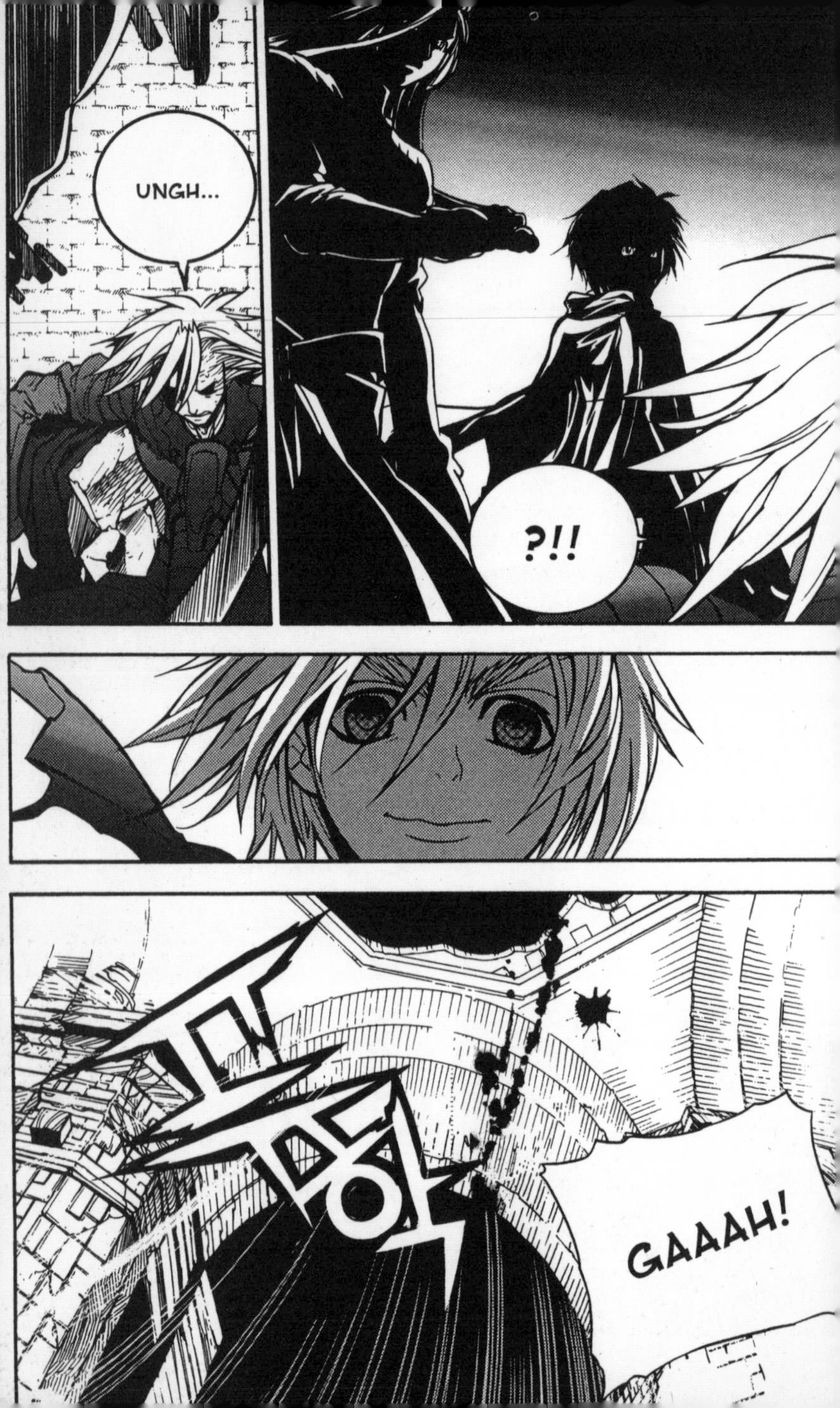
UNGH...
?!!
GAAAH!

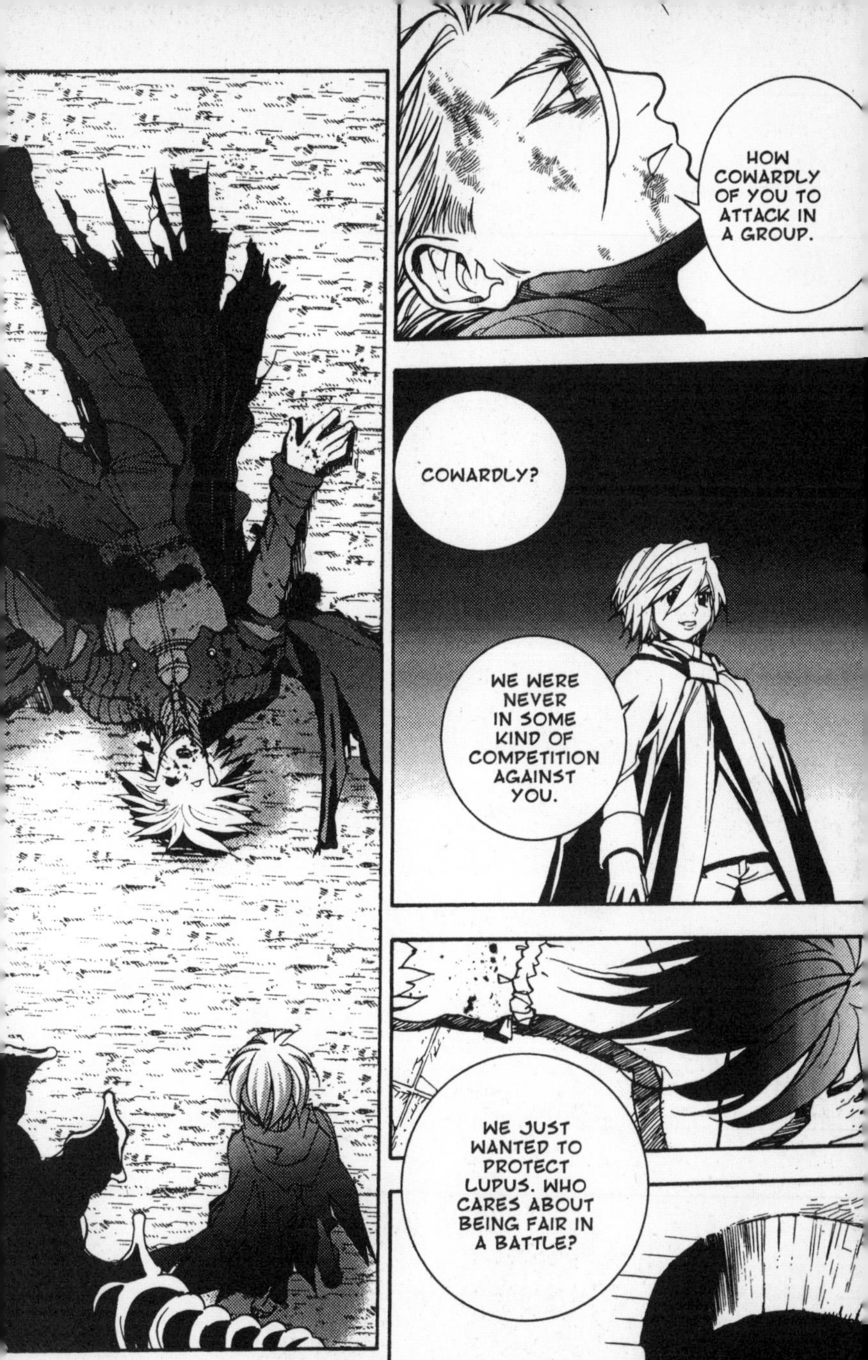
HOW COWARDLY OF YOU TO ATTACK IN A GROUP.
COWARDLY?
WE WERE NEVER IN SOME KIND OF COMPETITION AGAINST YOU.
WE JUST WANTED TO PROTECT LUPUS. WHO CARES ABOUT BEING FAIR IN A BATTLE?

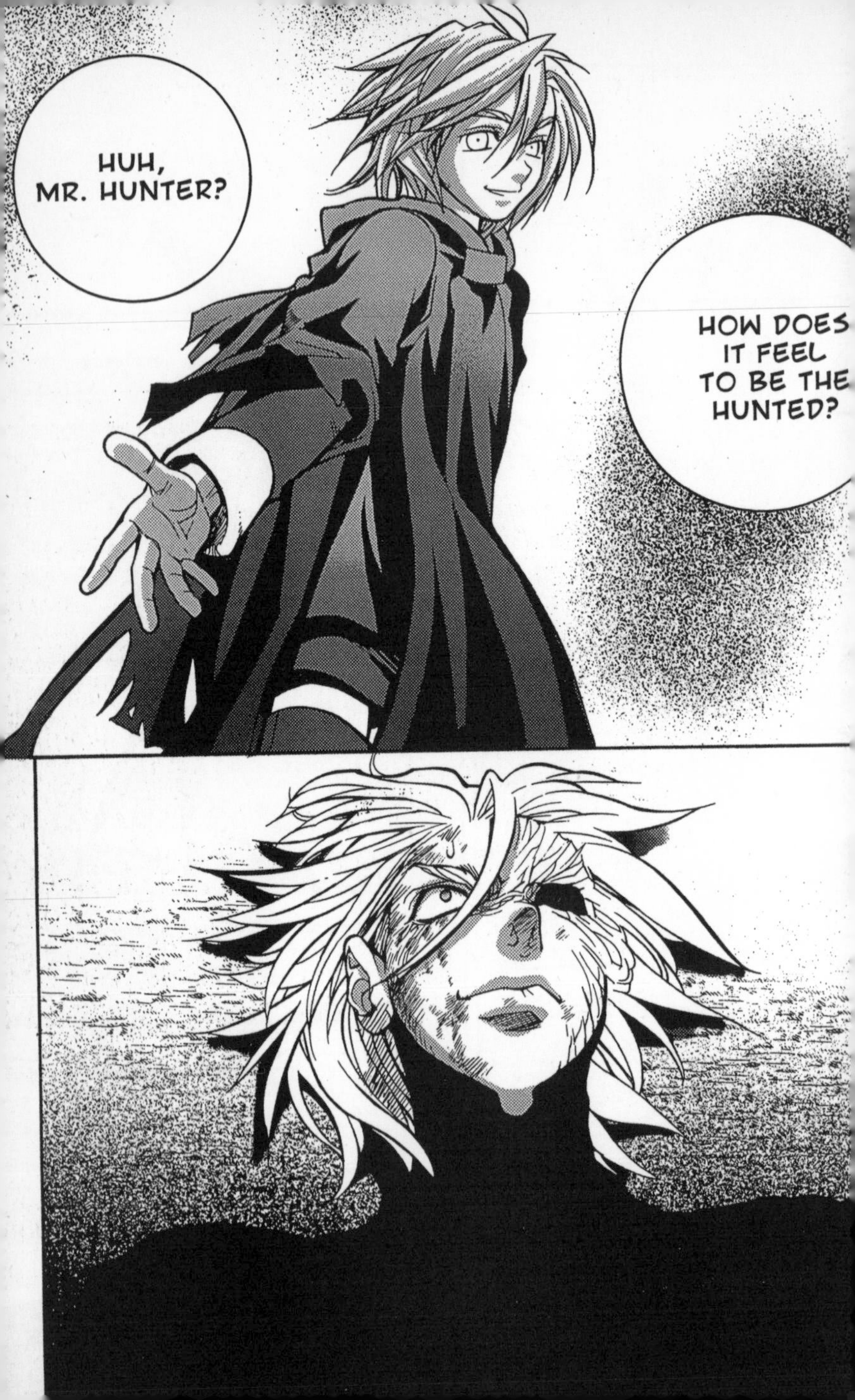
HUH, MR. HUNTER?
HOW DOES IT FEEL TO BE THE HUNTED?

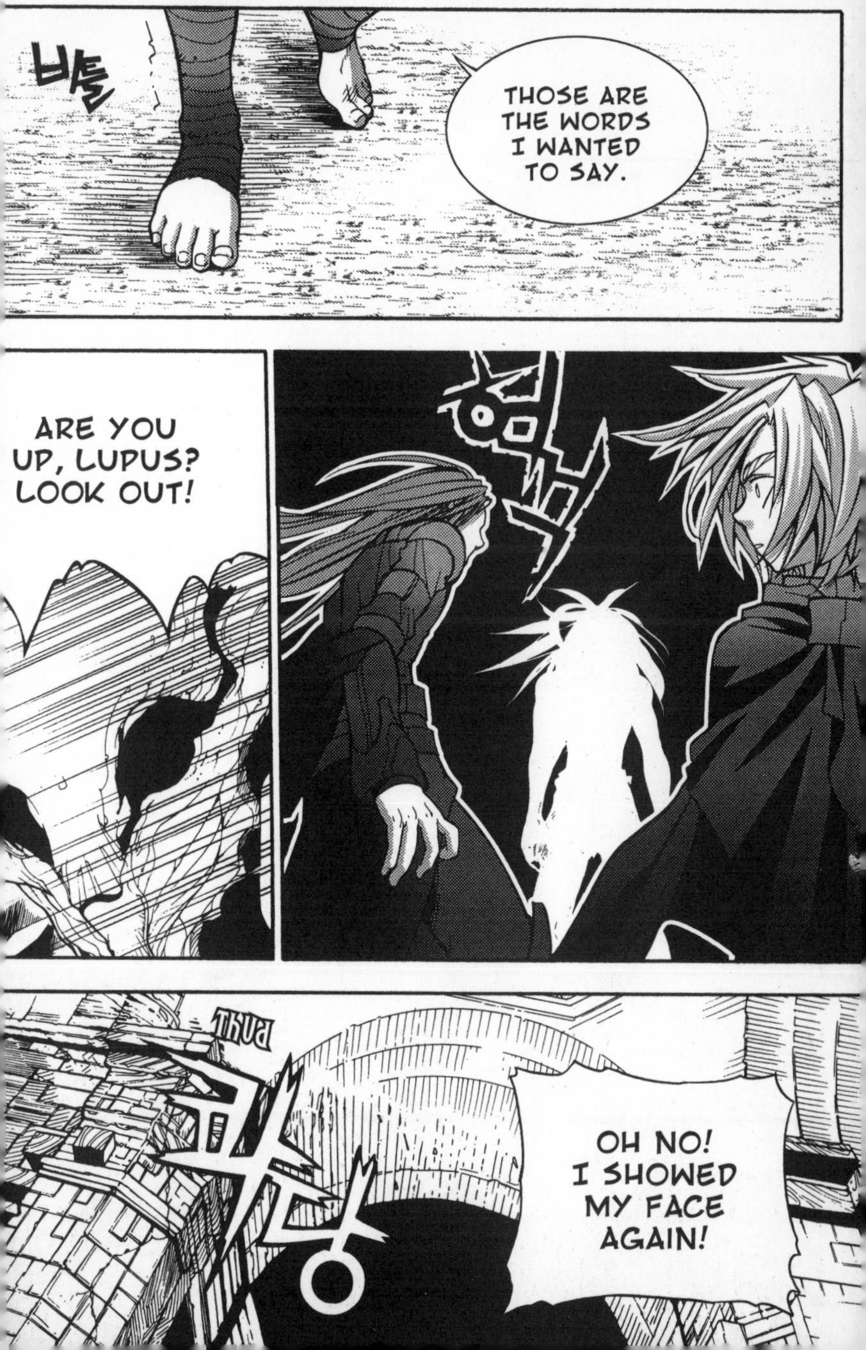
THOSE ARE THE WORDS I WANTED TO SAY.
ARE YOU UP, LUPUS? LOOK OUT!
OH NO! I SHOWED MY FACE AGAIN!

I'LL ASK YOU JUST ONE THING.

WHY DID YOU RAISE YOUR SWORD AGAINST LOYAL SERVANTS TO THE FOURTH WORLD?

WHY DID THE POWERS ABOVE KILL OFF MY FATHER?

SHEESH, YOU ANNOY ME 'TIL THE END. I'M A PUPPET, BUT THAT MEANS NOTHING TO ME.

I DON'T CARE ABOUT ALL THAT STUFF, AND I DIDN'T AIM TO GO AFTER YOUR FATHER.

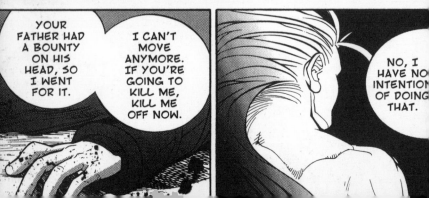

YOUR FATHER HAD A BOUNTY ON HIS HEAD, SO I WENT FOR IT.

I CAN'T MOVE ANYMORE. IF YOU'RE GOING TO KILL ME, KILL ME OFF NOW.

NO, I HAVE NO INTENTION OF DOING THAT.

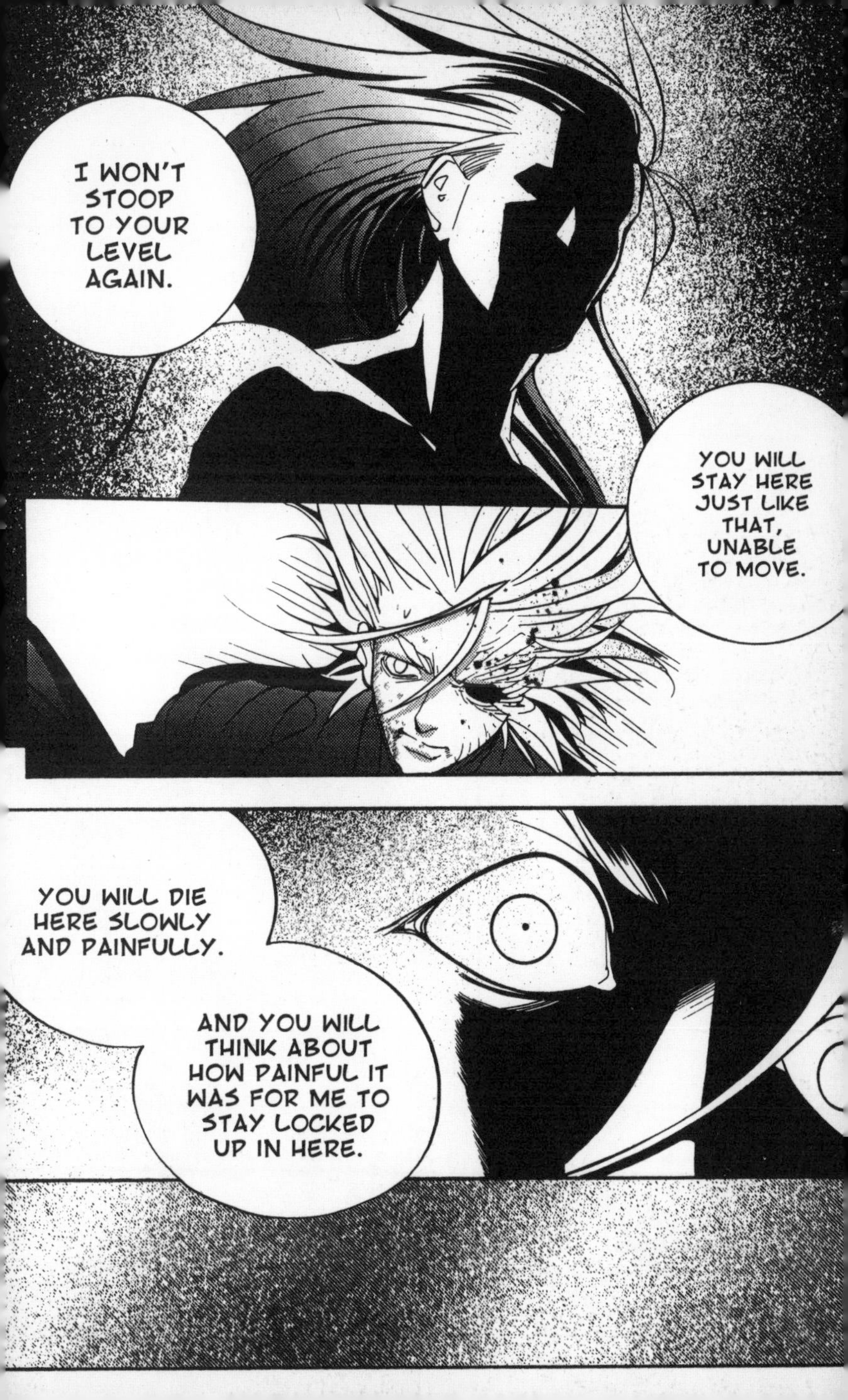
I WON'T STOOP TO YOUR LEVEL AGAIN.
YOU WILL STAY HERE JUST LIKE THAT, UNABLE TO MOVE.
YOU WILL DIE HERE SLOWLY AND PAINFULLY.
AND YOU WILL THINK ABOUT HOW PAINFUL IT WAS FOR ME TO STAY LOCKED UP IN HERE.

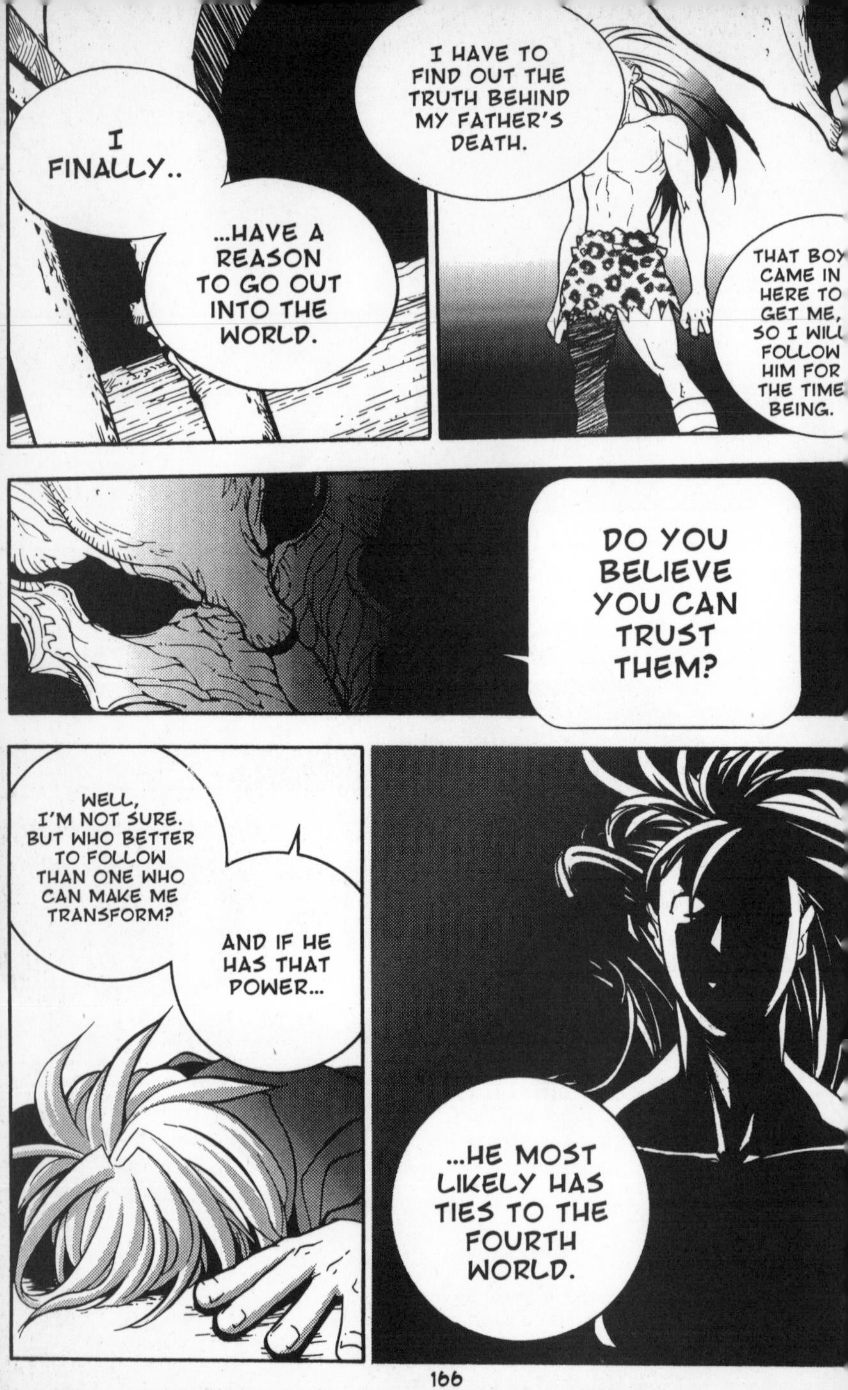
I FINALLY..
...HAVE A REASON TO GO OUT INTO THE WORLD.
I HAVE TO FIND OUT THE TRUTH BEHIND MY FATHER'S DEATH.
THAT BOY CAME IN HERE TO GET ME, SO I WILL FOLLOW HIM FOR THE TIME BEING.
DO YOU BELIEVE YOU CAN TRUST THEM?
WELL, I'M NOT SURE. BUT WHO BETTER TO FOLLOW THAN ONE WHO CAN MAKE ME TRANSFORM?
AND IF HE HAS THAT POWER...
...HE MOST LIKELY HAS TIES TO THE FOURTH WORLD.

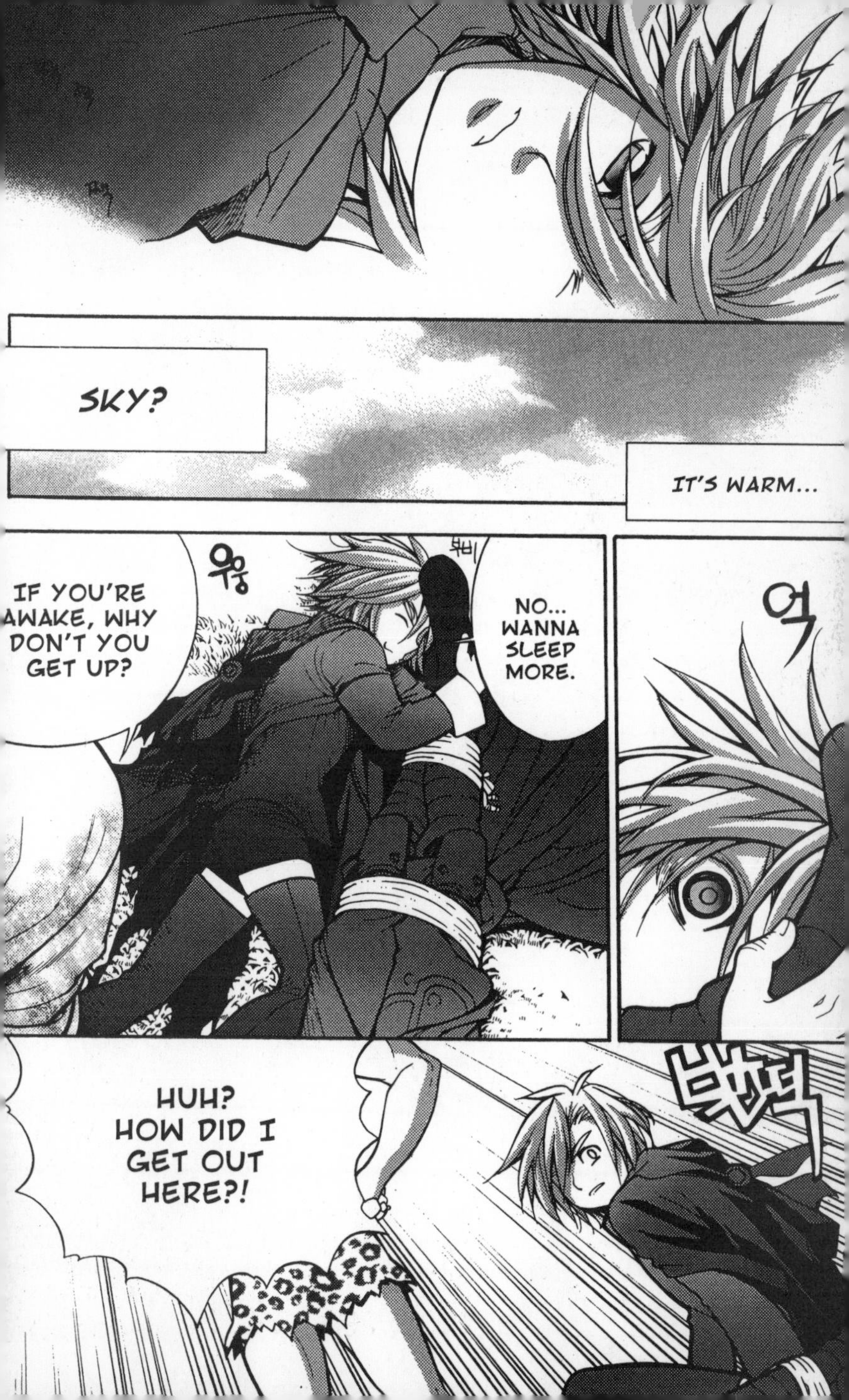
SKY?
IT'S WARM...
우웅
IF YOU'RE AWAKE, WHY DON'T YOU GET UP?
NO... WANNA SLEEP MORE.
억
HUH? HOW DID I GET OUT HERE?!

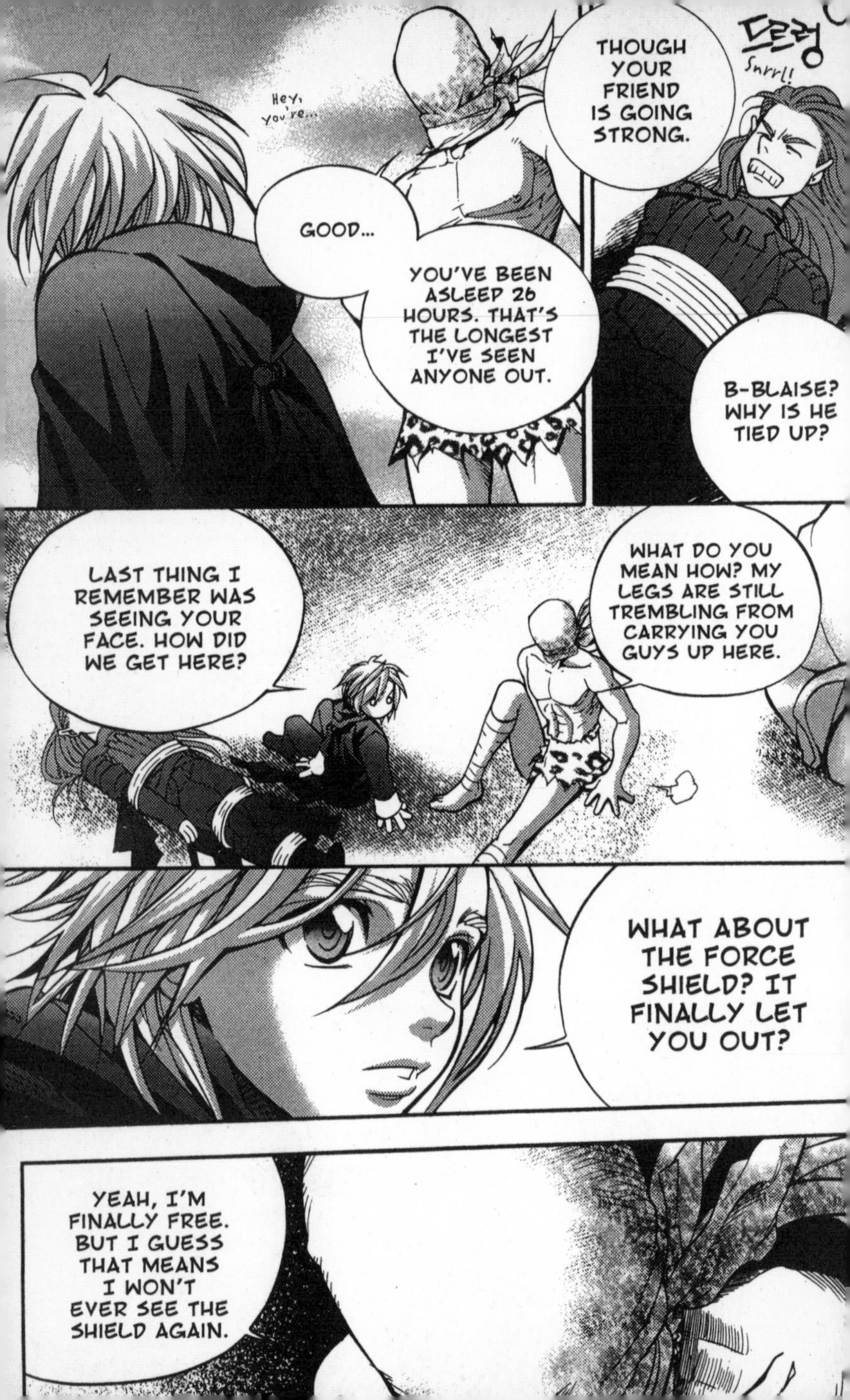
Hey, you're...
GOOD...
YOU'VE BEEN ASLEEP 26 HOURS. THAT'S THE LONGEST I'VE SEEN ANYONE OUT.
THOUGH YOUR FRIEND IS GOING STRONG.
드르렁
Snrrl!
B-BLAISE? WHY IS HE TIED UP?
LAST THING I REMEMBER WAS SEEING YOUR FACE. HOW DID WE GET HERE?
WHAT DO YOU MEAN HOW? MY LEGS ARE STILL TREMBLING FROM CARRYING YOU GUYS UP HERE.
WHAT ABOUT THE FORCE SHIELD? IT FINALLY LET YOU OUT?
YEAH, I'M FINALLY FREE. BUT I GUESS THAT MEANS I WON'T EVER SEE THE SHIELD AGAIN.

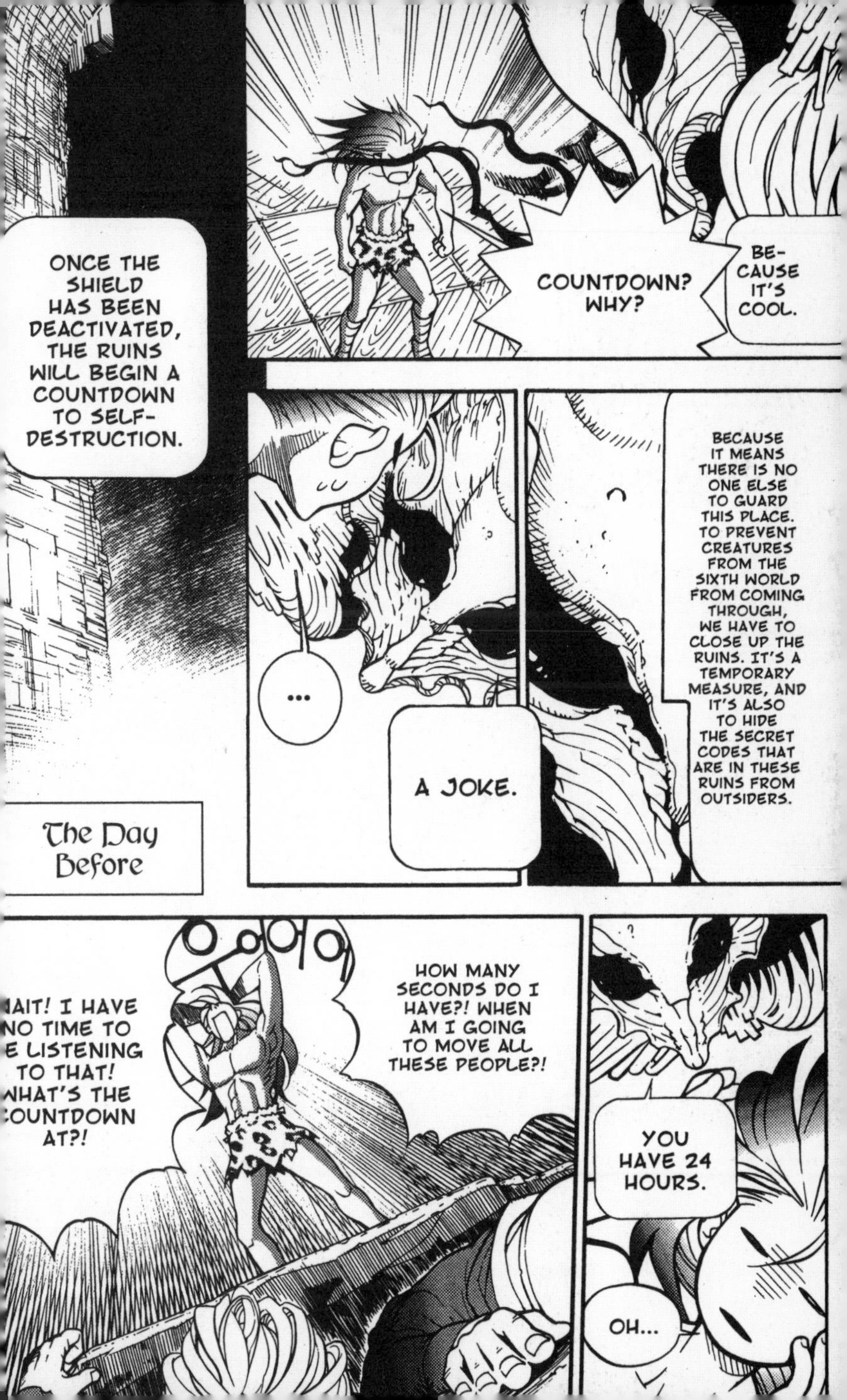

ONCE THE SHIELD HAS BEEN DEACTIVATED, THE RUINS WILL BEGIN A COUNTDOWN TO SELF-DESTRUCTION.
The Day Before
COUNTDOWN? WHY?
BE-CAUSE IT'S COOL.
...
A JOKE.
BECAUSE IT MEANS THERE IS NO ONE ELSE TO GUARD THIS PLACE. TO PREVENT CREATURES FROM THE SIXTH WORLD FROM COMING THROUGH, WE HAVE TO CLOSE UP THE RUINS. IT'S A TEMPORARY MEASURE, AND IT'S ALSO TO HIDE THE SECRET CODES THAT ARE IN THESE RUINS FROM OUTSIDERS.
AIT! I HAVE NO TIME TO E LISTENING TO THAT! HAT'S THE OUNTDOWN AT?!
HOW MANY SECONDS DO I HAVE?! WHEN AM I GOING TO MOVE ALL THESE PEOPLE?!
YOU HAVE 24 HOURS.
OH...

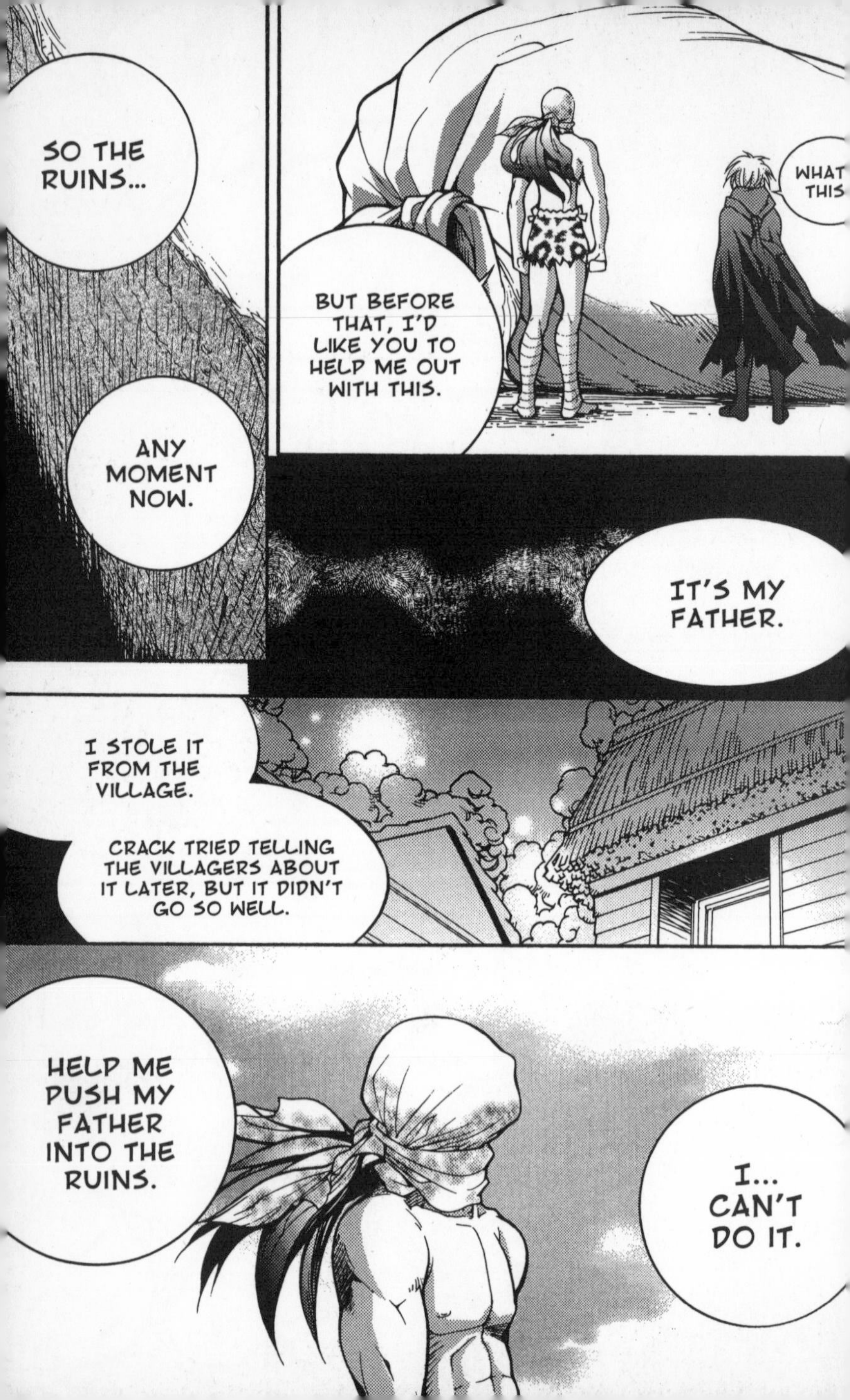
SO THE RUINS...
ANY MOMENT NOW.
WHAT THIS
BUT BEFORE THAT, I'D LIKE YOU TO HELP ME OUT WITH THIS.
IT'S MY FATHER.
I STOLE IT FROM THE VILLAGE.
CRACK TRIED TELLING THE VILLAGERS ABOUT IT LATER, BUT IT DIDN'T GO SO WELL.
HELP ME PUSH MY FATHER INTO THE RUINS.
I... CAN'T DO IT.

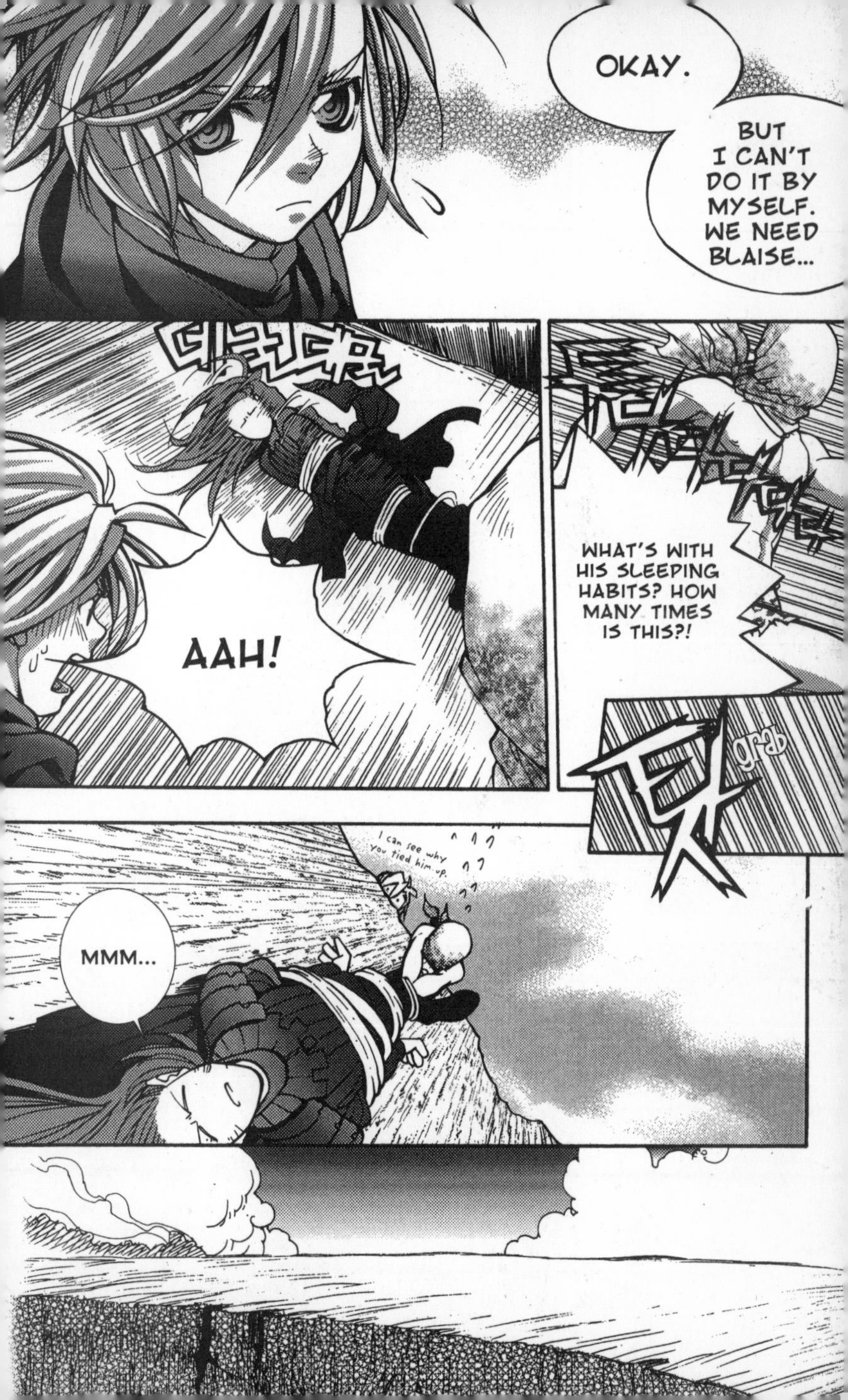
OKAY.
BUT I CAN'T DO IT BY MYSELF. WE NEED BLAISE...
AAH!
WHAT'S WITH HIS SLEEPING HABITS? HOW MANY TIMES IS THIS?!
grab
I can see why you tied him up.
MMM...

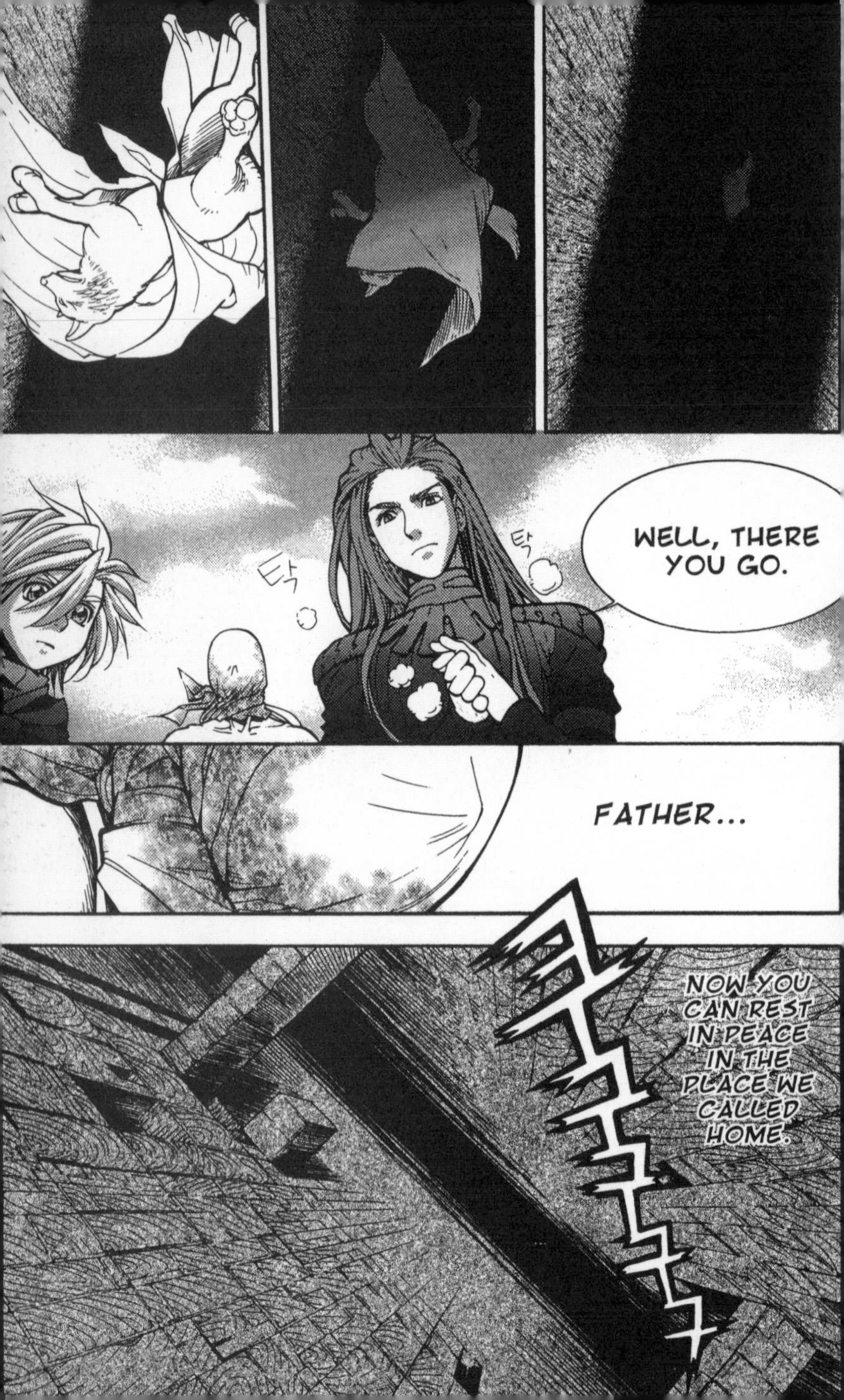
탁
탁
WELL, THERE YOU GO.
FATHER...
NOW YOU CAN REST IN PEACE IN THE PLACE WE CALLED HOME.

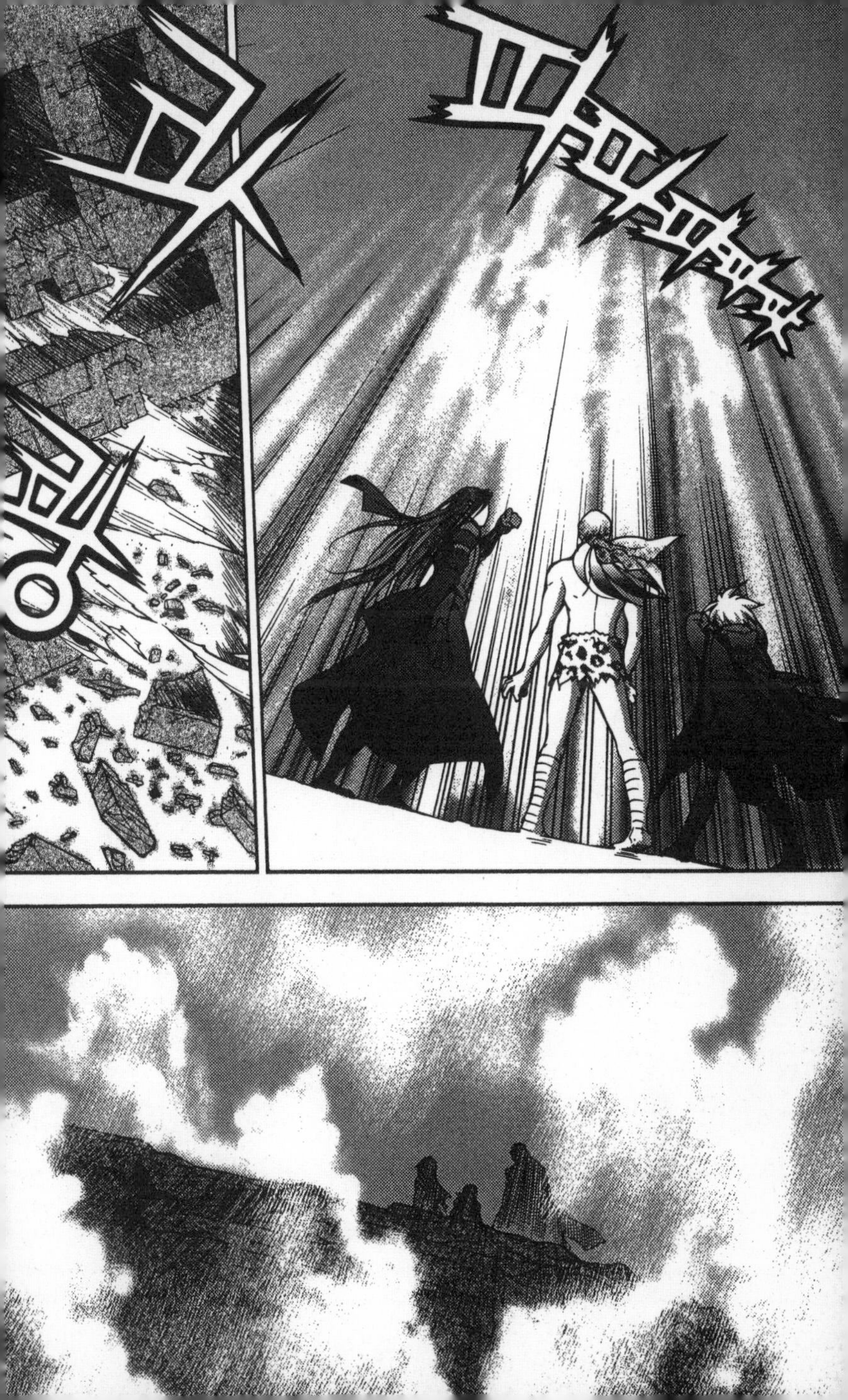

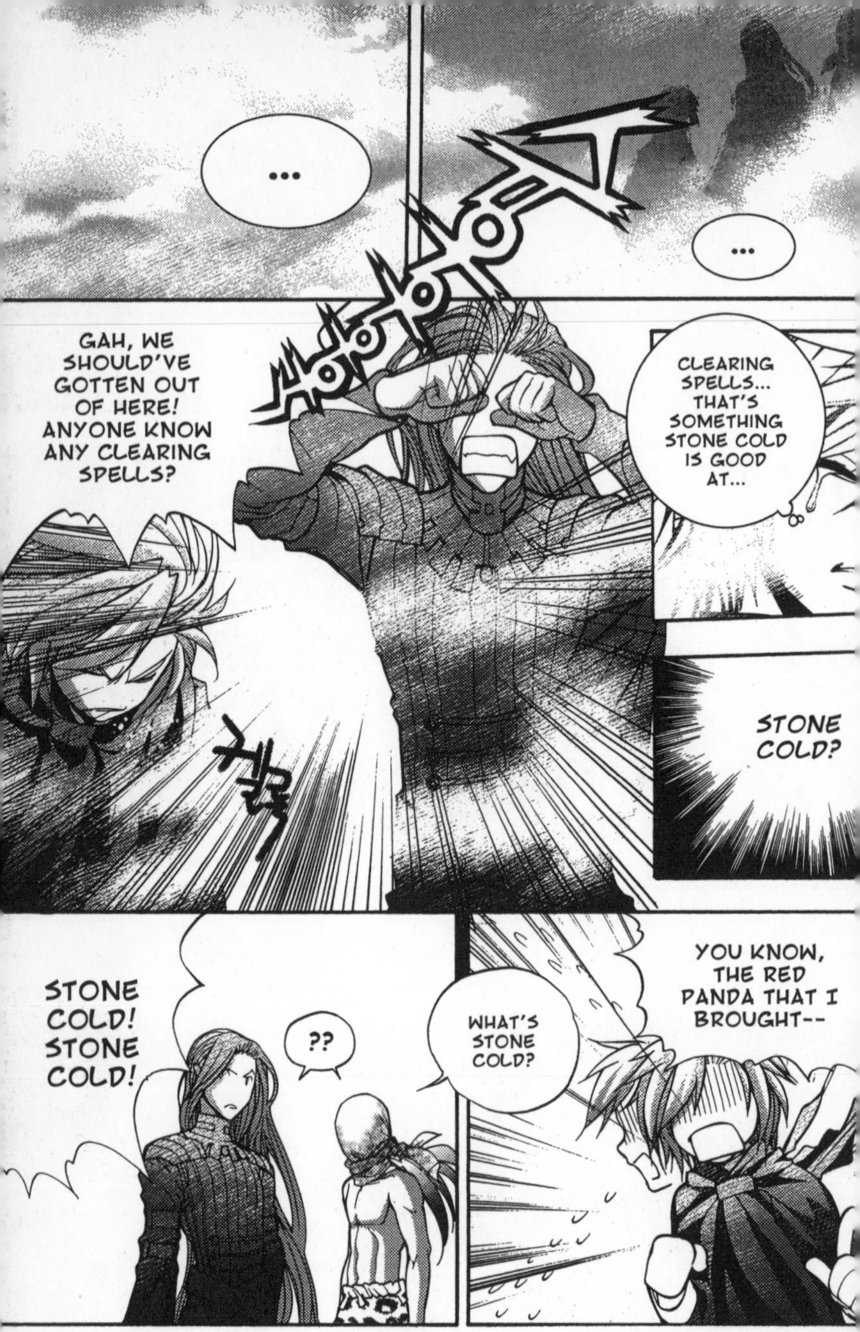
...
...
GAH, WE SHOULD'VE GOTTEN OUT OF HERE! ANYONE KNOW ANY CLEARING SPELLS?
CLEARING SPELLS... THAT'S SOMETHING STONE COLD IS GOOD AT...
STONE COLD?
STONE COLD! STONE COLD!
??
WHAT'S STONE COLD?
YOU KNOW, THE RED PANDA THAT I BROUGHT--

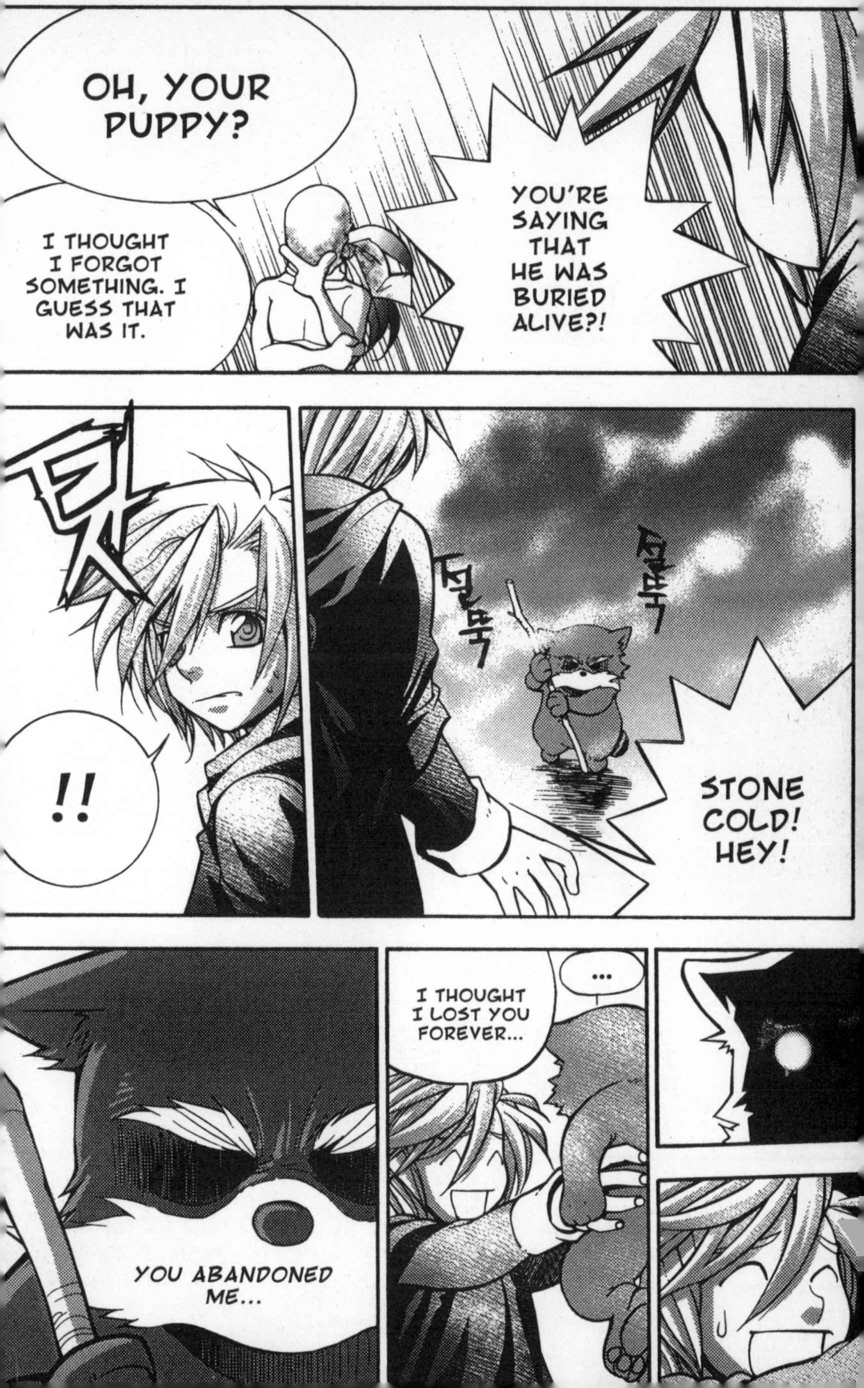
OH, YOUR PUPPY?
I THOUGHT I FORGOT SOMETHING. I GUESS THAT WAS IT.
YOU'RE SAYING THAT HE WAS BURIED ALIVE?!
!!
STONE COLD! HEY!
YOU ABANDONED ME...
I THOUGHT I LOST YOU FOREVER...
...

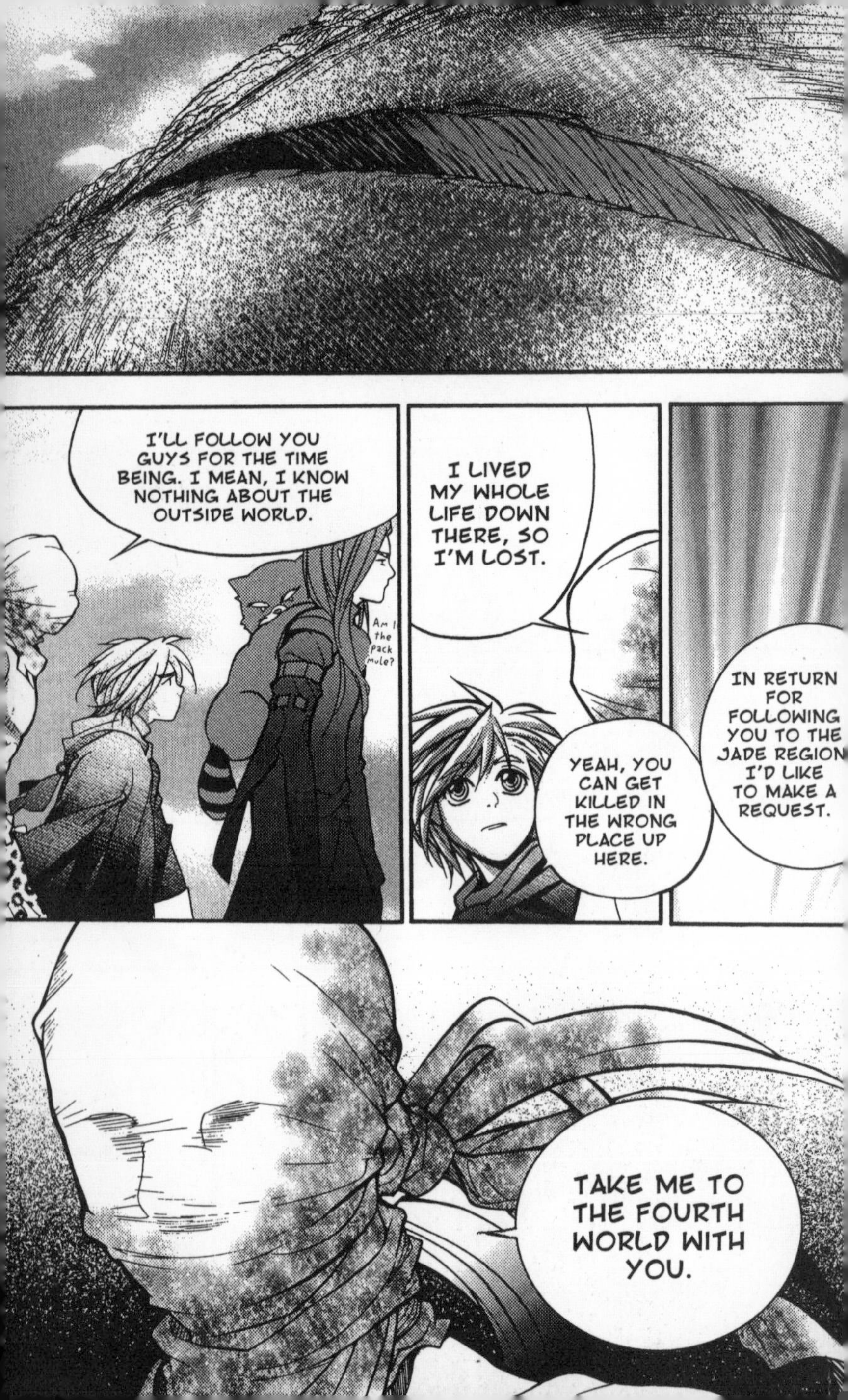
I'LL FOLLOW YOU GUYS FOR THE TIME BEING. I MEAN, I KNOW NOTHING ABOUT THE OUTSIDE WORLD.
Am I the pack mule?
I LIVED MY WHOLE LIFE DOWN THERE, SO I'M LOST.
YEAH, YOU CAN GET KILLED IN THE WRONG PLACE UP HERE.
IN RETURN FOR FOLLOWING YOU TO THE JADE REGION I'D LIKE TO MAKE A REQUEST.
TAKE ME TO THE FOURTH WORLD WITH YOU.

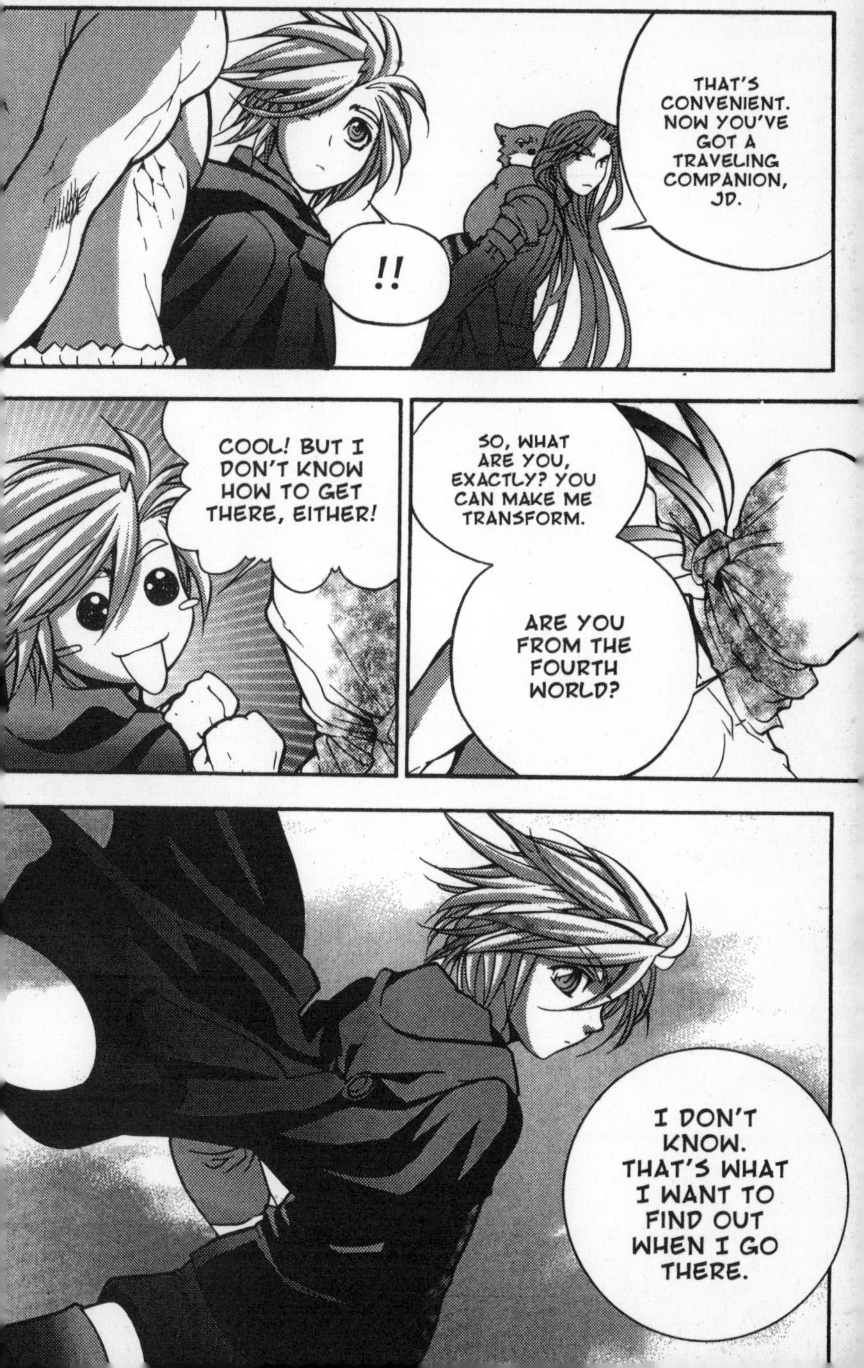
!!
THAT'S CONVENIENT. NOW YOU'VE GOT A TRAVELING COMPANION, JD.
COOL! BUT I DON'T KNOW HOW TO GET THERE, EITHER!
SO, WHAT ARE YOU, EXACTLY? YOU CAN MAKE ME TRANSFORM.
ARE YOU FROM THE FOURTH WORLD?
I DON'T KNOW. THAT'S WHAT I WANT TO FIND OUT WHEN I GO THERE.

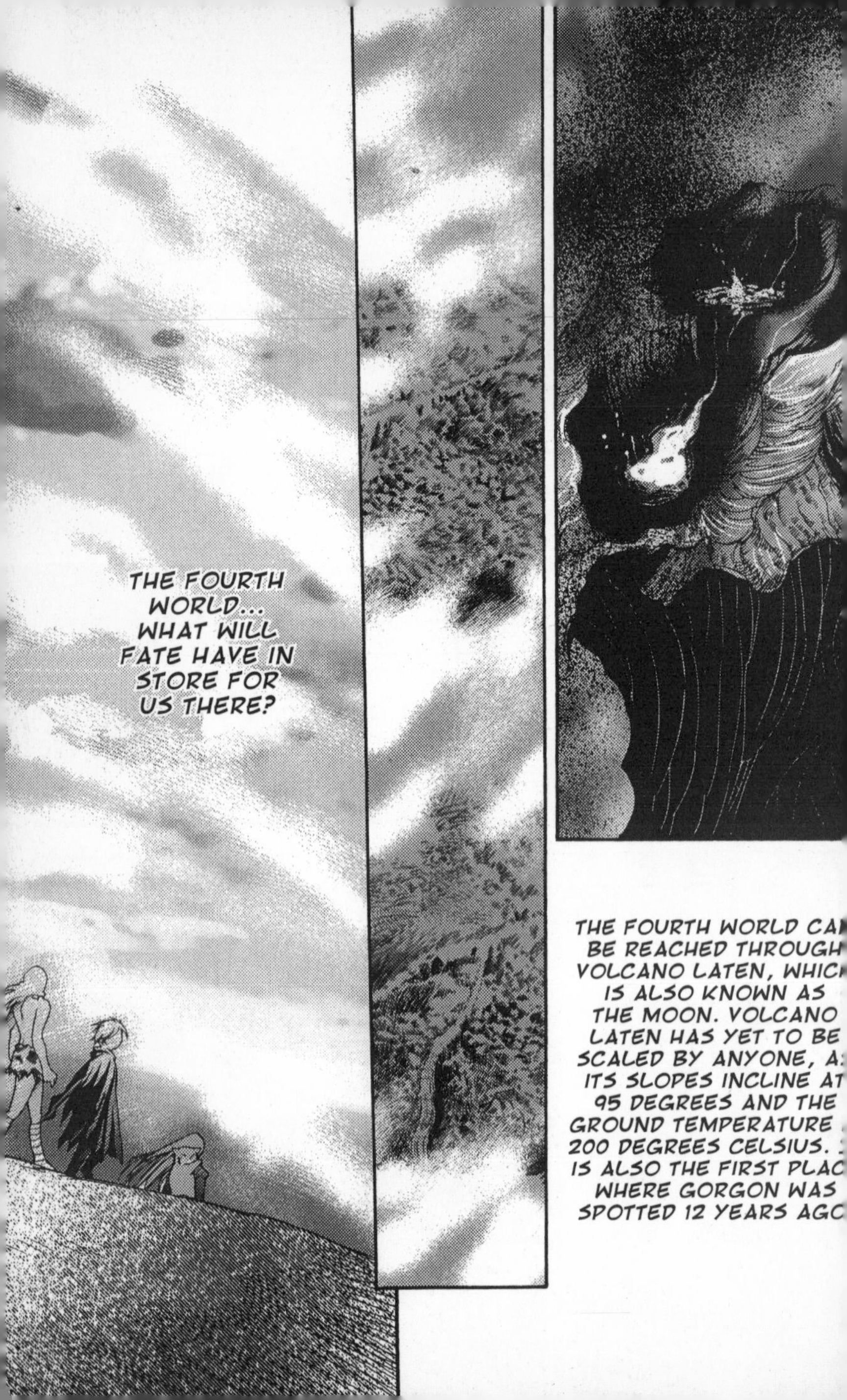
THE FOURTH WORLD... WHAT WILL FATE HAVE IN STORE FOR US THERE?
THE FOURTH WORLD CA BE REACHED THROUGH VOLCANO LATEN, WHIC IS ALSO KNOWN AS THE MOON. VOLCANO LATEN HAS YET TO BE SCALED BY ANYONE, A ITS SLOPES INCLINE AT 95 DEGREES AND THE GROUND TEMPERATURE 200 DEGREES CELSIUS. IS ALSO THE FIRST PLAC WHERE GORGON WAS SPOTTED 12 YEARS AGO

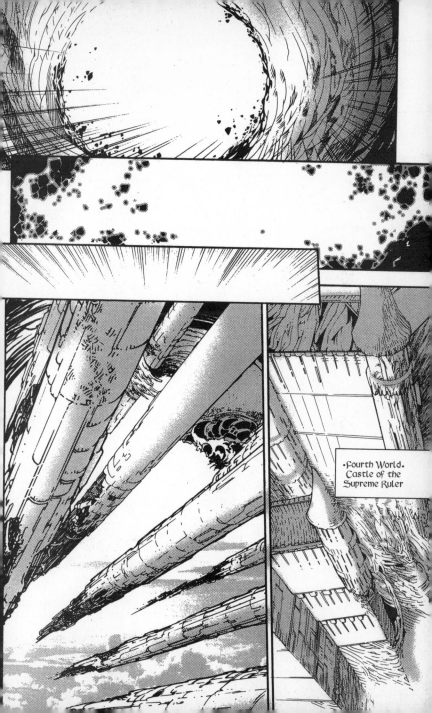

•Fourth World•
Castle of the
Supreme Ruler

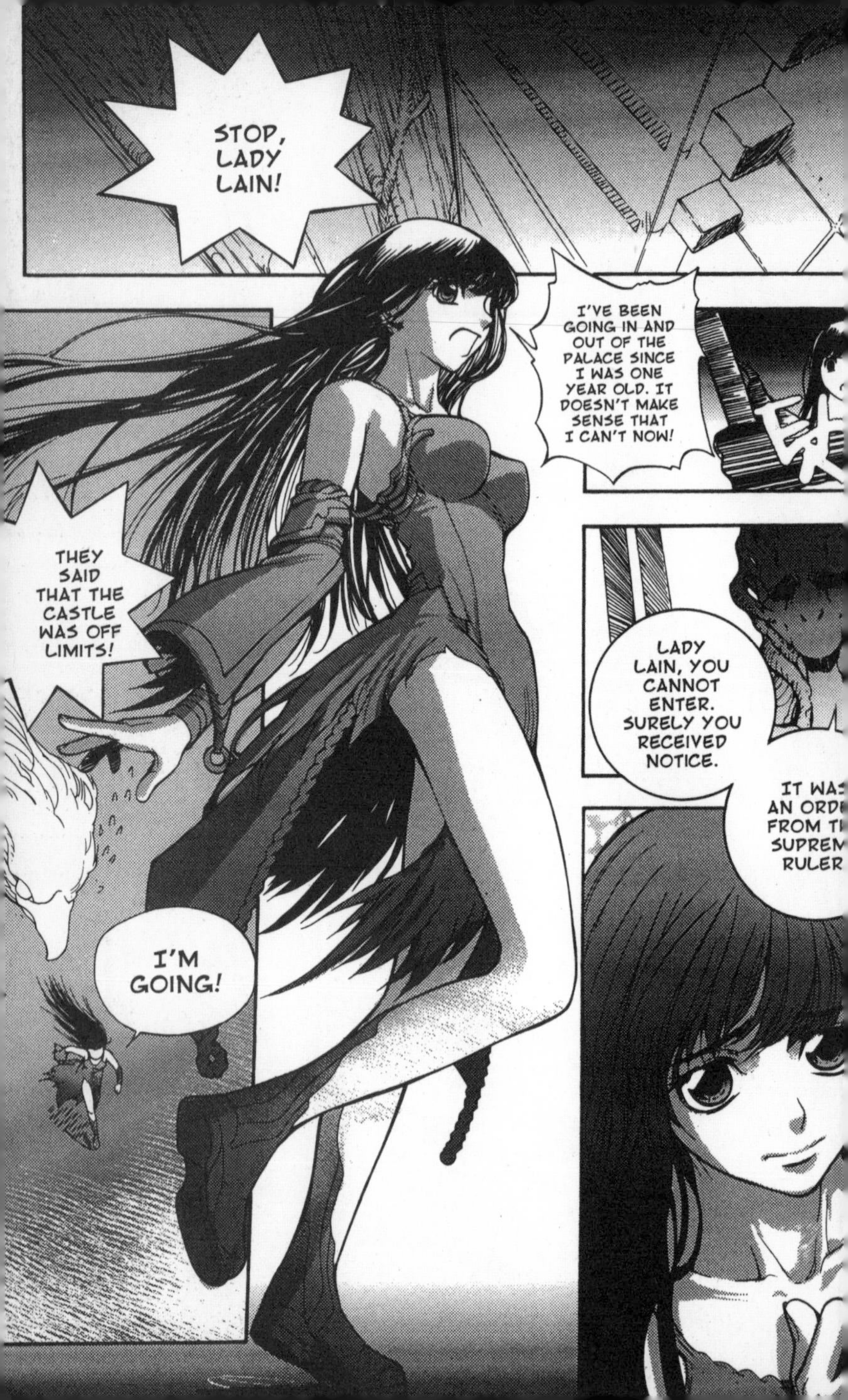
STOP, LADY LAIN!
I'VE BEEN GOING IN AND OUT OF THE PALACE SINCE I WAS ONE YEAR OLD. IT DOESN'T MAKE SENSE THAT I CAN'T NOW!
THEY SAID THAT THE CASTLE WAS OFF LIMITS!
I'M GOING!
LADY LAIN, YOU CANNOT ENTER. SURELY YOU RECEIVED NOTICE.
IT WAS AN ORDE FROM T SUPREM RULER

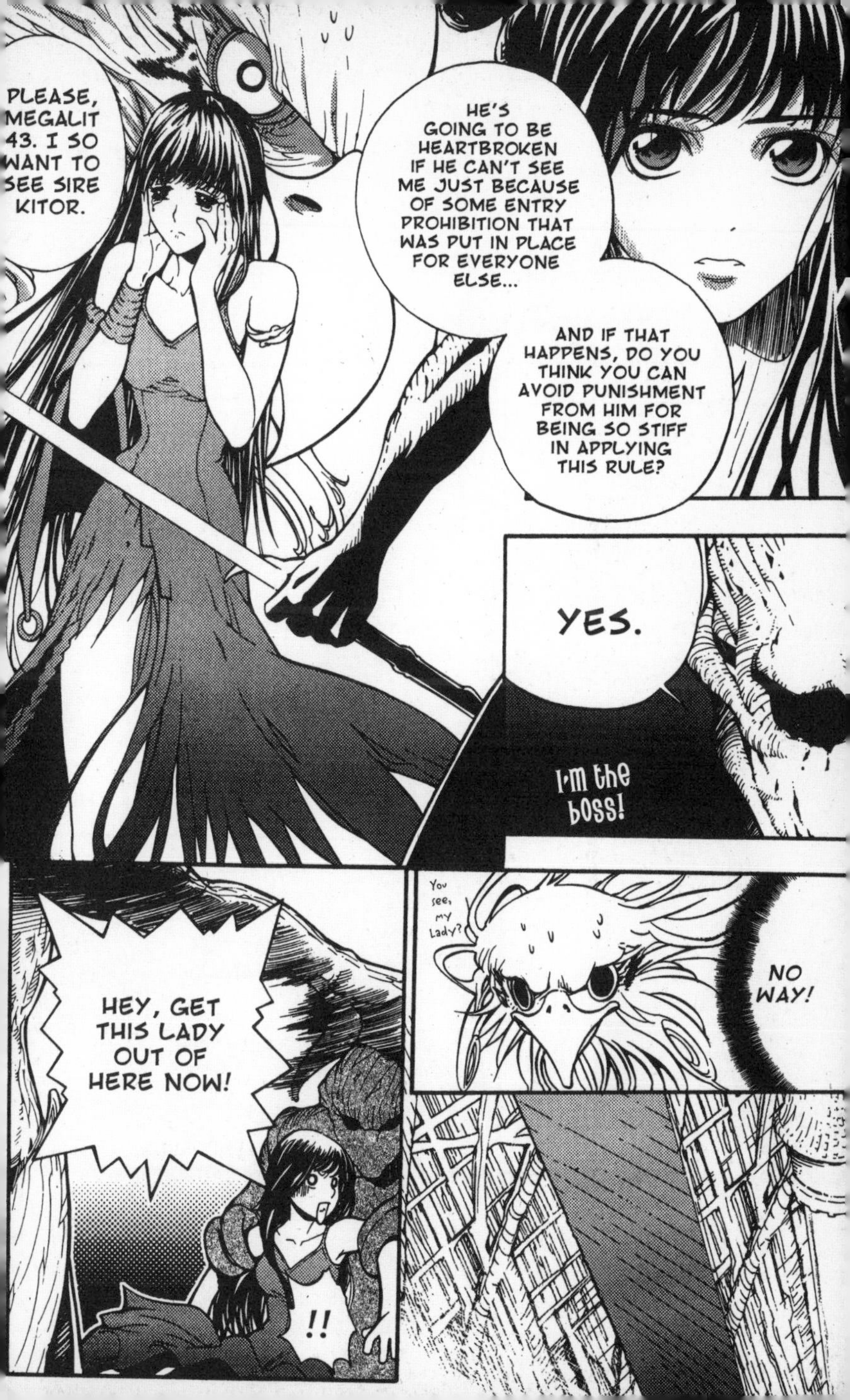
PLEASE, MEGALIT 43. I SO WANT TO SEE SIRE KITOR.
HE'S GOING TO BE HEARTBROKEN IF HE CAN'T SEE ME JUST BECAUSE OF SOME ENTRY PROHIBITION THAT WAS PUT IN PLACE FOR EVERYONE ELSE...
AND IF THAT HAPPENS, DO YOU THINK YOU CAN AVOID PUNISHMENT FROM HIM FOR BEING SO STIFF IN APPLYING THIS RULE?
YES.
I'm the boss!
HEY, GET THIS LADY OUT OF HERE NOW!
!!
You see, my Lady?
NO WAY!

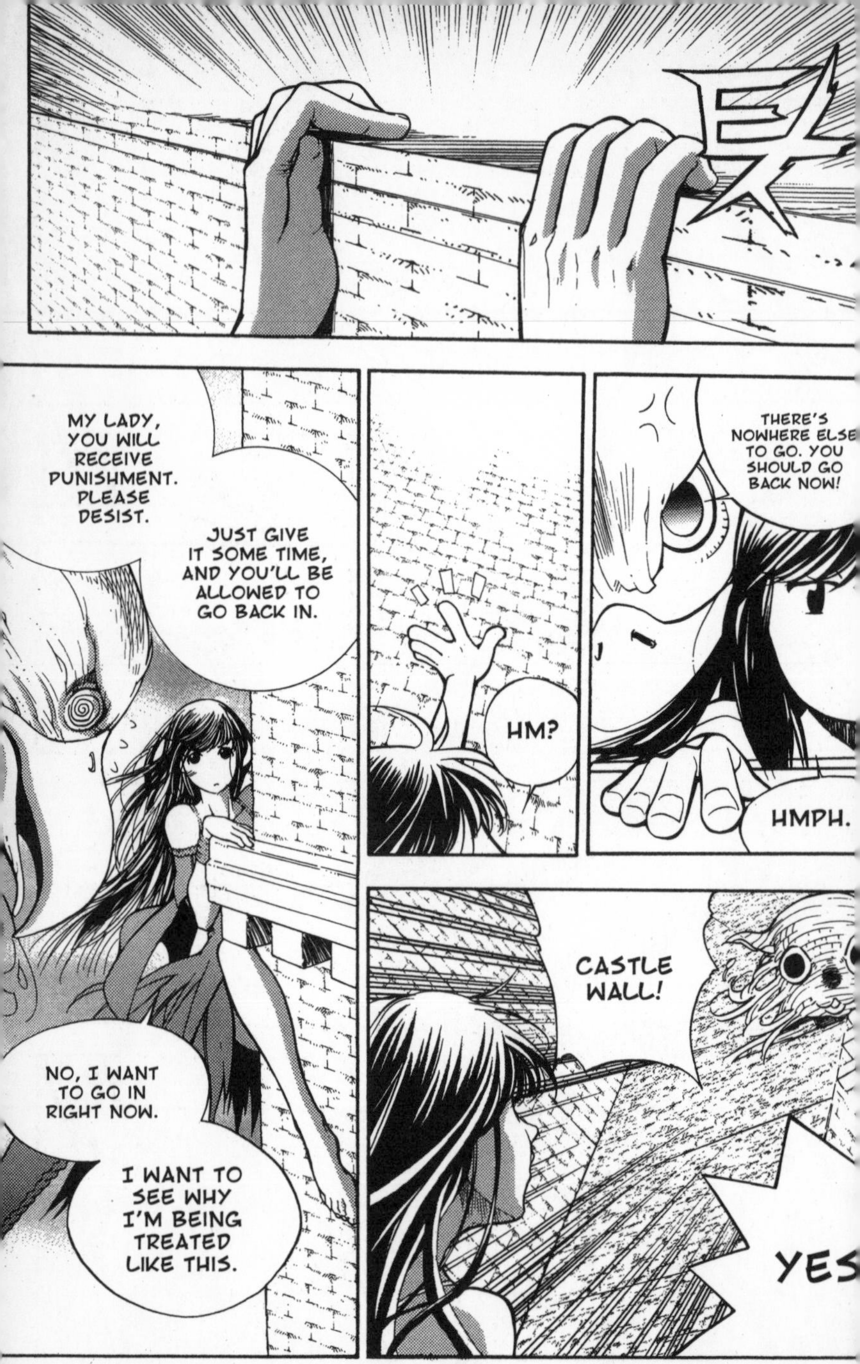
MY LADY, YOU WILL RECEIVE PUNISHMENT. PLEASE DESIST.
JUST GIVE IT SOME TIME, AND YOU'LL BE ALLOWED TO GO BACK IN.
NO, I WANT TO GO IN RIGHT NOW.
I WANT TO SEE WHY I'M BEING TREATED LIKE THIS.
HM?
THERE'S NOWHERE ELSE TO GO. YOU SHOULD GO BACK NOW!
HMPH.
CASTLE WALL!
YES

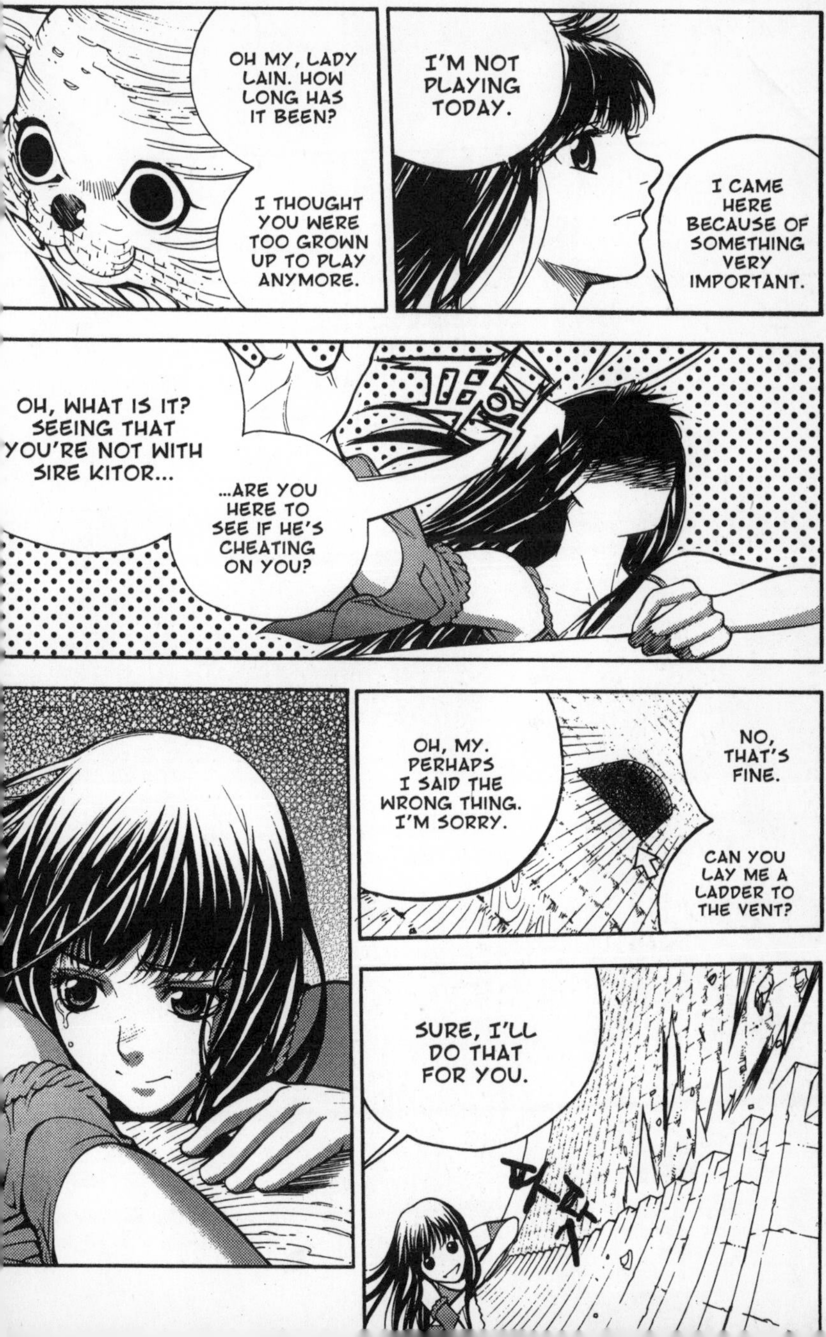
OH MY, LADY LAIN. HOW LONG HAS IT BEEN?
I THOUGHT YOU WERE TOO GROWN UP TO PLAY ANYMORE.
I'M NOT PLAYING TODAY.
I CAME HERE BECAUSE OF SOMETHING VERY IMPORTANT.
OH, WHAT IS IT? SEEING THAT YOU'RE NOT WITH SIRE KITOR...
...ARE YOU HERE TO SEE IF HE'S CHEATING ON YOU?
OH, MY. PERHAPS I SAID THE WRONG THING. I'M SORRY.
NO, THAT'S FINE.
CAN YOU LAY ME A LADDER TO THE VENT?
SURE, I'LL DO THAT FOR YOU.

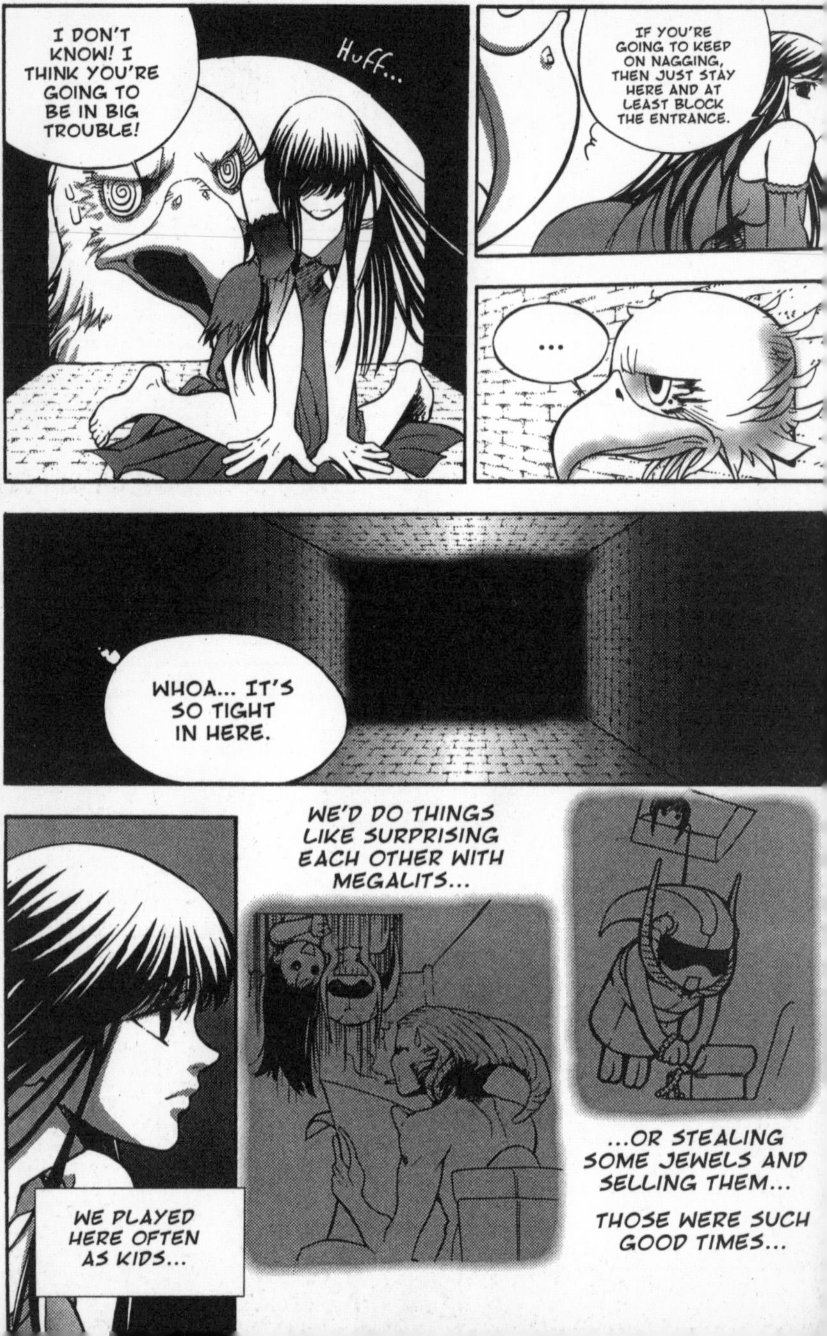
I DON'T KNOW! I THINK YOU'RE GOING TO BE IN BIG TROUBLE!
HUFF...
IF YOU'RE GOING TO KEEP ON NAGGING, THEN JUST STAY HERE AND AT LEAST BLOCK THE ENTRANCE.
...
WHOA... IT'S SO TIGHT IN HERE.
WE PLAYED HERE OFTEN AS KIDS...
WE'D DO THINGS LIKE SURPRISING EACH OTHER WITH MEGALITS...
...OR STEALING SOME JEWELS AND SELLING THEM...
THOSE WERE SUCH GOOD TIMES...

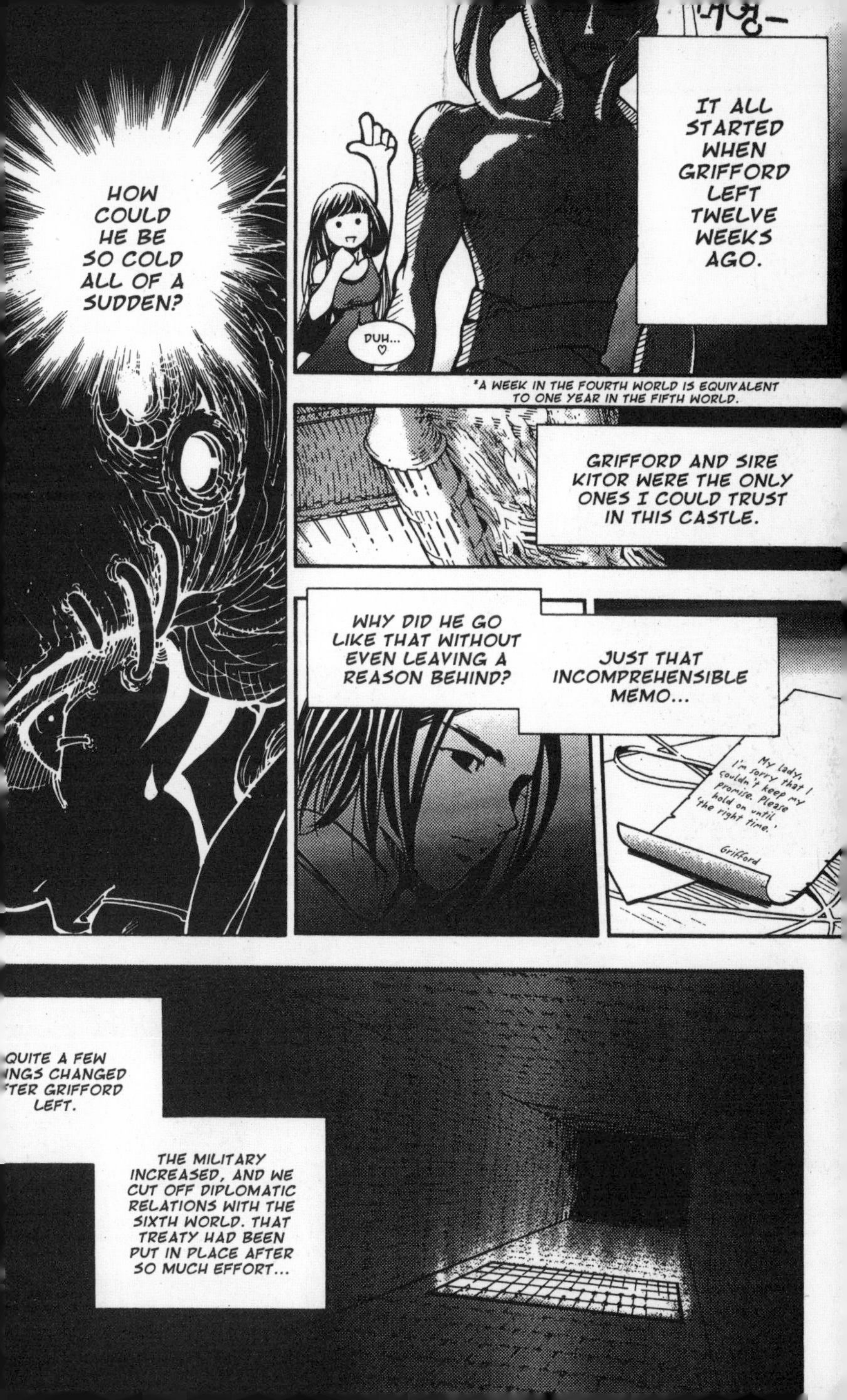
HOW COULD HE BE SO COLD ALL OF A SUDDEN?
IT ALL STARTED WHEN GRIFFORD LEFT TWELVE WEEKS AGO.
DUH... ♡
*A WEEK IN THE FOURTH WORLD IS EQUIVALENT TO ONE YEAR IN THE FIFTH WORLD.
GRIFFORD AND SIRE KITOR WERE THE ONLY ONES I COULD TRUST IN THIS CASTLE.
WHY DID HE GO LIKE THAT WITHOUT EVEN LEAVING A REASON BEHIND?
JUST THAT INCOMPREHENSIBLE MEMO...
My lady, I'm sorry that I couldn't keep my promise. Please hold on until 'the right time.'
Grifford
QUITE A FEW INGS CHANGED TER GRIFFORD LEFT.
THE MILITARY INCREASED, AND WE CUT OFF DIPLOMATIC RELATIONS WITH THE SIXTH WORLD. THAT TREATY HAD BEEN PUT IN PLACE AFTER SO MUCH EFFORT...

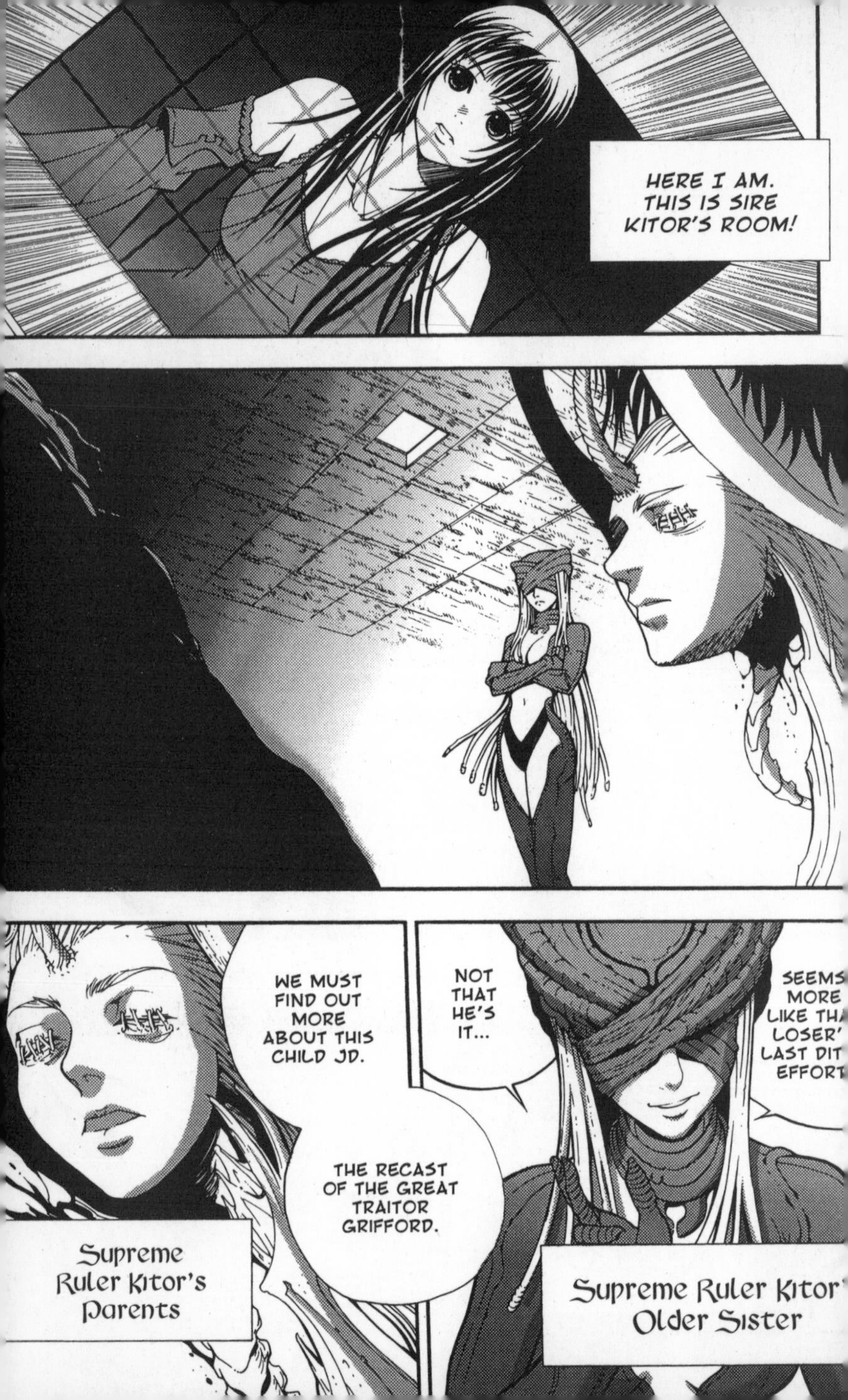
HERE I AM. THIS IS SIRE KITOR'S ROOM!
WE MUST FIND OUT MORE ABOUT THIS CHILD JD.
THE RECAST OF THE GREAT TRAITOR GRIFFORD.
Supreme Ruler Kitor's Parents
NOT THAT HE'S IT...
SEEMS MORE LIKE THA LOSER' LAST DIT EFFORT
Supreme Ruler Kitor' Older Sister

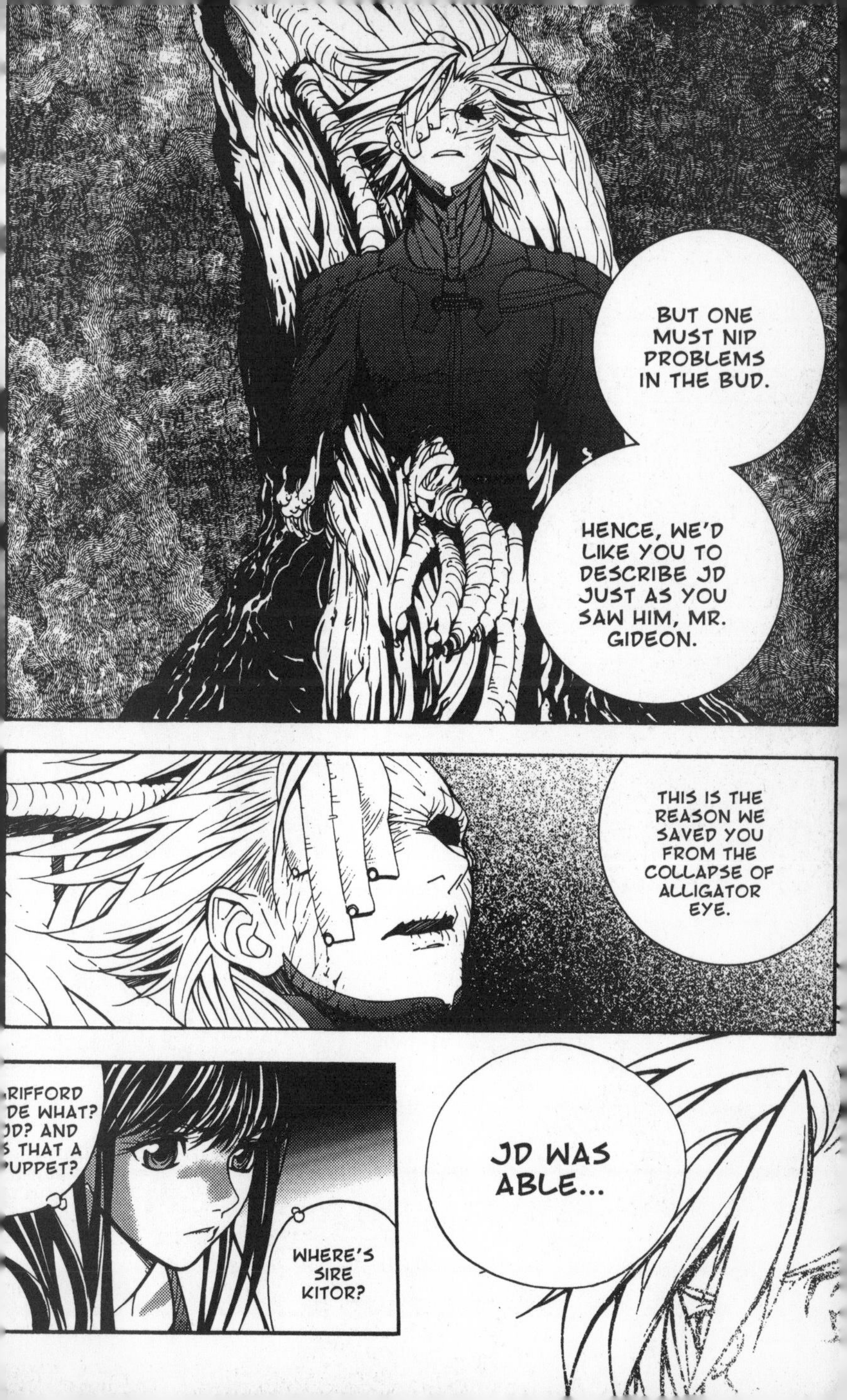

BUT ONE MUST NIP PROBLEMS IN THE BUD.
HENCE, WE'D LIKE YOU TO DESCRIBE JD JUST AS YOU SAW HIM, MR. GIDEON.
THIS IS THE REASON WE SAVED YOU FROM THE COLLAPSE OF ALLIGATOR EYE.
RIFFORD DE WHAT? JD? AND S THAT A UPPET?
WHERE'S SIRE KITOR?
JD WAS ABLE...

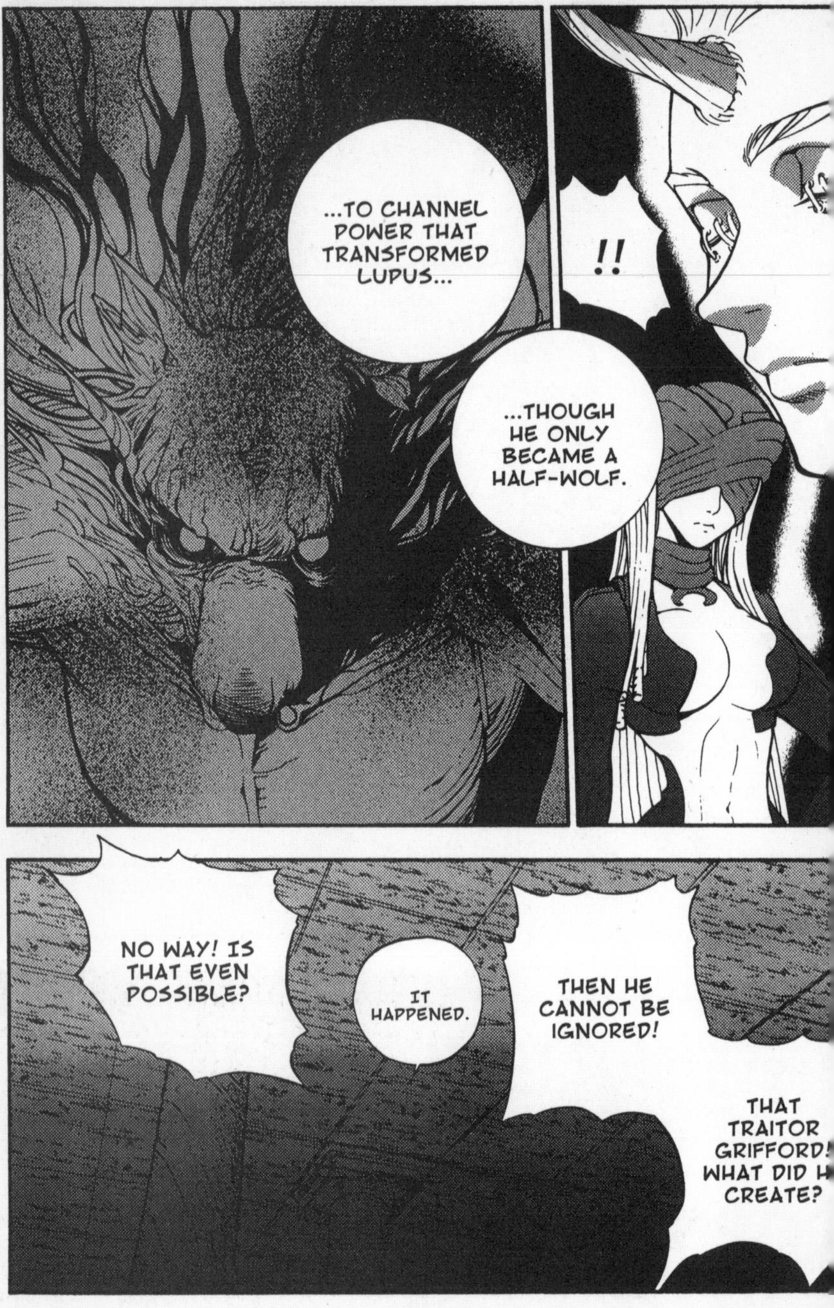

...TO CHANNEL POWER THAT TRANSFORMED LUPUS...
!!
...THOUGH HE ONLY BECAME A HALF-WOLF.
NO WAY! IS THAT EVEN POSSIBLE?
IT HAPPENED.
THEN HE CANNOT BE IGNORED!
THAT TRAITOR GRIFFORD! WHAT DID H CREATE?

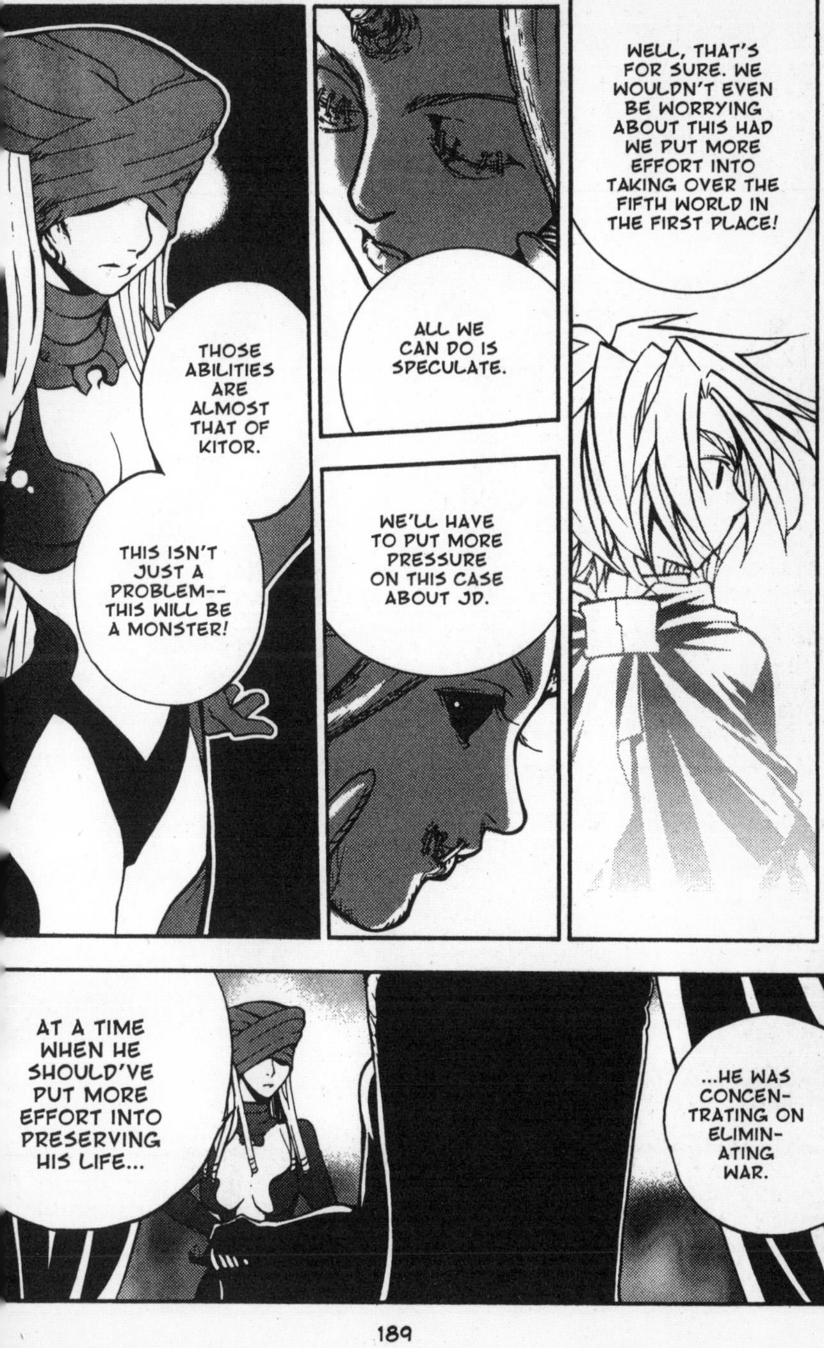
THOSE ABILITIES ARE ALMOST THAT OF KITOR.
THIS ISN'T JUST A PROBLEM--THIS WILL BE A MONSTER!
ALL WE CAN DO IS SPECULATE.
WE'LL HAVE TO PUT MORE PRESSURE ON THIS CASE ABOUT JD.
WELL, THAT'S FOR SURE. WE WOULDN'T EVEN BE WORRYING ABOUT THIS HAD WE PUT MORE EFFORT INTO TAKING OVER THE FIFTH WORLD IN THE FIRST PLACE!
AT A TIME WHEN HE SHOULD'VE PUT MORE EFFORT INTO PRESERVING HIS LIFE...
...HE WAS CONCENTRATING ON ELIMINATING WAR.

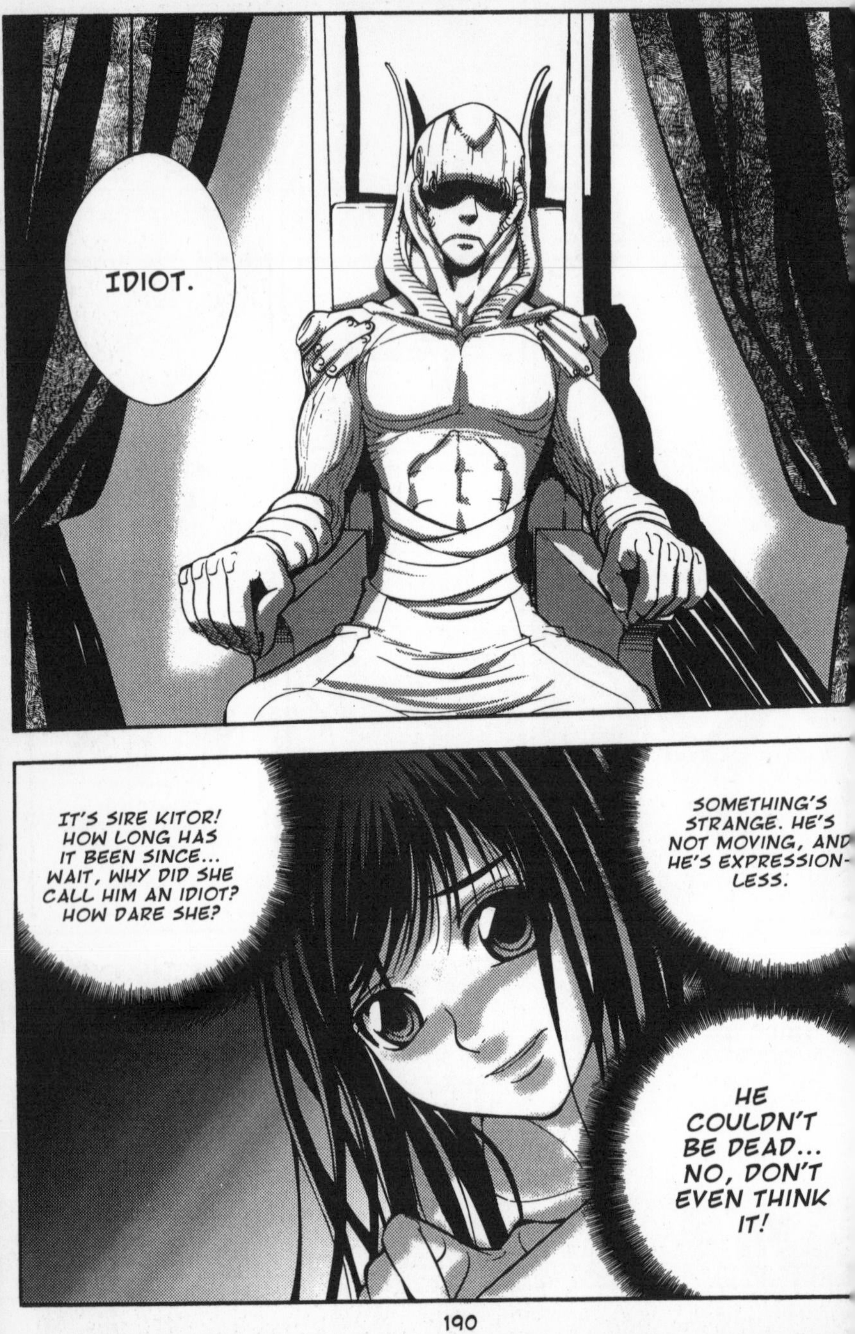
IDIOT.
IT'S SIRE KITOR! HOW LONG HAS IT BEEN SINCE... WAIT, WHY DID SHE CALL HIM AN IDIOT? HOW DARE SHE?
SOMETHING'S STRANGE. HE'S NOT MOVING, AND HE'S EXPRESSION-LESS.
HE COULDN'T BE DEAD... NO, DON'T EVEN THINK IT!

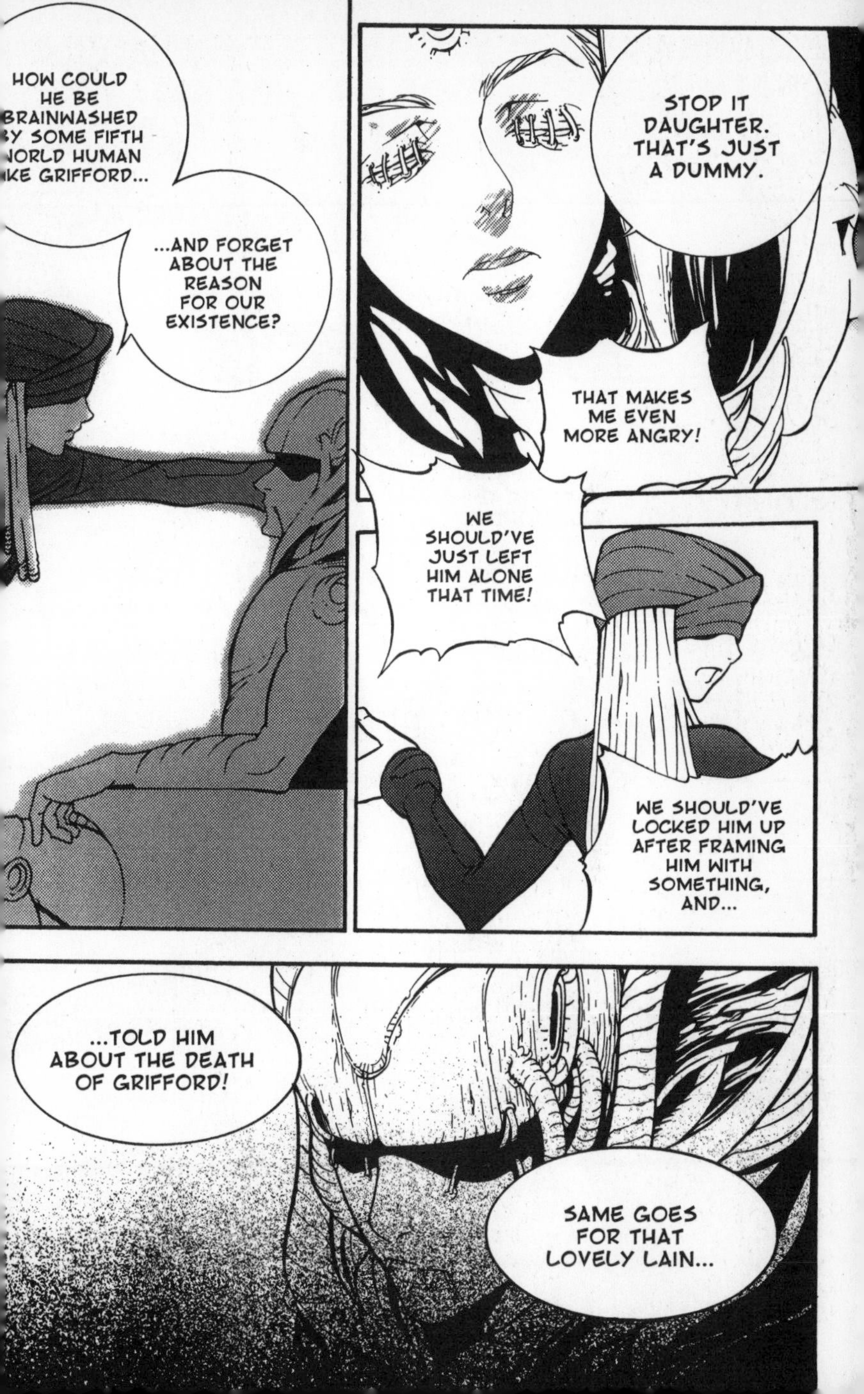
HOW COULD HE BE BRAINWASHED BY SOME FIFTH WORLD HUMAN LIKE GRIFFORD...
...AND FORGET ABOUT THE REASON FOR OUR EXISTENCE?
STOP IT DAUGHTER. THAT'S JUST A DUMMY.
THAT MAKES ME EVEN MORE ANGRY!
WE SHOULD'VE JUST LEFT HIM ALONE THAT TIME!
WE SHOULD'VE LOCKED HIM UP AFTER FRAMING HIM WITH SOMETHING, AND...
...TOLD HIM ABOUT THE DEATH OF GRIFFORD!
SAME GOES FOR THAT LOVELY LAIN...

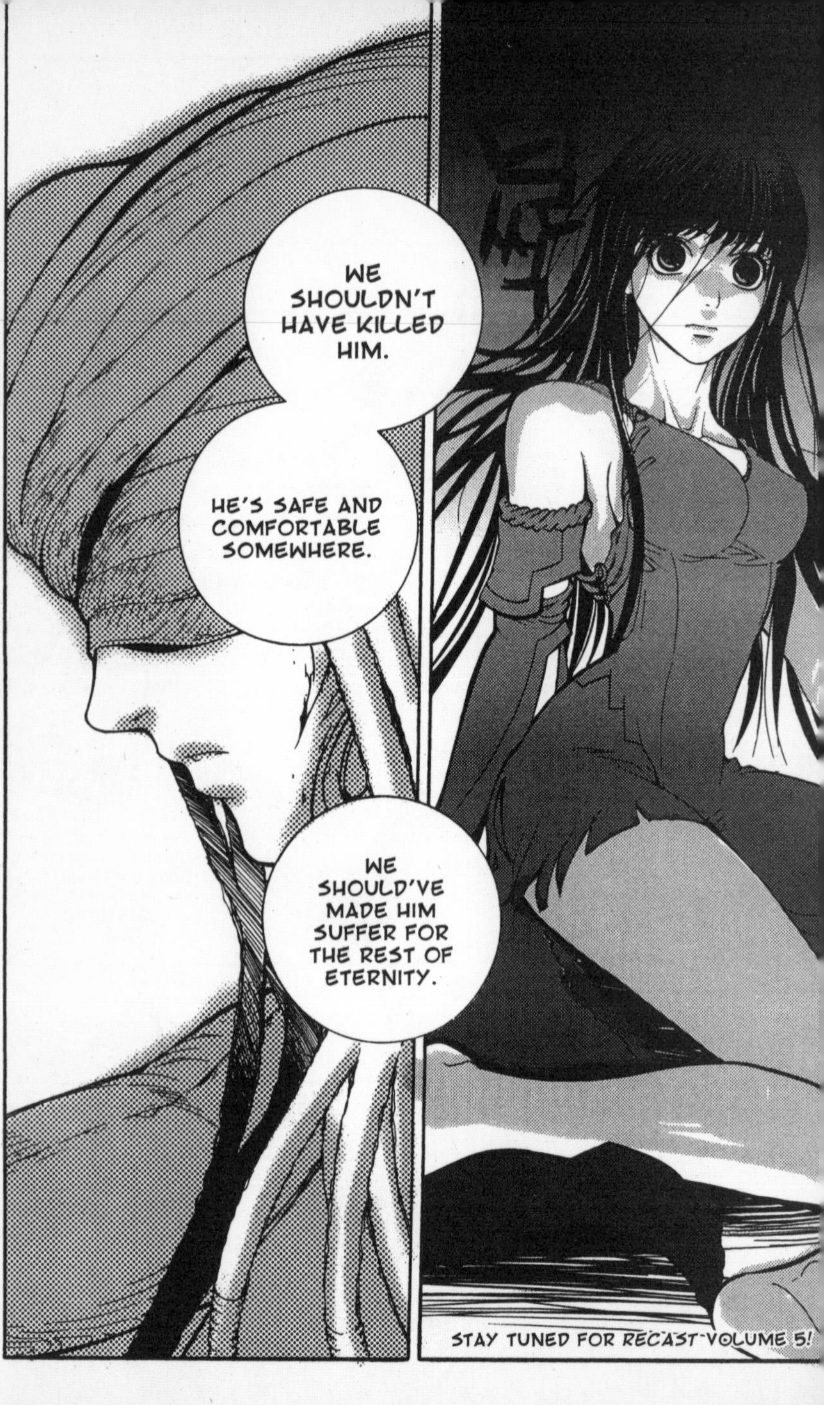
WE SHOULDN'T HAVE KILLED HIM.
HE'S SAFE AND COMFORTABLE SOMEWHERE.
WE SHOULD'VE MADE HIM SUFFER FOR THE REST OF ETERNITY.
STAY TUNED FOR RECAST VOLUME 5!

## CORNER CALLED
## UINATION CORNER

### NTRODUCING FOUR COMICS
### ROM ELEVEN YEARS AGO!

CTUALLY RAN OUT OF TIME AND
N'T HAVE ANYTHING ELSE TO FILL THE
ACE WITH. AND NOW I'M SHOWING
NGS THAT I REALLY SHOULDN'T...

REALLY LIKE WATCHING MOVIES, BUT
ER THE PAST YEAR, I'VE BEEN ABLE
SEE ONLY FOUR MOVIES IN THE
EATERS. AND I'D RATHER NOT WATCH
OVIES IN THINGS LIKE DIVX FORMATS--
E WHOLE EXPERIENCE FALLS SHORT
AT WAY. AND WHEN I TELL MYSELF
AT I'LL WATCH IT LATER ON DVD,
SOMETIMES LOSE INTEREST, AS IT
COMES SOME OLD MOVIE THAT
OPLE NO LONGER CARE ABOUT.
' FRIENDS TEASE ME BY SAYING,
OU STILL DIDN'T WATCH IT?"

SHUT UP, FRIENDS.
O, I'M JUST KIDDING. THANKS
R PLAYING WITH ME.)

2004,3

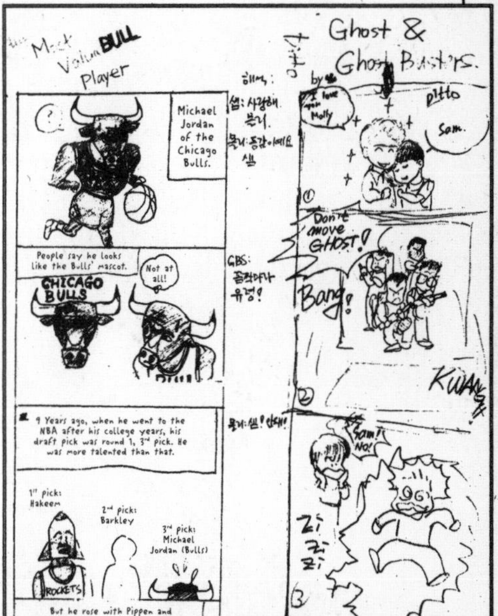
Most ValuaBULL Player
Michael Jordan of the Chicago Bulls.
People say he looks like the Bulls' mascot.
CHICAGO BULLS
Not at all!
9 Years ago, when he went to the NBA after his college years, his draft pick was round 1, 3rd pick. He was more talented than that.
1st pick: Hakeem
2nd pick: Barkley
3rd pick: Michael Jordan (Bulls)
ROCKETS
But he rose with Pippen and Grant and cemented his position as one of the Big Bulls.
the Most ValuaBULL Player #1 end
Ghost & Ghost Busters.
Ditto
Sam.
Don't move GHOST!
Bang!
KWANG
Sam! NO!
1500$.
UU~

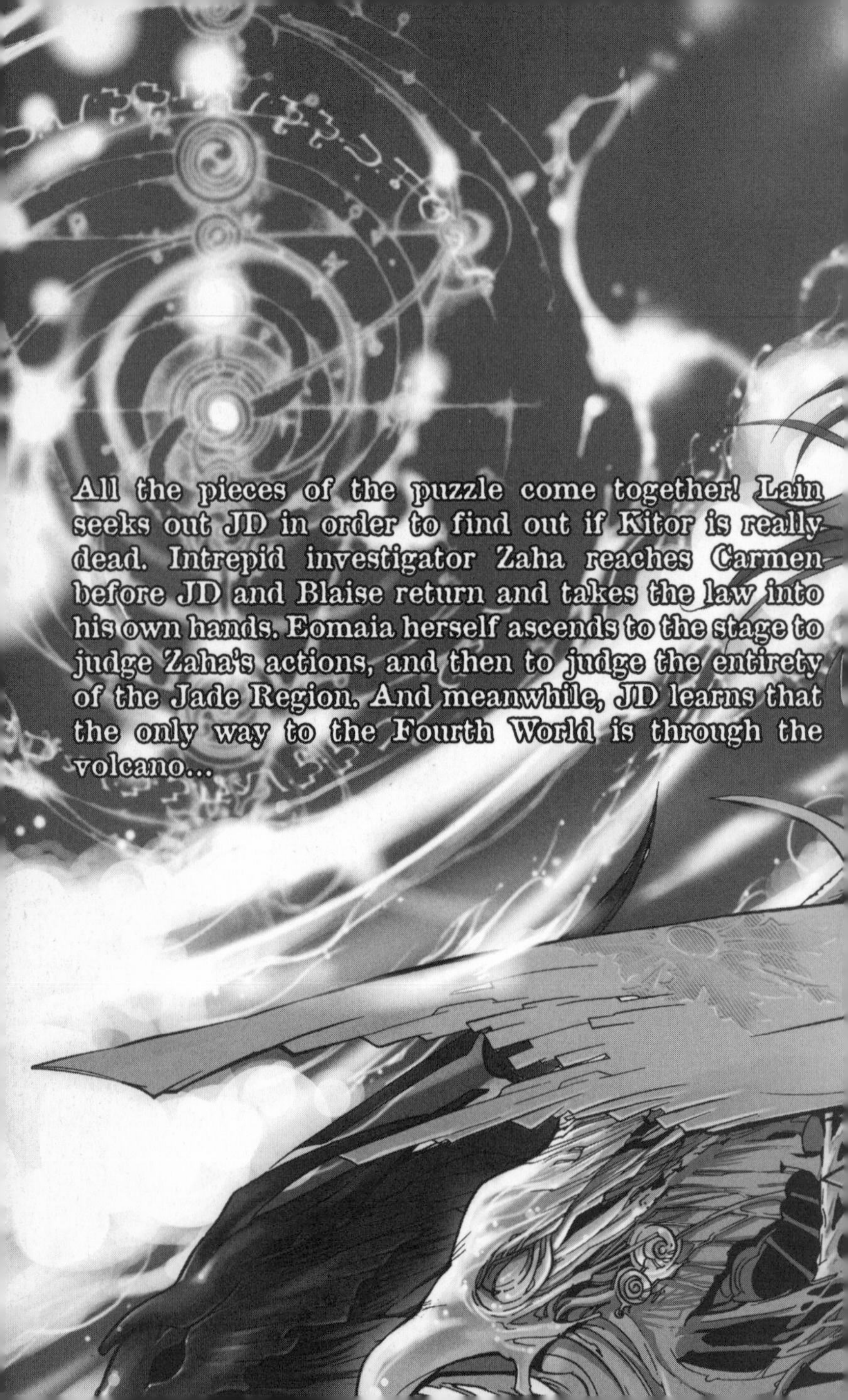

All the pieces of the puzzle come together! Lain seeks out JD in order to find out if Kitor is really dead. Intrepid investigator Zaha reaches Carmen before JD and Blaise return and takes the law into his own hands. Eomaia herself ascends to the stage to judge Zaha's actions, and then to judge the entirety of the Jade Region. And meanwhile, JD learns that the only way to the Fourth World is through the volcano...

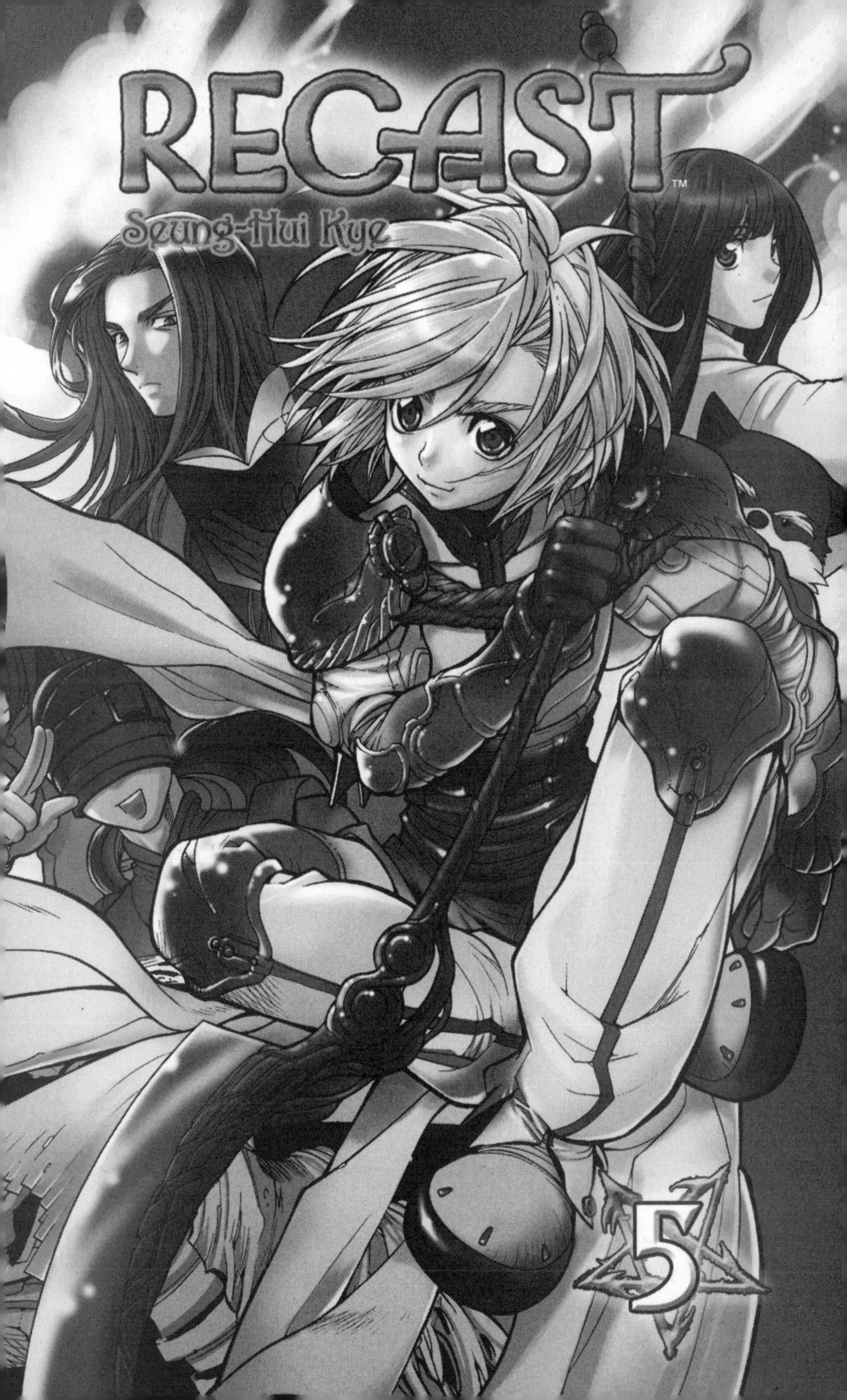
RECAST™
Seung-Hui Kye
5

# TOKYOPOP.com

## WHERE MANGA LIVES!

**JOIN** the **TOKYOPOP community:**
www.TOKYOPOP.com

### COME AND PREVIEW THE HOTTEST MANGA AROUND!

CREATE...
UPLOAD...
DOWNLOAD...
BLOG...
CHAT...
VOTE...
LIVE!!!!

### WWW.TOKYOPOP.COM HAS:

- Exclusives
- News
- Contests
- Games
- Rising Stars of Manga
- iManga
- and more...

## TOKYOPOP.COM 2.0 NOW LIVE!

漫画革命

Dramacon: © Svetlana Chmakova and TOKYOPOP, Inc.

# MISSING™
## KAMIKAKUSHI NO MONOGATARI

2

## ANYONE WHO MEETS *HER* DISAPPEARS

When Kyoichi, a.k.a. "His Majesty, Lord of Darkness," disappears, his friends in the Literature Club suspect he's been spirited away by a girl posing as his girlfriend. Their desperate investigation quickly spirals into a paranormal nightmare, where a fate worse than death waits on the "other side"...

MYSTERY

T
TEEN
AGE 13+

© Gakuto Coda and Rei Mutsuki/Media Works

FOR MORE INFORMATION VISIT: WWW.TOKYOPOP.COM